The Levellers

Politics, culture and society in early modern Britain

General editors
PROFESSOR ANN HUGHES
PROFESSOR ANTHONY MILTON
PROFESSOR PETER LAKE

This important series publishes monographs that take a fresh and challenging look at the interactions between politics, culture and society in Britain between 1500 and the mid-eighteenth century. It counteracts the fragmentation of current historiography through encouraging a variety of approaches which attempt to redefine the political, social and cultural worlds, and to explore their interconnection in a flexible and creative fashion. All the volumes in the series question and transcend traditional interdisciplinary boundaries, such as those between political history and literary studies, social history and divinity, urban history and anthropology. They thus contribute to a broader understanding of crucial developments in early modern Britain.

Already published in the series

Black Bartholomew's Day DAVID J. APPLEBY
The 1630s IAN ATHERTON AND JULIE SANDERS (eds)
Reading and politics in early modern England GEOFF BAKER
Literature and politics in the English Reformation TOM BETTERIDGE
'No historie so meete' JAN BROADWAY
Republican learning JUSTIN CHAMPION
This England: Essays on the English Nation and Commonwealth PATRICK COLLINSON
Cromwell's major-generals CHRISTOPHER DURSTON
The spoken word ADAM FOX and DANIEL WOOLF (eds)
Reading Ireland RAYMOND GILLESPIE
Londinopolis PAUL GRIFFITHS and MARK JENNER (eds)
Brave community JOHN GURNEY
'Black Tom': Sir Thomas Fairfax and the English Revolution ANDREW HOPPER
The boxmaker's revenge PETER LAKE
The politics of the public sphere in early modern England
PETER LAKE AND STEVEN PINCUS (eds)
Henry Neville and English republican culture GABY MAHLBERG
Royalists and Royalism during the Interregnum JASON McELLIGOTT AND DAVID L. SMITH (eds)
The social world of early modern Westminster J. F. MERRITT
Laudian and Royalist polemic in Stuart England: ANTHONY MILTON
Courtship and constraint DIANA O'HARA
The origins of the Scottish Reformation ALEC RYRIE
Catholics and the 'Protestant nation' ETHAN SHAGAN (ed.)
Communities in early modern England ALEXANDRA SHEPARD
and PHILIP WITHINGTON (eds)
The later Stuart Church, 1600–1714 GRANT TAPSELL (ed.)
Civic portraiture and political culture in the English local community ROBERT TITTLER
Aspects of English Protestantism, c. 1530–1700 NICHOLAS TYACKE
Charitable hatred ALEXANDRA WALSHAM
Crowds and popular politics in early modern England JOHN WALTER

The Levellers

Radical political thought in the English Revolution

RACHEL FOXLEY

Manchester
University Press

Copyright © Rachel Foxley 2013

The right of Rachel Foxley to be identified as the author of this work has been asserted by her in accordance with the Copyright, Designs and Patents Act 1988.

Published by Manchester University Press
Altrincham Street, Manchester M1 7JA, UK
www.manchesteruniversitypress.co.uk

British Library Cataloguing-in-Publication Data is available

Library of Congress Cataloging-in-Publication Data is available

ISBN 978 0 7190 9660 0 paperback

First published by Manchester University Press in hardback 2013

This paperback edition first published 2014

The publisher has no responsibility for the persistence or accuracy of URLs for any external or third-party internet websites referred to in this book, and does not guarantee that any content on such websites is, or will remain, accurate or appropriate.

Printed by Lightning Source

Contents

ACKNOWLEDGEMENTS—vii
LIST OF ABBREVIATIONS—ix
NOTE ON CONVENTIONS—xi

Introduction: Levellers and historians	1
1 Consent and the origins of government	20
2 The appeal to the people	51
3 The laws of England and the 'free-born Englishman'	91
4 Religion, politics, and conscience	119
5 Levellers and the army: England's freedom, soldiers' rights	150
6 Levellers into republicans?	194
Conclusion	230

BIBLIOGRAPHY—235
INDEX—254

Acknowledgements

This book grew out of a PhD dissertation supervised with exemplary care, tact, and efficiency by John Morrill. Glenn Burgess and Quentin Skinner were generous examiners, and all three have offered valuable advice on subsequent work, some of which has found its way into this book. I am immensely grateful to all of them.

My PhD was funded by the British Academy, with additional support for completion of the thesis provided by Trinity College, Cambridge. A junior research fellowship at Clare Hall, Cambridge allowed me to start work on the book, and a term of partial leave funded by the Research Endowment Trust Fund of the University of Reading, awarded by the Faculty of Arts and Humanities, enabled the final completion of the typescript.

Parts of Chapter 3 appeared in a different form as 'John Lilburne and the Citizenship of "Free-Born Englishmen"', *Historical Journal* 47 (2004), 849–74, © Cambridge University Press: reprinted with permission. Parts of Chapters 1 and 2 appeared in a different form as 'Problems of Sovereignty in Leveller Writings', *History of Political Thought* 28 (2007), 642–60. I am grateful to Imprint Academic for permission to reprint.

I am extremely grateful to the anonymous readers for Manchester University Press for their perceptive advice, and also to Stephen Taylor and Elliot Vernon for their careful comments on Chapters 1 and 6 respectively. The series editors and the staff of Manchester University Press have made the process much easier through their efficiency. In the slow evolution of this book, I have accumulated indirect debts to many colleagues and friends, and to audiences who have heard parts of this material presented in a variety of forms and offered valuable feedback. Among those who have provided the context – rumbustious or supportive as the case may be – for my academic life from PhD onwards I must single out Jason McElligott, Elliot Vernon and Phil Baker among early modernists, and Barnita Bagchi, Barbara Graziosi, Johannes Haubold and Naomi Hetherington as the most supportive and stimulating of friends in other fields. Robin Osborne's enthusiasm and encouragement at undergraduate level laid the foundations for my graduate study, although it has been a long way from 'What was new in the eighth century?' to the Levellers.

My family have been patient and supportive bystanders in the writing process, and Tara Dakini has prodded me towards completing the project. My partner, Anna, has suffered the side-effects of this book for far too long, and has been unaccountably patient with it and with me. I can only offer her my love and thanks, and promise not to make such heavy weather of the next book.

Abbreviations

AD	*A Declaration of the Engagements, Remonstrances, Representations, Proposals, Desires and Resolutions from His Excellency Sir Tho: Fairfax, and the general Councel of the Army.* (1647; E.409/25)
Brailsford	H. N. Brailsford, *The Levellers and the English Revolution* (London: Cresset Press, 1961)
CJ	*Journals of the House of Commons*
CP	C. H. Firth (ed.), *The Clarke Papers: Selections from the Papers of William Clarke* (London: Royal Historical Society, 1992 reprint, vols 1–2)
CSPD	*Calendar of State Papers Domestic*
Frank	J. Frank, *The Levellers: A History of the Writings of Three Seventeenth-century Social Democrats: John Lilburne, Richard Overton, William Walwyn* (Cambridge, Mass.: Harvard University Press, 1955)
Gentles	I. Gentles, *The New Model Army in England, Ireland and Scotland, 1645–1653* (Oxford: Blackwell, 1992)
H&D	W. Haller and G. Davies (eds), *The Leveller Tracts 1647–1653* (Gloucester, Mass., 1964)
LJ	*Journals of the House of Lords*
MMT	J. R. McMichael and B. Taft (eds), *The Writings of William Walwyn* (Athens, Ga. and London: University of Georgia Press, 1989).
ODNB	*Oxford Dictionary of National Biography* (Oxford: Oxford University Press, 2004)
Wolfe	D. M. Wolfe (ed.), *Leveller Manifestoes of the Puritan Revolution* (New York: Nelson, 1944)
Woodhouse	A. S. P. Woodhouse (ed.), *Puritanism and Liberty* (London: J. M. Dent, 1992 edn.)
Woolrych	A. Woolrych, *Soldiers and Statesmen: The General Council of the Army and Its Debates, 1647–1648* (Oxford: Clarendon Press, 1987)

Note on conventions

Dating is Old Style but the year is taken to begin on 1 January. Quotations from primary sources are reproduced with the original spelling and punctuation, except that the spelling of i/j, v/u, and vv/w has been modernised. Pre-1700 works were published in London unless otherwise specified.

Introduction
Levellers and historians

The Levellers can seem uncannily modern. '[W]hatever our Fore-fathers were; or whatever they did or suffered, or were enforced to yeeld unto; we are the men of the present age ...', proclaimed the *Remonstrance of Many Thousand Citizens* in July 1646. These citizens, speaking perhaps through the voices of William Walwyn or Richard Overton, and just beginning to cohere into a movement which would later become known as the Levellers, rejected the precedents and obligations of the past and sought 'naturall and just libertie, agreeable to *Reason*'.[1] With such bold claims, the Leveller writers detached themselves from their own past, and spoke a language which is quite comprehensible to us now. That air of modernity is reinforced by the fact that the inertia of English and British constitutional history leaves Leveller demands for the abolition of the power of the monarchy and the House of Lords not only comprehensible but actually relevant, while other preoccupations – arbitrary detention, equality before the law, religious toleration – may again speak to resurgent contemporary concerns. This apparent modernity is, of course, not entirely an accident: we have, through multiple lines of descent and of rediscovery, become the heirs of many of the ideas which the Levellers began to articulate. Where that is the case, there is certainly no harm in tracing these ideas back through their development and analysing the particular ways in which the Levellers spoke of them.[2]

However, it is also true that those processes of modern rediscovery and reassessment of the Levellers have given us a version of the Levellers which is suspiciously, unhelpfully modern. The great effort and confusion and tension inherent in the attempt – by some Levellers at some times – to initiate a new era, free of the bonds that had fettered their forefathers, is written out of the account, while their provocatively glib assertion of that new era is accepted at face value. The major narrative monographs on the Levellers and the Leveller leaders, which date from 1916 to 1961, are peppered with admiringly anachronistic appropriations of the Levellers: as 'democrats' ('social' or 'liberal' according to taste), and as secularists.[3] These descriptions were applied with a degree of self-consciousness about what they implied: the Levellers were 'born in the wrong century', were 'strangely modern'; in short, they were

1

indeed an 'anachronism'.⁴ Rather than explain how this anachronism was possible, these authors tended to see the Levellers as the fountainhead of modern traditions, situating them historically in relation to their future rather than their past or even their present. Pease marvelled at a Leveller 'ideal of democracy that perhaps only the twentieth century can parallel'; for Zagorin, the Levellers 'at the very birth of political democracy stated its full theoretical implications'; for Robertson, the Levellers were 'the first democratic party in the modern world'.⁵ Many more recent authors distinguish themselves from this tradition of appropriation only by apologizing for the fact that they too use these terms.⁶

One strand within the twentieth-century recovery of the Leveller movement, and of civil war radicalism more generally, was the work of Marxist historians, at its most influential in Christopher Hill's *The World Turned Upside Down* of 1972. Hill distinguished between the two revolutions of the mid-seventeenth century, the one which succeeded and the second which never came to pass. The Levellers were placed in an uncomfortable position between the first revolution and the second, the bourgeois revolution which ultimately protected property and entrenched the new authority of the propertied classes, and the radical revolution which might have overturned them. While Hill conceded the Levellers a place in a plebeian radical tradition, and in the fluid world of the radical groupings which were 'overturning, questioning, revaluing' English society in the 1640s and 1650s, he felt that the Diggers spoke more directly to twentieth-century socialists, and followed C. B. Macpherson in assessing the Leveller version of 'democracy' as a rather exclusive one. Ultimately, the moments when the Leveller leaders wrote of the poor and mean confounding the mighty did not entirely outweigh their defence of the 'men of small property', but of property nonetheless.⁷ One solution to the problem was to divide the Leveller movement into two 'wings', and to attribute to an under-documented, diffuse wing which tended towards the 'true Levellerism' of the Diggers a concern with property issues which was most clearly seen only in reflection, in the accusations of the Levellers' enemies.⁸ The Levellers' spirit of egalitarianism still pointed forwards, in ways which excited other socialist historians, including Brailsford, but the main branch of the Leveller movement had failed to pursue the more radical conclusions which even its seventeenth-century enemies saw as entailed by its arguments.

This Marxist historiography may ultimately have been ambivalent about the Levellers, but Hill's celebration of the radicalism of the English revolution in 1972 has seemingly been the foundation for popular perceptions of the movement and the broader radical context ever since. The annual Burford Levellers' Day has been running since 1975; Caryl Churchill's play, *Light Shining in Buckinghamshire*, dates from 1976. More recent popular representations have been less distinguished, but again tend to merge Levellers in a celebratory way with other civil war radicals and army men.⁹ At the other end of the interpretative spectrum, web searches reveal a great fondness for the Levellers among American libertarians, offering a very different present-centred and enthusiastic take on Leveller thought. Insofar as the Levellers retain a place in the popular imagination, they do so as admirable radicals – of whatever kind – cruelly defeated by Cromwellian forces of reaction.

But in the scholarly literature, times have changed since the 1970s, and the Levellers have changed with them. The revisionist historians who have rewritten the history of the seventeenth century have questioned almost every aspect of the historical reputation of the Levellers. While these historians have never been a unified school, the cumulative effect of their work has been a sharp challenge to the incorporation of the English revolution into Whiggish narratives of constitutional progress, or indeed Marxist expositions of the unfolding historical dialectic. The Levellers as understood by such earlier histories did not pass muster with revisionist historians. Equally, the revisionists' seventeenth century – at its most extreme an 'unrevolutionary England' falling into an almost accidental, or perhaps backwardly religious, civil war – seems to have little place for the radicalism of the Levellers. This may begin to explain why there has been no scholarly monograph in English on the Levellers for half a century.

Revisionist historiography has, of course, enormously enriched our sense of the political contexts in which the Leveller movement arose. In doing so, it has offered new insights into the Levellers and, as a post-revisionist response has grown up, revisionism itself has also taken newer directions which have been fruitful for the study of the Levellers. We now have a much fuller sense of the ways in which the Leveller leaders played a part in broader political networks, and of the intricacies of radical politics within the New Model Army, for example. But the Levellers have been diminished, too. Their importance and their distinctiveness have been played down, and readings of their thought have placed them within the revisionists' 1640s by emphasizing their religious over their political motivations, or by bringing out apparently nostalgic or conservative strains within their thought. The problem of 'radicalism in a traditional society' has been placed in the path of any historian approaching them.

Recently, however, there has been renewed interest in the radical thinkers of the period.¹⁰ Post-revisionist historians have worked hard to build a more complex picture of political debate and political conflict in the earlier seventeenth century, and civil war radicalism now has a more plausible background, although its evolution in the 1640s and 1650s was undoubtedly rapid and unpredictable. It is thus a good moment to reassess the Levellers, to bring them back from the margins of revisionist historiography, and to see where they now fit in the landscape of 1640s England.

The Levellers

The Leveller movement was important. Even the most ardent defender of a cosy and consensual political world in early Stuart England must concede that Charles I was publicly tried and executed in 1649 – not killed in a corner – and that his demise was followed not by the hasty installation of a more pliable Stuart or any other substitute monarch, but by a four-year republican regime, however improvised, reluctant, and ultimately unsuccessful. These were, of course, the acts of minorities, and minorities whose authority lay only in the sword; but they were acts which had become debatable, proposable, and (in the most minimal sense) defensible over the course of the 1640s. Political events turned a ratchet of radicalization for some, even while they drove others to seek refuge in hopes of restoration. The Levellers did not ultimately support the trial and execution of the king, and they were effectively crushed by the republican authorities, but their writings helped to develop the language and arguments which enabled a king to be tried for high treason, and their mobilization of their supporters made such radical tendencies visible on the streets of London as well as on the bookstalls.

Revisionist treatments of the Levellers and the later 1640s cannot wipe out the contribution of the Levellers to the radicalization of parliamentarian political thought. But the actual contribution of the Levellers to radicalization where it really mattered – in the army – has been much challenged by revisionists. The most plausible case for the Levellers' impact on events used to rest on their supposed personal influence on the men of the New Model Army. It is now clear that the Levellers' relationship with radicalism in the army was less straightforward than used to be thought, and that the politicization of the army, while very real, had its own drivers and its own character. Revisionists may have cast doubt on old assumptions about personal cooperation between army radicals and civilian Levellers – although hints of such connections certainly remain – but, as I show in Chapter 5, there was significant interplay between army radicalism and Leveller thought, and army-related newsbooks continued to report on and sympathize with Leveller fortunes and 'Leveller' aims even after the army mutineers' defeat at Burford in 1649.[11] Our assessment of the Levellers' influence on their contemporaries cannot depend purely on their personal networks. Our renewed awareness of the burgeoning of cheap political print in the civil war period helps us to understand how it was that the Levellers were able to mobilize large numbers of people to protest, to petition, and to follow the fortunes of the Leveller leaders, particularly the immensely popular John Lilburne; this was as much the case in the army as elsewhere.

Part of the Levellers' significance lay in the way in which they mobilized their supporters and issued documents and demands in the name of 'many thousands' of the people. They first claimed to do this in mid-1646, and the traditional histories of the Levellers reflected this. Frank placed the 'conception' of the 'Leveller party' in mid-1646, and Pease its 'birth' 'as a political party

Introduction

with an entity and platform of its own' in August 1647. Revisionists, however, have objected to the notion of the Levellers as a 'party' and pointed out that no contemporary referred to a grouping under the derogatory term 'Levellers' until November 1647, and then it was used of army men as much as of civilians.[12] Again, although we do have evidence of treasurers gathering weekly subscriptions for the activities of the group, this refers to the petitioning campaign of January 1648, rather than to anything earlier, or to a more enduring 'party' organization.[13] All of this is true. The Levellers were a 'movement' rather than a 'party'; indeed, in accordance with the political taboos of a period when 'party' meant faction, and any fixed designation implied commitment to a sectional and corrupt interest rather than the public good, the Levellers would always present themselves as a slice of the population distinguished only by their commitment to the people's rights and liberties. Of course, this self-presentation may have disguised rather more formal organizational continuity. But even so, the Levellers were a shifting group of people gathered relatively informally around core writers and organizers, redefining their programme around a succession of documents (petitions or 'Agreements of the People') through meetings and discussions, and defining themselves as a group, if at all, through reference to the last key document they had subscribed to. As emerges particularly in Chapter 5, the Levellers and those of a radical temper in the New Model Army were only ever part of a broader audience for different varieties of radical argument in the 1640s; that means that the contours of the Leveller movement itself cannot be pinned down very neatly, but it also indicates the potential for large numbers of people to align themselves with the Leveller 'movement' and its figureheads at times of crisis.

The movement coalesced around its leaders and their writings. Thanks to recent research by David Como we are now more certain that the three major Leveller leaders, John Lilburne, Richard Overton, and William Walwyn, were already in active collaboration by the autumn of 1645.[14] The historians of the Leveller movement had indeed already pieced together a plausible picture of cooperation between Lilburne and Walwyn from around this time, and had seen possible links with Overton too; from the next summer, a further burst of publications in Lilburne's defence confirmed these links, and landed Overton, too, in prison.[15] The Presbyterian castigator of the sects and the radicals, Thomas Edwards, was bracketing together '*Lilburne, Overton,* [the printer William] *Larner,* and the rest of that generation' in their political views by the end of 1646.[16] Revisionists have questioned the coherence of the movement both by casting doubt on the chronology of its development and the timing of any public recognition of it as a group, and by absorbing the Levellers into a broader view of the political scene of 1640s London. For some revisionist historians, the Leveller movement was not the only or the defining network which people were involved in: rather than a coherent group of devoted activists, individual 'Levellers' might be allies or clients of more important political patrons, aligned (not necessarily as a group) at one time or another with one or another faction in Parliament, or the city, or the army.[17] In this broader range of networks and connections, different Leveller leaders might be actively involved in different alliances at one time, supporting different strategies or ends and on good terms with different figures beyond the 'Leveller' movement.[18] Such work has been immensely helpful in situating the Leveller leaders within broader political networks, and thus casting light, too, on the ways in which their thought emerged from the radical Independent tendency within parliamentarianism, and may have been linked with the radical thought of others – such as Henry Marten – whom we do not consider as Levellers. However, while the richer description of the workings of parliamentarian politics which recent historiography has given us can help us to locate the Levellers within their intellectual and political contexts, it need not dissolve them into an undifferentiated part of that complex political world.[19] So while Walwyn's name may not automatically have been linked with Lilburne's and Overton's in late 1646 or early 1647, all three men certainly felt committed to the petitioning campaign of spring 1647, in which Walwyn orchestrated petitions which were intended, among other things, to free Lilburne and Overton from prison.[20]

The Levellers were distinctive in their thought and their demands. That is not to deny that some of their fundamental arguments – notably on the origins of political power in the people – were shared with and derived from radical parliamentarian thought; that was a crucial influence. But the Levellers united round more distinctive and radical visions of the political future than this broader coalition was prepared to support. Their questioning of the ultimate and unchallengeable power of Parliament in favour of the underlying sovereignty of the people themselves drew on Presbyterian as well as Independent ideas. Some of the army's advocates who echoed such views about the resistance of Parliament in 1647 had little interest in the vision of political life which the Levellers developed, preferring to trust to the sword and the saints rather than the consciences of the people as a whole. Leveller thought was not cut off from the thought of anti-monarchical parliamentarians and Independent advocates of parliamentary supremacy, or from the thought of army radicals in 1647 and republicans after 1649: there were indeed many points of contact. Nonetheless, Leveller thought never fused with any of these strands, and developed in its own directions.

The Levellers' historical importance rests on their ideas as well as their actions. Taking it as axiomatic that ideas are the product of their times, Leveller thought would surely remain worthy of historical study even if its contemporary impact – positive and negative – had been considerably less than it was.[21] Some revisionist approaches to the Levellers have challenged the traditional characterization of their thought, seeing aspects of Leveller thinking as fundamentally nostalgic, conservative, or 'localist'.²² This is a misguided reading, but it is based on some genuine features of Leveller thought. There is a much-vaunted problem of the place or possibility of 'radicalism' in the 'traditional society' of early modern England. It is true that 'radicalism' is not – and could not have been – a seventeenth-century concept, and that the authority of custom and precedent shaped people's thinking profoundly.²³ Those, like the Levellers, who were recognizably 'radical' in their desire to change some of the fundamental ordering principles of existing society, naturally not only expressed themselves in, but genuinely thought in and through the discourses of their time. Their vision of a very differently ordered politics was expressed through a reimagining of the past and the present as much as the future. A fictive past (of Anglo-Saxon liberties or of an original human state of benign government) could yield a present which still had embedded within it fundamental principles of equality and liberty; once people recognized those fundamental principles they could shape the future accordingly, avoiding the 'usurpations' and tyrannies of the recent past.²⁴ It was not just rhetorical sleight of hand to speak of fundamental or even ancient liberties, or the birthright of the English law, rather than self-consciously demanding radical change; and it does not render the Levellers merely nostalgic. This conception of past, present, and future was a substitute for the 'transfer mechanism' to a better society which J. C. Davis has seen as one of the requirements of early modern radicalism.²⁵ Indeed, Davis and Conal Condren both see the Levellers using innovative or transformative means to achieve the restoration of true order which they desired.²⁶ I would simply add that this 'restoration' was a profoundly far-reaching and imaginative one, which we can well describe as 'radical'; the same could be said of the Levellers' innovative and uniform version of 'localism' in the third Agreement of the People.

THE LEVELLER MOVEMENT

In the 1640s, England was convulsed by two civil wars, which culminated in the defeat of the royalists and the execution of Charles I on 30 January 1649. It was in the middle of this turbulent decade, with the parliamentarians nearing victory in the first civil war, that the Leveller movement began to emerge. Post-revisionist historiography has encouraged us to see genuine conflict on matters of political principle in the parliamentary turbulence of the earlier seventeenth century, and recent historians of the civil war have discerned radical ideas and energies right at the outset of the English events, in the later 1630s and early 1640s.²⁷ Even historians of a more revisionist temper would concede that the civil wars fought across the three kingdoms generated a new world of political polemic and an outburst of print; saw the breakdown of effective enforcement of press censorship and religious conformity; and brought the usual pressures and dislocations of war to local populations. Leveller ideas did not spring from nowhere in the mid-1640s, but it was only under circumstances like these that they could be developed in collaboration by a group of people, publicized widely, and used as a justification for popular political action which exerted real pressure on the direction of political events.

This study focuses on the Levellers' thought, rather than on the strategic and organizational aspects of the Levellers' history, their wider network of supporters, or the narrative of the political battles they fought over their years of activity. Consequently we will often be dealing with the writings of the major Leveller leaders – John Lilburne, Richard Overton, William Walwyn, and to a lesser extent John Wildman.[28] These were men of the middling sort, who between them had had considerable education; they or their families were incomers to London, making their way in the world of artisans, merchants, and lawyers structured by the City's regulatory companies and a complex and busy legal system; and they were religiously unorthodox, with links to the gathered congregations which promoted the most challenging forms of puritan expression (see Chapter 4). Walwyn, a younger son of a gentry family, in his forties in the 1640s, was the oldest, the most prosperous, and the most securely ensconced in the City's structures of regulation and privilege, as a freeman of the Merchant Adventurers' company. He remained the most cautious and well connected of the Leveller leaders, enduring only one spell of imprisonment, in 1649, when the perceived danger of the Levellers as a group to the new regime outweighed his own prudent withdrawal from the group's activities.[29] Lilburne and Overton were in their early thirties in the years of Leveller activity up to 1649, and Wildman turned twenty only near the start of the civil war; these men, like many of their followers, were much more insecurely placed in London and chafed more against its authorities. Overton and Wildman both appear to have attended Cambridge (Lilburne and Walwyn, by contrast, being autodidacts who claimed ignorance of Latin);[30] Lilburne and Overton were both deeply involved in the puritan separated congregations of the baptists, Overton in Amsterdam, and also both involved in the printing or smuggling of illicit works related to their religious views;[31] Wildman appears to have operated on the edges of the legal profession, and was able to supplement Lilburne's amateur interest in the law.[32] Lilburne was apparently the only one of the four to have served in the parliamentarian forces.

In spite of their overlapping concerns, the Leveller leaders were men of very different temperaments. Our sense of their characters rests largely on their individual writings, whether before or alongside the Leveller movement. Richard Overton, perhaps fittingly, is the figure of whom we have the least secure knowledge; his writings attacked their targets 'sometimes in a Comick, and otherwhiles in a Satyrick stile', and rather than creating a consistent persona, he delighted in appropriating popular pamphlet formats and inventing characters to dramatize his message.³³ His probable attendance at Cambridge and his General Baptist confession of faith nevertheless give us two reference points which help us to interpret his peculiar mixture of learned pastiche and popular form in his attacks on religious persecution. His reinvention of the Elizabethan 'Martin Marprelate' as 'Martin Marpriest' aligned him with radical critics of the church who did not observe puritan literary decencies. His heterodox beliefs (discussed further in Chapter 4) seem to have grounded his optimistic account of human rationality – but also the despair he felt when these hopes were betrayed by the ignorance and brutishness of the people. While he enjoyed mocking the pretensions of the learned, his political works have characteristic passages of abstract philosophizing which can seem rather close to the sophistry he condemned.

Walwyn's literary persona was quite different, although he too used popular forms to striking effect in his writings advocating religious toleration, particularly his sequence of colourful satirical attacks on Thomas Edwards, who had attacked the sects and Walwyn himself in his *Gangraena*. Walwyn's contributions to co-authored Leveller works may be quite extensive, but until he was imprisoned with the other Leveller leaders in 1649 he avoided putting his name to political works; the *Manifestation* of 1649 displays the same rhetoric of openness and plainness that characterized his tolerationist writing. Judging by both his own and his enemies' accounts, he played a central role in organizing petitioning, particularly the campaign of spring 1647 when Lilburne and Overton were in prison. While his rational and humane writing is notable for its gentleness, we should not underestimate his effectiveness as a political operator. According to his enemies, his 'devout, specious, meek, self-denying, soft and pleasant' style was merely a cover for his 'sligh, cunning and close subtlety'.³⁴

John Lilburne was already a well-known figure in the puritan and parliamentarian cause by the time these men began to come together as the core of the Leveller movement. He had been whipped, pilloried, and imprisoned for his activities in support of John Bastwick, one of the three famous puritans who had their ears cropped in 1637 for their polemic against the Laudian bishops; he had subsequently been rescued from a possible death sentence by a high-profile parliamentarian intervention, when imprisoned by the royalists in the first civil war. His flair for a self-publicist martyrdom, partly based on his reading of Foxe's *Book of Martyrs*, had already been displayed both in person and in print by the time he began the series of disputes around which the Leveller movement was eventually to crystallize.³⁵ His apparently endless turbulence drew the scorn of his critics, who accused him of being 'a professed Enemy to every present Government whatsoever it be', just as a rainbow is always on the other side of the sky from the sun.³⁶ Whether or not Lilburne sought trouble, he certainly always seemed to find it, and protest about his treatment. Even his sometime ally Henry Marten exasperatedly called him 'a man that always dwelt upon a hill in a house of glass'.[37] Lilburne's extraordinary record of repeated punishments and imprisonments, often stemming from disputes which fused personal animus with political significance, became the vehicle for his exposition of the wrongs done to 'free-born Englishmen' and the rights due to them. Lilburne himself, looking back at his public career and writings, divided them up into four stages, each involving a 'contest' with a different authority: the bishops (during his association with Bastwick), the House of Lords, the Commons and Lords jointly, and finally, after the execution of Charles I in 1649, the Council of State which acted as an executive body for the governing 'Rump' Parliament.[38] These last three stages involved collaboration with the other Leveller leaders, and formed the core of the Leveller movement's history, although we should not neglect the extent to which, initially, Lilburne's battles were those of the 'Independent' faction.[39]

Parliamentarian politics had been fractured from early in the civil war period, and divisions hardened between the 'political Independents', who generally took an aggressive line on the conduct of the war against the king, and the 'political Presbyterians', whose eagerness to find a swift settlement with the king was accompanied by a commitment to rebuilding a non-episcopal but coercive national church. Lilburne was heavily involved in Cromwell's battles against Presbyterian commanders and their sluggish attitude to the war, while Walwyn was involved in the war effort at Salters' Hall.[40] Lilburne made contact with the radical Independents of this group by the summer of 1645, and by the autumn David Como has detected a 'propaganda collective' in which Lilburne, Overton, and Walwyn were all involved, waging a battle in print against the Presbyterian party.[41] The Leveller leaders' strenuous objections to the imposition of religious uniformity, as well as their developing political tenets, motivated this struggle (see Chapter 4). The autumn of 1645 was significant for the development of Leveller thought, too: pamphleteers, some connected with Lilburne and some not, began to articulate the implications of a radical notion of parliamentary representation, which made MPs answerable to their electors outside Parliament, though through unclear mechanisms (see Chapter 2). This shift in the understanding of representation was the precondition for the Levellers' issuing of an 'appeal to the people' outside Parliament in 1647.

The political conflicts of this period, once Parliament's victory over the king was as good as secured at Naseby in June 1645, were over the terms of the treaty with the king which was to be hammered out. While extensive limits on the king, and perhaps even on his successors, might be on the agenda of both Presbyterians and Independents, the assumption was that the basic constitutional architecture of king and Privy Council, House of Lords and House of Commons, would remain. Lilburne and his colleagues challenged this, although sometimes only implicitly, from the outset. They had no truck with notions of a mixed constitution, instead asserting the supremacy of the House of Commons. When Lilburne was imprisoned by the authority of the House of Lords from the summer of 1646, the three men were spurred on in their protests not only against the judgement of a commoner by lords, but also against the status of the Lords themselves, derived from the arbitrary patronage of the monarchy rather than from popular consent. In his defence of Lilburne, Overton too incurred the anger of the authorities and was committed to Newgate.

The *Remonstrance of Many Thousand Citizens* of July 1646 was an early summation of Leveller radicalism on the constitution, and indicated themes which were to be much more fully developed, by the Levellers themselves and by those who took control of the revolution in 1648–49, executing the king and abolishing the House of Lords. We do not know the authors of the *Remonstrance*, but it was part of the literature which clustered around the case of John Lilburne and it was printed by Overton. It urged Parliament to realize that it was possible for a 'Nation to be happy without a King', and to abolish the veto and legal privileges of the Lords and end their sitting as a separate, unelected chamber.[42] The attitude towards Charles I hardened in the prudently anonymous *Regall Tyrannie Discovered* of January 1647, which all but spelt out the demand for his execution.[43] The petition of 11 September 1648 reiterated the demand at just the point when it could serve as one focus for a growing army campaign for regicide, and offer a sketch of an alternative constitution after the king's death.

The Levellers did not regard the regicide as a triumph, however, because, in taking up one side of their programme, the army grandees had ignored the other set of ideas in the 1646 *Remonstrance*. That 'remonstrance' was administered by the people 'to their owne House of Commons', and it voiced the Levellers' growing impatience with and distrust of elected MPs who seemed to be failing in their duties of representation. Having asserted the supremacy of the House of Commons precisely because that power (unlike that of king and lords) was derived from the consent of the people, Lilburne and his colleagues now divided constitutional 'supremacy' from ultimate sovereignty, and moved towards the view that a House which had betrayed the trust of its electors could be held accountable by them. In the spring of 1647, Lilburne and Overton were to launch an explicit 'appeal to the people' from their imprisonment – something which had no established mechanism and could effectively be a call to rebellion. Walwyn, in the meantime, was promoting a major petitioning campaign, another way in which the people might hope to hold their own Parliament accountable.

The year 1647 was the year of the New Model Army's politicization, faced with a Parliament which wanted to disband it and which saw its petitioning as treasonable. The predicaments of the Levellers and of the army radicals chimed with each other, and the Levellers attempted to gain the army men's support in 1647. The extent of personal contacts between civilian Levellers and army radicals is unclear, and as I show in Chapter 5, aspects of their thought remained distinct. However, the political ideas developed by the Levellers resonated with the army and can be seen reflected in the army's demands. At the Putney debates in the autumn, representatives of the rank and file debated the principles of political settlement with their officers, on the basis of two remarkable papers of demands: *The Case of the Armie Truly Stated*, and the first 'Agreement of the People'. The *Case* called for manhood suffrage, a demand which Lilburne had been hinting at and developing since the autumn of 1646. Indeed, in December 1646 Lilburne had argued that 'the poorest that lives' should have a vote, anticipating Colonel Rainborough's memorable plea in the great debate on the franchise at Putney that 'the poorest hee that is in England hath a life to live as the greatest hee'.[44] The first Agreement of the People, also tabled by the radicals, was an elegant and concise proposal for the fundamentals of a settlement. It established a mode of limiting the power of future parliaments (through the explicit reservation of powers by the people) which had already been hinted at in Leveller thought, and which the Levellers were to return to in subsequent manifestoes, whether framed as 'Agreements of the People' or not. More remarkably still, it was not a settlement which was to be imposed: it was to be ratified by the subscription of the people, inside and outside the army, asserting their inviolable ownership over their own consciences (the first reserve) and their superiority over their elected representatives. The first Agreement of the People was the radicals' attempt to find a settlement which would unite the interests of civilians and soldiers; it was taken up by the Levellers in London, and although other petitioning campaigns intervened, two further Agreements of the People were propounded, the second in the regicide crisis of 1648–49, and the third on May day in 1649 as a challenge to the new regime.

The Levellers had a significant role in making the establishment of a commonwealth without a king thinkable and justifiable, both through their attacks on the power of the monarchy and through their insistence on the supremacy of the House of Commons. The Levellers were organized and active in 1648 – the year of the second civil war, which turned some of the army men decisively against Charles I. Their great petition of 11 September became one of the focal points in the campaign which led to the trial and execution of Charles I. But the 'free state' which was established in 1649 struggled to find legitimation precisely because it was not constructed according to the principles of popular consent which the Levellers stipulated. Although the Leveller leaders had been involved in consultations at Whitehall at the end of 1648, the second Agreement of the People, which resulted from these negotiations, was sidelined and then dropped. Instead, the new regime consisted of the purged continuation of the apparently perpetual Long Parliament, and its Council of State, and Lilburne and some of his fellow Levellers soon proved to be among their most immediate and dangerous enemies. Lilburne, Walwyn, Overton, and Thomas Prince were taken into custody; mutiny in the army was crushed shortly after the issuing of the third Agreement of the People in May 1649; and Lilburne was put on trial for his life at the Guildhall in the autumn. That should have ended the movement, but Lilburne used all his popularity and persuasive power to convince the jury to acquit him, and lived to endure another trial in 1653 where he achieved the same result. In Chapter 6, I consider the more subtle afterlife of the Leveller movement, in the political ideas which the more oppositional republican writers of the 1650s may have inherited from it.

The Levellers' constitutional and religious demands were accompanied by a roster of social and economic complaints and demands. The Levellers were always opposed to forms of monopoly, and sought to break the grip that priests and lawyers as well as monopolizers of trade had on people. Both religion and the law should be accessible to people in English, so that ordinary people could understand their salvation and defend their rights without professional help. The abolition of tithes was part of this programme in religion; in the law, various reforming measures were proposed and the driving motive was to eradicate arbitrary power and the persistence of differential privileges in the legal system, as well as mitigating the harshness and inefficiency of the system. While the eradication of monopolies such as that of the Merchant Adventurers was pursued as a matter of principle, it formed part of a set of ideas about poverty and the economy which were well intentioned but patchy. A genuinely systematic concern for the poor was shown by the Levellers' opposition to the levying of indirect taxes rather than a proportional income tax; the Levellers also intermittently showed concern to reverse or prevent enclosures and eradicate base tenures.

LEVELLER THOUGHT AND THE LANGUAGES OF POLITICS

The Leveller leaders were pamphleteers, who went into print frequently and often reactively, with a mixture of shorter and longer, more immediate and more considered works. Historians or political theorists looking for a cogent, cohesive, and consistent political theory in particular Leveller works, or even spanning the Levellers' collective output, have sometimes found these writings frustrating. I do not share this frustration. The writings reveal the Levellers' thought developing and being worked out, effortfully, in real time, with all the revealing loose ends and blind alleys that involved. The Leveller leaders did not write lengthy and deliberate political treatises, and hence they did not work out and define terms of art to structure their arguments, unlike contemporaries such as Hobbes or Harrington. Their more urgent writing reflected the language of the political debates taking place around them and the assumptions of their contemporaries. That is not to say that they did not innovate: Chapters 1–3 present their political thought in the context of contemporary political arguments and languages, showing the ways in which they forged original arguments. But they did so largely in language which was common coin at least among groups of their contemporaries. A study of the Levellers' political language is thus a study of the political languages of the mid-seventeenth century more broadly.

These 'languages of political thought' have been the subject of much methodological discussion, and are sometimes even seen as constituting the proper subject of history of political thought, taking precedence over the particular arguments and articulations of them found in any given thinker's work.[45] Certainly, a sense of the texture of political argument and expression which surrounded an author is essential to any historical interpretation of his or her thought. Available patterns of argument and the vocabulary which habitually expressed them did not have such a stranglehold on these writers that they could not make original arguments, but they were the matrix out of which those arguments grew. They also provided the linguistic tools with which authors could communicate with their audience, even if their ultimate aim was to reshape their readers' beliefs and concepts.[46]

The world of politics in seventeenth-century England was not one of stable, uncontested paradigms and and discrete political languages. While historians have been able to pick out different types of discourse which fed into political debate, emanating from different specialist conceptual fields such as the common law or theology, for example, the fusion of these elements was complex. The choice of one type of language over another might signal a commitment to one vision of politics over another – but it might not. Each of these 'languages' was itself complex and contested: as we will see in Chapter 3, the language of the common law could certainly offer scope for radical interpretations as well as complacently conservative ones. We thus do not need to find Leveller thinking more 'genuine' when conducted in one linguistic mode than in another, or be suspicious about 'radicals' using an apparently 'conservative' language:[47] the Levellers found themselves surrounded by a complicated meld of different ways of thinking and talking about politics, and they naturally thought in and through these languages. Although I have separated out some of these elements here (considering natural law in Chapter 1, common law and positive law more generally in Chapter 3, theology in Chapter 4, and classical republicanism in Chapter 6), Leveller pamphlets often blended these elements relatively seamlessly. In this they merely reflected the argumentative world they grew from, where it was similarly common to draw on multiple vocabularies and modes of argument almost in the same breath.

There has been debate among historians about whether Leveller ideas came to them from 'above' or 'below' – whether they filtered down from high political theory, or were part of a persistent but only patchily recorded tradition of popular radicalism.[48] Recent scholarship emphasizes both the relatively high educational status of at least some of the Leveller writers, and the availability of 'high' traditions of thought in translation and in the controversial literature of the English Revolution.[49] I want to offer a word of caution here. It is important that we do not simply reverse the poles of the argument and align the Levellers with elite rather than plebeian traditions. The work of Adam Fox, Tim Harris, and Jonathan Barry, among others, has alerted us to the difficulty of drawing any sharp distinction between elite and popular culture in this period.[50] The popular and elite ends of the cultural spectrum fed each other and interacted with each other in far more complicated ways than used to be assumed; and there was a vast territory between the two, in which the 'middling sort' played an important part. Living on 'the lower fringes of the social and educational elite'[51] at a time when written news and polemic was devoured by many less educated than themselves, the Levellers did not have to go far to find material which fed their thinking and found its way into their writing. In this sense, they found their sources not above or below them, but around them, in great abundance. In Chapter 1, we will plunge into the world of parliamentarian argument – argument which was disseminated across the social spectrum in the appeal to the consciences of those who might fight for the Parliament – and consider the ways in which the Levellers drew on, challenged, and developed Parliamentarian thought.

NOTES

1 *A Remonstrance of Many Thousand Citizens* (1646), pp. 4–5.

2 For a defence of the proposition that ideas can be traced across texts from different periods, see M. Bevir, 'Are there perennial problems in political theory?' *Political Studies* 42 (1994).

3 The five key monographs on the movement and its leaders are: T. C. Pease, *The Leveller Movement* (Gloucester, Mass.: Peter Smith, 1965: originally published in 1916); M. A. Gibb, *John Lilburne the Leveller: A Christian Democrat* (London: Lindsay Drummond, 1947); Frank (1955); P. Gregg, *Free-born John: A Biography of John Lilburne* (London: Phoenix Press, 2000 reprint); and Brailsford (1961); H. Shaw, *The Levellers* (London: Longman, 1968) is a shorter introduction; in French we may add M. M. Gimelfarb Brack, *Liberté, Égalité, Fraternité, Justice! La vie et l'oeuvre De Richard Overton, Niveleur* (Berne: P. Lang 1979); O. Lutaud, *Cromwell, Les Niveleurs et La République*, 2nd edn (Paris: 1978). The Levellers as 'democrats': Pease, *Leveller Movement*, p. 149; Wolfe, 'Introduction', p. 12; D. B. Robertson, *The Religious Foundations of Leveller Democracy* (New York: Columbia University Press, 1951), p. 121; H&D, 'Introduction', p. 35; Brailsford, p. 118 on Lilburne's 'liberal democracy', p. 275 on the Levellers' 'classless political

democracy'; Frank, pp. 4, 245, 252, 254, classing the Levellers as 'social democrats'; G. E. Aylmer (ed.), *The Levellers in the English Revolution* (London: Thames & Hudson, 1975), 'Introduction', p. 9; P. Zagorin, *A History of Political Thought in the English Revolution* (London: Routledge & Kegan Paul, 1954), pp. 13–15, 17, 23, 28–9, 41. The Levellers as secularists: Pease, *Leveller Movement*, p. 217; Woodhouse, p. 48; Frank, p. 247.

4 Frank, pp. 251–6; Pease, *Leveller Movement*, p. 217.

5 Pease, *Ibid.*, p. 149; Zagorin, *A History of Political Thought*, p. 41; Robertson, *Religious Foundations of Leveller Democracy*, p. 121.

6 A. Sharp, 'Introduction', in Sharp (ed.) *The English Levellers* (Cambridge: Cambridge University Press, 1988), p. xii–xiii, discusses the objections to calling the Levellers democrats, before concluding that he sees them as 'liberal democrats'; D. Wootton, 'The Levellers', in John Dunn (ed.) *Democracy: The Unfinished Journey 508 BC to AD 1993* (Oxford: Oxford University Press, 1992), p. 73, regards the term as a 'harmless' anachronism. A. C. Houston, 'A way of settlement: the Levellers, monopolies and the public interest', *History of Political Thought* 14 (1993), 383–4, emphasizes the historically inappropriate nature of the term 'democracy', but concludes that forward-looking elements in Leveller thought perhaps made them 'democrats in spite of themselves'. J. C. Davis, 'The Levellers and democracy', *Past & Present* 40 (1968), 174–80 has held out against the use of the term, arguing that constitutional arrangements which we might call democratic were for the Levellers a means to an end rather than desirable in themselves.

7 C. Hill, *The World Turned Upside Down: Radical Ideas During the English Revolution* (Harmondsworth: Penguin, 1987), pp. 14–15, 38; C. Hill, *The Century of Revolution, 1603–1714*, 2nd edn (London: Routledge, 1980), pp. 110–11; C. B. Macpherson, *The Political Theory of Possessive Individualism: Hobbes to Locke* (Oxford: Clarendon Press, 1962), pp. 107–59; B. Manning, *The English People and the English Revolution, 1640–1649*, 2nd edn (London: Heinemann, 1991), pp. 378, 423.

8 Hill, *The World Turned Upside Down*, pp. 114, 118–23.

9 *The Devil's Whore* (UK mini-series, Channel 4, 2008).

10 A. Hessayon and D. Finnegan (eds), *Varieties of Seventeenth- and Early Eighteenth-century English Radicalism in Context* (Farnham: Ashgate, 2011); G. Burgess and M. Festenstein (eds), *English Radicalism, 1550–1850* (Cambridge: Cambridge University Press, 2007); J. Gurney, *Brave Community: The Digger Movement in the English Revolution* (Manchester: Manchester University Press, 2007); more popular or introductory works include A. Bradstock, *Radical Religion in Cromwell's England: A Concise History from the English Civil War to the End of the Commonwealth* (London: I. B. Tauris, 2011); E. Vallance, *A Radical History of Britain: Visionaries, Rebels and Revolutionaries: The Men and Women Who Fought for Our Freedoms* (London: Little, Brown, 2009). Literary scholars arguably resumed the focus on radical texts earlier, with contributions such as N. Smith, *Literature and Revolution in England, 1640–1660* (New Haven and London: Yale University Press, 1994); D. Norbrook, *Writing the English Republic: Poetry, Rhetoric, and Politics, 1627–1660* (Cambridge: Cambridge University Press, 1999); N. McDowell, *The English Radical Imagination: Culture, Religion and Revolution, 1630–1660* (Oxford: Oxford University Press, 2003).

11 M. A. Kishlansky, 'The Army and the Levellers: the roads to Putney', *Historical Journal* 22:4 (1979), p. 796; and see Chapter 5 below.

12 Frank, p. 77; Pease, *Leveller Movement*, p. 156; B. Worden, 'The Levellers in history and

Introduction

memory, c.1660–1960', in M. Mendle (ed.) *The Putney Debates of 1647: The Army, the Levellers and the English State* (Cambridge: Cambridge University Press, 2001), pp. 280–2; J. S. Morrill and P. Baker, 'The case of the armie truly re-stated', in M. Mendle (ed.) *The Putney Debates of 1647*, p. 119; Kishlansky, 'The Army and the Levellers: the roads to Putney', p. 797, n.

13 N. Carlin, 'Leveller organization in London', *Historical Journal* 27:4 (1984).

14 D. R. Como, 'An unattributed pamphlet by William Walwyn: new light on the prehistory of the leveller movement', *Huntington Library Quarterly* 69:3 (2006), 370.

15 Frank, pp. 55, 63–6.

16 T. Edwards, *The third part of Gangraena. Or, A new and higher discovery of the errors, heresies, blasphemies, and insolent proceedings of the sectaries of these times* ([28 December] 1646; E.368[5]), p. 156.

17 J. Peacey, 'John Lilburne and the Long Parliament', *Historical Journal* 43:3 (2000), 625–46.

18 J. S. Morrill and P. Baker, 'The case of the armie truly re-stated', in M. Mendle (ed.) *The Putney Debates Revisited* (Cambridge: Cambridge University Press, 2001), pp. 119–20.

19 Como, 'An unattributed pamphlet', 371.

20 See Chapter 5 for further discussion.

21 For contemporary reaction against the Levellers, see P. Baker, 'Rhetoric, reality, and the varieties of civil-war radicalism', in J. S. A. Adamson (ed.) *The English Civil War: Conflict and Contexts, 1640–49* (Basingstoke: Palgrave Macmillan, 2009), 202–24; M. Sampson, 'A story "too tedious to relate at large"? Response to the Levellers, 1647–1653', *Parergon*, 5 (1987), 135–54.

22 J. S. Morrill, *The Revolt of the Provinces: Conservatives and Radicals in the English Civil War, 1630–1650* (London: Allen & Unwin, 1980), pp. 100–1 (comparison with the Clubmen); J. S. Morrill, 'The army revolt of 1647', in A. C. Duke and C. A. Tamse (eds) *Britain and the Netherlands: Vol. VI, Law and Society* (The Hague: 1977), p. 55; B. Kümin, 'Gemeinde und Revolution: die kommunale Prägung der englischen Levellers', in H. Blickle (ed.) *Gemeinde und Staat im Alten Europa* (Munich: 1998), 361–96; contrast R. Tuck, *Philosophy and Government 1572–1651* (Cambridge: Cambridge University Press, 1993), pp. 242–3.

23 J. C. Davis, 'Radicalism in a traditional society: the evaluation of radical thought in the English commonwealth 1649–1660', *History of Political Thought* 3 (1982), 193–213; J. C. Davis, 'Reassessing radicalism in a traditional society: two questions', in G. Burgess and M. Festenstein (eds) *English Radicalism, 1550–1850* (Cambridge: Cambridge University Press, 2007), 338–72; C. Condren, 'Radicals, conservatives and moderates in early modern political thought: a case of Sandwich Islands syndrome?', *History of Political Thought* 10 (1989), 525–42; C. Condren, 'Afterword: radicalism revisited', in G. Burgess and M. Festenstein (eds) *English Radicalism, 1550–1850* (Cambridge: Cambridge University Press, (2007), 311–37 and G. Burgess, 'Radicalism and the English Revolution', in G. Burgess and M. Festenstein (eds) *English Radicalism, 1550–1850* (Cambridge: Cambridge University Press, 2007), 62–86.

24 See my forthcoming chapter, 'Radicalism in early modern England: innovation or reformation?', in B. Bagchi (ed.) *The Politics of the Impossible: Utopia and Dystopia Reconsidered* (Delhi: Sage publications).

25 Davis, 'Radicalism in a traditional society'.
26 C. Condren, 'Afterword: radicalism revisited', p. 317; J. C. Davis, 'Reassessing radicalism', p. 358.
27 D. Cressy, *England on Edge: Crisis and Revolution 1640–1642* (Oxford: Oxford University Press, 2006); J. Adamson, *The Noble Revolt: The Overthrow of Charles I* (London: Weidenfeld & Nicolson, 2007) works in a revisionist framework but offers an intriguing picture of his protagonists' vision of an aristocratic 'commonwealth'.
28 For fuller biographical and individual studies of these men, see *ODNB*; Gibb, *John Lilburne*; Gregg, *Free-born John*; MMT; A. L. Morton, 'A still and soft voice', in his *The World of the Ranters: Religious Radicalism in the English Revolution* (London: Lawrence & Wishart,1970), 143–96; B. Taft, 'Journey to Putney: the quiet Leveller', in G. J. Schochet, P. E. Tatspaugh, and C. Brobeck (eds) *Religion, Resistance, and Civil War* (Washington: Folger Institute Center for the History of British Political Thought, 1990), 63–81; Gimelfarb Brack, *Liberté, Égalité, Fraternité, Justice!*; D. R. Adams, 'Religion and reason in the thought of Richard Overton, the Leveller' (PhD dissertation, University of Cambridge, 2003); M. P. Ashley, *John Wildman, Plotter and Postmaster. A Study of the English Republican Movement in the Seventeenth Century* (London: Jonathan Cape, 1947). Lilburne's self-documentation in print and in interaction with the authorities mean that the details of his life are much more securely known than for the others, where historians have resorted to more conjecture in piecing together the narrative.
29 MMT, pp. 37–8.
30 J. Venn and J. A. Venn, *Alumni Cantabrigienses: A Biographical List of All Known Students, Graduates, and Holders of Office at the University of Cambridge, from the Earliest Times to 1900*, 2 parts in 10 vols (Cambridge: Cambridge University Press, 1922–54), III.289 Richard Overton matriculated sizar at Queens', 1631; IV.408 John Wildman of Norfolk matriculated sizar at Corpus Christi, 1637.
31 See Chapter 3; D. R. Como, 'Secret printing, the crisis of 1640, and the origins of civil war radicalism', *Past & Present* 196 (2007), 37–82; D. R. Adams, 'The secret printing and publishing career of Richard Overton the Leveller, 1644–46', *The Library* 11:1 (2010), 3–88.
32 ODNB.
33 Walwyn, *Writings*, 405–6.
34 [Price et al.], *Walwins Wiles*, 2–3.
35 J. R. Knott, *Discourses of Martyrdom in English Literature, 1563–1694* (Cambridge: Cambridge University Press, 1993), pp. 144–50.
36 Canne, *Lieut. Colonel J. Lilburn*, 23–4.
37 S. Barber, *A Revolutionary Rogue: Henry Marten and the English Republic* (Gloucestershire: Sutton Publishing, 2000), p. 15.
38 Lilburne, *The Innocent Man's Second-Proffer* ([22 October] 1649; 669.f.14/85), single sheet.
39 Peacey, 'John Lilburne and the Long Parliament'.
40 MMT, pp. 20–1.
41 Como, 'An unattributed pamphlet', p. 370.
42 Wolfe, pp. 115–17.

43 Brailsford, pp. 117–18.

44 *CP*, vol. 1, p. 301.

45 J. G. A. Pocock, 'Languages and their implications: the transformation of the study of political thought', in his *Politics, Language and Time: Essays in Political Thought* (London: Methuen, 1972), pp. 24–5.

46 Q. Skinner, 'Some problems in the analysis of political thought and action', in J. Tully (ed.) *Meaning and Context: Quentin Skinner and His Critics* (Cambridge: Cambridge University Press, 1988).

47 G. Burgess, 'Protestant polemic: the Leveller pamphlets', *Parergon*, n.s. 11 (1993), 45–67; G. Burgess, *The Politics of the Ancient Constitution: An Introduction to English Political Thought, 1603–1642* (Basingstoke: Macmillan, 1992), pp. 90–3; A. Sharp, 'John Lilburne's discourse of law', *Political Science* 40 (1988), 18–33; J. G. A. Pocock, *The Ancient Constitution and the Feudal Law: A Study of English Historical Thought in the Seventeenth Century. A Reissue with a Retrospect.* (Cambridge: Cambridge University Press, 1987), pp. 125–6.

48 C. Hill, 'From Lollards to Levellers', in M. Cornforth (ed.) *Rebels and Their Causes: Essays in Honour of A. L. Morton* (London: Lawrence and Wishart, 1978) hypothesized 'a continuing underground tradition' of radical and heretical belief which 'burst into the open in the 1640s' in the Levellers and others (pp. 56, 62).

49 N. McDowell, *The English Radical Imagination*; D. Wootton, 'From rebellion to revolution: the crisis of the winter of 1642/3 and the origins of civil war radicalism', *English Historical Review*, 105 (1990), 654–69; S. D. Glover, 'The Putney debates: popular versus élitist republicanism', *Past & Present*, 164 (1999), 47–80; Adams, 'Religion and reason', pp. 85–93 on Richard Overton, cautioning against over-emphasizing Overton's scholarliness.

50 J. Barry, 'Literacy and literature in popular culture: reading and writing in historical perspective', and T. Harris, 'Problematising popular culture', in T. Harris (ed.) *Popular Culture in England, c. 1500–1850* (Basingstoke: Macmillan, 1995), 1–27; A. Fox, *Oral and Literate Culture in England, 1500–1700* (Oxford: Clarendon Press, 2001).

51 D. Wootton, 'Leveller democracy and the Puritan Revolution', in J. H. Burns and M. Goldie (eds) *The Cambridge History of Political Thought 1450–1700* (Cambridge: Cambridge University Press, 1991), p. 413; G. E. Aylmer, 'Gentlemen Levellers?', *Past and Present* 49 (1970), 120–5.

Chapter 1

Consent and the origins of government

The Levellers are often credited with a ground-breaking social contract theory: believing that England's civil wars and political conflicts had reduced the nation to a state of nature, they devised an entirely new means of reconstituting a polity out of the mass of newly ungoverned individuals. They did this by drawing up an 'Agreement of the People', to be subscribed by individuals, setting out the extent and nature of the powers which the people agreed to transmit to their future governors. On this view, the Levellers not only produced the first proposed written constitution for England (albeit one which was never implemented), but did so by bringing out of the fictive past the original act of consent which, in parliamentarian theory, was the foundation of all legitimate government. The Levellers, the story goes, not only embraced the most alarming consequences of parliamentarian consent theory by appealing beyond Parliament to the ultimate authority of the people, but took the theory to its logical conclusion by seeking to reconstitute a polity from scratch through the actual, written consent of its members.

The Levellers did, of course, appeal beyond Parliament to the people; and they did seek settlement (at some points) through successive versions of the 'Agreements of the People', which would be validated by popular subscription rather than simple implementation by the parliamentary authorities. The parliamentarian consent theory derived from the natural law tradition was indeed the foundation of these elements of Leveller thought. But the nuts and bolts of consent theory could be used to build theories which were markedly different in character, and this was not simply a question of some being bolder or more radical than others. Parliamentarian thought was not monolithic, and it is only by unpicking the divergent strands within parliamentarian thought that we can really see the distinctiveness of the Levellers' contribution. Wootton has argued that all the essential positions articulated by the Levellers were prefigured in earlier 'radical' parliamentarian tracts, and there is some truth in this.[1] The individual elements of Leveller thought were all at least hinted at in earlier parliamentarian writing. What was original about the Levellers was their synthesis of two positions which had previously belonged to different, often mutually exclusive, tendencies within parliamentarian thought.

In these first two chapters, I will explore the particular character of the Levellers' thought about the origins and nature of government, challenging some of the grander claims which have been made for the Levellers as theorists, while trying to give a fuller sense of their refashioning of the parliamentarian materials, and of the distinctive and powerful view of political life that their theory expressed. The Agreements of the People may not have been 'social contracts', and the Leveller appeal to the people was not intended either to return the nation to, or rescue the nation from, a state of nature: but they were both powerful expressions of the Levellers' troubled but insistent emphasis on the underlying political power of the people. Again, the Leveller theory was not a simple 'radicalization' of parliamentarian theory; but in its attempt to combine the sovereignty of an elected chamber with the ongoing political engagement of the people outside Parliament, it was an expression of the complicated impulses and allegiances of passionate parliamentarians who came to fear the tyranny of parliaments as much as that of kings. This was what led to the Levellers' attempt to meld two largely separate streams of parliamentarian thought: parliamentary sovereignty and the appeal to the people.

THE ORIGINS OF POLITICAL POWER

Early modern thinking about the state of nature is perhaps most familiar to us from Hobbes's grim picture of 'continuall feare, and danger of violent death; And the life of man, solitary, poore, nasty, brutish, and short'. The state of nature, the condition of humans before or without government, had been discussed by both Catholic and Protestant thinkers in the natural law tradition, and had come to be a crucial building-block in theories of government by consent. Hobbes's desperate reading of it had its antecedents, but it was also highly polemical, justifying the people's willing surrender of freedom and rights in favour of the protection offered by the 'Mortall God' Leviathan, the sovereign power.[2]

In spite of Hobbes's royalist tendencies, however, the theory of an original state of nature in which people were free and equal was far more employed by parliamentarians than by royalists. Hobbes had found a mechanism for transmuting freedom and equality into a robustly absolutist state, but many royalists avoided such suggestive starting-points altogether. Parliamentarians were much more likely to exploit these ideas, but, like Hobbes, they used them as a starting-point for drawing their desired conclusions about the current constitution. The people, when they consented to government, must have built in a protection for themselves, in the form of some right of resistance against the king, to be exercised by their lesser magistrates. Like Hobbes's people, they gave up much of their freedom and equality when they entered the governed state; they just drove a harder bargain.

Parliamentarians were thus in agreement on two crucial shared principles: that legitimate political authority was only originally established by the consent of its subjects; and that in that process of consent, restrictions might be placed on the exercise of power. However, the immediate source of political power was not a matter of complete agreement among parliamentarians. Many (sometimes called the 'Presbyterian' thinkers) insisted on 'designation theory': the view that political power itself was derived directly from God, only its form or location being subject to human consent. These authors were careful not to locate the power in the people themselves even at the point before they had determined the form of their government. If the people had consented to government by kings, then, the power passed directly from God to those kings; political power was not actually derived from the people, but the people simply 'designated' their ruler. While designation theory was perfectly compatible in theory with a people's choice of democracy or aristocracy rather than monarchy, the English constitution was clearly a monarchy, whether mixed or unmixed, limited or absolute. Designation theory had the consequence that the power the monarch held within the English constitution must be understood to be derived immediately from God, not simply transferred from the people. This meant that the monarch had an independent and divinely sanctioned power which could not be reduced to the rights or power of the people, and effectively excluded any possibility of parliamentary sovereignty.[3]

A very different emphasis is seen in those writers who did place power originally in the people, and saw the people as not just consenting to the use of power over them, but actually consenting to the use of their *own* power over them – effectively transferring their own power to their rulers. Henry Parker was a key exponent of this view, arguing that 'Power is originally inherent in the people, and it is nothing else but that might and vigour which such or such a societie of men containes in it selfe.'[4] More radical parliamentarian works challenging the constitutional place of the king and moving towards parliamentary sovereignty also used this theory of the people's 'constituent authority'. The authors of *Remonstrans Redivivus* asserted that 'originally the Supreme power being in the whole people, Parliaments were by them constituted to manage the same'.[5] These theorists of original popular power did not, of course, deny that power ultimately derived from God; but they saw that power as divinely implanted in the people as part of the natural order. God 'hath originally founded all authority in the people'; the people then delegated

Consent and the origins of government

it for its right use. So, concluded the anonymous pamphlet *Touching the Fundamentall Lawes*, the 'universall and popular authority, that is in the body of the people' could be exercised by Parliament.[6]

The Levellers were unequivocal believers in the original political power of the people. For them, political power was simply that power which was inherent in the people, now exercised on their behalf by government. Parliament's power was 'the same Power that was in our selves, to have done the same'.[7] They had no truck with the designation theorists' belief in the king's possession of political power immediately from God, and were correspondingly willing to follow parliamentarian theorists of constituent authority in the direction of an assertion of parliamentary sovereignty. However, this did not mean that their thinking about the people's original power was of exactly the same nature or led them to exactly the same conclusions as the arguments of men like Parker.

We can start to see the particular quality of the Levellers' thinking about the people's power if we look at the glimpses the Levellers give us of an original state of humankind. The Levellers did not use the term 'state of nature',[8] but Overton and Lilburne, in the early phase of Leveller cooperation in 1646, did both include passages in their works which sketched out the natural state or moral progress of humanity. The two men were profoundly different thinkers, and their narratives here are very different in tone. Overton almost equated the divine with 'nature', and certainly read divine intentions through nature, whereas for Lilburne the presence of God as the only legitimate absolute ruler was crucial. This makes the similarities in their views even more striking, and it is those similarities which I will explore here.

The postscript to Lilburne's *Free-man's Freedom Vindicated* of June 1646 laid out that God – by his 'unlimited' and 'soveraign will' – had given to his creature mankind 'the soveraignty (under himselfe) over all the rest of his Creatures', and made him a rational creature. However this sovereignty certainly did not extend to fellow human beings: all human beings since Adam and Eve 'are, and were by nature all equall and alike in power, digni[t]y, authority, and majesty, none of them having (by nature) any authority, dominion or majesteriall power, one over or above another'.[9] The equality of individuals and their lack of political power over each other are unsurprising: they are standard elements in discussions of the state of nature in the natural law tradition. But Lilburne also suggested a very positive picture of the attributes of life in a state of nature in that list of equally distributed qualities: 'power, dignity, authority, and majesty'. People may not be able to exercise their natural authority and power over each other, but they possess these qualities in and over themselves, and perhaps in relation to the rest of creation.

In *An Arrow Against All Tyrants*, dating from October 1646, Overton gave a similarly positive picture of the attributes of natural man. The primary purpose of the passage was to set out principles which demonstrated that parliamentary power could never have been unlimited; but within this context, the exposition was ambitious, covering (as the title page glossed it) 'the originall rise, extent, and end of Magisteriall power, the naturall and Nationall rights, freedomes and properties of Mankind'. While Overton's picture was set out in a more technical language of 'self-propriety', in many ways it meshed rather well with Lilburne's view of the dignity and majesty of people in a state of nature. For Overton, 'every man by nature [is] a King, Priest and Prophet in his owne naturall circuite and compasse'.[10] While he emphasized the boundaries of each natural person's 'selfe propriety', which meant that no one must be 'an encroacher & an invader upon an other mans Right', the picture of each person enjoying their own 'naturall, innate freedom and propriety' was a very positive one, and the insistence on the language of 'propriety' as well as that of freedom connoted a certain power that each person has over their own little domain. Like Lilburne's, Overton's natural people seem to have dignity, authority, and majesty. These hints that some kind of power is a natural attribute of all people are reinforced by Overton's comments about the source of the power which the House of Commons exercises: it is the 'natural Soveraignity' of the people, their 'naturall rights and powers'.[11]

This state of nature is poles apart from the pessimistic visions of those rare royalists (such as Hobbes and also Dudley Digges) who were prepared to work from the same premise of original equality and liberty. Naturally, they emphasized the brutality of the state of nature in order to show that the break from it needed to be absolute and irrevocable. But among parliamentarians, too, the terms on which people agreed to leave the state of nature were as crucial as the original liberty and equality which they enjoyed before that point, and those terms would similarly depend on what was a rational bargain to make so as to escape a particular version of the state of nature. Lilburne and Overton, however, said little to indicate what the disadvantages of this original state were, and presented it as remarkably benign. Correspondingly, the governed state which they endorsed was designed to protect rather than to obliterate many of the features of the original state of nature.

The natural state of humans was not confined to the prehistoric past in these Leveller accounts. The Levellers did not, after all, talk about the 'state of nature', but about the *law* of nature. Even when they specified the 'originall' or 'prime' law of nature, the operation of this law was not necessarily confined to the prepolitical past. The Leveller discussions of the natural endowments of humankind are punctuated by present-tense verbs unsuited to a fable about the distant past. Thus, for Overton, 'To every Individuall in nature, is given an individuall property by nature' and just as we 'are delivered of God by the hand of nature into this world, every one with a naturall, innate freedom and propriety', 'even so are we to live'.[12] Overton was not setting out a historical progress from lawless freedom to government, but a set of propositions about the natural rights we all possess, and the circumstances under which we might want to depute them. Even when Lilburne did offer a historical account of natural rights, he brought in an intrusive present-tense verb to indicate that the state of affairs he described was not confined to the past: Adam, Eve and all their descendants 'are, and were by nature all equall and alike in power'.[13] The Levellers were not invoking a 'state' of nature, confined to a hypothetical or historical past, but the natural attributes of humans and the provisions of the law of nature.

The transition from a state of nature to a governed state was a transaction which, by definition, involved the people bargaining away or transferring to their governors some of the freedoms, rights, or powers they had in the state of nature. But that was not the emphasis of the Levellers' accounts. Overton's opening lines set out the individual's essential 'selfe propriety', which was 'not to be invaded or usurped by any'. This was not a description just of the state of nature; it continued to be the case that there was a core of 'rights and liberties' which simply could not be 'communicated', as they were too essential to each person's being and well-being. None of nature's original gifts to each person could be transferred without that person's consent, but some could not be transferred at all.[14] As we will see in Chapter 4, this reservation of rights to the individual protected each person's spiritual integrity as well as their physical safety.

This all raises the question of how clearly demarcated the state of nature might be from political society, and what processes or transactions produced that political society. An attractive state of nature does not easily justify a decision to enter into a radically different social organization via a social contract. Rather, as in many political origin-narratives, including those of Hooker and Grotius, we might expect any change to be precipitated at least partly by less dramatic factors such as sociability and a growth in social complexity requiring regulation – drawing on the Aristotelian account.[15] Yet these factors are barely touched on in Leveller accounts: Levellers did cite the Golden Rule, and the Ciceronian dictum that we are not born for ourselves alone, but any notion of sociability here is very thin. The other motivation for government which we might expect to find emphasized, at least in authors with a gloomier picture of human nature, is the corruption of human nature: the view, most influentially stated by Augustine, that it was the Fall which brought about the necessity for human government. One of the last joint Leveller statements, the rather defensive *Manifestation* issued from prison in 1649, responded to the slander of anarchy by defending the need for government: 'the pravity and corruption of mans heart is such that there could be no living without it'; the Levellers, they insisted, sought good government, not the indisputable evils of 'Confusion'. It is true that Leveller thought by 1649 displayed on occasion a deep disillusionment with human nature.[16] However, even in the Levellers' late thought, corruption was more often brought on by the exercise of power than cured by submission to it; it is likely that the Levellers' very genuine belief in good government rather than anarchy was being defended in slightly disingenuous terms in the *Manifestation*. Walwyn, the chief drafter of the spring *Manifestation*, issued his personal reply to the accusations of his enemies in the summer of 1649, and found room in it to praise Montaigne's innocent cannibals, suggesting a rather more positive view of the natural state of mankind.[17] In general, Leveller references to the natural or divine purposes of government were optimistic, even where they tacitly suggested some disharmony in the state of nature: 'solid peace and true freedome ... is the end of the primitive institution of all governments'.[18] Peace, and certainly freedom, were not unknown before government; they simply needed refining and securing. While Lilburne and Overton did employ narratives of moral decline and the Fall, they did not link these with the need for government per se; rather, they linked them with the rise of illegitimate, tyrannical government.

Lilburne's postscript to *Londons Liberty in Chains* (1646) is a suggestive example of this. Here he stated that when God originally created man in his own image (that is, endowed with reason and understanding), he 'made him not Lord, or gave him dominion over the individuals of Mankind, no further then by free consent, or agreement, by giving up their power, each to other, for their better being'. It seems that *consensual* government may be part of God's original dispensation. What was not part of God's benign dispensation was the 'Lordship' or 'Soveraignty' which rules by 'Will, and Prerogative'. It was due to the Fall, and the corruption of human reason, that man 'became tyrannicall, and beastly in his principles and actions', and hence started to impose this form of government on others.[19] Within this moral history of mankind, it seems that government by consent might, for Lilburne, be part of the innocent, prelapsarian state of mankind. In a sense, Lilburne, like the Diggers, was here advocating a return to an original moral innocence. For him, Christ's work as 'the Restorer and Repairer of mans losse and fall' enabled human reason to be recovered and exercised in legitimate government.[20]

While Overton did not offer a sequential moral narrative of history, he did seem to hold a similar view to Lilburne's. In *A Defiance Against All Arbitrary Usurpations*, he talked of (the English) people's being 'naturally of themselves noble and free', but explained that people had degenerated and become 'grosly ignorant of themselves, and of their own naturall immunities, and strength too, wherewith God by nature hath inrich'd them ... being void of the use of Reason for want of capacitie to discern, whereof, and how far God by nature hath made them free'. People thus corrupted thought 'usurpation, and tyranny, better then naturall freedome and property'.[21] Overton drew a sharp distinc-

Consent and the origins of government

tion between innocent freedom and sinful tyranny. Tyranny was clearly not all government, but government which did not comply with the requirements of consent, and under which people became slavish and failed to exercise 'their natural immunities' against overweening power. Presumably, under a government which was the result of the people's enlightened consent, people retained their 'naturall freedom and property'.

We might posit the view that government by consent was seen by the Levellers as an expression of the secondary laws of nature, in accordance with the will of God to see people in properly governed societies; and we might fill in the gaps in the Leveller accounts and suggest that ultimately humans *did* need to leave the state of nature because their self-propriety, though prescribed by the law of nature, was subject to violations which could only effectively be prevented by human, governmental enforcement. These views were standard, and the Leveller accounts are not incompatible with them. Nonetheless, it is striking that the Levellers did not express such views. Rather, they emphasized the division not between initial freedom and subsequent government, but between that initial freedom, perhaps extended into government by consent, and a later stage of wicked tyranny. And, in a way which was typical of the Levellers throughout their careers as a movement, they were far quicker to identify the sins of the governors than those of the governed. For this reason, at least in these optimistic early accounts, sin figured not as the cause of coercive government, but as a sign of its eventual corruption.

It is instructive to contrast the Levellers' account of human nature and government with that of Henry Parker, the parliamentarian theorist often credited with breaking away most decisively from historical justifications in favour of a theory of natural law. While the Levellers certainly did learn from Parker's contract theory, the character of their thought was strikingly different. Parker's theory – laid out most clearly in his *Jus Populi* of 1644, but already present in his earlier propaganda works – was of a decisive, artificial contract of government, arising out of the fallen nature of mankind. Human 'jurisdiction', as opposed to divine 'order', 'derives not it self from Nature, unlesse we mean corrupted nature'.[22] Although Parker mentioned in passing that the people had reserved rights to themselves out of Parliament as well as in Parliament, what he emphasized was the principle of self-preservation which must be embedded in any constitution formed by consent, and which was effectively vested in Parliament by the people when they contracted to be governed. For Tuck, what divided Parker from the Levellers was that Parker's was a theory of collective natural rights rather than individual natural rights.[23] But I think the difference is also that Parker's collective right of self-preservation – the supreme law of *salus populi*, the safety of the people – was not a simple carrying-over of the people's prepolitical rights. It was, rather, part of the bargain they made when they entered government, and it – or the means of defending it – became institutionalized through that contract. The contract abrogated other original rights, but it enshrined that one. Consequently, it was the contract, rather than an idyllic picture of original natural rights, which was important to Parker. For the Levellers, it was not simply the principle of consent, but the original natural rights themselves, which were key. The Levellers did at least sometimes indicate that some original rights were surrendered when the people transferred their powers to their governors, but they placed the emphasis on those rights which survived. The transition to benign, consensual government was not a decisive break, but simply a development of the right and natural state of things.

CONSENT AND CONTRACTS

Modern scholars have been keen to see the Levellers as exponents, or even originators, of a social contract theory: a theory which explains not only how a society chooses and subjects itself to its governors through a political contract, but one which explains how society itself is created out of a multitude of free individuals. So, for Frank, the Levellers are 'the first of the thinkers of the Puritan Revolution who state clearly the theory of the social compact'.[24] Brailsford, too, sees the reduction of society to a 'state of nature' and its reconstitution by a 'new social contract' as the 'discovery' which the Levellers 'bequeathed to posterity'.[25] For Hampsher-Monk, similarly, 'The Agreements of the People were social contracts' designed to bring people back out of the state of nature into which England had degenerated.[26] Höpfl and Thompson's important 1979 critique of over-schematized readings of the history of contract theory offers many salutary warnings to a reader of the vocabulary of consent, contract, and natural law in the Leveller writings, but still gives the Levellers a pivotal role in achieving 'a conjuncture of covenant (their term was "agreement") and individual natural right'.[27] While their account is rightly sceptical about the centrality of a 'state of nature' to Leveller thought, their emphasis on the role of individual rights and individual consent places the Levellers a step beyond the resistance theorists who had primarily derived their arguments from the political covenants made by communities. One dissenting voice in the scholarship is Gleissner, who suggests that Hooker's far less rigid natural law account of the growth of human society via consent but motivated by sociability may have been an important influence on the Levellers. His downplaying of 'apparent references to a social contract' in Leveller writings and his emphasis on a more gradual consensual process based on a positive view of human nature tallies well with my reading of the Levellers' state of nature. The influence of Hooker on Overton and Lilburne may not be attested, but Nicholas McDowell has shown that William Walwyn was certainly receptive to Hooker's optimistic view of human rationality.[28]

Consent and the origins of government

The emphasis which the Levellers placed not only on the natural freedom but also on the natural authority of human beings was designed to underpin their account of the nature of political power. As we have seen, not all parliamentarian theorists subscribed to a theory of the 'constituent authority' of the people; for some, the people had the power to 'designate' their governors, but political power itself came not from the people but from God. The Levellers, however, followed Henry Parker in their insistence that political power was nothing other than the original power of individuals. How, then, did that power come to be exercised by governors?

There is no definitive Leveller account of an originary moment when free individuals yielded up (some of) their natural rights and transferred (some of) their natural power to put themselves under government. This is, in itself, a striking fact. While the Levellers' emphasis falls insistently on the processes of consent which make any government legitimate and give it its power, these processes are not pinned down to a single moment in time. The (original) constitution of any legitimate political authority must indeed take place 'by the mutuall consent of a People',[29] but we are told nothing about how this could come about from a state of nature. Lilburne offers an endearingly indecisive account of how governments come to have dominion over people: 'by institution, or donation, that is to say, by mutuall agreement or consent – given, derived, or assumed, by mutuall consent and agreement'.[30] Although Lilburne hints at the technical distinctions between different ways of acquiring governmental authority, it is telling that in the end they all seem to boil down to 'mutuall consent and agreement', and there is no elaboration which might enable us to pin the process down in time or detail.

The further the Leveller texts are examined, the harder it becomes to separate consent *to* political society from consent *in* political society. The Levellers systematically elided the difference between choosing a new Parliament and entering a governed state – or at any rate, those passages most easily read as accounts of the institution of government turn out on closer inspection to be about electing a House of Commons. Consider this account by Overton:

> And thus Sir, and no otherwise are you [Marten and his fellow MPs] instated into your soveraign capacity, for the free people of this Nation, for their better being, discipline, government, propriety and safety, have each of them communicated so much unto you (their *Chosen Ones*) of their naturall rights and powers, that you might thereby become their absolute Commissioners and lawfull Deputies, but no more; and that by contraction of those their severall Individuall Communications confer'd upon, and united in you, you alone might become their own naturall proper, soveraign power, therewith singly and only impowred for their severall weales, safeties and freedomes, and no otherwise: ... for no more can be communicated from the generall then is included in the particulars, whereof the generall is compounded.[31]

The elements we might expect from a social contract are here: the transfer of individuals' power, specifically designated as 'naturall', to a common political authority; the transition motivated by a desire for order, security, and property rights ('propriety'), as in many accounts of the transition from a 'state of nature' to government; the creation of a power which has genuine sovereignty and which somehow transcends and unites individual powers into a whole. Yet what is being talked about is not, apparently, the transition from a state of nature to a governed society, but the election of a House of Commons within the English constitutional system. Even within the polity, individuals retained and could exercise their individual, natural rights and powers. The ongoing operation of consent within governed societies is a feature of Leveller thought which blurs the line between any original state of nature and people's continued exercise of their natural rights in consenting to a government already in existence.

This transmission of natural powers between the people and their representatives in elections raises some puzzles of its own. As with the possible transition out of a state of nature, the motives here are not entirely clear, and there is a genuine question as to why the people do not exercise their own sovereign powers themselves, rather than handing them over. The authors of the *Remonstrance of Many Thousand Citizens* do offer an explanation for choosing MPs rather than exercising power directly: 'For wee might justly have done it our selves without you, if we had thought it convenient; choosing you ... for avoiding some inconveniences.'[32] The power held by the Commons is identical with the power originally held by the people; what occurs is a genuine (but conditional) transfer of power: 'we possessed you with the same power that was in our selves, to have done the same'.[33] It is less than clear exactly how the people could directly have exercised their original sovereignty, particularly given the variation in Leveller accounts on the question of the individual or collective nature of that original power. While in *An Arrow* Overton had been clear that the powers communicated by the people to the House of Commons were individual and transferred by individuals ('their *severall Individuall* Communications confer'd upon, and *united in you*'[34]), later, in *An Appeale*, he argued that these individual powers were united in being 'confer'd and conveyed by *ioynt and common consent*.... And so it is, that there is a *generall* communication amongst men from *their severall innate properties*'.[35] Whether either of these accounts left room for the people as a body to exercise their collective powers directly, without representatives, is doubtful, but in other places Overton spoke in terms which suggested that this might be possible. He spoke of the 'Commons of this Nation, having empowred their Body Representative ... with their own absolute Soveraignty'.[36] This could perhaps mean their individual self-proprieties, but the phrasing and the use of the word sovereignty more obviously suggests a collective popular sovereignty. The people were 'the Body Represented, (the true originall Soveraigne Authority of Parliaments) the free borne Commoners':[37] again we wonder whether the people could be their own sovereign authority, rather than being the Parliament's.

We saw in the last section that Lilburne and Overton displaced attention from the moment – if there was a single moment – when free individuals gave up their power and established governments to exercise it in their place, emphasizing instead the distinction between life, whether in the state of nature or under government, in which self-propriety was respected, and life under tyrannical rulers. Here we again see a rather curious displacement of the emphasis we would expect in social contract theorists – on the moment when free individuals contracted to enter society and live under government – in favour of a much more recent moment, which was merely one in a series of moments when the English people transferred some of their powers to their representatives by electing a new House of Commons.

This feels rather different from the parliamentarian consent theory which was developed in the early years of the war. The Levellers' use of consent theory did have some of the same functions, and place some of the same constraints on their thought, but the fundamental aims of parliamentarians in justifying resistance against the king in 1642–44, and Levellers in questioning the conduct of parliamentarian policy in 1645–46, were rather different. Arguments about the origins of political power in consent had one central use for the parliamentarian writers: they allowed them to argue that the king's power was not and never could have been unlimited. If people's natural freedom could be removed only by their own consent, then it followed that it could be removed only *as far as* they had consented.[38] Moreover, the restrictions on the king's power which parliamentarian writers emphasized were built into the constitutional structures of the nation through the original consent of the people; this meant that there was no need to build in any provision for the lapsing of the original agreement, as it already provided for all eventualities. The Levellers certainly agreed that consent had constitutional consequences, and their radical rethinking of the English constitution was based on ideas of consent as well as representation (discussed below). But they were also much more inclined to insist on rather more formless rights which were retained by the people or could be reclaimed in a less orderly way if a particular government forfeited its trust. In spite of these differences, the parliamentarian constitutional thought which emerged from consent theory was a major influence on the Levellers, and in the rest of the chapter I will examine the parliamentarian constitutional debates and the way in which they fed into the Levellers' views of the king, the House of Lords, and the House of Commons.

CONSTITUTIONS

Parliamentarian writers in the early stages of the war were largely arguing positions on the constitution which would allow them to act against the king, but these arguments led them to divergent constitutional conclusions. As the 1640s wore on, the parliamentarians' differences on constitutional matters grew more visible, and the Levellers were among those who pursued the logic of one line of parliamentarian argument to its conclusion in the exclusion of the king from sovereign power. An examination of parliamentarian constitutional debates shows some of the roots of Leveller anti-monarchism, but it also reveals that the Levellers were not comfortable with all the implications of this strand of parliamentarian thought. Indeed, as we will see in the next chapter, the supposedly more 'conservative' parliamentarian theorists of coordination in a system of mixed government had their own contribution to make to Leveller radicalism.

The monarchical element in the English constitution was undeniable: England had a king. The parliamentarian theorists set about analysing his place in the constitution, and in particular his relationship to the two Houses of Parliament. What they needed – and what the argument from consent helped them to achieve – was a convincing argument not only that the king's power was limited by divine or human law (something which royalists generally accepted), but also that these limits could be enforced upon the king by some human authority. Parliamentarians naturally rejected any hint that the English monarchy might be absolute, although natural law and consent theory offered two different routes to that rejection. The natural-law command enjoining self-preservation might simply make it illegitimate to accept submission to the power of an absolute monarchy, meaning that any such contract was void; alternatively, voluntary servitude might be possible, but was something that 'free people, and in their right wits' – such as the English – would never have consented to.[39] Parliamentarians took divergent routes to their conclusions, but in essence they all argued that the fundamental constitution – to which rational people had consented when they entered into a governed society – had not placed power in the king alone, but had distributed it among three 'estates': the people had wisely placed some of their power in the Houses of Parliament, enabling them, at least in an emergency, to limit and correct the king.

The parliamentarian theory of the three estates was in itself innovative: under the influence of the classical notions of the one, the few, and the many, the traditional 'three estates' (nobility, commoners, and clergy) were replaced by the king, Lords, and Commons.[40] The king was now one of the three estates – rather than ruling over a nation composed of these estates – and 'monarchy' was only one aspect of a classically interpreted 'mixed' constitution, alongside aristocracy and democracy. This did not, of itself, threaten the king's prerogative, or his sovereignty (at least as king-in-Parliament, if legislative sovereignty was intended). But it did provide the Houses of Parliament with some independent power within the constitution, which they could use to limit the monarch, rather than a power merely derived from royal power. The Protestant resistance theories of the sixteenth century, revived by the Scottish Covenanters in their resistance of the king since 1637, offered a model for resistance by 'inferior magistrates', including representative assemblies.[41]

From this point, parliamentarian theory developed in two broadly divergent directions. For some, the doctrine of 'coordination', whereby the three estates were to 'supply' each other's defects in an emergency, provided enough grounds for Parliament's resistance of the king. This option was particularly attractive to the 'Calvinist' or 'Presbyterian' thinkers, for whom the derivation of the king's power from God meant that the independent authority of the king within the constitution could not be sacrificed.[42] For scholars such as Franklin, this insistence on clinging on to a mixed sovereignty while also justifying Parliament's action against the king represents a failure of theoretical penetration.[43] Indeed, Philip Hunton, the most acute parliamentarian theorist of mixed monarchy, deliberately and decisively closed off all the usual argumentative routes by which Parliament could claim some constitutional right to act against the king within a coordinative mixed government. If a mixed monarchy was to be genuinely mixed and genuinely a monarchy, the monarch's power had to be 'not so great as to destroy the mixture; nor so titular as to destroy the Monarchy'.[44] The parliamentarian justifications of resistance either, in Hunton's view, provided too little justification of resistance, as they were too committed to coordination, or so much that they destroyed the existing mixed constitution. His solution was to maintain a genuinely mixed sovereignty by placing the decision to resist outside the constitutional framework, in the consciences of the people themselves. As we will see in the next chapter, Hunton was not alone among parliamentarian theorists of a mixed constitution in his willingness to call on the consciences of the people.

In spite of Hunton's strictures, many parliamentarians did try to maintain that coordination gave Parliament some right of resistance, without tipping over into the sovereignty of the two Houses over the king: they were simply too attached to the constitution as they understood it to reduce it to a single locus of sovereignty, and their current experience surely prompted them to think that a mixed constitution *without* any right of resistance in Parliament was, effectively, not very mixed at all. Hunton objected to the theory that ranged the king against the three estates of which he was now taken to be one, and which pointed out '*that one is lesse than three*',[45] on the grounds that this would overthrow the mixed nature of the government and allow a 'confederacy' of any two to make the third element 'a bare Cypher'.[46] But parliamentarians had great incentives to maintain both the possibility of coordination and its compatibility with resistance; and a theory which held that in times of emergency powers could be exercised which were not 'ordinary' powers was not out of line with existing constitutional understandings.[47]

The defenders of a genuinely mixed polity formed one strand of parliamentarian thinking on the constitution. For these thinkers, the king's power either remained qualitatively superior to that of the 'inferior magistrates' who were empowered to hold him in check in an emergency, or was similar in nature to that exercised by the two Houses. But – perhaps in vindication of Hunton's fears – another strand of parliamentarian thought developed, partly out of coordination theory and partly by going beyond it, which effectively demoted the king's power and elevated that of the two Houses.

The doctrine of coordination, however, ran deep, and even Henry Parker, Charles Herle and more radical anonymous authors paid lip-service to the mixture of powers, Herle tending more towards a genuine theory of coordination.[48] These authors were, however, drawn towards Bodin's view that any effective sovereignty could not be divided, and they went to some lengths to explain that the apparent multiplicity of sites of power in the English polity had to boil down, at least in moments of crisis, to one single locus of sovereignty. Parker was able to account for the apparent supremacy of the king and still settle the matter in favour of Parliament by citing a motto of Huguenot resistance theory: 'It is true, two supreames cannot bee in the same sence and respect, but nothing is more known or assented to then this, that the King is *singulis major*, and yet *universis minor*.'[49] In other words, even if the king was indisputably greater than an individual subject, all his subjects united – as they were in Parliament – were greater than him. Herle argued that a 'joint' supreme legislative power did not violate Bodin's principle of the indivisibility of sovereignty; legislation was shared between king and Parliament. However, he agreed with Parker that it was not the *making* of law, but the *interpreting* of it, which was the ultimate act of will required in the government of a state – and, like Parker, he placed that power in Parliament.[50]

The parliamentarian arguments which did most to pave the way for more outspoken denials of the king's sovereignty thus did so by moving one step towards a parliamentary absolutism. In an interpretation which was the mirror image of some royalist views of the king's extraordinary prerogative powers, these parliamentarians came to believe that even in a balanced polity made up of different elements, a final, arbitrary power of decision had to be located somewhere. Laws framed the life of a polity, but the authoritative interpretation of existing law and the determination of circumstances under which extraordinary powers might be invoked both involved the exercise of judgement. Hence, rather than rejecting arbitrary power completely, these authors conceded a necessary role for it, but located it in Parliament rather than in the king. Herle, in December 1642, expressed it thus:

it cannot be denyed nor avoyded, but that as the Government in the forme or qualification of it was, at first an act of the will, and so Arbitrary; so it remaining the *same* it must remaine some where a[r]bitrary still, else our forefathers should not convey that same government to us which they began, they cannot bind us in that wherein they were themselves free.[51]

If some arbitrary power was necessary somewhere in the state, this was the power to which Bodin's principle of indivisibility applied: 'the principle of ultimat resolution cannot be a *divided* one, for then it cannot *resolve*'.[52] The question for Herle was where this arbitrary power could safely and legitimately rest; his answer was 'where it was at first', that is, 'in the *consent* and *reason* of the state'; that is, in Parliament.[53] Such arguments certainly played a role in the Levellers' placing of supremacy in the House of Commons, and in their thinking about representation, as we will see below; but the Levellers were to set themselves up against 'all kindes of ... *Arbitrary Power*'.[54] Their growing distrust of the House of Commons had several causes, but the increasing willingness of parliamentarian writers to claim arbitrary power for it must have been one of them.

Such arguments were often articulated without any explicit discussion of where that left the king, but they naturally tended towards a diminution of the power of the king, and can be seen as one of the origins of parliamentarian anti-monarchism. Parliament proclaimed its loyalty to the king through the first civil war and beyond, and a majority were on the verge of restoring the king at the point when the Long Parliament was interrupted by Pride's Purge. But on the Independent and radical end of the parliamentarian spectrum, anti-monarchical feeling could develop, even before the events of 1647 and the second civil war crystallized these feelings for some of the future regicides. The Levellers participated in, and promoted, a broader development among radical parliamentarians.

While some of the mainstream parliamentarians – Parker particularly – by implication left the king very little of his power, some anonymous pamphleteers from the first crisis of the war years were prepared to be even more explicit. Both *Touching the Fundamentall Lawes* and *Remonstrans Redivivus* denied the reality of the king's supposed 'negative voice': 'there is no known or written law that gives him any', royal assent being a matter 'of honour' only; it is 'but matter of forme annext to his office and not left to his will'. Effectively, then, the king's role was merely honorary.[55] William Walwyn was one of the promoters of *Remonstrans Redivivus*, and a future Leveller leader is thus aligned, as early as the summer of 1643, with the denial of the veto power which was to become a hallmark of Leveller thought. Even more aggressive anti-monarchism was possible, and it did tend to go along with an emphasis on parliamentary sovereignty, rather than with a genuinely populist view of political life. This was true of the only truly outspoken anti-monarchist of the

The Levellers

early years of the war, the MP Henry Marten.[56] Prynne's *Fourth Part of the Soveraigne Power of Parliaments and Kingdomes*, printed by order of Parliament in 1643, collected historical examples intended, according to its title page, to show that kingdoms were entitled not only to resist their monarchs, but under some circumstances to 'censure, suspend, deprive them for their Tyranny.... and sometimes capitally to proceed against them'.[57] Prynne's theory of parliamentary sovereignty allowed Commons and Lords to act against the king in an emergency, legally but only temporarily, before the restoration of a balanced constitution.[58] Nonetheless, he brought into English civil war political thought, in the vernacular, potentially radical exempla of the deposition and even execution of kings, and allied them with one type of parliamentary sovereignty.[59]

As the first civil war drew to an end, Parliament had to deal both with the Scots, to whom the king surrendered himself, and with the defeated king himself. A complicated web of rival negotiations was set in motion, and the Independents struggled to fend off the threat of a Presbyterian settlement, while Charles spent most of 1646 in the hands of the Scots. That struggle was marked by an increasing radicalization of opinion on the fringes of Independency, both against the Scots and against the king. The Levellers participated in that radicalization, and indeed the *Remonstrance of Many Thousand Citizens* of July 1646 was the first Leveller text to make a claim to a mass following, a significant moment in the genesis of the group. The *Remonstrance* appeared when the king had been with the Scots only a couple of months. It attacked the king and his office in forthright terms, calling for Charles to be declared an enemy and for the House of Commons to resolve to have no more kings; it also set out the presumed thinking of those who wanted to extend the yoke of Presbyterian church government from Scotland to England, and objected to the self-righteousness of recent Scottish papers about their role in the parliamentarian victory.[60] In this combination of concerns it shared something with other radical parliamentarian writings of the time. Marchamont Nedham, the editor of the parliamentarian newsbook *Mercurius Britanicus*, was consistently anti-Presbyterian, and had finally pushed the authorities into repudiating and closing the publication in May 1646 when he crowned a series of mocking editorials against the king with a suggestion of his execution.[61]

In the autumn of 1646, as negotiations for handing over the king to the English Parliament came to a close, the tension became higher, and Independents continued to offer threats – more or less veiled – against the king, in the guise of challenges to the Scots' right to have a say in his treatment by his English subjects. This was the theme of Chaloner's 'speech without doors' on 26 October, orchestrated with the Independent grandees, and it was taken up and defended by Henry Marten in the subsequent controversy.[62] But Richard Overton plunged into the controversy too, with the anonymous *Unhappy*

Game at Scotch and English which came out at the end of November and which the House of Commons promptly ordered to be burnt. Like Chaloner, he was responding to recent Scottish papers which challenged England's sole right to dispose of the king, but the anti-monarchical conclusion was made more outrageously apparent than Chaloner or even Marten had made it. As far as Overton was concerned, the Scots and the king were conspiring 'to subjugate the neckes of the Free-men of England to your Scotch Monarchicall *Yoake of Bondage*', but those English free-men would defend their liberties in spite of 'Scot, King, or Keysar'.[63] *Regall Tyrannie Discovered*, published in January of the next year, was written in the same political context.

The Levellers' constitutional arguments evolved early and their views on the status of the king and the House of Lords drew on the more radical streams of Independent political thought. The Levellers made a very single-minded choice against coordination theory. They were firmly in Parker's camp, asserting parliamentary sovereignty, and indeed the sovereignty of a single, representative chamber, long before Parliament itself eventually did so. In discussions of the theory of government, the Levellers had no truck with the notion of mixed constitutions, although a version of it is detectable in Lilburne's suggestions that one might have to use the king to keep a balance against threats from elsewhere in the government; even the classical language of constitutional description is barely hinted at in Leveller writings, apart from a couple of denunciations of 'aristocratical' government.[64] Leveller anti-monarchism, in spite of later strategic compromises with royalism, was early and well developed; the Levellers had little patience with the parliamentarian fiction that they were fighting not against the king, but for him.

As we can see from the varieties of parliamentarian consent theory, the Levellers' commitment to government originating in consent, and even to the powers of that government stemming originally from the people, did not lead inevitably to such anti-monarchism. If government was made legitimate simply by the will of the people in assenting to their governors, that placed no necessary limitation on the constitutional structures, as long as a mechanism of consent was involved. An elective king or aristocracy might equally well be entrusted with sovereign power. This is a view which can be faintly discerned within Leveller thought at some points – particularly when parliamentary betrayal was at its height, in the Leveller view – but its implications were never integrated into Leveller thought. The 1646 *Remonstrance of Many Thousand Citizens* stated this theory most explicitly, arguing that

> if Kings would prove themselves Lawfull Magistrates, they must prove themselves to be so, by a lawfull derivation of their Authority, which must be from the voluntary trust of the People, and then the case is the same with them, as between the People & you [the House of Commons], they as you, being possessed of no more Power then what is in the People justly to intrust ...[65]

But the author of the *Remonstrance* did not represent Leveller thought more broadly in arguing that 'the case is the same' with any elected power, whether king or people.[66] As we will see, in other places, and particularly in Overton's *Arrow Against All Tyrants* of a few months later, it was clear that power could be transmitted from the people to an elected representative in a way that it could not be transmitted to an elected officer of any other kind. Indeed, an elected king was never mooted as an equally valid alternative to an elected representative; rather, it was assumed that he was in addition to that representative and had an additional line of responsibility to the people through that representative.

In practice, the Levellers were insistent that only a unicameral elected 'representative' could bear sovereignty. To see what their thinking was here, we will first consider their comments on the king and the House of Lords, before looking in more detail at what they meant by representation. The issue is, of course, slightly confused by the fact that the king and the House of Lords who were in existence were not elected – although the Levellers, on occasion, were not above using the arguments of other parliamentarians that an element of election and consent was present in the coronation of each successive king. Thus the Levellers' accounts of the illegitimacy of, or limits on, the power which they could exercise were often not accounts of the power which a magistrate could exercise under ideal circumstances. To be able to exercise legitimate power, kings would have to be elected by the people (presumably in a much fuller and more direct way than anyone could claim was currently the case), and – it was suggested on a couple of occasions – the Lords would have to cease to sit as a separate House and instead offer themselves for election for the Commons or new Representative. This solution was offered as a possibility by the *Remonstrance*, which optimistically suggested that it would solve the problem of the Lords' distinct 'interest' and give them 'one and the same interest'.[67] Tellingly, *Regall Tyrannie Discovered*, published in the following January, appeared less convinced, first repeating the demand that Lords should 'put themselves upon the love of their Country' and be elected to Parliament if they wished to exercise power, but then reiterating the unique legislative power of a Commons chamber, which would be compromised if it were augmented by Lords joining them.[68] Ultimately, these suggestions of a future legitimate role for the Lords in politics were dwarfed in Leveller literature by simple denunciations of the illegitimacy of lordly power. The Levellers' animus against the Lords was fuelled by the sufferings of Lilburne as that House proceeded against him, and there were no moments of ambivalence in which a more conciliatory line towards the Lords as a body was advisable. Consequently, the Leveller texts used all the possible lines of argument against them, sometimes invoking Norman Yoke notions of them as conquerors and usurpers and of their role in the hierarchy of society and landholding, but also, often in the same texts, making an argument about their arbitrary power, not founded in consent, which rendered the people 'slaves'.[69] Conceptual space for a legitimized role for a distinct class of lords was also used up by the Levellers' habit of appropriating the term for the people, and asserting that it was the people who were the only 'sovereign lord' over the House of Commons.[70]

The current illegitimacy of the king – unlike that of the Lords – could, in typically Leveller fashion, be glossed in such a way that current constitutional arrangements were not overtly repudiated but, rather, silently reinterpreted. Thus statements that the king was a mere chief officer deriving his power from the Commons were part of the Leveller strategy – to be explored more in the third chapter – of reading a true, underlying constitution which was legitimate into the present, in preference to admitting that they were seeking radical reform. Of course, there were calls for reform, or rather for the sweeping away of kingship, and they began early: the *Last Warning to All the Inhabitants of London* was railing against the delusions which induced people to hang on to kingly government as early as March 1646, and the drumbeat continued, although in a more moderated form, in the *Remonstrance* and *Regall Tyrannie Discovered*. The *Remonstrance* gave a damning account of kings as the 'continuall Oppressours of the Nation', but spoke of the status of kings in normative terms which might have allowed for good kings: kings were among 'the Officers of Trust in the Common-wealth'.[71] Similarly, *Regall Tyrannie Discovered* employed a rhetoric which equated kingship with tyranny, but nonetheless proved the tyranny of actual kings by situating them as mere supreme officers (not supreme powers) bound by contract.[72] Looking under 'king' in the book's index, we again find normative regulations about kings: 'King is intrusted', 'Kings subordinate to Lawes', 'King, no propriety in his Kingdome', 'Kings are lyable to be punished'; again, alongside objections to kings' 'tyrannical usurpation' and stipulations that kingship needed popular consent. In this way we can read statements about the status of the king as reflective of a permitted, if not ideal, Leveller constitution. They implied that the power of such a king – and of other legitimate magistrates – was different in kind from that of the Representative. Petitioners to the House of Commons might make this point particularly insistently, as in the autumn of 1648, when the choice between restoration and regicide was becoming stark, when the 11 September petitioners accused the Commons of 'putting him that is but one single person, and a publike Officer of the Common-wealth, in competition with the whole body of the people, whom ye represent; not considering that it is impossible for you to erect any authority equall to your selves'.[73]

REPRESENTATION AND THE THEORY OF PARLIAMENTARY SOVEREIGNTY

The Levellers thus took the power of the House of Commons to be different in kind from other magisterial power, even that of a legitimate king. Their grounds for this view again had their roots in parliamentarian thought, and particularly that stream of it which has generally been regarded as more 'radical': those theorists who, like Parker, accepted the people's constituent authority and tended towards a theory of ultimate parliamentary sovereignty. This tendency within parliamentarian thought was naturally highly controverted, and its proponents needed to ground it in a plausibly historical account of the nature of Parliament. Luckily, the development of the English Parliament had resulted in a view of the powers of parliamentary representatives which, reinterpreted, became extremely useful to those who wanted to make a case for the ultimate sovereignty of Parliament in the 1640s. Across Europe, parliaments and estates had evolved different views on the relationship between the representatives who sat in them and the communities which sent those representatives. Representatives might be empowered with *plena potestas* to make binding decisions on behalf of those communities, or they might need to refer matters back to their constituents, as in the Netherlands. While *plena potestas* might seem to enhance the status of the representatives themselves, it was often preferred by monarchs too, as it enabled them to manage parliaments and estates more effectively. In Castile and Poland monarchs had attempted to foist *plena potestas* onto representatives, in order to be able to use them more effectively, and clearly English monarchs also valued the (potential) manageability and usefulness of a Parliament which did not need to refer back to its constituents.[74] Thus the debate on *plena potestas* in England had long since yielded a broad consensus that the acts of the English Parliament could indeed be taken as the acts of the nation as a whole, without further consultation or conditionality.

In the context of the civil war, parliamentarians naturally made much of this doctrine, leaving royalists to protest that the powers handed over by the people to their representatives were in fact limited.[75] In combination with an enhanced notion of the importance of representation, this strand of thinking about Parliament enabled parliamentarians to argue that the Parliament, rather than the king, *was* essentially the nation, and its acts were the nation's acts. Parker, in his *Observations*, used this argument to counter the king's objection that Parliament was claiming 'an arbitrary unlimitable power'. Rather than denying the essential truth of the accusation, Parker sought to show that the only safe place for the necessary arbitrary power was in Parliament:

> That there is an Arbitrary power in every State somewhere tis true, tis necessary, and no inconvenience follows upon it; every man has an absolute power over himself;

but because no man can hate himself, this power is not dangerous, nor need [sic] to be restrayned: So every State has an Arbitrary power over it self, and there is no danger in it for the same reason.

Because Parliament was 'the State it self', it would do itself no harm.[76] Mendle's attribution to Parker of a theory of 'parliamentary absolutism' seems well justified.[77]

So alongside pragmatic arguments (for example, that a greater number of people 'see more' and are 'lesse swayable' than one[78] – an argument ultimately deriving from Aristotle), we find the much more sweeping claim that parliamentary sovereignty is simply the nation acting for itself, in a way so direct and natural as to be virtually unquestionable. For Parker, 'the Lords and Commons [in Parliament] represent the whole Kingdome'.[79] For Herle, the Lords had 'shares both of *trust* and *interest* in this *Supremacy* of power in Parliament', as '*conciliarii nati*, borne Councellours to the State'. Members of Parliament exercised 'trust and interest' essentially on their own behalf, as subjects: the interests of subjects

> as *Property, Priviledge,* &c. with which the Parliaments either ends or interest cannot thus dash and interfer, the Members are all subjects themselves, not only *intrusted* with, but self *interested* in those very *priviledges*, and *properties*.[80]

For Herle, the ways in which Parliament could be identfied with the people or kingdom verged on the mystical. He expressed a common view in talking of the 'common interest of the whole body of the Kingdome in Parliament'.[81] it was usual to think of the whole nation as present in Parliament. Here, as parliamentarians were to do more and more, he slipped into discussing Parliament without apparently including the king in it: this parliamentary interest was 'twisted with the Kings' for greater strength. In the two Houses resided 'the *Reason* of the *Kingdome*',[82] expressed in the votes and ordinances of Parliament.

The Levellers' constitutional thought was daring in its (tacit) exclusion of the king and the House of Lords from any share in sovereignty, but it followed on smoothly from these parliamentarian precedents. It was in the House of Commons, rather than the king or Lords, that the Levellers consistently located the supreme institutional power and authority of the nation. We have seen the importance that mixed government could take on in some strands of parliamentarian thought. Yet the Levellers, even when they seemed to concede a potential role for the king, did not use that language of mixed government. Rather, they advocated the supremacy of a unicameral, popularly elected 'representative', closely resembling the House of Commons. In line with this, they often insisted, throughout the existence of their movement, that the Commons was the 'supreme authority' of the nation. A selection of their petitions tells this tale most succinctly: *To the right honourable and supreme authority of this nation, the Commons in Parliament assembled* (the Large

Petition of March 1647); *To the Supream Authority of England, the Commons in Parliament assembled* (23 November 1647); *To the Supream authority of England, the Commons assembled in Parliament* (18/19 January 1648); *To the right honourable, the supreme authority of this nation, the Commons of England in Parliament assembled* (19 January 1649). If this was intended as flattery of the House, it was a very pointed flattery: the House of Commons did not, until shortly before the last of these petitions, accept that it was or claim to be the supreme authority of the nation. Indeed, the petitioners often laboured the point: in the past their petitions had been burnt 'for attributing the supream authority of this Nation to this Honourable House, which alone represents the people';[83] they would not have supported the parliamentarian cause 'but that we judged this honourable House to be the supream Authority of *England*'.[84] They were maddened by the House's own refusal to be clear on this point, and its 'indulgent *expressions concerning the King or Lords*'.[85] Once the Commons had voted itself supreme, on 4 January 1649 (in order to legislate for regicide), Leveller petitioners urged the MPs to stick to their resolve – and highlighted their own long-term advocacy of this position.[86]

The Levellers thus rejected theories of mixed government, and with them the notion that it might be coordination which legitimized the Parliament's war against the king. Instead, they developed the thought of the advocates of parliamentary sovereignty, extending it to exclude the Lords as well as the king from any share in that sovereignty. A unicameral elected representative was the only safe or legitimate repository for the supreme power. But why was it legitimate, and what was the nature of its power? The Levellers' answers to these questions underwent some changes as the 1640s wore on, and circumstances created some noticeable strains in the Levellers' thought.

Clearly, the legitimacy of the House of Commons as the locus of supreme power depended on election. That made it unique among the governing institutions already in existence, but there is little sign that the option of an elective monarchy in the future attracted Leveller writers. Elective kingship tended to be mentioned in a concessive tone, rather than hinted at as an appealing solution.

It was thus not consent alone, or even consent via the specific means of election alone, which rendered a sovereign power legitimate in the Levellers' eyes. As the 11 September 1648 petitioners explained, 'we judged this honourable House to be the supream Authority of *England*, as chosen by, and representing the People'.[87] Election was only ever fully envisaged as election to a 'representative', and only a representative body was seen as the appropriate vehicle for sovereign power. What was understood by representation, however, was not entirely stable, and at times the notion was put under such strain that the distinction between a betrusted representative and a mere officer became blurred.

Overton was the Leveller author who – in a characteristically philosophizing passage in his *Arrow against All Tyrants* in October 1646 – attempted to delineate the significance of representation most thoughtfully. For him, the act which constituted the House of Commons as legislative sovereign was not a simple handing over of delegated powers which could be recalled, but a much more organic extension of the powers of the people into their natural representatives. These representatives enjoyed a status entirely different from that of a mere executive officer – such as the king. Just human powers are 'implanted' by God 'in the creature, and from the creature those powers immediatly proceed; and no further'.[88] Overton insisted on the consequence that the people's 'natural Soveraignity'[89] could travel only as far as 'representers' – not as far as kings or the House of Lords: 'the Legislative power is not in the King himselfe, but only in the Kingdome and body Representative'.[90] This had important consequences:

> So that seeing the Soveraigne power is not originally in the King, or personally terminated in him, then the King at most can be but chief Officer or supream executioner of the Lawes, under whom all other legall executioners, their severall executions, functions and offices are subordinate; for indeed the Representers [sic] (in whom that power is inherent, and from whence it takes its originall) can only make conveyance thereof to their Representors, vicegerents or Deputies, and cannot possibly further extend it.[91]

The qualitatively different relationship between the people and the Representative meant that the people's inherent sovereign powers could be exercised by the Representative, but never by a mere officer such as the king. In Overton's hands, the theory of the people's constituent authority was combined with the theory of representation to offer a robust account of the limits of the transferability of power, and thus of legitimate constitutional forms. In addition to the standard parliamentarian view, retained and developed by the Levellers, that the people could not rightly give away so much power as would harm them, Overton thus argued that they could, in any case, only transfer their inherent power to those who represented them. Similarly substantial notions of representation are visible in other works from 1646 and early 1647.[92]

That Overton had in mind a substantial notion of representation was made clear in the summer of 1647, when his idealism about this representation had faded. When Overton's disillusionment with the existing House of Commons led him to appeal directly to the people (explored further in Chapter 2), the justification given was not parallel to any justification for resisting the king or Lords, but rather based on the special status of the Commons as a representative body, now 'degenerate'. The Commons had been able to exercise supreme power only *because* they were representative of the nation; now they had ceased to be representative they could no longer exercise that power. As Condren remarks, Overton 'protects the integrity of representation by improvising a distinction between true and false representation, only the latter clearly being challengeable'.[93] 'Representation' clearly has a substantial meaning here, even if the difficulty of explaining exactly what it is that qualifies the Commons as representative shows up in the circularity of Overton's argument:

> certainly tyrants and oppressors cannot be the Representers of the Free-men of *England*, for freedom and tyranny are contraries, that which representeth the one, doth not represent the other; therefore such as are the representers of *Free-men*, must be substantial and reall *Actors* for *freedome* and *liberty*, ...[94]

Rather than the natural relationship between the people and the House of Commons guaranteeing the representativeness and rightness of their rule, representation had become a test which the House had to pass. Yet, as Condren suggests, Overton's attachment to the concept is visible even in this tortuous rethinking.

In truth, the Levellers' unease at the behaviour of the House of Commons meant that, from the start, it was never quite possible to trust to the mysterious efficacy of representation. Mystery was increasingly shored up with mechanism: the almost organic flowing of the people's power into their representatives through election was displaced by a carefully limited process of selection and rotation which looked forward to the republican schemes of the 1650s. In a theme which became increasingly important in Leveller thought, the first *Agreement of the People* added rotation to election, to ensure that the MPs were meaningfully representative:

> they shall be in a capacity to tast of subjection as well as rule, & so shall be equally concerned with your selves, in all they do. For they must equally suffer with you under any common burdens, & partake with you in any freedoms; & by this they shal be disinabled to defraud or wrong you, when the lawes shall bind all alike, without priviledge or exemption ...[95]

The further the Levellers' disillusionment with the Long Parliament went, the more concerned they were to ensure that representation meant (more or less) identity: the MPs would simply *be* a tranche of the people, and all efforts possible were made to prevent them from becoming different by virtue of being MPs. The members of the legislature were to be subject to all the same laws as everyone else, and parliaments were to be short and frequent, in order to make sure that MPs lived under their own laws as well as making them.

If representation was not, after all, guaranteed by the people's election of a body of MPs, then erring MPs needed sharper reminders of their status as mere temporary recipients of the trust of the people. In his optimistic account of representation, Overton saw MPs as 'vicegerents' and 'deputies' genuinely acting in place of those they represented. But running alongside such positive views of representation, even in the same texts, was a more threatening current of reminders that even the powers of elected representatives were strictly secondary. Even in the *Arrow against All Tyrants*, where he set out his view of representation, Overton reminded the Commons that they were the people's 'absolute Commissioners and lawfull Deputies, but no more'.[96] The *Remonstrance of Many Thousand Citizens* had spoken to the House of Commons more sharply: 'Wee are your Principalls, and you our Agents'; the House's power was derived from the people's 'Trust and choice'.[97] Again, in *Regall Tyrannie Discovered*, which had emphasized the special status of the Representative as against the king as a mere officer, the House of Commons was nonetheless reminded that its power was 'meerly derivative', with a 'tacit Commission' to act for the good of its betrusters.[98] In the next chapter we will see how changing ideas about the significance of representation helped the Levellers, among others, to develop the notion that the people should hold their Parliament to account.

CONCLUSION

The Levellers were heavily indebted to parliamentarian theorists such as Henry Parker, whose arguments tended towards parliamentary sovereignty. For Parker, this view meant that Parliament's actions were not to be questioned or resisted by the population outside Parliament. In important ways, the Levellers took up this view; as we have seen, they certainly saw the House of Commons as the only possible institutional locus for supreme power or sovereignty, and did not contemplate the dividing of that sovereignty between institutions as the parliamentarian coordination theorists did. To modern readers the theory of representation might seem to belong to the other side of Leveller thought, and to be more compatible with a willingness to appeal from Parliament to the people outside Parliament, than with a strong view of parliamentary sovereignty. However, some early modern notions of representation might well foster a view in which the sovereignty of a representative House was immune from any challenge from its electors. The Levellers' emphasis on representation, then, may have hindered them in contemplating an appeal to the people rather than helping them. In the next chapter, we will see that parliamentarian theorists were divided over the question of whether any appeal to the consciences of the people could be made, even in an emergency. In this chapter we have seen the Levellers apparently following the lead of the parliamentary absolutists fairly faithfully. In the next chapter, we will see that the Levellers' growing fear of parliamentary tyranny conflicted with their passionate commitment to Parliament as the proper locus of supremacy in the state. The notion of appealing to the people, which began to be more prominent in their thought, was partly derived from the other strand of parliamentarian thought, that of the coordination theorists. The Levellers were creating a troubled but powerfully original synthesis of two aspects of parliamentarian thought which had hitherto often been mutually exclusive.

NOTES

1 D. Wootton, 'From rebellion to revolution: the crisis of the winter of 1642–3 and the origins of civil war radicalism', *English Historical Review* 105 (1990), 654–69.

2 T. Hobbes, *Leviathan*, ed. R. Tuck (Cambridge: Cambridge University Press, 1996), pp. 89, 120; J. P. Sommerville, *Thomas Hobbes: Political Ideas in Historical Context* (Basingstoke: Macmillan, 1992), pp. 37–8.

3 J. H. Franklin, *John Locke and the Theory of Sovereignty: Mixed Monarchy and the Right of Resistance in the Political Thought of the English Revolution* (Cambridge: Cambridge University Press, 1978), ch. 2.

4 H. Parker, *Observations upon some of his Majesties late Answers and Expresses*, 2nd edn (1642), p. 1.

5 *Remonstrans Redivivus: Or, an Accompt of the Remonstrance and Petition, Formerly Presented by Divers Citizens of London, to the View of Many* (25 July 1643), p. 4.

6 *Touching the Fundamentall Lawes, or Politique Constitution of this Kingdome, the Kings Negative Voice, and the Power of Parliaments* (1643), p. 13.

7 *A Remonstrance of Many Thousand Citizens* ([7 July] 1646), p. 3.

8 I use the term 'state of nature' for convenience when discussing the very few places where the Levellers do seem to be talking about the very first state of mankind, but for reasons discussed below, I think it is often misleading to impose the language of the 'state of nature' on Leveller thought.

9 John Lilburne, *The Free-mans Freedom Vindicated* ([16 June] 1646), p. 11.

10 Richard Overton, *An Arrow Against All Tyrants and Tyrany* ([20 October] 1646), p. 4.

11 Overton, *An Arrow*, pp. 4, 10.

12 Overton, *An Arrow*, p. 3.

13 Lilburne, *The Free-mans Freedom*, p. 11.

14 Overton, *An Arrow*, pp. 3–4.

15 Hooker's account is a complex and not entirely coherent one, closely following Aristotle at some points in its emphasis on sociability and a happy life, but also emphasizing at others the importance of artificial agreements which are needed to curb the effects of human sinfulness. Richard Hooker, *Of the Laws of Ecclesiastical Polity: Preface, Book I, Book VIII*, ed. A. S. McGrade, Cambridge Texts in the History of Political Thought (Cambridge: Cambridge University Press, 1989), pp. 87–99.

16 As an even later example, *The Engagement Vindicated & Explained, or the Reasons upon which Leiut. [sic] Col. John Lilburne, Tooke the Engagement* (22 January 1650), p. 6, states that 'Government it self is from God, or the prime Lawes of nature, without which by reason of mans corruption by the fall, he cannot live as a rationall Creature.' This statement melds the distinct views that government is a benign part of the divine order and that it is a remedy for human corruption. The text may well be by Lilburne, although its publication was presumably designed to expose him to charges of hypocrisy for taking the Engagement.

17 Augustine, *The City of God against the Pagans*, ed. R. W. Dyson (Cambridge: Cambridge University Press, 1998), p. 942 (Book XIX, ch. 15); W. Walwyn, *A Manifestation*, in MMT, p. 339; Walwyn, *Walwyns Just Defence*, in MMT, pp. 399–400, on Montaigne's account of 'innocent Cannibals'.

18 Wolfe, p. 139 (Large Petition, March 1647).
19 Lilburne, *Londons Liberty in Chains* ([October] 1646), 'A postscript', p. 17.
20 Lilburne, *Londons Liberty*, 'A postscript', pp. 18–20, quotation at p. 18.
21 Richard Overton, *A Defiance Against All Arbitrary Usurpations* ([9 September] 1646), p. 2.
22 Henry Parker, *Jus Populi* (1644), pp. 3–4.
23 R. Tuck, *Natural Rights Theories: Their Origin and Development* (Cambridge: Cambridge University Press, 1979), pp. 147–51.
24 Frank, p. 142.
25 Brailsford, p. 376.
26 I. Hampsher-Monk, 'The political theory of the Levellers: Putney, property and Professor Macpherson', *Political Studies* 24 (1976), 417.
27 H. Höpfl and M. P. Thompson, 'The history of contract as a motif in political thought', *American Historical Review* 84 (1979), 940.
28 R. A. Gleissner, 'The Levellers and natural law: the Putney debates of 1647', *Journal of British Studies* 20 (1980–81), 78–9; N. McDowell, *The English Radical Imagination: Culture, Religion, and Revolution, 1630–1660* (Oxford: Oxford University Press, 2003) pp. 83ff.
29 Wolfe, p. 265: petition of January 1648.
30 Lilburne, *The Free-mans Freedom*, p. 11.
31 Overton, *An Arrow*, p. 4.
32 *A Remonstrance of Many Thousand Citizens*, p. 3.
33 *A Remonstrance of Many Thousand Citizens*, p. 3.
34 Overton, *An Arrow*, p. 4 (my emphasis).
35 Richard Overton, *An Appeale from the Degenerate Representative Body the Commons of England Assembled at Westminster: to the Body Represented, the Free People in General* ([17 July] 1647, p. 6 (my emphasis).
36 Overton, *An Arrow*, p. 5.
37 Overton, *An Appeale*, p. 10.
38 Herbert Palmer et al., *Scripture and Reason Pleaded for Defensive Armes* (1643), p. 39.
39 Palmer, *Scripture and Reason*, pp. 25, 40; *Touching the Fundamentall Lawes*, p. 5. The author of *Touching the Fundamentall Lawes* may perhaps have had specific, possibly non-European, societies in mind in talking of voluntary servitude: nations which, 'though they have an equall right in Nature to all the Laws of Nature and Equity, yet having fundamentally subjected themselves by their politique Constitutions unto a Regal servitude, by Barbarisme or the like they have thereby much disabled and disvested themselves of that common benefit'. On the question of absolutist thought in early Stuart England, see J. Daly, 'The idea of absolute monarchy in seventeenth-century England', *Historical Journal* 21:2 (1978); G. Burgess, 'The divine right of kings reconsidered', *English Historical Review* 107 (1992); G. Burgess, *Absolute Monarchy and the Stuart Constitution* (New Haven: Yale University Press, 1996); J. P. Sommerville, 'Richard Hooker, Hadrian Saravia, and the advent of the divine right of kings', *History of Political Thought* 4 (1983); J. P. Sommerville, *Politics and Ideology in England, 1603–1640*

The Levellers

(London: Longman, 1986); J. P. Sommerville, 'Ideology, property and the constitution', in R. P. Cust and A.Hughes (eds) *Conflict in Early Stuart England: Studies in Religion and Politics, 1603–1642* (Harlow: Longman, 1989). Daly and Burgess have argued that an absolutist theory of sovereignty was absent in early Stuart England (with the possible exception of Sibthorpe and Mainwaring); Sommerville has argued that there were advocates of monarchical absolutism (as opposed to simply rejection of any right of subjects to resist) in the period. For our purposes here, the important point is the parliamentarian rejection of any potential absolutist theory, whether or not such a theory was actually advocated in England; many parliamentarians were well able to *imagine* an absolutist theory which claimed unbounded rights for the king over the lives, liberties and property of his subjects, and they could be quick to see traces of it in the arguments of their opponents, even where modern historians might not agree.

40 M. J. Mendle, *Dangerous Positions: Mixed Government, the Estates of the Realm, and the Making of the Answer to the 19 Propositions* (Alabama: University of Alabama Press, 1985), charts the contested emergence of this reinterpretation of the three estates, and the assimilation of it to classical categories, in the sixteenth and seventeenth centuries. In the mid-century crisis, it was revived by the Scottish Covenanters and then in Parker's *Case of Shipmony*, before being adopted by royalist propagandists in the *Answer to the XIX Propositions*; Mendle argues that it then became a hindrance to parliamentarian theorists, who largely abandoned it.

41 I. M. Smart, 'The political ideas of the Scottish covenanters, 1638–88', *History of Political Thought* 1:2 (1980), 169.

42 Tuck, *Natural Rights Theories*, pp. 144–5, naming Rutherford and Hunton; Franklin, *John Locke*, pp. 33–48, discussing Burroughes, Bridge, and Hunton; W. M. Lamont, *Marginal Prynne, 1600–1669* (London: Routledge and Kegan Paul, 1963), pp. 91–2 contrasts Calvinist thinking with Covenant theology, putting Prynne on the Calvinist side. See below in this chapter for the differing views on the origin of political power which underlie this classification of the authors.

43 Franklin, *John Locke*, p. 49. In Franklin's view, even Hunton did not entirely resolve this problem.

44 Philip Hunton, *A Treatise of Monarchie* (1643), pp. 25–6.

45 [Charles Herle], *A Fuller Answer to a Treatise Written by Doctor Ferne, Entituled, The Resolving of Conscience* ([29 December] 1642), p. 3.

46 Hunton, *Treatise*, p. 28.

47 It can, indeed, be argued that some strands of parliamentarian argument essentially appropriated, and applied to parliaments, much of the standard pre-civil war understanding of the powers of the monarch.

48 Parker, *Observations*, p. 23; M. Mendle, *Henry Parker and the English Civil War: The Political Thought of the Public's 'Privado'* (Cambridge: Cambridge University Press, 1995), p. 98 on the contrast between Herle and Parker; G. Burgess, *British Political Thought, 1500–1660: The Politics of the Post-Reformation* (Basingstoke: Palgrave Macmillan, 2009), p. 197 on Herle as theorist of coordinative and mixed monarchy. *Touching the Fundamentall Lawes* attributed 'supreame Government' to 'the King and Parliament' before going on to argue that Parliament was unbound by written law: pp. 5, 7–8.

49 Parker, *Observations*, p. 8; J. H. M. Salmon, *The French Religious Wars in English Political Thought* (London: Clarendon Press, 1959), p. 82.

50 Parker, *Observations*, pp. 43–4.
51 [Herle], *A Fuller Answer*, p. 17.
52 [Herle], *A Fuller Answer*, p. 15.
53 [Herle], *A Fuller Answer*, p. 17.
54 *A Remonstrance of Many Thousand Citizens*, pp. 5, 8.
55 *Touching the Fundamentall Lawes*, p. 9 (mispaginated as 7; misprint 'honoer' corrected); *Remonstrans Redivivus*, pp. 4–6, quotation at p. 5.
56 Burgess, *British Political Thought*, p. 231.
57 W. Prynne, *The Fourth Part of the Soveraigne Power of Parliaments and Kingdomes* (1643), title page.
58 Lamont, *Marginal Prynne*, pp. 101–6, 117.
59 Wootton, 'From rebellion to revolution', p. 661, draws attention to the fact that the 'Appendix' to Prynne's work contained the first English translation of all the 'key secular arguments for tyrannicide' of the *Vindiciae, Contra Tyrannos*.
60 *A Remonstrance of Many Thousand Citizens*, in Wolfe, pp. 119, 123–4.
61 *Mercurius Britanicus* no. 92, 28 July–4 August 1645, p. 825; no. 129, 4–11 May 1646, p. 1110; no. 130, 11–18 May 1646, p. 1111.
62 Thomas Chaloner, *An Answer to the Scotch Papers* (1646); [Henry Marten], *A Corrector of the Answerer to the Speech out of Doores* (1646); Henry Marten, *The Independency of England Endeavoured To Be Maintained* (1648) develops the theme; D. Scott, *Politics and War in the Three Stuart Kingdoms, 1637–49* (Basingstoke: Palgrave Macmillan, 2004), pp. 126–7; Burgess, *British Political Thought*, pp. 232–4.
63 [Richard Overton], *Unhappy Game at Scotch and English* ([30 November] 1646), pp. 10, 21; Overton later acknowledged authorship: Frank p. 99 and note.
64 John Lilburne, *The Legall Fundamentall Liberties* ([8 June] 1649), p. 29 (H&D p. 416): note that Lilburne's specific argument is for the need to use both king and Parliament against the *army*; cf. John Lilburne, *Jonah's Cry out of the Whales belly* ([26 July] 1647), p. 8: Lilburne on 22 June 1647 advising Cromwell to deal with the king as a balance against a tyrannical Parliament. In neither case is Lilburne discussing an ideal and permanent constitutional balance. *Remonstrance of Many Thousand Citizens*, in MMT, p. 225; John Lilburne, Thomas Prince and Richard Overton, *The Picture of the Councel of State* (1649), p. 39 (Overton's narrative).
65 *A Remonstrance of Many Thousand Citizens*, p. 13.
66 The authorship of the *Remonstrance* is unclear, and although it was printed by Overton, it may not have been written by him: D. R. Adams, 'The secret printing and publishing career of Richard Overton the Leveller, 1644–46', *The Library* 11:1 (2010), 3–88; for Adams's sceptical view on Overton's authorship of the text, see D. R. Adams, 'Religion and reason in the thought of Richard Overton, the Leveller' (PhD dissertation, University of Cambridge, 2003), pp. 334–8, 212.
67 *A Remonstrance of Many Thousand Citizens*, p. 7.
68 *Regall Tyrannie Discovered* ([6 January] 1647), pp. 92–3, 98.
69 [Walwyn], *Just Man in Bonds* (1646), in MMT, pp. 218–19; *A Pearle in a Dounghill* ([30 June] 1646), pp. 3–4.

The Levellers

70 *Regall Tyrannie*, p. 11.

71 *A Remonstrance of Many Thousand Citizens*, pp. 4–5.

72 *Regall Tyrannie*, pp. 9, 38.

73 *To the Right Honorable, the Commons of England in Parliament Assembled* (11 September 1648), in Wolfe, p. 285.

74 H. G. Koenigsberger, *Estates and Revolutions: Essays in Early Modern European History* (Ithaca and London: Cornell University Press, 1971), ch. 7, 'The powers of deputies in sixteenth-century assemblies', pp. 176–210; A. Marongiu, *Medieval Parliaments: A Comparative Study* (London: Eyre and Spottiswood, 1968), pp. 223–8; M. A. R. Graves, *The Parliaments of Early Modern Europe* (Harlow: Pearson Education, 2001), pp. 160, 175–7; on England, E. S. Morgan, *Inventing the People: The Rise of Popular Sovereignty in England and America* (New York and London: Norton, 1988), pp. 39ff.

75 Morgan, *Inventing the People*, p. 70; he suggests that the Levellers followed royalist argument on this point.

76 Parker, *Observations*, p. 34.

77 Mendle, *Henry Parker*, p. 70.

78 [Herle], *A Fuller Answer*, p. 16.

79 Parker, *Observations*, p. 9.

80 [Herle], *A Fuller Answer*, pp. 5, 16.

81 [Herle], *A Fuller Answer*, p. 7.

82 [Herle], *A Fuller Answer*, p. 8.

83 Wolfe, p. 237 (petition of 23 November 1647).

84 Wolfe, p. 283 (petition of 11 September 1648).

85 Wolfe, p. 284 (petition of 11 September 1648).

86 Wolfe, p. 326 (petition of 19 January 1649).

87 Wolfe, p. 283 (petition of 11 September 1648).

88 Overton, *An Arrow*, p. 4.

89 Overton, *An Arrow*, p. 10.

90 Overton, *An Arrow*, p. 11.

91 Overton, *An Arrow*, p. 11. See C. Condren, *The Language of Politics in Seventeenth-Century England* (Basingstoke and London: Macmillan, 1994), p. 66, for the distinction between accountable 'officers' and unaccountable representatives in Leveller thought.

92 Overton, *A Defiance*, pp. 7, 15, 17; *Regall Tyrannie*, pp. 38–9.

93 Condren, *The Language of Politics*, p. 66.

94 Overton, *An Appeale*, p. 12.

95 *An Agreement of the People for a Firme and Present Peace* ([3 November] 1647), p. 8.

96 Overton, *An Arrow*, p. 4.

97 *A Remonstrance of Many Thousand Citizens*, p. 3.

98 *Regall Tyrannie*, p. 99.

Chapter 2

The appeal to the people

In 1642, parliamentarians and royalists had embarked on a virtual war of 'paper bullets' to mobilize opinion and rally support for the real war which was to come. As the fighting began, they continued to publish, with parliamentarian authors outlining their views of the constitution and its origins in order to reassure their followers about the rightness of resistance against the king. During the war years, the parliamentarian coalition came under enormous strain, and by the time Parliament had won the war, observers saw within Parliament two rival factions or parties, the 'Presbyterians' and the 'Independents', the successors (broadly) of earlier 'peace' and 'war' parties. In the last chapter we saw that these factions developed differing accounts of the relationship of the king to the other two 'estates' in Parliament, the Presbyterians preserving the independent power of the king within a coordinative mixed monarchy, the Independents stressing the ultimate power of judgement of the Parliament, or House of Commons, which could be argued partly due to the role of Parliament as a representative embodiment of the will of the nation. 'Independent' thinkers laid the foundations for the theory of parliamentary sovereignty which the Levellers came to develop, and as the first civil war came to an end, Levellers were among the radical Independents who began to spell out the potential conclusion for Charles I and for monarchy in England.

It is easy to see this strand of radical Independent thinking as the foundation of Leveller radicalism, but in this chapter we take a second look at the 'Presbyterian' coordination theorists and at the radicalization of parliamentarian thought towards and after the end of the first civil war, in which the Levellers participated and which forged the Levellers as a group. The Presbyterian theorists' refusal to derive political authority from the original power of the people has made them seem rather conservative, as has their commitment to the role of the king: it was these theorists who provided the underpinning

The Levellers

of the political Presbyterians' opposition to regicide when it came. However, I will argue here that they contributed one crucial element to the radicalism of Leveller political thought: the appeal to the people.

It was 1647 before the imprisoned Leveller leaders Lilburne and Overton declared in print that they were 'appealing' from the jurisdiction of the House of Commons to the people at large. But Lilburne and Overton's move drew on five years of parliamentarian thinking which had, in different contexts, hinted at or allowed for some appeal to the consciences of the people if government broke down or threatened the 'safety of the people' which it was supposed to protect. This trail leads from radical 'war party' parliamentarians alarmed by the lack of appetite for the war in its first winter in 1642–43, through a selection of Presbyterian thinkers who proved remarkably open to the possibility of some role for the people's consciences in emergencies, to the sharpening of dissatisfaction with Parliament among enthusiastic parliamentarians, including the incipient Leveller movement, around the end of the first civil war. The Leveller leaders' appeal to the people was thus a realization of a possibility which had stirred comment by parliamentarians, as well as hostile royalists, from the early stages of the war. However, the parliamentarian thinkers who developed these implications at the earlier stages were not, by and large, those whom royalists or modern commentators would expect. It was not those who had a strong belief in the original power of the people who contemplated allowing the people this emergency political role. The Levellers, by contrast, were strong believers in the original power of the people, and the parliamentary supremacy which they saw as derived from it. Consequently, they faced significant difficulties in trying to reconcile the appeal to the people with their conviction that the representative chamber was the only place where institutional supremacy could reside. The implications of this are explored later in the chapter, and the chapter concludes with a discussion of the nature of the Leveller appeal to the people, and its implications for their thought about the social contract and the state of nature.

1642: THE ROYALIST CHALLENGE

No sooner had the civil war started in the autumn of 1642 than parliamentarians became divided. A war conducted as an 'armed negotiation' led to fears of a premature peace which more committed parliamentarians would see as a sell-out. The first of these crises of war and peace, over the winter of 1642–43, generated a significant number of parliamentarian pamphlets which reacted against the dangers of an undesirable settlement by articulating radicalized parliamentarian positions. As David Wootton has pointed out, these radical parliamentarian publications foreshadowed all the key elements of Leveller thought, including the deposition of kings and an appeal to the people against the potential betrayals of Parliament.¹ This may seem in danger of reducing the Levellers' thought to a mere reiteration, expansion, or application of the earlier arguments of radical or 'war party' parliamentarians. However, this is an oversimplification, for two reasons. Firstly, the Levellers' struggles with the inadequacy of the Long Parliament pushed them to combine two strands of parliamentarian thinking which had been largely separate. The earlier 'radicals' had generally either advocated a fuller assumption of parliamentary sovereignty or contemplated the possibility of appealing to the people against a corrupt Parliament – but they had not developed both ideas simultaneously. Indeed, appealing to the people against Parliament was fundamentally at odds with parliamentary sovereignty, if that sovereignty was taken to be absolute not only against competing claims from the king but also against competing claims from the people – which was the view upheld by the advocates of parliamentary sovereignty. Secondly, it is far from simple to distinguish 'radicals' from 'conservatives' in parliamentarian ranks. Perhaps in more concrete terms, those who formed the 'war party' and wanted to defeat the king militarily were more radical than those who defended the position and honour of the king and opposed regicide. But the theoretical arguments which they used in favour of their positions had implications which were untidy and sometimes uncontainable, and an argument used in one context to try to moderate parliamentarian thinking might prove to offer the means for 'radicalization' of parliamentarian argument at a later date. For this reason, I will here consider 'radical' and more mainstream parliamentarian works alongside each other, focusing instead on the more complex divide between theorists of parliamentary sovereignty and theorists of an appeal to the people.²

From the start of the war, parliamentarian theories of government by consent, especially those in which political power came originally from the people themselves, were an irresistible target for royalist writers. Henry Ferne was in the vanguard of the royalist campaign, and he chose to interpret parliamentarian theories as theories of the reassumption of power from the king by Parliament.³ He was quick to challenge parliamentarians about the logical consequences of this: if Parliament had reassumed power originally given to the king, surely the people might also 'reassume' (from Parliament) the power which was originally theirs? The consequences were vividly imagined:

> We see the danger, if (as it is now said, for the justifying of this power of resistance, The King will not discharge his trust, and therefore it falls to the representative body of the people to see to it, so) the People being discontented, and having gotten power shall say, The Members of the two Houses do not discharge the trust committed to them, they do not that for which they were chosen and sent for, then may the multitude by this rule and principle now taught them take the Power to themselves, it being claimed by them, and ... overthrow King and Parliament, fill all with rapine and confusion, draw all to a Folkmoot, and make every Shire a severall Government.⁴

The Levellers

Such a powerful challenge to Parliament could not go without an answer: parliamentarian theorists tackled it directly.

There was, of course, a plausibility to Ferne's overall line of argument. Much as parliamentarians tried to place the right of resistance within the constitution provided for by the original consent of the people to government, they were still arguing for emergency powers for Parliament – powers which looked suspiciously like those exercised by the king under normal circumstances. At some points, parliamentarians came dangerously close to endorsing Ferne's view of the reassumption of royal power by Parliament. Palmer and the other ministers who wrote *Scripture and Reason* insisted that what was involved was not any taking away of the king's power, but simply the temporary 'use' or administering of a part of it.[5] In general, however, Palmer and others preferred to argue for powers which were specifically annexed to Parliament 'by Law',[6] rather than admit any need to use something which was inherently a royal power. Herle denied the charge that the parliamentarians were legitimating a reassumption of power; rather, he argued a theory of reservation of power to the Parliament within the supreme power, which was a coordinative, mixed monarchy.[7] Even Parker, seen by Sirluck as committed to the model of parliamentary reassumption of the king's power outlined by Ferne, in fact tended to view the mechanism as one of reservation rather than resumption: when the people made the agreement to be ruled, 'some things they have reserved to themselves out of Parliament, and some thing [sic] in Parliament'.[8] The consequence of the 'derivative' quality of the king's power was not the possibility of its resumption, but the fact of its limitation:

> if our Kings receive all royalty from the people and for the behoofe of the people, and that by a speciall trust of safety and libertie expressely by the people limited, and by their owne grants and oathes ratified, then our Kings cannot be sayd to have so unconditionate and high a proprietie in all our lives, liberties, and possessions ...[9]

The people had 'intrusted their protection into the Kings hands irrevocably';[10] the limits to the king's power could and had to be enforced *within* the constitution set up by the original agreement, not by going back on that agreement. Jeremiah Burroughes, although as we will see he flirted with the *popular* resumption of power, used a typical parliamentarian move – the separation of royal power from the king's person – to assert that nobody 'hath attempted to take any power away from the King, that Law hath given him'.[11] In other words, resumption of power was simply not at issue: the physical resistance which was appropriate in cases of abuses of 'civill and natural' government was precisely that resistance which was built into the laws of the land – acting *through* those was the remedy justified by God and nature.[12]

Up to this point, parliamentarians of all stripes could largely agree. Ferne's challenge was nonsensical because Parliament had not, in fact, taken it upon itself to recover any power previously given to the king. Nonetheless, parliamentarians had further responses to Ferne's challenge which diverged significantly, some accepting in some circumstances the possibility of appealing to the people's consciences and letting them exercise their political judgement directly, rather than through their governors; others rejecting vehemently Ferne's suggestion that their arguments should or might lead to any direct exercise of power by the people.

It was often the more radical users of natural-law theory – those who saw the Parliament as exercising the people's own constituent authority – who resisted most vehemently the possibility of a popular resumption of power. This could be achieved by holding the line of parliamentary sovereignty, a move which may seem desperate and unconvincing to a modern democrat, but which rested on deeply held ideas about Parliament which should not be dismissed as special pleading. We saw in the last chapter how these notions of representation underpinned arguments for the supremacy of Parliament made by both Henry Parker and the Levellers; here it is important to note how such ideas militated against the notion of appealing to the people. Parker invoked the traditional fiction that the whole kingdom was present in Parliament to argue against any possibility of the people's appealing against their Parliament. The people and the Parliament were not 'severall', he insisted, because 'the Parliament is indeed nothing else, but the very people it self artificially congregated, or reduced by an orderly election, and representation, into such a Senate, or proportionable body'.[13] The way in which Parker developed and underpinned this point is interesting. While admitting that there were differences between Parliament and the 'rude bulk of the universality', he insisted that in political essentials – 'in power, in honour, in majestie, in commission' – Parliament was not to be distinguished from the 'universality' it represented. Therefore, he reasoned, the Parliament was more 'representative' than the king – who was only a second-best as a representative of the people, though he sometimes had to take on that function. The 'supreme reason or Judicature' of the state thus rested in Parliament, largely because the 'interests' of Parliament were virtually identical with those of the people.[14] In his *Observations* he cited it as a 'maxime' that 'a community can have no private ends to mislead it, and make it injurious to itselfe', and proceeded from this maxim to argue that no Parliament could be injurious to a whole kingdom – at least, as long as it was a 'Parliament freely elected'.[15] Parliament could be described as a 'community' because of its relationship of free election with the people; and because it was – more or less – *the* community of the kingdom, it could not hurt the kingdom, which would be to hurt 'itselfe'.

The early modern interpretation of 'representation' and election, then, made Parliament (in modern terms) less, rather than more, accountable. So, for Herle,

> as their *interests* with us tye them more to do *a right*, so our *elections* of them tye us more to suffer what they doe if not *a right:* because, what *they* do *we* do in them ... our judgements are not enthralled, 'tis our interests are entrusted and so, subjected to their decisions: our judgements are not infallibly guided from either erring with them or differing from them, but bound up in, and superseded by theirs from gaine-saying or ressistance ...[16]

Although Herle added that there might be pragmatic reasons for any man to expect Parliament's decision to be better than his own,[17] his main argument was that Parliament's actions simply were the subject's own actions.

For Parker, the assertion that the people might act against Parliament was a violation of the understanding of the nature of Parliament itself: 'The vertue of representation has been denied to the Commons, and a severance has beene made betwixt the parties chosen and the parties choosing.'[18] In early modern terms, 'representation' did not imply the separation of the electors and the elected, but rather their unity. Parker admitted that recently the people had become 'prone to withdraw themselves from their representatives, ... yet there can be nothing under Heaven, next to renouncing God, which can be more perfidious and more pernitious in the people than this'.[19] The idea of 'perfidy' may not be entirely comfortable within Parker's argument – in a sense, it ought not to be *possible* for the people to act against their representatives if they are so united with them by representation – but the extent of Parker's outrage is clear. This is more comprehensible in the light of the account of the origins of parliaments which precedes this passage. In Parker's view, the 'motions of the peoples moliminous body' needed regulating; assemblies such as parliaments were the only way in which 'the people may assume its owne power to do itself right without disturbance to it selfe, or injury to Princes'.[20] In these assemblies 'the whole community in its underived Majesty shall convene to do justice'; in order to prevent the sheer size of the *actual* whole community making this unworkable, 'by vertue of election and representation, a few shall act for many'.[21] It is likely that for Parker, even when these 'few' acted, they were still exercising the 'underived' power of the whole community. In short, a strong assertion of parliamentary sovereignty tended to go along with a denial of the possibility of direct popular intervention in politics – and this should not surprise us.

This held true for radical advocates of parliamentary sovereignty in the crisis of 1642–43. Two of these works, *Remonstrans Redivivus* and *Touching the Fundamentall Lawes*, both clearly rejected the negative voice of the king, but they also both repudiated any right of subjects outside Parliament to resist its authority. *Remonstrans Redivivus* straightforwardly located all power in Parliament, 'from whose judgements there is no appeale, being presumed ever to intend the proper interest of the Common-wealth'.[22] We should note that the future Leveller leader William Walwyn was one of those involved in the production of *Remonstrans Redivivus*. As late as March 1646, he referred back to its arguments with approval – if perhaps offering an overly charitable retrospective interpretation of it as standing against all arbitrary power. If he was in accord with all of its arguments at the time of its production, he had a long way to travel before endorsing any Leveller appeal to the people.[23] It is true that *Remonstrans Redivivus* was, consciously and rather defensively, challenging Parliament to live up to its own declarations and assume the power belonging to it; but in spite of its promoters' doubts about the performance of Parliament, it left no conceptual space open for the will of the nation or the people to be expressed anywhere except in Parliament.[24]

Touching the Fundamentall Lawes, an anonymous pamphlet from February 1643, is a more complex case. It has been read as endorsing the power of the people outside Parliament, alongside its willingness to assert the supremacy of Parliament itself at the expense of the king.[25] However, the author's treatment of this question of the scope for popular action is compressed and is framed in answer to a question about subjects resisting the *king*, rather than in response to Ferne's provocative idea of them resisting their own Parliament. Essentially, it was merely a treatment of the perennial question within resistance theory about who was qualified to resist, and the answer it gave was conventional. The author admitted that individual subjects might, of course, resist wilful attack by people who happened to be kings or magistrates; but 'Every Subject taken *divisim*, and apart from the whole, is to suffer under abused authority [i.e., when the abuse was exercised in the name of the office and not merely by the person who happened to hold the office], and to obey passively, rather than to breake union or cause confusion.' What has misled modern commentators is the combination of two elements in this passage: the profound identification of Parliament with the people and the interests of the people, and the glimmer of distrust in Parliament which ends the pamphlet on an ambivalent note. The people 'divisim' could not resist abuse of authority; but the people were only undivided when they were in their Parliament: 'the representative body of the Common-wealth, (which is all men conjunctim)', might, unlike individuals, resist abuse of office. At this stage in the exposition, no third possibility was visible: there was no state where the people were a collective entity able to exist and act independently of their representative body. Popular resistance, for this author, *was* resistance by Parliament. And yet the hint of a division between people and Parliament then opens up, treated with an awkwardness which echoes Parker's uncomfortable consideration of the possibility of the withdrawal of the people from their representatives. The 'people ... or their trustees', the author said, must resist wicked rulers. Like Parker, the author of *Touching the Fundamentall Lawes* spoke highly of the original power of the people, and made clear that it was the people's own power –'that universall and popular authority, that is in the body of the people' – which was put into the hands of their representatives. Perhaps the people *were* a 'body' which might not, after all, be identical with their representative body, and they might 'expect and chalenge' their representatives to provide for their safety rather than betraying them. But whether that legitimate demand could actually be expressed by any form of popular action against Parliament, or repossession of the people's power, was a question that remained unvoiced at the end of the pamphlet.[26]

It may seem surprising that it was often precisely those authors who *did* believe that the Parliament was exercising the people's own power who resisted the idea that the people themselves, outside Parliament, could have a role in national politics. A strong belief in the original transfer of power from the people to their governors may have made it more important to reject Ferne's accusation that a popular reassumption of power, with all which that might entail, was a logical consequence of their thought. But more importantly, those authors who wanted to reach a conclusion which privileged Parliament over the king had to explain why that should be the case, and they reached for explanations which legitimized parliamentary power through its intimate connection with the popular power which was its source. Mechanisms of election and, more intangibly, the notion of representation were invoked to do this work.[27] But since the very impulse for invoking the people's power was to legitimate parliamentary sovereignty, these authors were naturally reluctant to admit that the people's power could now be exercised anywhere other than in Parliament itself.

There are a couple of exceptions to this rule, which point towards the possibilities opened up in Leveller argument later in the 1640s, but also highlight some of the difficulties of combining these positions. Jeremiah Burroughes was, as Sirluck remarks, one of the most forthright propounders of 'parliamentary supremacy over positive law', following Parker's defence of equity and of Parliament as the interpreter of that equity. In his systematic 'Brief Answer' to Ferne, he emphasized the binding nature of original contracts, 'explicite or implicite', and rested his assertion of Parliament's powers purely on the contents of the resulting fundamental constitution. No parliamentary reassumption of power from the king had taken place, and the king was simply being prevented from acting illegally, rather than being stripped of any legally held powers. Parliament's own powers included legislative power and the power to interpret law, so there was no clear criterion for transgression of the power given them – their power was, in a sense, arbitrary in any case.[28] Indeed, for Burroughes, Parliament's interpretation of law was 'binding to us for obedience'.[29]

All of this militated against any doctrine of the popular resumption of power from the Parliament, but nonetheless, Burroughes reluctantly worked out a direct answer to Ferne's challenge. He conceded that Parliament might do things which were 'unjust', and that in that case the 'law of nature' might possibly 'allow of standing up to defend our selves'. This recourse to the law of nature necessitated the abandonment of the original contract of government, and was thus a step to be taken only in the most extreme circumstances: 'It is hard to conceive it possible, that a Parliament can so degenerate, as to make our condition more grievous by unjust acts, then it would be if the power in a Kingdom should return to the law of nature, from whence at first it rose.' In Burroughes's theory, parliamentary sovereignty was so absolute that only catastrophe could open it up again to the people who had originally constituted that government; and when this did happen, they would exercise their power only for a brief moment: they would 'discharge them of that power they had, and set up some other'.[30] Nevertheless, it was the people's action, not the government's betrayal, which would take the decisive step of dissolving the polity into the law of nature, allowing a new one to be constituted.

Plaine English, believed to be the work of the parliamentary army chaplain Edward Bowles, provides an interesting intermediate case between proponents of parliamentary sovereignty and defenders of popular action. The work was published in January 1643, amidst pressure for peace by petitioners and London crowds, and with Parliament already drafting peace proposals in response.[31] Bowles raised the possibility of popular resistance against Parliament not merely in reply to Ferne, but in the immediate context of the threat of a too-easy accommodation, and confronted the question of betrayal by Parliament relatively directly. While he set out no constitutional theory, his desire for a strong settlement led him to question the status quo, criticizing those who were too 'possest with the Majestie nay with the Deitie of a King' and suggesting – as few consent theorists did – that if the dangerous extent of the king's established prerogatives prompted the question 'how farre we are obliged by any acts or graunts of our ancestours, giving away their and our liberty', it could be answered 'to our advantage'.[32] Desperate to prevent an early parliamentarian accommodation with the king, which he thought would be no guarantee of safety at all, Bowles raised the question – though it was only a question – whether, in the event of such a parliamentarian sell-out, the people 'may resume (if ever yet they parted with a power to their manifest undoing) and use their power so farre as conduces to their safety'. A series of avoidances or notes of caution marked Bowles's discussion: his parenthetical comment hinted at reservation rather than resumption of power; he assumed that any betrayal by Parliament could only be the result of members' being absent from the Houses, not the action of a full Parliament; and, in the end, he gave no final answer to his own question of whether in such a case the people could resume power. But his discussion was vivid in its imagination of the people's predicament. He wrestled with the question of whether they would feel able to submit to the (conventional) consequences of passive obedience –

to 'hang or flye' – strongly suggesting that these could not be tolerated;[33] and while he rejected the 'Monster of a Democracy', he promoted instead a new 'Association' of the well-affected which would unite the efforts of individuals in Parliament's true cause.[34] Bowles was one fervent parliamentarian whose perception of danger from Parliament forced him to contemplate resistance to it, even while he asserted that Parliament itself was the protector of liberty and religion.

With a couple of slightly troubled exceptions, then, advocates of parliamentary sovereignty against monarchical power tended to reject the possibility of the people's appealing against their own Parliament, even though they often emphasized the power of the people as the original source of Parliament's authority. The converse was also true: those who did contemplate a role for the people outside Parliament could often do so because they did not hold such a strong view of parliamentary sovereignty, even though they might also hold a less emphatic view of the original power of the people. This, indeed, means that supposedly more 'conservative' parliamentarians are in some ways closer to the 'radical' Leveller notion of appeal to the people than were the advocates of a parliamentary sovereignty derived from original popular power. This holds true of three significant 'Presbyterian' works: Philip Hunton's *Treatise of Monarchie* (1643); *Scripture and Reason*, a work jointly authored by Herbert Palmer and other ministers; and the Scottish Covenanter Samuel Rutherford's *Lex, Rex*.

Hunton's work was credited with revolutionary potential in the later seventeenth century, although modern commentators have tended to emphasize its caution in avoiding any reinterpretation of the balance of the constitution in favour of Parliament;[35] *Scripture and Reason*, in contrast, is counted by Sirluck and Wootton in the ranks of the radical pamphlets which accepted the popular reassumption of power.[36] The premises of these two tracts, if not the exact conclusions, prove to be very similar. Both were fully committed to the coordination of the three estates, rejecting the possibility of parliamentary sovereignty. For Palmer, each of the three estates had a negative voice, each expressing part of the collective reason of the body politic.[37] The reason for the freedom of Parliament, or indeed just one of the Houses of Parliament, to act for the safety of the state was that, as coordinate powers, they were all charged with this responsibility, the fundamental law of the state (and of all states).[38] Thus, in spite of the potential for Parliament to act alone if necessary, there is no argument here for parliamentary sovereignty; supremacy was mixed. The ministers accepted the theory of coordination for its own sake, seeing that it gave *enough* power to Parliament to resist; but they did not use coordination as a stepping-stone to arguing a two-against-one, *'universis minor'* view of parliamentary authority over the king. Hunton, too, resisted any move from genuine coordination towards parliamentary sovereignty. He agreed, too, that it was the duty of other estates to prevent the monarch if he should 'exorbitate' and act illegally, but, crucially, he felt that where this arose, there could be 'no Constituted, Legall, Authoritative Judge of the fundamentall Controversies arising betwixt the three Estates' – unlike the parliamentarian theorists who had laboured so hard to show that Parliament was the final arbiter.[39]

This was the point at which Hunton's theory became most distinctive: he concluded that under circumstances of breakdown and conflict between the elements of the mixed constitution, the only judge would be the consciences of the people as they decided which side to support. This was far from being a radical appeal over the heads of Parliament to the fundamental power of the people: Hunton had denied that the people, after having consented to government, were left with any of that right or power which had qualified them to perform that act of consent. His argument did not rest on any claim of residual or ultimate sovereignty in the people, and was framed so as not to be vulnerable to the claim that he was licensing the people's resumption of a power which had formerly been theirs. But it is striking that a refusal to simplify the complexity of the constitution and to award ultimate power to Parliament left Hunton, like other ministers of religion, appealing directly to the consciences of the people – even if this was only to choose which of their leaders to follow.[40] Indeed, Hunton made very explicit the nature of the power which the people might exercise under these circumstances: it was, specifically, a 'morall' power rather than a civil one. Hunton had no truck with the idea that any civil powers were reserved by the people to themselves in their act of consent, though limits might be set on the monarch by that act; indeed, he refrained from seeing the power of the monarch as the transferred power of the people, steering a course which seems closer to designation theory. The only power which the people did 'reserve to themselves' was 'not a Formall Authoritative Power, but a morall Power, such as they had originally before the Constitution of the Government'.[41] Their exercise of that power of judging in such constitutional emergencies was 'beyond the Government' and 'the Appeale must be to the Community, as if there were no Government'.[42] That was, however, a counterfactual: there was still a government, and by acting as if there were no government, the people were acting to save the fundamentals of their government – in which the monarch, and not the community appealed to, had the supreme power. Rather than a doctrine of the dissolution of government, Hunton's position is better understood as a theory either of reserved (moral) powers, powers which no government could ever have claimed to remove from the people, or as a theory of the freedoms which persist (as Hobbes agreed) in the gaps between the authoritative commands of the state. As Hunton puts it, 'in a Case which transcends the frame and provision of the Government they are bound to, People are unbound, and in state as if they had no Government' – not because they have been released from any of the obligations their government *can* bind them to, but simply because in the case at issue their government has no authority to command their consciences.[43] Indeed, it is the 'Lawes and Government' the individual is sworn to which 'bindes him' to exercise his own conscience in such cases.[44] The crux of Hunton's argument is that a mixed monarchy would be destroyed if there were a judge constituted *within* the frame of government – it would no longer be genuinely a monarchy or genuinely mixed, as that judge would be effectively supreme. The moral consciences of the people are appealed to precisely because, being outside the frame of government, they cannot unbalance it.

The role that the consciences of the people outside Parliament played in *Scripture and Reason* was rather different. For Hunton, Parliament had the authority to act to curb a king exceeding his own authority, but did not have the authority to issue a binding command to the people to follow it; this was a determination which they had to come to in their own consciences.[45] Since the people were not freed from all bonds of government, the question they were to decide was limited in scope: which of the warring estates to follow. They could not free themselves from the leadership of the three estates altogether. Palmer and his co-authors, in contrast, did not keep the people's action so strictly circumscribed, and countenanced the possibility of the people's acting without Parliament. The fundamental law of the state was its preservation, and so if king, Lords and Commons conspired to destroy the state, 'even the Body of the People, should (by vertue of the power which each State hath for its necessary safety) have Authority sufficient to defend themselves'. Similarly, if there was a dispute between the three estates – regarded by the authors as coordinate – 'who can be Judge between them? or who can amongst men decide the difference but the Body of the People? Exercising their understanding and consciences to judge who is in the right ...?' Thus it was not just the representative body of the state which could act for the collective self-defence of the state, but 'any considerable part of the Body (with them, or) even without them'.[46] They were aware of the probable hostile perception of this as a step towards 'Cantoning and Folkmoots', and insisted that only the worst tyranny would lead people to resort to such extreme behaviour.[47] Even so, in *Scripture and Reason* we find a text which is conventional in forms and aims, and in much that it says to justify the parliamentarian cause, but which seems entirely committed to the principle that all necessary means (if not explicitly forbidden by God or the original agreement made to constitute a government) might be used to save the state from danger, including the action of the people without other constituted authority if necessary. And again, it is clear that the possibility of the people's acting without Parliament went along with, and perhaps rested upon, the assertion of coordination and the denial of parliamentary sovereignty.[48]

The appeal to the people

Samuel Rutherford's *Lex, Rex* of 1644 has been depicted as one of the most 'radical' of the major parliamentarian or Covenanter works, and several scholars have seen its arguments as an important influence on the Levellers.[49] This 'radicalism', however, involved his pushing against the boundaries of Presbyterian theory rather than breaking them outright. Rutherford's bitterness against Charles I was notable, and he was insistent on strict limitations on the king's power; he perhaps went as far as was possible within a coordination theory in disabling the king of any independent power; even the divinity of royal office was emphasized partly to restrain its incumbent. The role of the people's original consent was made central to Rutherford's account of the limited power of the king; like Parker, he felt that (Scottish and English) parliaments were more direct 'representatives' of the people than the king was.[50] Rutherford, however, was far from endorsing any populist view of political life. He carefully hedged even the version of 'constituent authority' which he gave, so that it came as close as possible to a designation theory of the origins of royal power. The original collective of the people had 'devolved their power' to their rulers, but this was a power which they had possessed only 'virtually', rather than 'formally': it was theirs to confer, but not theirs to exercise.[51] While a popular form of government would be legitimate, such a democracy derived its power no more directly from the people than any other kind of government, and it could never consist of the entire mass of the people ruling itself: it was, rather, a multitude of people designated for power from out of the community, just as a monarchy or aristocracy might be.[52] Resistance was undertaken by the 'estates', effectively the Scottish or English parliaments, rather than by private men.[53]

While Rutherford's attitude to the king himself (although not the kingly office) was sharp, it is his comments on the possibility of the community acting against their Parliament which have been seen as a possible source for later Leveller radicalism. When Rutherford considered the question of whether the people could take back power from their representatives, it was in response to the Scottish royalist Maxwell's challenge (a parallel to Ferne's in England). Maxwell sought to open up a gap between the precedents set by Buchanan and Parker, emphasizing a populist element in Buchanan's account of legislation so as to imply that Parker's absolute commitment to the unquestionable legislative sovereignty of Parliament could not hold, and was dissolved into an endless recourse to the approval of the people. Rutherford's reply aimed to vindicate Parliament's authority, insisting that any parliamentary measure which was justly commanded was indeed binding and irrevocable; it was only where fiduciary power was abused that there was any question of its not being binding. The concession which Rutherford then made, that if that power was abused 'the people' might resist, was again far from a populist endorsement of the reclamation of original, individual powers. The 'people' who resisted were the 'particular Corporations' who reclaimed their 'fountain-power' of electing representatives: as Coffey has shown, this is a federalist theory in the mould of Althusius, rather than an individualist foreshadowing of Locke – or, we might add, of the Levellers.[54]

From as early as the winter of 1642–43, then, there were dissatisfied radical parliamentarians who could, when pushed, envisage the people's being tempted to take some kind of action against their own Parliament. However it was more mainstream thinkers who began to theorize this type of popular action: Presbyterian theorists who rejected the strong theory of the people's constituent authority and upheld the office of the king within a coordinative mixed constitution. Clearly these authors did not provide a simple template for Leveller views. From 1645, some of these hints in parliamentarian thought were developed in a selection of pamphlets, some of which were part of a coordinated campaign on behalf of Lilburne. These new challenges to Parliament's authority were not theoretically uniform, and we may again be surprised that some authors who participated in this moment of radical dissatisfaction with Parliament, which seems so closely linked with the origins of the Leveller movement, still hankered after a return to the old balance of king, Lords and Commons. What they did have in common, however, was their understanding of representation, and it was this which finally enabled the incipient Leveller movement to fuse two very different strands of parliamentarian thought: the supremacy of Parliament and the appeal to the people.

1645: THE CRISIS OF REPRESENTATION

In Chapter 1 we saw that the notion of representation was key to the Levellers' enormously radical constitutional thought, which effectively remade one of the three estates – the House of Commons – into the supreme legislative power, offering to other magistrates only a strictly subordinate executive role. In this chapter we have seen that those parliamentarians who were most inclined to emphasize the special status of the representative chamber tended to equate it with the nation itself, and conclude that it was a safe resting-place for arbitrary power. Representation was understood in ways which rendered any appeal to the people unnecessary: their interests simply could not be distinct from those of their representatives.

Ultimately, the Levellers were to reverse the logic of representation, arguing that it created an obligation on MPs to represent their electors faithfully. The Levellers' emphasis on the capacity and duty for political judgement of all 'free-born Englishmen' might seem at odds with that older notion of a representation which simply wrapped up the hypothetical judgements of subjects in the acts of the House. And yet the language which had become associated with the English Parliament's *plena potestas* could be read as a powerful validator of the political role even of the lowliest in the nation. It was commonplace to assert that Parliament not only represented the kingdom, but *was* the kingdom: 'everie Englishman is entended to bee there present'; the Parliament 'consisteth of the king, and of all that within the land are subject unto him: for they are all there present, either in person or by such as they voluntarily have derived their very personal right unto'.[55] The Levellers' proposals for a vast expansion of the franchise were a gloss on, and were validated by, the traditional idea that the voices of all Englishmen were heard – virtually – in the House of Commons.

The development of Leveller thought was not a purely theoretical process, of course. Leveller views on the authority of the Commons varied in response to political developments and, in particular, to the impact of those developments on the Leveller leaders themselves. In 1645, Lilburne found himself repeatedly examined and proceeded against by the authority of the House of Commons, at the instigation of Prynne and Bastwick. Such proceedings seemed to reflect the dangerous Presbyterian influences which might sway the House of Commons in religious and political settlement, and, consequently, writings by the future Leveller leaders in 1645 emphasized limits on the power of the Commons and of Parliament. From September, indeed, the notion of limitation began to be accompanied in Leveller-related texts by hints at the possibility of appealing to the people to enforce such limits.

At this juncture in the mid-1640s, the parliamentarian voices beginning to explore such possibilities were not homogeneous, although they were clearly moved by common impulses and there may have been connections between them. *England's Miserie, and Remedie*, an anonymous text from September 1645, was picked out by Sirluck, among others, as the first to develop the hints about the popular resumption of authority which we have examined in the radical fringes of pamphleteering in 1642–43.[56] This pamphlet was written in support of Lilburne, but its authorship is unclear and it has precocious elements of classical republican language which are not typical of the Leveller authors at this period (see Chapter 6). The Leveller authors themselves were developing a strong critique of Parliament which involved a rejection of its binding power. *England's Miserie, and Remedie* and *Englands Birth-right Justified*, another anonymous work in support of, and possibly by, Lilburne, both quoted the work of the parliamentarian poet George Wither, whose writing at this time was increasingly concerned with the dishonesty and treachery of many supposed parliamentarians, including members of the House of Commons. A more explicitly argued case for the people's entitlement to act outside and against Parliament if necessary was put into print at this time by William Ball of Barkham, whose work has been linked by Peacey to the campaign on Lilburne's behalf, and who himself had links with Henry Marten.[57] In the autumn of 1645, there was thus a significant burst of writing by parliamentarians prepared to take a radical view of the rights of the people against their Parliament.

The immediate occasion for some of this writing was the recruiter elections which were held for vacant seats from late 1645, which enabled those who had become dissatisfied with the House of Commons to plead for an influx of new MPs who would keep their faith with their electors. Lilburne's imprisonment by the House of Commons in July provided another spur. Recruiter elections might tilt the balance of the House, but they would not cleanse the House of the existing MPs hostile to Lilburne and uncommitted to the final stages of the war effort. As well as pleading with the electorate to make a wiser choice of MPs than they had done previously, these works took the opportunity to criticize the limited scope for the people to hold their elected House to account for its supposedly deepening corruption. *Englands Birth-right* suggested that the principle of the recruiter elections should be regularized and extended: the free-men of England should have the chance to fill vacant seats once a year, 'but also to renue and inquire once a yeere, after the behaviour and carriage of those they have chosen'. The author suggested an even more inventive means of bridging the gap between the elected representatives and the 'private men' who had often been the source of the best measures enacted in Parliament: allowing 'every free-man of England' who was capable of the task to serve 'the Civill State' for a year in any office or place of trust which was appropriate, with pay if necessary.[58]

These works did not necessarily break the mould established for the earlier 1640s and combine their defence of the people's power with a radical constitutional vision of the supremacy of Parliament. William Ball and George Wither both, in their distinctive ways, clung to a nostalgic vision of the pre-civil war constitution restored and rebalanced, with a full role for the king if he could come to recognize its nature and fulfil it without violating the people's liberties.[59] In contrast, Marchamont Nedham, possibly the author of the anonymous *Englands Miserie and Remedie*, had recently issued a mocking 'Hue and Cry' after the supposedly runaway king in his newsbook *Mercurius Britanicus*, and was soon to hint at his deposition and execution – even though he did then go on to serve the king.[60] These authors who began to explore the possibility of resistance against Parliament were writing as parliamentarians (Ball had been a royalist but became a recruiter MP in the Long Parliament in 1646 and addressed his book to the parliamentarian army officer Skippon), but their writing emerged from a culture of criticism of Parliament which was royalist as well as parliamentarian and which comprehended different parliamentarian perspectives. Discerning the specific positioning and motives of these authors is not easy. Ball has been seen as an ally of Marten, but clearly did not share his early anti-monarchism; according to Peacey, Ball's works of the mid-1640s belong to the campaign in support of Lilburne, but according to Tuck they were 'clearly designed to defend the Clubmen's actions' and were notably different from the Leveller version of the appeal to the people.[61] George Wither was an energetic parliamentarian, but one whose emphasis on honesty and on reconciliation did not directly align him with a particular parliamentarian faction; it was partly through chance that he found himself on the receiving end of the displeasure of the Presbyterians in 1646.[62]

Whatever their specific motivations, these accounts tended to provide a basis for the people's potential action against Parliament by developing the notion of representation. This was particularly prominent in Wither's writing, as Norbrook has noted, although Wither was rather inclined to blame the degeneracy of the whole nation, rather than just that of its representatives: the House was corrupt and in need of purging as much because it *did* represent the body of the people as because it failed to.[63] Nonetheless, one of the faults of the MPs was that they had lost sight of the relationship of representation by which they acted for the body of the people, and forgotten that they themselves were drawn from and part of that same body; consequently they tended to 'conceiv[e] themselves so invested with an irrevocable Trust, that they are above controule'.[64] The works which quoted Wither took up his interest in representation, and particularly his observation that the House of Commons was merely the shadow or reflection of the people.[65] This notion of representation implied the priority of the represented. Wither's most consistent demand was for the House of Commons to purge itself of its corrupt members, but he increasingly imagined ways in which the people might speak back to their Parliament, and hinted – in the passage quoted in *England's Miserie, and Remedie* – that those represented by Parliament might hold that Parliament 'to a strict account', or even that God would intervene on behalf of the people by raising 'a *lawfull-power*'.[66] A year later he argued from analogy with Parliament's resistance against the king: 'Why, may not we as justly question them,/ Who break their *trust* to *us*; as, *you* do *him*?'[67] *England's Miserie, and Remedie* itself built on the observation of the priority of the represented over the representers by arguing that Lilburne could not only appeal from the thin House which had condemned him to a fuller House, but from that House to the people. The argument offered was that sovereignty lay in the people (as Buchanan had said), but it rested on the notion of grades of representation, with the people's essence only fully representable by themselves.[68]

William Ball's bold argument for the direct exercise of popular power was, like Wither's, embedded in a constitutional argument which was, ostensibly, carefully balanced. Like Wither's, it too emphasized the logic of representation, in which the represented were ultimately superior to their representers. Ball was well aware that for some parliamentarians the notion of representation bolstered parliamentary absolutism, but he insisted that representation, properly understood, implied accountability: 'the word *Represent* inferres as much, for to represent, or *alterius vices gerere* doth not import (as some would have it) to be an absolute *Judge or Umpire* in all things, (for then he doth not represent, or *vices gerere*, but is absolute, and independent)'. This accountability, for Ball, was enacted by the authority of the 'essentiall' part of the kingdom (as opposed to the Representative), by virtue of the natural right which they had always retained, rather than handing it over to their representatives. But, like Rutherford, he imagined it exercised only by the 'Counties, Cities, and Townes corporate' which originally elected MPs, not by the essential body of the kingdom collectively or individually. Nonetheless, Ball's argument was remarkably bold in its explicit concession that subjects defending themselves against a conspiracy by their king and Parliament might actually raise arms in their own defence.[69]

The autumn of 1645 thus saw the development of parliamentarian arguments – some of them in support of Lilburne – which emphasized the responsibilities and accountability of representation. The body represented – the people – could claim to be the essence of the state; the members of the House of Commons could not.[70] Ultimately, the people (at least in their corporations) could look to their own defence, in spite of or against their corrupt representatives. The Levellers were to pick up these arguments and develop them further, particularly from 1647, when Lilburne and Overton explicitly appealed over the heads of the House of Commons to the people themselves. However, their commitment to parliamentary government made this move more difficult for them than we would expect, and they did not immediately and permanently adopt the radical account of the significance of representation.

In the summer and autumn of 1645, Lilburne had found himself victimized by Presbyterians within the House of Commons. By the spring of 1646, however, the greatest Presbyterian threats appeared to be bearing down on Parliament from the outside – from the Scots, now holding the king and hoping to extract an agreeable settlement from him, and from the City of London – while the House of Commons, unlike the Lords, was willing and (narrowly) able to hold off the most alarming Presbyterian proposals.[71] In addition, the House of Lords became Lilburne's new persecutor, and he appealed to the House of Commons to come to his defence. The high period of the Levellers' endorsement of the absolute sovereignty of the House of Commons thus followed one period of scepticism, and preceded another more vehement one. Walwyn's *Word in Season*, distributed by Lilburne himself, illustrated the potential relationship between representation and absolute authority, arguing that MPs were 'absolutely Free to follow the dictate of their own Understandings and Consciences' regardless of outside pressure, as no one exerting that pressure would be elected as they were. 'Consider', Walwyn warned those outside Parliament who were dissatisfied with its actions, 'whatever you are, you are but a part of the whole people, it is impossible that you can give the

The appeal to the people

sense and mind of all the Commons of England.' In writing this, Walwyn invoked the persistent view that the people of England *were* virtually present in the House of Commons, and that the members thus had *plena potestas* to act without referring back to those who had sent them. MPs should thus act with complete freedom, though always conscientiously, in acting for the good of the people according to their trust.[72] A trace of similar views is seen in a 1646 petition from Overton cannily praising the *'legall regality'* of *'this most Soveraigne House'*, and urging MPs to act for Overton and thus the other commoners whom they represent.[73] These two examples are clearly both strategic uses of the notion of parliamentary sovereignty; Walwyn indeed had in 1645 remarked most pointedly on the dubious views of those who held 'that a Parliament being once chosen, have power over all our lives estates and liberties, to dispose of them at their pleasure'.[74] He was unlikely to have reverted to that view himself within so short a time, and it was not long before the Leveller leaders were again seeking strategies of containment of the House's power; by early 1647, Lilburne and Overton had settled on the idea of appealing beyond the House of Commons to the people themselves. Before examining that appeal in more detail, we will consider the ways in which the Levellers' notions of representation and popular sovereignty developed from 1645 through to the final collective statement of Leveller principles in the third *Agreement of the People* of May 1649.

The traditional English conception of *plena potestas*, along with the idea of representation, was an important building-block in the Leveller theory of the supremacy of the representative chamber. Naturally, as the Levellers became more distrustful of the actions of the House of Commons, and tried to justify resistance to it, the idea that the whole nation was there present and that the House could therefore do what it liked became an argumentative difficulty. It was, however, hard to reject completely, and the Levellers were surprisingly slow to make this step (a point also noted by Conal Condren[75]), partly because they were in danger of leaving themselves with no justification for the supreme position of the House of Commons within all their constitutional proposals. Thus, in a relatively early work by Lilburne in 1645, a protestation of the limited powers of the Commons sat uncomfortably alongside the assumptions of *plena potestas*:

> I look upon the House of Commons, as the supream Power of England, who have residing in them that power that is inherent in the people, who yet are not to act according to their own wils and pleasure, but according to the fundamentall constitutions, and customes of the Land, which I conceive provides for the safety and preservation of the people.[76]

This quotation is hard to harmonize with any over-simple view of the Levellers as consent theorists for whom the people's transfer of power was limited, conditional, and revocable. Lilburne does *not* say that the Commons is limited in its actions because it is exercising the people's power; indeed, he draws no causal connection between the House wielding the people's power and the House being limited and obliged to act for the people's safety. Quite the reverse. The Commons exercises the people's power, 'yet' it cannot act just as it wills. In order to limit its exercise of the people's power, Lilburne has to bring in a quite extraneous factor: the 'fundamentall Constitutions and Customes of the Land'. It is these which provide for the people's safety.

The Levellers were thus problematically attached to the idea of the House of Commons *being* the people, representing the people, and exercising in some rather organic and direct way the sovereign power of the people. This meant that the Levellers were sometimes less concerned than are modern commentators to pin down exactly where sovereignty lay. Overton could claim in an apparently untroubled way that 'the Parliament & whole Kingdom whom it represents' is the supreme power, seeing their power as so interfused that a decision between them need not be made.[77] Leveller petitioners declared that 'there can be no Liberty in any Nation where the Law giving power is not solely in the people or their Representatives'.[78] The Commons and the people seemed to be so identified that the power inherent in the people was present in the Commons almost without explanation. Modern commentators have struggled to come up with formulations which do not diminish the complexity of the Leveller view, Wootton fleshing out the Levellers' principle of 'popular sovereignty' as 'the ultimate supremacy of the people and the legal sovereignty of the Commons', and Scott speaking of the Levellers' key demand as 'popular self-government through representatives'.[79] These formulations draw on the Levellers' own attempts to find a formulation which might allow for the representatives to be corrected by the people, but also explain the validity of an uncorrupt Representative's exercise of popular power. Lilburne's *Just Mans Justification* offered an early example of such a clarification in June 1646, speaking of 'that underived Majesty and Kingship, that inherently resides in the People, *or the state universall*, (the representation or derivation of which, is formally and legally in the *State [elect or] representative*, and none elce'.[80] Similarly, *Regall Tyrannie Discovered* explained that 'the absolute Supream Power is the People in generall, made up of every individuall, and the legall and formall supream Power is only their Commissioners, their collective or representative Body, chosen by them, and assembled in Parliament'.[81] These neat formulations articulated the 'legal and formal' transaction of 'representation or derivation' by which the people's inherent power or majesty came to be exercised by the House of Commons. 'Underived' or 'absolute' power remained in the people themselves, and the House had only the shadow of it. Nonetheless, although both these strikingly parallel passages might seem to subordinate parliamentary power rather aggressively to the original power of the people, they are both designed in context to legitimate the elected chamber's power against that of the king and other mere 'officers', who are to be accountable to Parliament, or to the people through Parliament. They do not succeed in eliminating the mystery of organic representation; only the elected chamber can 'formally' exercise the people's power, even if it does so only derivatively. Indeed, 'formal' power might, in the hands of other parliamentarian authors, be valorized precisely as the only kind of power which could be effectively exercised, whatever its ultimate origins in the (perhaps merely virtual) power of the people.[82] Overton, drawing a line between the 'Members Representative' and 'the Body Represented' in his *Appeale* later in 1647, fleshed out the 'Body Represented' as '(the true originall Sovereigne Authority of Parliaments) the free borne Commoners', still leaving open the question of whether sovereignty was temporarily transferred to parliaments by the electors or whether it remained in the people even while parliaments exercised it.[83]

The Levellers' increasing uneasiness about the dangers of a too-monolithic parliamentary sovereignty did issue, by the final Agreement of the People in May 1649, in some proposals which sought to provide a halfway house between the sovereignty of the people and that of their representatives in Parliament. They proposed the annual election of public officers for 'Counties, Hundreds, Cities, Towns or Boroughs'; the election and removal of almost all military officers by local electors; and the election of ministers of religion by their parishioners.[84] This development has often been characterized as revealing a Leveller interest in 'decentralization': for Gentles, the third Agreement presented 'a radically libertarian England, a decentralized federation of the localities'; for Frank, the new developments in this version of the Agreement were aimed at 'securing a maximum decentralization of power'; for Roberts, the Levellers 'wanted more than "devolution" or "decentralisation"; they sought a flow of power from the parishes outwards which would leave the central authority at the furthest (and weakest) point of its scope'.[85] The appearance of these measures only in the third Agreement, however, should warn us against seeing decentralization in and of itself as a fundamental in Leveller thought. In particular, it would be a mistake to see this type of 'decentralization' as another version of the 'localism' stressed by revisionists, or even of the quasi-republican local participatory ethos which more recent historical work has made much of.[86] It may or may not be true that the Levellers' democratic tendencies were fostered by their own experiences of participation and self-government in parish vestries, London wards, and sectarian congregations.[87] But even if this was important in the formation of Leveller attitudes to government, the Levellers' vision of politics was national, and I will argue in the next chapter that much of Lilburne's thought and language, in particular, was dependent on the assertion of the status of the individual within the nation, rather than within any local community, corporate body, or congregation. Indeed, all the novel types of election proposed in the third Agreement, including the election of ministers of religion in parishes, were dependent on the national franchise: 'none be chusers but such as are capable of electing Representatives'.[88] There was to be no return to the existence of a patchwork of divergent local franchises and privileges.

These late-emerging 'decentralizing' proposals should be read as solutions to the escalating problem of the tension between popular and parliamentary sovereignty in Leveller thought. They answered, to some extent, the need to bypass the betrayals of trust of so-called 'Representatives', without dissolving government into a formless, institutionless popular sovereignty. Presumably, even for the Levellers at their most desperate and/or idealistic in the third Agreement, direct popular sovereignty was unimaginable, and its 'inconveniences' insuperable. The inherent sovereignty of the people needed to be exercised through and by institutions, and if Parliament was looking increasingly incapable of doing so, the Levellers turned to the idea of dispersing that innate sovereignty more widely, through the local and functional institutions which in any case needed to exist. They thus kept popular sovereignty and the notion of representation, but it was a much more fluid and dispersed version of representation.

THE APPEAL TO THE PEOPLE AND THE CONTINUITY OF GOVERNMENT

As we have seen, royalists insinuated that parliamentarian thought would lead by a process of analogy and extrapolation to the people's 'reclaiming' their power from Parliament and acting against their elected representatives. This royalist view was somewhat mischievous and misguided: it attributed to parliamentarian thinkers a theory of the resumption of power (by Parliament from the king) which they did not endorse; and it ignored not only the strategic power of an unbending parliamentary absolutism, but also its plausibility in terms of contemporary notions of representation. In addition, it was often those parliamentarians who were most sceptical about the popular origins of power and least sceptical about the role of the monarchy who did allow some role for popular action in their political thought, whereas those who believed that Parliament exercised the people's power were, in fact, more likely to insist that *only* Parliament *could* exercise it.

Leveller thought was deeply committed to the legislative supremacy of an elected representative, but as we have seen, after some conceptual struggle it reversed the logic of representation so that it placed obligations of loyalty not on the represented but on the representers. Leveller writers located the original and originary sovereignty in the people, and left unclear its status and location while it was actually being exercised by a Parliament. These elements fused in the Levellers so that, under pressure of circumstance, they came to appeal directly to the people outside Parliament in ways that echoed the royalist predictions.

Lilburne and Overton began to articulate their appeal to the people from the beginning of 1647. The balance of parliamentary power had tipped decisively against the Independents and their allies, although votes could still be close.[89] The Scots handed over Charles I to the protection of the English Parliament, and the Scottish army withdrew from the north, leaving the political Presbyterians in England with unprecedented freedom of manoeuvre – a freedom which they proceeded to exploit with tactless and counterproductive enthusiasm. The year 1647 was to become a year of extraparliamentary politics and resistance to Parliament, on the part of not just the Leveller movement, but also of the New Model Army. But the Levellers' exploration of the theory and practice of the appeal to the people began with their own case. Lilburne and Overton had 'appealed to the Right Honourable the House of Commons' as their 'legall and proper Judges' to mitigate the harshness of the Lords' treatment of them, but this had borne little fruit; their eventual appearances before Marten's committee in November 1646 had not presaged any reversal of their fortunes.[90] At a dead end in their explorations of parliamentary procedure, they turned to more novel procedural measures: the appeal to the people. Lilburne, with characteristic expansiveness, called on 'all in *England*, that are not willing to be slaves' to join him in a 'grand petition' to the Commons against the Lords in his case.[91] By January 1647, this 'grand petition' had metamorphosed into a 'formal Appeal to all the Commons of the Kingdome of *England*, and Dominion of *Wales*', copies of which were issued the next month under the title *Out-cryes of Oppressed Commons*; Overton's *Appeale* of July 1647 was also a document which embodied the Levellers' appeal to the people, and the notion was frequent in the Levellers' works over the year.[92] The 'Agreements of the People' were to provide a more formal mechanism for appealing to the political judgement of the people, and whatever the origins of the notion of such an Agreement, it was one which the civilian Leveller movement could rally round on the basis of ideas which they had already developed.[93]

The Levellers' appeal to the people was a call for concerted extraparliamentary action, even violence, expressed through the metaphor of legal procedure.[94] Unsurprisingly, the political theory behind it was not always very clearly articulated. It is, however, clear that in some respects it did enact royalist fears with remarkable fidelity: the spectre of the resumption of the power which the people had originally transferred became real. The Levellers were prepared to say that the power entrusted to elected representatives could be forfeited, precisely because it was a 'trust'. The people were to reclaim the Parliament's ever 'revokable' power.[95] In this, of course, the Leveller theory represented an advance beyond the speculations of the Presbyterian theorists who had allowed for an appeal to the people's consciences without conceding that it was possible for them to exercise actual political power, even temporarily. The Levellers were also prepared to countenance – and exploit – the argument that their own appeal to the people was merely the logical extension of the Parliament's action against the king: they could hardly be blamed 'if we for our preservation shall tread in the Parliament [sic] steps by *appealing to the People* against them, as they did against the King'.[96] In this they showed considerable sleight of hand. The appeal to the people was a notion they had derived from the Parliament's Book of Declarations. This was in line with the whole rhetorical strategy of the *Out-Cryes*, which was packed with citations of parliamentary declarations, intended to demonstrate that the Levellers' appeal to the people was consistent with and indeed entailed by parliamentarian principles of self-preservation. However, the parliamentary *Remonstrance* of 2 November 1642 had been protesting against, rather than endorsing, the king's charge that by publishing declarations Parliament had appealed to the people.[97] The *Out-Cryes* seized on the fact that the same passage went on to plead 'let the people judge every man within his own breast of the persons that they have trusted, and of the persons that they have not trusted', to determine which in fact had appealed to the people. This, in itself, seemed usefully to be an appeal to the people. More substantially, the Levellers took the Protestation of May 1641 as a clear example of Parliament's 'appealing to the people, and craving their aid and assistance to helpe to preserve them'.[98] The Levellers – here at least – interpreted parliamentarian thought in a radical direction and then claimed it for themselves. While claiming to endorse parliamentarian thought, they adopted precisely the royalist interpretation of it which Parliament had been rejecting.

On another point, however, the Leveller texts did not endorse the royalist interpretation. There is something of a consensus in the secondary literature that, from the summer of 1647, the Levellers believed that government had been dissolved and the people returned to a state of nature from which they could emerge only by means of a social contract – the Agreement of the People.[99] The Levellers' tactic of appealing to the people is taken to be legitimated by their belief that government had dissolved. This view needs serious modification in the light of the detail of the Leveller texts supposedly expounding it, and the story turns – again – on Lilburne's use of the same page from the Parliament's Book of Declarations.

The notion of the dissolution of government into the 'originall' or 'prime' law of nature does occur in a few Leveller texts, and is linked to the idea of appealing to the people. However, these references do not add up to the doctrine standardly attributed to the Levellers. Not until September 1649 did a Leveller (Lilburne) unequivocally say that 'we are put into that originall state or chaos of confusion; wherein lust is become a law, ... all our ancient boundaries and land-marks, are puld up by the roots, and all the tyes and bonds of humane society in our English horizon totally destroyed and exterpated'.[100] In another of his pamphlets from the same month, Lilburne made the interesting admission that he had concluded at the time of the Windsor negotiations over the Officers' Agreement that there was no legitimate government in existence – but that he had kept his mouth shut out of a misguided (and, we might add, uncharacteristic) tact.[101] This hardly supports the view that the Levellers had regarded the government as dissolved since 1647, let alone that they had publicly said so and founded the Agreements of the People on that basis. His claim is supported by *A Plea for Common-Right and Freedom*, dated 28 December 1648, with Lilburne as its lead signatory, which specifically accused the army of 'breaking all Authoritie' through Pride's Purge.[102] Before he walked out of the army's negotiations earlier in the month, Lilburne still appeared to regard the securing of an Agreement as dependent on *not* arguing that government had been dissolved and must be reconstituted from scratch: even if he himself believed that that was the job the Agreement would do, he did not think that others would necessarily view it in that light.

All the texts from earlier in the Levellers' career which invoked the idea of the dissolution of government fell short of saying that government *had* been dissolved. They were also all (at least jointly) by Lilburne, and they referred directly to Parliament's Remonstrance of 2 November 1642, which used the phraseology 'dissolving of the whole frame and constitution of the Civill policy and government ... into the originall Law of nature', and linked this to 'an Appeal to the people'.[103] I want to suggest that this passage gave Lilburne a snippet of polemical vocabulary which was not picked up by other Leveller leaders and which remained peripheral to Leveller thought. Leveller appeals to the people to act for their self-preservation presumed, as the Parliament's own invocation of *salus populi* had done, that the English polity could still be saved, not that it had been dissolved; and their invocations of the people's natural powers expressed a belief in the exercise of those natural rights even within constituted society – at least in a state of ongoing emergency such as the 1640s.

Lilburne did directly apply the idea of the dissolution of authority leading to the need for a newly constituted structure in one context: that of the army. The passage most often cited as an explicit statement that government had dissolved and England had returned to the state of nature in fact says nothing of the kind: it is talking about the army only, not the nation or government.[104] When the idea was applied to national government, the tone was far more cautious, and the most that was declared before Lilburne's pronouncements of September 1649 was that the the actions of Parliament were (in danger of) leading government to be dissolved. The most positive statement of this, from February 1647, was a pre-emptive defence against a parliamentarian charge that the *Levellers* were dissolving government by appealing directly to the people. It retaliated by arguing that the Parliament, and not the Levellers, was destroying the civil government by allowing will and lust to rule in the place of law; but there is no statement that government *had* now been dissolved.[105] Other passages invoked the *danger* of the dissolution of government – but as a conditional, not a statement of fact,[106] or as a plea to the authorities not to dissolve the government into the law of nature.[107]

The Levellers worked hard to avoid the implication that the appeal to the people was lawless, either following from or causing the dissolution of the polity. Parliament had thrown the charge of appealing to the people and dissolving the polity back onto the royalists:

> Do they not rather Appeale unto them [the people] as Judges, who decline the highest Court of Judicature within this Kingdome, and having recourse to the people, arraigne and condemne before them the judgments and Resolutions of that Court [Parliament] from whence there can be no Appeal but by dissolving of the whole frame and constitution of the Civill policy and government of this Kingdome into the originall Law of nature?[108]

Levellers, like royalists, had to explain how it was possible to appeal from the highest court in the land without dissolving the polity. Lilburne's argument about the Protestation was useful here: he could claim that the people had already been sworn, by this very court, to maintain liberties and their defenders against any threat to them.[109] The *Out-Cryes* danced around the parliamentary text, accepting that 'legally there can be no appeale' from the High Court of Parliament, and that 'in law we have no higher appeale' than the House of Commons.[110] Insisting that all that the authors desired was 'the benefit of the knowne and unrepealed Lawes of the Land', and to *'save our selves, Lawes, Liberties and Freedomes'*, they threw the charge of dissolving government at Parliament. Lilburne expanded this vocabulary in *Rash Oaths unwarrantable*, arguing that people could use *'extraordinary and rationall means'* to preserve themselves if 'ordinary and legall' ones were not available.[111] Elsewhere he had noted that one should not have recourse to 'extraordinaries' where remedies were available by 'an ordinary course in law', but the implication there was that extraordinary courses (in that case, an appeal to the House of Commons as the supreme judicature and last refuge for popular appeal) did fall within constitutional provision in some way.[112] Even in moving beyond that last (legal) refuge, though, Lilburne was reluctant to let go of all law, insisting that it was not in the Parliament's power to do away with as fundamental a law as Magna Carta.[113] Extraordinary measures were legitimated by reason and nature, rather than being more technically and nationally 'legal', but they were used in order to restore the law of the land to full efficacy.

We have seen that in the crisis of 1642–43 there were rare parliamentarian thinkers who resembled the Levellers in both advocating unmixed parliamentary sovereignty and conceding, however hypothetically or minimally, the potential for an appeal to the people. Burroughes accepted that the appeal to the people resulted in the dissolution and reconstitution of government, and was correspondingly unwilling to contemplate the possibility; Bowles's more pragmatic treatment of the issue avoided the question of a return to the state of nature although it hinted at the resumption of power. Lilburne's discussion of extraordinary means certainly seems to resort to the *laws* of nature, but does not appear to imply a return to the *state* of nature. Overton, who appealed to the commoners alongside Lilburne, and who provided a characteristically philosophical parsing of the meaning of that appeal, resisted more explicitly still the idea of the dissolution of political authority. In his *Appeale from the degenerate Representative Body ... to the Body Represented The free people in general*, of 17 July 1647, Overton turned to the legal metaphor of an appeal from a lower to a higher court to explain why his appeal did not threaten a return to a dangerous state of nature. Overton did regard the betrusted power of the House of Commons as forfeit, due to its actions, and he juxtaposed that verdict with an account of the natural inherence of power in individuals and their choosing of deputies to wield these powers for their well-being. What happened when they forfeited that power was that the 'Authority', 'magistracy', 'power', or 'Soveraign power' reverted to the people, where it originated. Why, then, did Overton not use the language of reversion to the law of nature?

Just as Overton often seems to be discussing the constituting not of government itself, but of a particular representative, so he could discuss the dissolution of a particular representative through the forfeiting of their trust without concluding that the people were left in a state of nature. Rather, he saw an almost organic flowing back and forth of sovereign power between the two possible sites of sovereignty: the people and a representative. Legitimate political power was not dissolved: it simply flowed back to the people where it originated. Overton adapted the office/person distinction to maintain his claim that power was not dissolved but displaced: he was appealing 'not at all from the *power*, but from the *persons*, not forsaking the *power*, but *following* of it in its *retreat* to the *Fountaine*'.[114] Appealing to the people was not appealing '*from* that *Soveraign power*, but *to* that *Soveraign power*'.[115] Like the Parliament's office/person distinction, this was partly a propaganda move, but it clearly also reflected a view in which the people's natural sovereignty was hard to place either in a 'state of nature' or under government. While the flowing back of power to the people might make us think of a return to the state of nature, the insistence that what is reverted to is also a form of 'magistracy' or 'Soveraign power' makes this way of understanding Overton's argument seem inappropriate.

Lilburne and Overton's appeal to the people was issued early in 1647 and repeated during the turbulent events of that year. From the spring of 1647,

Parliament faced a much more threatening act of resistance to its authority, as the army rejected disbandment proposals and ultimately banded together in explicit resistance of them. Leveller and army activities that year began to mirror each other, and army radicals and civilians sought out support from each other, as we will see in Chapter 5. This meant that army men and their political supporters were also theorizing about the limits of parliamentary power and the circumstances under which it could be disobeyed. While the army men tended to exalt the power of Parliament (see Chapter 5), the army's actions in 1647 needed some form of justification. Army supporters tended to trace the corruption of the Parliament to some minority within it. For an army supporter like John Goodwin, disobedience to these Parliament-men in a case of necessity should not be construed as disobedience to Parliament itself. Just as Parliament had professed itself still loyal to the kingly office while fighting Charles I, Goodwin argued that parliamentary authority could be respected while the orders of Parliament were disobeyed. Goodwin had been bold in 1642 in arguing that the mobilization against the king involved some legitimate examination of the king's orders by the consciences of private men. In 1647 he made an extensive argument on similar lines to justify the army's actions in disobedience to Parliament.[116] Like Overton, then, Goodwin was effectively maintaining the continuity of authority, even if that authority had temporarily departed from Parliament. The two men were similar, too, in suggesting that while Parliament was in breach of its duty to protect the people, there might still be one institutional locus of the people's power: the army. Indeed, as Goodwin sardonically remarked, 'to say to a Junto of Parliamentary Grandees, ye are wicked; requires an Army at least in the Reere.' According to Overton, the army was now 'the only *formall and visible Head* that is left unto the people for protection and deliverance'.[117]

Army men and Levellers came together more formally in the autumn of 1647. Only a few months after Overton had voiced his version of the appeal to the people, a remarkable constitutional document was presented to the General Council of the Army. The first Agreement of the People, of October 1647, was born partly of an attempt to knit army and civilian radicalism together, and the extent of any distinctively Leveller contribution to it is unclear (see Chapter 5). Nonetheless, it became the focus of a civilian Leveller campaign, and the Levellers returned to the device on two more occasions, publishing revised Agreements in December 1648 and May 1649 (both moments when they were seeking army support).[118] In all three versions, the Agreement was intended to settle the nation not as the basis for a treaty process or through immediate enactment by Parliament, but, in the first instance, through its subscription by the people themselves. That is the basis for the scholarly view that the Agreements were social contracts, brought out of the fictive past and put into written form in the present to found a new polity. The second Agreement even specified that only those who had subscribed it were to be electors, apparently enacting the process of individual consent to a system of government quite literally.[119]

This interpretation of the Agreements is hard to sustain, given that, as we have seen, the Levellers did not believe that England had been returned to a state of nature, at least before the time of Pride's Purge in December 1648. The view may have been present in radical army circles from earlier on – Francis White was excluded from the army council in 1647 for stating that there was no power in England except the sword. But we have no evidence that this was a consistent view in the army/civilian-radical circle from which the first *Agreement* emerged. What is more, the documents themselves did not aspire to constitute a polity from scratch. The wording of the first two Agreements and their associated documents certainly gave no hint of any such grandiose intention. There was no principled assertion of the original power of the people to create a polity; no statement of the purposes of society or government; no assertion that this was an originary moment and the foundation of something new. The preamble and letters recommending the 1647 Agreement, substantially repeated in the second and even the third, made quite clear the purpose of the device. The civil war was caused, fundamentally, by 'uncertainty', and the purpose of the Agreement was to rule out future wars by a definitive clarification of the constitutional position. However dishonest it may seem to historians, or to the Levellers' contemporaries, the Agreement presented itself as a clarification of the existing constitution of the nation, not as a new one.

There was no suggestion, let alone a statement, that the nation had returned to a state of nature. The keynote was of modified continuity: the preamble to the Agreement's articles stated that:

> since therefore our former oppressions, and scarce yet ended troubles have beene occasioned, either by want of frequent Nationall meetings in Councell, or by rendring those meetings ineffectuall; We are fully agreed and resolved, to provide that hereafter our Representatives be neither left to an uncertainty for the time, nor made uselesse to the ends for which they are intended.[120]

The Agreement's main purposes were to clarify the powers of an existing institution – Parliament, or at least the House of Commons – and to make it more effective in its fulfilment of its ends. The short conclusion to the Agreement's text clarified the position of the Agreement in English constitutional history: the authors were determined to vindicate their rights, inspired by the example of 'our Ancestors, whose bloud was often spent in vain for the recovery of their Freedomes, suffering themselves, through fradulent [sic] accommodations, to be still deluded of the fruit of their Victories'. The same was not to happen this time round. The ancient cycle of assertion and suppression of these 'native Rights' was finally to come to an end with a definitive, unalterable codification.[121]

The Agreement was thus conceived of as momentous, but it placed itself within the nation's history rather than cutting itself off from it. The constitutional status of the Agreement was not entirely clear, but it was clearly distinguished from statute law, which depended on the whim of a single Parliament and could be changed by a subsequent one. The gaining of the real 'agreement of the people', through their subscriptions to the document, would secure for the Agreement the status of a fundamental constitutional law. (This undertheorized claim naturally drew criticism at Putney.[122]) That fundamental law, however, was designed to confirm and protect the existing 'native rights' of the English people.

Exactly how outrageous was the claim that the 1647 Agreement merely vindicated and 'cleared' the rights which the people had always been owed? The document was brief and steered well clear of specific constitutional machinery. The first three of the positive clauses tellingly referred to 'Parliament' rather than to the Leveller 'Representative', making relatively uncontroversial demands for the dissolution of the present Parliament and biennial meetings on a revised system of parliamentary seats. In the fourth positive article parliaments metamorphosed into 'Representatives' – the Levellers' sovereign version of the House of Commons – and the clause quietly abolished the 'negative voice' of the Lords and the king, insisting that the unicameral Representative has power 'inferiour only to theirs who chuse them'. But the king and the House of Lords were not explicitly abolished; they might continue to exist as 'Magistrates' appointed by the Representative. The striking innovation of the Agreement was its stipulation of powers which were 'expresly, or impliedly reserved by the represented to themselves', a category under which five items were listed. That there *were* powers which could not be transferred to the Representative was implicit and sometimes explicit in earlier Leveller writings, particularly in the case of powers over religion (see Chapter 4). The Agreement developed the parliamentarian argument that any original contract of government, made by consent, could be taken to have reserved (to the people or, more usefully, to the Parliament) those powers which were necessary to safeguard *salus populi*. In the Agreement's version, the people reserved these powers even from their Representative. The reserved powers might well be interpreted as expressions of certain natural rights, or of natural equality, and in that way the Agreement's reserves again blurred the line between the state of nature and the governed state.[123]

The radicalism of the first two Agreements, then, lay in their content rather than in their form, and they did not claim to be refounding the polity. Only the third Agreement, of 1 May 1649, revealed grander ambitions:

> We the free People of *England*, to whom God hath given hearts, means and opportunity to effect the same, do with submission to his wisdom, in his name, and desiring the equity thereof may be to his praise and glory; Agree to ascertain our

Government, to abolish all arbitrary Power, and to set bounds and limits both to our Supreme, and all Subordinate Authority, and remove all known Grievances.

Here finally the Levellers went beyond remedying 'the uncertaintie of our Government' and clarifying the constitution ('ascertain our Government'), declaring that they were actively abolishing, limiting, removing.[124] They were, after all, setting out to change the constitution. Why now? The declaration of supremacy by the House of Commons, the trial and execution of the king, the institution of a Council of State, and the abolition of the office of king and of the House of Lords had all taken place in the previous six months. The taboo on innovation had been comprehensively smashed by the shapers of the new regime; and in any case, the Levellers could claim that what they were keen to 'abolish' was the arbitrary power of the indisputably new regime rather than the old one. Indeed, some have seen the spring and summer of 1649 as a time when Leveller sympathizers were drawn to royalism as a preferable alternative to the new dispensation.[125]

What is the significance of the new tone of the third Agreement? For Gentles, the Levellers under pressure of circumstance 'threw realism to the winds' and 'at last showed what moved them most'.[126] But changed circumstances could change beliefs as well as tactics. We should not view the third Agreement as the expression of all the wild hopes and outlandish theories the Levellers had always harboured but never previously dared to express. And if it was feeling its way towards a theory of the state of nature and the social contract, it failed to get there: again, there was no hint that government and society had been dissolved into a state of nature, and the proposal was to 'ascertain' a constitution which modified, perhaps very significantly, the existing one, rather than proceeding upwards from basic principles to build a new one.

CONCLUSION

For all the Levellers' concern to assert the locus of legislative sovereignty as the House of Commons, they were unable to commit themselves very fully to that conclusion. As we saw in Chapter 1, in asserting the original liberty and rights of individuals, the Levellers seem to have given them a 'property' over which they could exercise their own private sovereignty. Why people should want to surrender that original power, the Levellers never made very clear; and increasingly they imagined that power being not so much surrendered as exercised *through* representatives who would never fully possess it. This view of the people's power grounded their 'appeal to the people' in 1647.

As we have seen, however, this development was not an easy or inevitable one. Many of the theorists who had been prepared to countenance some role for the exercise of the people's consciences in a crisis of governance had not been those who saw the people as the origin of political power; some of them

The Levellers

stressed quite clearly that the people themselves could not hold and exercise political power, and that the exercise of their judgements in an emergency was simply dependent on their status as conscientious human beings, not as bearers of political power. These parliamentarian authors were also generally not advocates of parliamentary supremacy; even in 1645, Wither and Ball were nostalgic at least for the idea of a constitutional balance including the monarch. What the writers of 1645 developed further than the earlier parliamentarian writers was the notion of representation, which was appropriated from the theorists of parliamentary sovereignty and remade so that it implied not the absoluteness of Parliament but its accountability.

The theoretical roots for much of Leveller thought were in the tradition of Independent parliamentarian thought. In keeping with this tradition, the Levellers removed sovereignty from the king and placed it in Parliament (in their case, a reformed elected chamber) on the basis of the people's original power. But they participated in the broader reinterpretation of the implications of representation, and thus came to combine a theory of parliamentary supremacy with the notion of appeal to the people. It was not a comfortable combination, and the Levellers were in danger of leaving themselves with a theory in which the only remedy for abuse of parliamentary power was an appeal to the people, but the only thing the people could then do was elect a new Parliament. Their thinking on the reserved powers which could be settled – with or without an Agreement of the People – did not solve this problem of enforcement. The demands of the third Agreement of the People for a more distributed system of power, and the insistence on frequent elections, were ultimately the only institutional remedies the Levellers could produce.

Both these remedies exemplify what is powerful about the Levellers' vision of politics: the extent to which the people retained the sovereign power which was theirs by birth, even when they were living under government. Through local and national elections, the people's natural, original, sovereign power would continually refresh and reanimate the supreme Representative. This insistence on the reservation of relatively extensive natural (and equal) rights, together with the continued exercise of genuine political power by the people even under government, were ample grounds for suspicion for their enemies within parliamentarianism. Ireton, airing his views in direct debate with the army and civilian radicals at the Putney debates, was alarmed by their tendency to 'flie for refuge to an absolute naturall Right, and ... deny all Civill Right'.[127] Their enemies saw the Levellers not as contractarians, but as contract breakers, and they had some grounds for that view.[128]

That enemy view was not entirely correct. The Levellers' refusal to imagine one single decisive break between the state of nature and an artificial world of politics cut both ways. It meant that they could always appeal to a natural right; but it also meant that they could do so *without* denying all civil right. They did not agree that they were invoking a dangerous liberty, outside government, law, and social bonds. For them, the appeal to the law of nature was not necessarily an appeal beyond the law and constitution of England. The law of nature was often invoked to reinterpret and reinforce the law of England as they believed it truly existed. The equal rights and sovereignty which individuals were born into were not obliterated once a constitution was in place; as we will see in the next chapter, Lilburne's assertion of the rights of 'free-born Englishmen' was a powerful way of channelling those natural rights through the language of English law.

NOTES

1 E. Sirluck, 'Introduction', in E. Sirluck (ed.) *The Complete Prose Works of John Milton, Vol II: 1643–1648* (New Haven: Yale University Press, 1959), esp. pp. 45–7 on the appeal to the people; D. Wootton, 'From rebellion to revolution: the crisis of the winter of 1642/3 and the origins of civil war radicalism', *English Historical Review*, 105 (1990), 654–69.

2 Where I distinguish 'radical' from more 'mainstream' documents, I am distinguishing between 'radical' works which were clearly intended to support the 'war party', and which may have been marginal or virtually unnoticed in parliamentarian debate, and more 'mainstream' documents which played a significant part in parliamentarian propaganda, whatever their political tendency.

3 Henry Ferne, *The Resolving of Conscience* (Cambridge, 1642), p. 18.

4 Ferne, *The Resolving of Conscience*, pp. 29–30.

5 Herbert Palmer et al., *Scripture and Reason Pleaded for Defensive Armes* (1643), pp. 29, 34–5.

6 Palmer et al., *Scripture and Reason*, p. 47.

7 Sirluck, 'Introduction', pp. 42–3.

8 Henry Parker, *Observations upon some of his Majesties late Answers and Expresses*, 2nd edn (1642), p. 8; Sirluck, 'Introduction', p. 42.

9 Parker, *Observations*, p. 5; see also p. 2 on the 'derivative' quality of the king's power.

10 Parker, *Observations*, p. 8.

11 Jeremiah Burroughs, *The Glorious Name of God, the Lord of Hosts ... With a Post-Script, Briefly Answering a Late Treatise by Henry Ferne* (1643), 'A briefe Answer', p. 7 bis.

12 Burroughs, *The Glorious Name of God*, 'A briefe Answer', p. 9.

13 Henry Parker, *Jus Populi* (1644), p. 18.

14 Parker, *Jus Populi*, pp. 18–19.

15 Parker, *Observations*, p. 22.

16 [Charles Herle], *A Fuller Answer to a Treatise Written by Doctor Ferne, Entituled, The Resolving of Conscience* ([29 December] 1642, p. 18.

17 [Herle], *A Fuller Answer*, p. 19.

18 Parker, *Observations*, p. 15.

19 Parker, *Observations*, p. 16.
20 Parker, *Observations*, pp. 14–15.
21 Parker, *Observations*, p. 15.
22 *Remonstrans Redivivus: Or, an Accompt of the Remonstrance and Petition, Formerly Presented by Divers Citizens of London, to the View of Many* (25 July 1643), p. 4.
23 I. Russell-Jones, 'The relationship between theology and politics in the writings of John Lilburne, Richard Overton and William Walwyn' (DPhil dissertation, University of Oxford, 1987), pp. 78ff., 145–8; MMT, 'Introduction', p. 20; V. Pearl, *London and the Outbreak of the Puritan Revolution: City Government and National Politics, 1625–43* (Oxford: Oxford University Press, 1961), pp. 260–1. In his *Whisper in the Eare* of March 1646 Walwyn wrote that 'my next publike businesse was with many others, in a remonstrance to the Common Councell, to move the Parliament to confirm certain infallible maximes of free Government: wherein the power of Parliament was plainly distinguished from the Kings Office, so plainly, that had it taken effect: few men after due consideration thereof, would through error of judgement have taken part against the Parliament, or have befriended arbitrary power, as too too many did for want of light.' MMT, pp. 176–7.
24 *Remonstrans Redivivus*, sig. A2v, defensively protesting that the tract is intended to reflect rather than question Parliament's wisdom. Sirluck, 'Introduction', p. 40, offers a different assessment of the significance of the tract: *Remonstrans Redivivus* gave 'an extreme and lucid statement of the natural law theory', argued without any reliance on precedent or constituted authority but backed up by references to the Book of Declarations: 'In short, this would be adaptable, with scarcely a word changed, to the needs of the Levellers and the New Model when they marched to teach the people's representatives the will of the people.' (Sirluck does not note Walwyn's part in the petition.)
25 J. L. Malcolm (ed.), *The Struggle for Sovereignty: Seventeenth-century Political Tracts*, 2 vols (Indianapolis: The Liberty Fund, 1999), vol. 1, p. 263. The author 'places final authority in the people themselves, not in the Parliament', following Wootton, 'From rebellion to revolution', p. 663, who places a similar interpretation on the author's reference to the authority that is in the body of the people.
26 *Touching the Fundamentall Lawes, or Politique Constitution of this Kingdome, the Kings Negative Voice, and the Power of Parliaments* ([24 February] 1643), p. 13.
27 R. Tuck, *Philosophy and Government 1572–1651* (Cambridge: Cambridge University Press, 1993), pp. 230–1 on Parker's emphasis on election and representation, as part of his non-Presbyterian parliamentarian theory. Tuck sees this theory as a fundamentally republican theory of hegemony by an aristocratic council (Parliament). For most of the parliamentarian authors at this stage, the two Houses – Commons and Lords – had both to be comprehended within the argument; 'representation' might serve to include the Lords in the legitimacy which came from wielding the power of the population as a whole, if the nobility were understood as an 'estate' of the realm present as, or represented by, the peers in Parliament.
28 Burroughs, *The Glorious Name of God*, 'A briefe Answer', pp. 9, 7 bis, 12.
29 Sirluck, 'Introduction', p. 38.
30 Burroughs, *The Glorious Name of God*, 'A briefe Answer', p. 10.
31 M. J. Braddick, *God's Fury, England's Fire: A New History of the English Civil Wars* (London: Allen Lane, 2008), pp. 254–60.

32 E. Bowles, *Plaine English, or, a Discourse Concerning the Accommodation, the Armie, the Association* (1643), pp. 7, 13.

33 Bowles, *Plaine English*, p. 20.

34 Bowles, *Plaine English*, pp. 25, 27.

35 J. Peacey notes that according to Anthony Wood, compiling his *Athenae Oxonienses* in the 1680s, the *Treatise of Monarchy* 'hath been and is still in great vogue among many persons of commonwealth and levelling principles', and that the work was republished twice in 1689: *ODNB*, s.v. 'Hunton, Philip'.

36 Sirluck, 'Introduction', p. 47; Wootton, 'From rebellion to revolution', p. 663.

37 Palmer, *Scripture and Reason*, pp. 53, 22, 14.

38 Palmer, *Scripture and Reason*, pp. 42–4, 53.

39 Philip Hunton, *A Treatise of Monarchie* (1643), p. 28.

40 On the conscientious aspect of Hunton's theory, and on its possible contradictions, see J. H. Franklin, *John Locke and the Theory of Sovereignty: Mixed Monarchy and the Right of Resistance in the Political Thought of the English Revolution* (Cambridge: Cambridge University Press, 1978), pp. 39–48. Also note that as Hunton was not a theorist of 'constituent authority', this action by the people was not, by definition, a resumption of their power. On Hunton's theory as a parliamentarian case built on premises opposed to Parker's, see M. J. Mendle, *Henry Parker and the English Civil War: The Political Thought of the Public's 'Privado'* (Cambridge: Cambridge University Press, 1995), pp. 98–100; on his ultimate aim of the restoration of a functioning mixed monarchy, rejecting parliamentary sovereignty as a solution, see W. Lamont, *Marginal Prynne, 1600–1669* (London: Routledge and Kegan Paul, 1963), pp. 90–106; J. Sanderson, *'But the People's Creatures': The Philosophical Basis of the English Civil War* (Manchester: Manchester University Press, 1989), pp. 30–1.

41 Hunton, *Treatise*, p. 18.

42 Hunton, *Treatise*, p. 29.

43 Hunton, *Treatise*, p. 18. Mendle, *Henry Parker*, p. 99 appears to suggest that the situation released people from former obligations to their government into a 'pre-political' state, which is clearly not Hunton's view.

44 Hunton, *Treatise*, p. 73.

45 Hunton, *Treatise*, pp. 68, 73.

46 Palmer, *Scripture and Reason*, pp. 53 (mispaginated '5'), 54, 15.

47 Palmer, *Scripture and Reason*, p. 59 (mispaginated '51').

48 Evidently the possibility of an appeal to the people rests on a denial of parliamentary sovereignty in the trivial sense that if Parliament always had power and capacity to decide every question correctly, the people would never be called upon to intervene. However, it is striking that many of the theorists who allowed the possibility of appeal to the people did not accept parliamentary sovereignty even as a solution under normal circumstances to the location of sovereignty, with a possibility of popular appeal in case of abuse: they were much more strongly committed to a mixed constitution.

49 J. Coffey, *Politics, Religion and the British Revolutions: The Mind of Samuel Rutherford* (Cambridge: Cambridge University Press, 1997), p. 171 with footnote; Woodhouse, p. [66]; P. Zagorin, *A History of Political Thought in the English Revolution* (London: Routledge & Kegan Paul, 1954), pp. 5–6.

50 Coffey, *Politics, Religion and the British Revolutions*, pp. 150, 163, 170, 173–4.

51 Samuel Rutherford, *Lex, Rex* (1644), pp. 10, 50.

52 Rutherford, *Lex, Rex*, pp. 52–3.

53 Coffey, *Politics, Religion and the British Revolutions*, p. 177.

54 Rutherford, *Lex, Rex*, p. 152; Coffey, *Politics, Religion and the British Revolutions*, pp. 178–81.

55 G. Griffiths (ed.), *Representative Government in Western Europe in the Sixteenth Century* (Oxford: Clarendon Press, 1968): Sir Thomas Smith, p. 547; Richard Hooker, p. 613.

56 Sirluck, 'Introduction', pp. 134–5; G. Burgess, *British Political Thought, 1500–1660: The Politics of the Post-Reformation* (Basingstoke: Palgrave Macmillan, 2009), pp. 226–7, citing Wootton.

57 J. Peacey, 'John Lilburne and the Long Parliament', *Historical Journal* 43:3 (2000), 633–4; S. Barber, *A Revolutionary Rogue: Henry Marten and the English Republic* (Stroud: Sutton, 2000), pp. 10, 32 and notes.

58 *Englands Birth-Right Justified* ([10 October] 1645), pp. 33 [48–9].

59 William Ball, *Tractatus de Jure Regnandi, & Regni* (1645), pp. 1–2, 5–10; Ball reluctantly concludes that the king's negative voice may be overridden, however; on Wither, see D. Norbrook, *Writing the English Republic: Poetry, Rhetoric, and Politics, 1627–1660* (Cambridge: Cambridge University Press, 1999), pp. 153–5, but also 149–50 on republican possibilities.

60 *Mercurius Britanicus* no. 92, 28 July–4 August 1645, p. 825; no. 129, 4–11 May 1646, p. 1110; no. 130, 11–18 May 1646, p. 1111. For discussion of the authorship of *England's Miserie, and Remedie* and *Vox Plebis*, see Chapter 6.

61 Tuck, *Philosophy and Government, 1572–1651*, pp. 242–3.

62 J. Gurney, 'George Wither and Surrey politics, 1642–1649', *Southern History* 19 (1997), 87.

63 Norbrook, *Writing the English Republic*, p. 141; G. Wither, *Letters of Advice: Touching the Choice of Knights and Burgesses*, 2nd edn (1645), p. 3.

64 Wither, *Letters of Advice*, pp. 4–5, 12.

65 G. Wither, *Vox Pacifica* (1645), p. 199; quoted in *England's Miserie, and Remedie* (1645), p. 8, and referred to pp. 1–2; *Englands Birth-Right Justified* (1645), p. 34 (using phrases derived from Wither even outside the section directly quoted).

66 G. Wither, *The Speech Without Doore. Delivered July 9. 1644 in the Absence of the Speaker* (1644), sig. A, page 14; G. Wither, *Opobalsamum Anglicanum* (1646), pp. 2ff.; Wither, *Vox Pacifica*, p. 199.

67 Wither, *Opobalsamum Anglicanum*, p. 8.

68 *England's Miserie, and Remedie*, pp. 3–4.

69 Ball, *Tractatus de Iure Regnandi, & Regni*, pp. 13, 15.

70 Wither, *Vox Pacifica*, p. 199.

71 D. Scott, *Politics and War in the Three Stuart Kingdoms, 1637–49* (Basingstoke: Palgrave Macmillan, 2004), p. 120; A. Woolrych, *Britain in Revolution, 1625–1660* (New York: Oxford University Press, 2002), pp. 347–8.

72 MMT, p. 202.
73 Richard Overton, *An Arrow Against All Tyrants and Tyrany* (1646), p. 17.
74 Walwyn, *Englands Lamentable Slaverie* (1645), in MMT, p. 147.
75 C. Condren, *The Language of Politics in Seventeenth-century England* (Basingstoke and London: Macmillan, 1994), pp. 65–6.
76 John Lilburne, *The Copy of a Letter From Lieutenant Colonell John Lilburne to a Freind* [sic] ([25 July] 1645) p. 14 [mispaginated 41].
77 Overton, *An Arrow*, p. 10.
78 Wolfe, p. 237: petition of 23 November 1647.
79 D. Wootton, 'Leveller democracy and the puritan revolution', in J. H. Burns and M. Goldie (eds) *The Cambridge History of Political Thought 1450–1700* (Cambridge: Cambridge University Press, 1991), pp. 433, 427; J. Scott, *Commonwealth Principles: Republican Writing of the English Revolution* (Cambridge: Cambridge University Press, 2004), p. 249.
80 Lilburne, *The Just Mans Justification* ([6 June] 1646), p. 14. The exact reading of the word(s) between 'State' and 'representative' is unclear; 'Elector' is the word found here in the 1647 edition of the text (E.407/26), p. 17. I suspect this may be a slip for 'the state elect or representative'.
81 *Regall Tyrannie Discovered* ([6 January] 1647), pp. 38–9.
82 See above in this chapter for Samuel Rutherford's use of this vocabulary; see also OED, s.v. 'formal'.
83 Richard Overton, *An Appeale from the Degenerate Representative Body the Commons of England Assembled at Westminster: to the Body Represented, the Free People in General* ([17 July] 1647), p. 10.
84 *An Agreement of the Free People of England* ([1 May] 1649), pp. 6–7.
85 I. Gentles, 'The Agreements of the People and their political contexts, 1647–1649', in M. Mendle (ed.) *The Putney Debates of 1647: The Army, the Levellers, and the English State* (Cambridge: Cambridge University Press, 2001), p. 171; Frank, p. 207; S. Roberts, 'Local government reform in England and Wales during the Interregnum', in I. Roots (ed.) *Into Another Mould: Aspects of the Interregnum* (Exeter: University of Exeter Press, 1998), p. 51.
86 For revisionist work on 'localism', see J. S. Morrill, *The Revolt of the Provinces: Conservatives and Radicals in the English Civil War, 1630–1650* (London: Allen & Unwin, 1980); for early counter-arguments stressing the national political horizons at least of gentry prior to the war, see C. Holmes, 'The county community in Stuart historiography', *Journal of British Studies* 19:2 (1980), 54–73. See P. Lake, '"The monarchical republic of Queen Elizabeth I" (and the fall of Archbishop Grindal) revisited', in J. F. McDiarmid (ed.) *The Monarchical Republic of Early Modern England: Essays in Response to Patrick Collinson* (Aldershot: Ashgate, 2007), p. 134, for an acute comment on the relationship between the localist and republican interpretations.
87 As suggested by B. Kümin, 'Gemeinde und Revolution: die kommunale Prägung der englischen Levellers', in H. Blickle (ed.) *Gemeinde Und Staat Im Alten Europa* (Munich: R. Oldenbourg, 1998), pp. 361–96.
88 *An Agreement* (1649), p. 6.

89 Scott, *Politics and War*, pp. 132–4; Woolrych, *Britain in Revolution*, pp. 350–3.

90 John Lilburne, *An Anatomy of the Lords Tyranny* ([6 November] 1646), p. 8; Overton appeared on 3 November, Lilburne on 6 November.

91 Lilburne, *An Anatomy*, pp. 19–20.

92 John Lilburne, *The Oppressed Mans Oppressions Declared* ([30 January] 1647), p. 38; *The Out-Cryes of Oppressed Commons* ([28 February] 1647), p. 1, addresses itself to all men in England and Wales who have not resolved to be slaves, the group whom Lilburne promised to appeal to.

93 See below, Chapter 5, for consideration of the army and civilian genesis of the first *Agreement of the People* in 1647.

94 Tuck, *Philosophy and Government*, pp. 242–3, has suggested that the Levellers' appeal to the people, unlike William Ball's, did not contemplate armed force but merely fresh elections. However, it seems clear that, in order to reclaim the Parliament's power and bring these elections about, moral pressure verging on crowd violence or army mutiny was contemplated.

95 *A Remonstrance of Many Thousand Citizens* (1646), p. 3; *Regall Tyrannie*, title page; *Out-Cryes*, p. 17

96 *Out-Cryes*, p. 14.

97 *An Exact Collection of all Remonstrances, Declarations, Votes, Orders, Ordinances, Proclamations, Petitions, Messages, Answers, and Other Remarkable Passages betweene the Kings most Excellent Majesty, and his High Court of Parliament* (1643; part 2), p. 690.

98 *Out-Cryes*, pp. 14–15; cf. Lilburne, *An Anatomy*, pp. 19–20 on the significance of the Protestation. D. M. Jones, *Conscience and Allegiance in Seventeenth-century England: The Political Significance of Oaths and Engagements* (Rochester: University of Rochester Press, 1999), pp. 116–9; 273–4; the Protestation did of course assert loyalty to the King's 'royal person, honour and estate' as well as to reformed religion, the privileges of Parliament and the liberties of the subject, and did not necessarily exclude future royalists; what appears to have appealed to the Levellers is the language binding individuals to use 'all good ways and means' 'with my life, power, and estate' to defend these, even though the oath restricted this to 'as far as lawfully I may'.

99 Frank, p. 142; Brailsford, p. 376; I. Hampsher-Monk, 'The political theory of the Levellers: Putney, property and Professor Macpherson', *Political Studies* 24 (1976), 417. J. C. Davis has rightly expressed scepticism about the importance of the Agreements, arguing that they were 'only a device, never an article of faith': J. C. Davis, 'The Levellers and Christianity', in B. Manning (ed.) *Politics, Religion and the English Civil War* (London: Edward Arnold, 1973), pp. 239–40.

100 *An Outcry of the Youngmen and Apprentices of London* ([29 August] 1649), p. 8.

101 John Lilburne, *Strength out of Weaknesse* ([19 October] 1649), p. 5. Note that it is the army, rather than the betrayals of Parliament itself, which has 'reduced us into the Originall state or Chaos of Confusion, *wherein every mans lusts becomes his Law*'. It is not entirely clear whether Lilburne dates this breaking of the magistracy of the nation to Pride's Purge or before (see p. 4 for his accusation that the Grandees themselves were prepared to say Parliament was invalid even before Pride's Purge.)

102 John Lilburne et al., *A Plea for Common-Right and Freedom* ([28 December] 1648).

103 *An Exact Collection*, p. 690. These concepts were evidently in common circulation:

Parliament was defending itself against an accusation by the king that it was dissolving government by appealing to the people.

104 John Lilburne, *Jonahs Cry Out of the Whales Belly* ([26 July] 1647), p. 13: the phrase 'being now dissolved into the originall law of Nature' clearly refers to the army, left without legitimate command (according to the radicals) by the betrayal of Parliament: 'Yet now he [Fairfax] and his Army ... being now thereby dissolved into the originall law of Nature, hold their swords in their hands for their own preservation and safety.' The passage goes on to explain that by the law of nature the *army* are now attempting their own preservation against Parliament, and making new arrangements to be governed, *as an army*, by their own consent. While the betrayal of Parliament might be thought to imply that the nation, too, was free of its government, the pamphlet does not say so, and the immediate need for self-preservation according to the law of nature did, of course, apply particularly to the army, which had been threatened with disbandment. Scholars who apparently take this passage as a reference to the dissolution of national government include: Wolfe, p. 33; Brailsford, p. 236; Hampsher-Monk, 'The political theory of the Levellers', p. 417; J. S. Morrill in R. L. Greaves and R. Zaller (eds) *Biographical Dictionary of British Radicals in the Seventeenth Century*, 3 vols (Brighton: Harvester Press, 1982–1984), s.v. 'Lilburne'; and A. Sharp's entry on Lilburne, *ODNB*. Lilburne's interpretation of the army's actions in making the Solemn Engagement in terms of a resort to 'the prime Laws of Nature' is repeated in John Lilburne, *An Impeachment of High Treason against Oliver Cromwell and ... Ireton* ([10 August] 1649), p. 2.

105 *Out-Cryes*, p. 14.

106 John Lilburne, *The Legall Fundamentall Liberties* ([18 June] 1649), p. 7, here reprinting a 'Plea' from June 1648. Lilburne, in a dense passage of legal wrangling and invective, argues that 'if you shall stop my proceedings at Common Law against Master *Wollaston* the Jaylour of *Newgate*, ... You are so far from punishing the criminous, that you justifie the wicked, ... and dissolve the whole frame and constitution of the Civill Policy and Government of this Kingdom into the originall Law of Nature, which crime you taxe the King with, 1 *par. Book. Decl. pag.* 690.' He does not say that this has already happened; and if it was a major part of Leveller thinking that it *had* happened, for more important reasons than Lilburne's lawsuit, he would hardly have been able to make this conditional sally here. The same phrasing appears, again conditionally, on p. 18, at the end of Lilburne's 'Plea'. The passage on p. 7 is cited by Hampsher-Monk, 'The political theory of the Levellers', p. 417, as a statement that England had returned to a state of nature.

107 Wolfe, p. 272: 'Oh dissolve not all Government into the prime Lawes of nature, and compell us to take the naturall remedy to preserve our selves' (petition of 18 January 1648).

108 *An Exact Collection*, p. 690.

109 Lilburne, *An Anatomy*, pp. 19–20.

110 *Out-Cryes*, p. 14.

111 Lilburne, *Rash Oaths Unwarrantable* ([31 May] 1647), p. 20. The italicized words are presumably a quotation from the parliamentary Book of Declarations, but I have not been able to locate it in the document of 19 May 1642 which Lilburne cites on this page.

112 Lilburne, *An Anatomy*, p. 10.

113 Lilburne, *Rash Oaths*, p. 28.

The Levellers

114 Overton, *An Appeale*, p. 6.

115 Overton, *An Appeale*, p. 7.

116 [John Goodwin], *The Army, Harmlesse* (1647), pp. 15–26; John Goodwin, *Anti-Cavalierisme, or, Truth Pleading As well the Necessity, as the Lawfulness of this present War* (1642), p. 18.

117 [Goodwin], *The Army, Harmlesse*, pp. 12–14; Overton, *An Appeale*, p. 27.

118 See P. Baker and E. Vernon (eds), *The Agreements of the People, the Levellers and the Constitutional Crisis of the English Revolution* (Basingstoke: Palgrave Macmillan, forthcoming 2012) for further discussion of this series of documents and the relationship between Leveller and army-related versions.

119 John Lilburne, *Foundations of Freedom; Or an Agreement of the People* ([15 December] 1648), p. 5; E. Vallance, *Revolutionary England and the National Covenant* (Woodbridge: Boydell and Brewer, 2005), p. 148.

120 *An Agreement of the People for a Firme and Present Peace* ([3 November] 1647), p. 2.

121 *An Agreement of the People*, pp. 5–6.

122 Cromwell, *CP* 1.237, saw the Agreement as a factional document which could claim no authority over other possible proposals; but arguably even if it had achieved the subscription of a large majority of the population, it might logically still be subject to change in future referendums, or by future generations. The Engagements debate at Putney questioned the basis for breaking existing engagements, while hoping to make a future one unbreakable.

123 *An Agreement of the People*, pp. 4–5. Freedom of conscience, freedom from impressment, and the stipulation that laws must not destroy the safety and well-being of the people seem to be founded on natural rights; equality before the law on natural equality; the oblivion clause is more politically immediate.

124 *An Agreement of the Free People*, pp. 2–3.

125 Gentles, 'The Agreements of the People', pp. 172–3.

126 Gentles, 'The Agreements of the People', pp. 171, 174. Frank, p. 205, also comments on the lack of diplomatic constraints on the Leveller leaders as they constructed the third Agreement while imprisoned in the Tower, any chance of influence on the army leadership a forlorn hope.

127 Ireton, *CP* 1.301.

128 J. W. Gough, *The Social Contract: A Critical Study of Its Development* (Oxford: Clarendon Press, 1936), p. 89, notes this tension between natural rights and contract, and aligns the Levellers with the natural right argument, but still sees them as proponents of 'a kind of actualized social contract'.

Chapter 3

The laws of England and the 'free-born Englishman'

We have seen how Leveller writers, including Lilburne, invoked the law of nature to ground their arguments for government by consent and, if necessary, to appeal to the people to vindicate their rights against an abusive government. For the Levellers, the law of nature underlay and underpinned the national laws, and I have argued that – in spite of the arguments of many writers on the Levellers – the Levellers did not believe that the national laws had been abrogated and England returned to a state of nature. It was perfectly reasonable to appeal to the law of nature, even within a polity, as a safeguard, a corrective, or an interpreter of the national, positive laws, without believing that those laws were thereby annulled. Indeed, the persistent power of the laws of England, alongside the laws of nature, was precisely the tissue which held the polity together even when its supreme governmental body, the representative of the commons, forfeited its trust. The conventional eulogy – famously voiced by Pym – of the laws of England as the nerves and sinews which bound together the political body could easily have been echoed by the Levellers.

Early Stuart England was a culture saturated by law, as seen in frequent litigation and in the legal education common among the gentry. Historians have emphasized the enormous role which the language of the common law played in political argument, though the political tendencies it came to express were not uniform and have been very differently interpreted.[1] Nonetheless, the Levellers' use of the language of the common law – especially Coke – has tended to be treated as an apparent anomaly requiring explanation or excuse by all sides in these debates.[2] As we will see later, the Levellers' relationship with the common law was indeed complex, and although they invoked it, they equivocated about its authority, making full use of the flexible relationship of the common law with statute, reason, and natural law (when they did not simply reject it). However, the law offered much more than simply a convenient rhetorical covering to Leveller thought. What it contributed was often

The Levellers

not strictly legal or procedural argument, but rather a language in which to think about the rights of Englishmen. In Lilburne's hands, this became a way of arguing about citizenship and political equality. This was the distinctive contribution of Lilburne's writing to the movement, and this chapter focuses on him.

Lilburne's prolific writings did much to set the tone of the movement and to appeal to a wide audience of potentially radical readers. We have already discussed his view of the original state of mankind and his account of government by consent, but these discussions are far from characteristic of Lilburne's writing as a whole. Lilburne's rousing, emotive, but also somewhat repetitive writings revolved around the concept of the 'free-born Englishman'. He appealed to his audience as free-born Englishmen, and depicted himself as the archetype of the free-born Englishman, whose persecutions and sufferings were the index of the state of the nation. The 'free-born Englishman' was not merely a rhetorical trope, but a key term in Lilburne's evolving political theory, which credited all free-born Englishmen with uniform political rights. He founded this novel claim on the supposedly ancient 'birthright' of the common law. This chapter traces Lilburne's development of this language and the thinking which it expressed, and after considering the attitudes of Lilburne and the other Leveller leaders to the status of English law, it concludes by examining Lilburne's argument for political inclusiveness as a basis for the expansion of the franchise.

In the debate over the historical or theoretical basis of early modern and Leveller thought, the common law has tended to be consigned to the 'conservative' and historical end of the spectrum, as we will see below. Lilburne's colleagues in the Leveller movement appeared to agree, at least early in their linked careers, with Walwyn famously reproving Lilburne for his faith in Magna Carta. Lilburne has thus sometimes been seen as lagging behind his colleagues in theoretical terms, a figurehead and demagogue who left the real intellectual work to his colleagues, and who sometimes embarrassed them with his autodidact legal ramblings.[3] This view, I think, is profoundly wrong. Not only did Lilburne participate with his colleagues in developing natural law arguments, as we have already seen, but he used the materials of the common law tradition to forge a parallel theory of the English polity which had novel and radical force.

THE RIGHTS AND LIBERTIES OF 'FREE-BORN ENGLISHMEN'

The collocation 'free-born Englishman' was not common before Lilburne. Its novelty may have been overlooked by historians because it subsequently became so ubiquitous; and the familiar ingredients of the phrase – the idea of 'free-born' status, and the appeal to patriotism – must have been reassuring to contemporaries too. Lilburne himself had been nicknamed 'free-born John' at the time of his earliest public defiance of the authorities in 1638, long before he had adapted the idiom to his particular political uses.[4] The usual context for the expression was not 'free-born Englishman', but 'free-born subject'. The phrase 'free-born subject' was the correlate of the standard parliamentarian (and pre-civil war) call for the 'liberties of the subject' – the topic avowedly at issue, for example, in the debates leading up to the Petition of Right.[5] Indeed, even more radical pamphleteers did not completely abandon this vocabulary – which makes it very notable how far Lilburne himself did abandon it, and how early. In Lilburne's early writing we do find references to 'subjects', and in January 1645, in a hint of things to come, he referred to 'freeborne English Subjects'.[6] By the summer of 1645, however, he seems to have found his own language which avoided the word 'subject' altogether, replacing it with the notion of the 'free-born Englishman'. Lilburne created a consistent language in which 'subjects' became 'Englishmen'. The modern opposition between subjects and citizens might push us towards taking Lilburne's linguistic shift as a move in the direction of a notion of citizenship, and the details of Lilburne's language support such a view. The transformation of 'subjects' into citizens is marked by the appearance of the term 'Englishman' as much as by the disappearance of the word 'subject'. Cognates of the word 'subject', when they did recur in later Leveller writing, were clearly pejorative: to be subjected was to be vassalized or enslaved; one could only be 'subjected' to a power which was arbitrary.[7] The logic of Lilburne's elimination of the word 'subject' in favour of 'Englishman' is borne out by this later development.

Who were Lilburne's 'free-born Englishmen'? In talking of the 'free-born' and of 'free-men' or 'free men', Lilburne might be thought to be distinguishing these men from others who fell outside this status. I think it is clear, however, that these terms are inclusive rather than exclusive in their force.

It has been well demonstrated by Thomas, Hampsher-Monk and Wende that the term 'free-born' was not used by Leveller writers to distinguish a select group of Englishmen from the remainder, as C. B. Macpherson had argued. All Englishmen were taken to be free-born. One opponent of the Levellers remarked that it was redundant to talk about free-born Englishmen, asking rhetorically, 'are there any Englishmen that are not Free-borne?'[8]

There is more scope for confusion with 'free-men', as the term has two different meanings. To be a freeman of a guild or company, and hence of a city, was certainly to be a member of an exclusive group. Such status was connected to a locality, however, and not to the nation as a whole. So when Lilburne talks about 'freemen of England' we can be fairly sure that he does not mean only those men who were freemen in the narrower sense. This broader sense of 'freeman' is exactly parallel with 'free-born'. One of Lilburne's favourite references was to chapter 29 of Magna Carta, which set out what could not be done to a 'free man'. Keith Thomas's discussion shows that the status contrasted with freedom in the seventeenth-century texts was either slavery or villeinage. Since villeinage had effectively ended, the 'free men' referred to in Magna Carta included all Englishmen.[9] Coke's discussion of the 'liber homo' of Magna Carta chapter 29 included in it even villeins, 'saving against their lord', and made no other exclusions.[10]

Even in contexts where we might expect the narrow meaning of 'freeman' to be dominant, Lilburne and his associates often either used, or clearly invoked, the broader meaning. Lilburne reprinted a petition, on behalf of 'all the freemen of England', which complained that charters of incorporation to specific merchants 'disfranchis[e] ... all other the free-borne people of England'.[11] Playing consciously on the narrower and broader meanings of 'free-man', Lilburne lamented that 'the poor *Weavers*, though Free-men of *London*, are not only in miserable poverty, but in the miserablest slavery (in the City where they by name are Free-men)'.[12] In Leveller idiom, the status of Englishman could even be used to *override* the status distinctions of London politics. In *Londons Liberties in Chains*, Lilburne's co-author urged London freemen to demand the right to elect the Lord Mayor; he justified his own interest in the topic by saying that though he was not a citizen of London, 'yet [he was] no stranger, nor forreigner, but a free-man of England who hath freely hazarded all, for the recovery of the common Liberty, and my Countries freedom'.[13] In fact, as a non-citizen of London the writer *was* technically a 'foreigner': this was the word used to describe English residents in London who were not freemen of the city.[14] But his status as 'a free-man of England' outweighed, for him, the fact that he was not a freeman of London.

In his writings specifically on London – where he avoided spelling out exactly which 'free-men' he was talking about – Lilburne was again driving at inclusiveness, although he surely drew on his readers' familiarity with the assertion of the liberties of the privileged freemen of the city. The whole thrust of his argument was against the exclusiveness of 'these Prerogative-Monopolizing Patentee-men of London'; 'the Prerogative-Monopolizing arbitrary-men of London'. Their offensive activities took place through their

> Patentee-Monopolizing Companies, Corporations and Fraternities. So that to speak properly, really, and truly, their Brotherhoods are so many conspiracies to destroy and overthrow the lawes and liberties of England, and to ingrosse, inhance, and destroy the trades and Franchises of most of the Freemen of London.[15]

These 'conspiracies' and 'monopolies' of private interest were diametrically opposed to the Leveller ideal of the common good as exemplified in the equal freedoms of individuals. Carlin points out that this makes the Levellers very different from the guild-members who agitated *within* their corporations in these years; Houston is, I think, right to assert that Lilburne did attack monopolies and the company system directly, as part of this campaign against private interests.[16] Lilburne himself pointed to his own writings as demonstrations of 'the unjustnesse of Corporations and Monopolies, which are both sons of one father'.[17]

The inclusive force of Lilburne's insistence on calling Englishmen 'free-born' and 'free-men' is clear. The assumption that Englishmen were free and not bond was not controversial. What was controversial was the assertion that the free status of Englishmen gave them, as individuals, political status. Sir Thomas Smith had written that the lowest class of free men 'have no voice or authoritie in our common wealth, and no account is made of them but onelie to be ruled, not to rule other'.[18] Henry Ireton, at the Putney debates in 1647, was quite prepared to put free Englishmen into that category. The Levellers' innovation was not in saying that all Englishmen were free men, but in drawing extensive conclusions about political rights from that.

One way in which Lilburne fleshed out the status of free-born Englishmen and gestured towards the rights which they all possessed was through his use of the term 'denizen'. The phrase 'free denizen' was another alternative for 'free-born Englishman', and denizen in this context simply meant 'inhabitant'. Thus Lilburne amplified his claim to be a free-man with the phrase 'a free-borne Denizen of England'.[19] Again, Lilburne referred to good laws made for the protection of 'all the free Denizens' of the country.[20]

Denizen, however, had a technical legal meaning as well; and as the *Oxford English Dictionary*'s examples show, this was familiar enough to be usable figuratively as well as literally. Coke, giving a false etymology, summed up the two meanings:

> he that is borne within the King's liegeance is called sometime a Denizen, quasi deins nee, born within ... But many times ... Denizen is taken for an Alien borne, that is infranchised or denizated by Letters Patents.[21]

In the latter case there are two things to notice: firstly, that the denizen only gained rights like those of an English person by being formally granted them; and secondly, that the denizen never gained *all* the rights of a native subject. Thus the definition of the phenomenon in *Les Termes de la Ley*: 'where an Alien born becommeth the Kings subject, & obtaineth the Kings letters patents for to enjoy all priviledges as an Englishman, but if one be made denizen, he shall pay customes & divers other things as aliens'.[22] Cowell was even more explicit about the status of denizens: the word

> signifieth in our common law, an Alein [sic] that is infranchised here in England by the Princes Charter, and inabled, almost in all respects, to doe as the Kings native subjects doe, namely to purchase, and to possesse lands, to be capable of any office or dignitie.
>
> Yet it is said to be short of naturalisation, because a stranger naturalised, may inherit lands by descent, which a man made, onely a Denizen cannot.[23]

One useful connotation of this technical sense of 'denizen' was that it implied freedom. An alien became a denizen by being 'infranchised', being made free or granted freedoms. This literal meaning was clear to at least some of Lilburne's contemporaries: Henry Cockeram's *Dictionary* defined 'Enfranchise' as 'To make free' and 'Disfranchise' as 'To make one lose his freedome'.[24] Cowell's *Interpreter* gave a suggestive definition of 'Enfranchisement':

> It signifieth in our common law, the incorporating of a man in any society, or body politicke. For example, hee that by Charter is made Denizen of England, is said to be enfranchised; and so is hee that is made a Citizen of London, or other City, or Burgesse of any Towne Corporate, because hee is made partaker of those liberties that appertaine to the Corporation, wherinto he is enfranchised. So a villaine is enfranchised, when hee is made free by his Lord, and made capable of the benefits belonging to Free-men.[25]

Thus being enfranchized meant several things: being made part of a group; being granted liberties belonging to the members of a particular body; and being literally made free, from a status regarded as a kind of servitude.[26] This set of associations was a powerful one for Lilburne to draw on, as he clearly did in his use of the term 'disfranchise', and the often linked term 'denizen'.

As well as using the noun 'denizen', apparently in its original sense of native inhabitant, Lilburne also used various versions of the word 'undenize' or 'undenizenize' to denote the removal of liberties. This was often linked with the notion of disfranchisement. For example, Lilburne discussed what might lead 'to the disfranchising me of being a Denizon and freeman of England'.[27] A supporter of Lilburne wrote that through the imposition of the Covenant in the army 'men of excellent publique principles' would be 'disfranchised, and undenized'.[28] In *Londons Liberty* Lilburne used the term 'disfranchise' to refer to the denial of a vote both to Londoners who were not livery men in choosing their MPs, and of those elsewhere falling short of the 40-shillings income required to vote:

> and this undenezing of those Corporations, is an undenezing to all the towns and villages adjacent, in which live thousands of people, that by name are free-men of England, and divers of them men of great estates in money and stock; which also are disfranchised and undenezed, by the fore-mentioned unrighteous Statute; because they have not in land 40s. *per annum* ...[29]

Thus references in almost modern vein to disfranchisement as the deprivation of a vote were linked with references to 'undenezing'. By depriving someone of a vote the authorities had made him less of a denizen. Someone who was 'undenezed' was pushed outside that group of people whose consent was considered essential to government.

Lilburne drew on the concept of the granting of a set of quasi-native rights to (foreign) denizens in order to reinforce his own conceptualization of just

The laws of England and the 'free-born Englishman'

such a coherent set of rights which belonged to natives by right and birth. Given that there was no bill of rights stating in a comprehensive way what was due to all native English subjects, the granting of denizen status was, in a way, a legal acknowledgement that there *was* a set of rights which accrued to native Englishmen precisely because of that status. The foreign-born denizen could be seen as being granted exactly that package, minus a couple of important entitlements.

When Lilburne used the word 'denizen' he blended its two meanings, combining the idea of a package of entitlements for Englishmen with the emotive appeal of the idea of being a native inhabitant of England, a denizen. Thus he lamented the result of monopolies as 'but an indenosonizing of a few, to undenosonize a many', and juxtaposed this with the comment that England was supposed to be 'a Kingdom governed by one Law made by universall and common consent'.[30] Thus a legal grant (a corporation's patent) made a few people into denizens, in the way that letters patent could 'indenosonize' an alien; the effect of this was to 'undenosonize' most people – not from rights that they had ever been *granted*, but from those rights due to them as denizens, native inhabitants who were supposed to be equal in the eyes of the law.

What were the uniform entitlements of Lilburne's free-born Englishmen? Wende has pointed out that the Leveller writers used a whole list of interchangeable terms, in both singular and plural forms, to denote what they were fighting for: rights, liberties, freedoms, free customs, privileges, property, safety, laws, immunities. On Wende's interpretation of Leveller thought, freedom was a composite, resulting from all these things. It would perhaps be more accurate to say that the Englishman's freedom consisted in his rightful claim to all of these things, hence its frequent identification with the liberty of every subject to enjoy the benefit of the law. Wende perceptively emphasizes this logical shift from plural liberties to the single 'liberty' of the law.[31] Lilburne's language actively remodelled individual legal freedoms into a more unified conception of a set of citizenship rights. Law was the mediating term in this transformation: freedoms under law retained their names but came to signify the single and universal freedom guaranteed by the law.

One unifying expression denoting the entitlements of an Englishman was 'birth-right'. Like the terms 'denizen' or 'freeman', which came to connote the role of citizen, 'birth-right' came to connote all that was due to a citizen. Sometimes Lilburne used the term of quite specific entitlements: he opposed monopolies 'that so all the people may injoy their birth right, free trade'.[32] But generally, birth-right comprehended all that an Englishman was entitled to claim under English law, and sometimes under higher authorities too: the 'inheritance of our Fathers, and the Birth-right of us and our children' is 'our Fundamentall Lawes and Liberties, Franchises and Priviledges, that God, Nature, and the just Customes of the Land in which wee live, hath given us'.³³ The term is an indicator of the crucial influence of the legal tradition, and specifically of Coke's interpretation of English law. In the speech which he reported himself as giving to the Committee of Examinations, Lilburne firstly declared: 'I am a free-man, yea, a free-borne Denizen of England', and he went on to quote Magna Carta to justify his rights: 'Sir, the Priviledges contained herein is my Birth-right and Inheritance'.³⁴ This followed Coke's Ciceronian assertion that the law was 'the best birth-right the subject hath', which Lilburne quoted directly elsewhere.³⁵ Lilburne found similar statements about birth-rights in the Parliament's *Book of Declarations*.³⁶ Parliament had declared 'That the law, and the ordinary course of justice, is the common birth-right of every subject of England'.³⁷ The association of this legal birthright with English birth was not spelt out by Lilburne, though it was constantly implied, but one legal textbook declared that 'the law is our birthright, to which an alien is collateral & a stranger, & therfore disabled to take any benefit thereby'.³⁸ Lilburne's vision of an essentially English inheritance of law was in accord with this.

Lilburne's use of terms such as 'privilege', 'immunity', 'liberty' and 'franchise' was part of this project of unifying the entitlements of English law. All of these terms denoted specific rights or exemptions granted piecemeal to individuals or bodies, and they were overlapping concepts. Cowell defined 'Franchise' as 'a priviledge, or an exemption from ordinary jurisdiction, and sometime an immunity from tribute'. A 'libertas' (literally equivalent to 'franchise') 'is a priviledge held by grant or prescription, whereby men enjoy some benefit or favour beyond the ordinarie subject'. In defining privilege he followed Cicero and others in seeing it as a 'privata lex' granted to one man. *Les Termes de la Ley* defined privileges as 'liberties and franchises graunted to an office, place, towne, or mannor, by the Kings great charter, letters patents, or act of Parliament'.³⁹ So, with all these terms, the inherited legal meaning was of specific privileges which specific persons or institutions possessed not through right but ultimately through grant. Lilburne's usage turned this on its head.

In Lilburne's writing, privileges, immunities, and franchises were due to all Englishmen. Lilburne referred to the 'priviledges' in Magna Carta as being his 'Birth-right and Inheritance'.⁴⁰ He declared that 'Englishmen have some priviledges to stand for if they were not fooles'.⁴¹ Since he had not impaired his own status as denizen and freeman of England, he 'ought to enjoy as great a priviledge in the enjoyment of the benefit of the law of England, as any free Denizon of England whatsoever, by what name or title soever he be called'.⁴² Again, Lilburne 'ought by the fundamentall lawes of this Land, to enjoy the benefit of all the lawes, liberties, priviledges, and immunities of a free-born man'. He reinforced the universality of these liberties by describing them as 'the liberties, immunities, and priviledges of all the Commons of England'.⁴³ *An Anatomy of the Lords Tyranny* was 'published to the view of all the Commons of England, for their information, & knowledge of their Liberties and Priviledges'.[44] In the same vein 'our Fundamentall Lawes and Liberties, Franchises and Priviledges' were mentioned in one breath.[45] According to the strict definition of these terms, some Englishmen would have some privileges, some others. In Lilburne's discourse, all Englishmen had the same privileges and liberties.

My argument, then, is that Lilburne's thought is rooted in a legalistic vocabulary, and can be seen to have developed largely through the medium of this vocabulary. In the course of its development, however, the fundamental logic of this language was changed. The roots of the argument developed by Lilburne may lie in the set of notions described by Conal Condren as 'liberties of office': liberties tied to an office or status because they are necessary for the fulfilment of the duties inherent in that status. The legal 'privileges' and 'franchises' claimed by individuals as their particular rights may have been seen as liberties of this kind. However, if Lilburne is exploiting the logic of this kind of 'liberty', the status to which the liberty is tied is that of an Englishman, or sometimes simply a man – which, as Condren himself comments, 'is to extend the notion of an office to, or even beyond, its limit'. Condren may be right that such extensions of the relevant 'offices' testify to the power of the language in warding off potential charges of rebelliousness, but they surely also begin to nudge at more modern notions of liberty, where it has an absolute value, freed from dependence on social roles. Liberty of office may leave traces in the importance which Lilburne attached to the status of Englishmen: if Condren is right, then the logic which led Lilburne to tie his claims to a status, albeit a universalizing one, is one which was rooted in persistent political languages of the period.[46] Such universalizing usages as Lilburne's, though, pushed this language to or beyond its logical limits. In Lilburne's writing, all Englishmen enjoyed identical political 'privileges' – which meant that they were hardly 'privileges' at all.

THE 'RADICAL' TRADITION OF COMMON LAW THOUGHT

Lilburne, of course, was not dealing with an unmediated tradition of medieval legal terms. His materials were not 'raw' but embedded in discourses which were already politically specific. Lilburne used Sir Edward Coke's writings extensively, and his usage of legal terminology was undoubtedly influenced by the particular cast given to it by Coke and others in the early seventeenth century. Lilburne was self-taught in legal matters, and his pretensions in the field were easy to mock. Prynne ridiculed him as an 'upstart monstrous Lawyer ... called to the Barre at *Newgate*, where he now practiseth', and 'this *Ignoramus*, who understands the Law, and *Magna Charta*, no more then a Jack-daw'.[47] Modern historians have been equally tempted to see the technical legal trappings of Lilburne's discourse as, ultimately, a mere invocation of contemporary categories to cover a more radical discourse of natural rights.[48] In spite of his noticeable errors in law and his evident desire to appeal to authority, however, Lilburne was drawing intelligently on a tradition which itself adapted and interpreted precedents and maxims for broader political application, sometimes in a notably radical way. Weston describes the supposed Saxon laws as 'a farrago of items from which Stuart Englishmen fashioned legal and constitutional principles of wide application', and notes the way in which their application was extended by the framers of the Petition of Right, including Coke.[49] Sacks has discussed the evolution of 'liberties' into 'the liberty of the subject', dating this shift in language to the late sixteenth and early seventeenth centuries, and linking it to a 'process of conceptual expansion' of other terms, particularly 'monopoly'.[50] Coke was a particularly prominent figure in this history of expansive legal interpretation, and Lilburne's use of Coke was alert to the political tenor of Coke's interpretations.

Modern scholarship on Coke has demonstrated that, however authoritative his pronouncements on the ancient laws of England were later taken to be, his legal writings were far from being neutral collations of the materials of the common law. His very understanding of the nature of the common law implied principles of interpretation and generalization which could not be neutral. If the common law was for Coke a system of artificial reason comprehending all that needed to be talked about in political life, as well as more narrowly legal matters,[51] then the new questions which might arise for the law's consideration would have to be answered from old materials, which meant, essentially, that they would have to be answered from principles taken to be exemplified in these old materials. This could be done unremarked, by a redefinition of vocabulary or the extension of the applicability of a maxim; it could be helped along by a newly coined 'maxim' or a tendentiously reported case; or it could be done in the name of the spirit or reason of the law.[52]

It is clear from Coke's parliamentary career in the 1620s as well as his writing that he became more and more concerned to assert the law's control over, or at least bounding of, royal prerogative.[53] In his fostering of the Petition of Right he used expansive arguments from legal premises to reach conclusions which were quite different from those reached earlier in his career.[54] Among his writings it is in the *Institutes*, parts II–IV of which were confiscated after his death and recovered and published by the Long Parliament for their own purposes, that Coke's most potentially radical legal interpretations are found.

Magna Carta drew from Coke in the second part of his *Institutes* the same generalizing impulses as it had during the framing of the Petition of Right. He invoked its authority to argue for the illegality of monopolies, on the grounds that the 'liberty of the subject' guaranteed by Magna Carta included the liberty to follow any trade. (His definition of monopoly in the third part of the *Institutes* as an institution by which persons or corporations other than the monopolists 'are sought to be restrained of any freedome, or liberty that they had before' seems suspiciously well-suited to the workings of this extremely tendentious argument).⁵⁵ Commenting on the famous chapter 29 of Magna Carta, which set out the legal limits on what could be done to a free man ('liber homo'), Coke not only extended the 'libertates' mentioned to specifics such as the right to trade, but also glossed the term, in one of its 'significations', as meaning 'the laws of the realme' *tout court*.⁵⁶ Similarly, he quoted an unexceptionable common-law maxim from Plowden's *Commentaries*, but then glossed it with a significant extra phrase – derived from Cicero – in his translation:

> *Le common ley ad tielment admeasure les prerogatives le roy, que ilz ne tolleront, ne prejudiceront le inheritance dascun*, the common law hath so admeasured the prerogatives of the king, that they should not take away, nor prejudice the inheritance of any: and the best inheritance the subject hath, is the law of the realme.⁵⁷

A defence of the property of individuals – itself a great concern for Coke – was thus transformed into an assertion of an equal property of all subjects in the law. This glossed version of the maxim was transplanted from Coke's work to lend support to Lilburne's case.⁵⁸

In spite of such examples, Coke had to be used carefully for Lilburne's purposes. There were limits to Coke's capacity to transform the connotations of legal language. Wende perhaps exaggerates the smoothness of the transition from Coke's understanding of legal terms to Lilburne's. Thus, while Wende even cites Coke himself to show that in the common law a 'freedom' was essentially a privilege enjoyed by some and not others, he sees as more important those statements in Coke which imply that the law has to be equal for all and that it cannot privilege any individual or group. On the contrary, Coke says, for example, 'that ecclesiasticall persons have more and greater liberties then other the king's subjects'.⁵⁹ Lilburne, I would argue, made a new and consistent egalitarian language out of these terms, where Coke had merely redefined or glossed them in particular instances.

How well Coke's vision could nourish Lilburne's, and how subtle the changes were which could make Coke's language into truly Lilburnian language, can be seen in one example. Lilburne was trying to make out of the materials available in English law a unified set of rights which applied not haphazardly and individually, but as a package and evenly to a whole section of the population. Magna Carta was a central foundation for this set of rights. An ally of Lilburne's made use of Coke for this purpose, declaring that

> the Reasons ... why it [Magna Carta] is called *Charta Libertatum Regni*, The Charter of the Liberties of *England* from the effect, *Quia liberos facit*, It makes us Free-men, and for the same cause it is called (*communis libertas*, common liberty) and *Le charter des franchises* ...⁶⁰

The Levellers

The passage of Coke from which this is taken did not translate the Latin phrases.[61] Here the writer has chosen translations which are slightly more emotive than the Latin might suggest: the Latin phrase 'liberties of the kingdom' is translated as 'liberties of England'; the Latin phrase which could simply mean 'because it makes [people] free' becomes fixed as a statement of essential transformation in English: 'It makes us Free-men'. Together these translations recall Lilburne's key phrase 'free men of England'. The 'liberties' and (a direct translation) *'franchises'* may be in the plural, but each man affected did not simply acquire a series of separate liberties, but was made a free man.

HISTORY, THEORY, AND LAW IN LEVELLER THOUGHT

Lilburne appealed constantly to the laws of the land, and often equated the liberty which was the due of all Englishmen with the 'birthright' of English law. But Lilburne's appeal to positive law and praise of the protections it offered were not always welcomed warmly by the other Leveller writers, and, as we have already seen in the last chapter, Lilburne and the other Leveller leaders also offered robust arguments not from the laws of England but from natural law. How the Levellers understood the relationship between positive and natural law, and how they understood the history and significance of English law itself, can tell us much about their thought.

The mixture of legal language and – to modern readers – much more eloquent arguments from natural law and natural rights in Leveller writings has led some scholars to suggest that legal language was deployed largely for strategic reasons.[62] On this view, natural law was the more 'radical' discourse, and was the real driver of Leveller thought, while arguments from the common law, in particular, were less threatening to a mid-seventeenth-century audience and could be used to mask the Levellers' real radicalism. This, of course, hardly explains why Walwyn would reproach Lilburne publicly for his praise of the English law. Consideration of the nature of Lilburne's writings also militates against seeing his choice of argument and language as cynically tailored to particular audiences: his publication, republication, annotation, and cross-referencing of his own works show that he considered his published writing as a single, ongoing oeuvre intended for an overwhelmingly consistent audience: precisely the inclusive audience of concerned free-born Englishmen.

Behind this question of expediency lies a deeper assumption: that natural law language was more radical and intellectually powerful than the language of the law, and that it was not ultimately compatible with it. Attributing a preference for arguments from natural law to the Levellers thus credits them with theoretical sophistication, and the ability to move away from merely 'historical' arguments for their political ends. Certainly, scholarship on the Levellers has leaned heavily in favour of seeing the fundamentals of their thought as based on natural law.[63]

The picture, of course, is then complicated by the question of how the different Leveller writers regarded the English law. Was it the law of the Norman conquerors, imposed on an English population as a key part of the 'Norman yoke' of tyranny, or was it English law, surviving in its essentials through the rupture of conquest, endorsed and maintained by rulers at least in part through the struggles of their subjects to claim their rights under it? Lilburne's use of Coke and the common law tradition naturally suggests a story of continuity, the common law fiction of custom existing 'time out of mind'. But Walwyn, in particular, embraced the theory of the Norman Yoke in the earliest phase of the Leveller movement. *A Remonstrance of Many Thousand Citizens* set out the theory: 'The History of our Fore-fathers since they were Conquered by the *Normans*, doth manifest that this Nation hath been held in bondage all along ever since by the policies and force of the Officers of Trust in the Common-wealth.' The inevitable conclusion was that the legal system was 'forced upon this nation by Conquest, and continued against Reason, and the weale of the People'.[64]

The interpretation of Magna Carta is an index of the differences between Lilburne and Walwyn, but it also illustrates the flexibility of thinking about the law, and the scope there was to reconcile Norman yoke thinking with more positive conceptions of the common law and the laws of England more generally. Walwyn, in what seems to be his first intervention in print on Lilburne's behalf, made a point of rebuking him for his high regard for Magna Carta. Magna Carta was 'but a part of the peoples rights and liberties' and was so narrow in its provisions for freedom that it was only 'deceitfully and improperlie Called Magna Charta, (indeed so called to blind the people)'. Contrast Coke's enthusiastic explanation (above) of the varying names for Magna Carta, appropriate in his view because the charter made people free. For Walwyn, Magna Carta was a small set of concessions 'wrestled out of the pawes of' (Norman) conquerors; it was the same parliaments who spent most of their time abridging liberties yet further, who when danger appeared could look no further than Magna Carta, 'calling that messe of pottage their birthright, the great inheritance of the people, the great Charter of England'. Even after this reproach, Lilburne continued to regard Magna Carta as all these things, and to give great significance to the Englishman's 'birthright' of the law, encapsulated in Magna Carta. On the face of it, this reveals a stark divide between Lilburne's historical mode of thought and Walwyn's more theoretical approach, which enabled him to step aside from the rights supposedly guaranteed by prescription and urge instead that Parliament legislate afresh: he complained that Parliament, 'when they might have made a newer and better Charter, have falne to patching the old'.[65]

Pocock and Hill developed a view of the constraints of common law thinking which made it out to be completely dependent on denying that the Norman Conquest formed a significant rupture in tradition. The Levellers, under the influence of Walwyn's unsentimental vision of the English past, were thus supposed to have adopted the idea of the Norman Yoke and split themselves off decisively from the common law tradition as it was seen in Coke, rejecting the common law itself as Norman.[66] In practice, however, the early division between Lilburne and Walwyn was not resolved simply by Lilburne accepting the rebuke of his senior and supposedly more theoretically minded colleague. There were means by which the divide between arguments from historical continuity and theoretical arguments enabled by the assertion of a break in legitimacy at the Conquest could be bridged. We see these bridging strategies in Lilburne's writing, but we also see Walwyn retreating from the strident Norman Yoke theory of his early work.

As we have seen, the Levellers shared the radical parliamentarian impulse to place sovereignty solely in Parliament – in their version, a reformed representative body based on the House of Commons. However, Parliament itself, and particularly a Parliament which had begun to justify its actions partly in terms of a parliamentary absolutism, with a sovereign Parliament ultimately exercising arbitrary power, soon began to seem a threat to liberties itself. Under these circumstances, the Levellers struggled to find more resilient safeguards for liberty than Parliament's will. Walwyn's willingness to seek solutions through Parliament's implementation of better statute law – law which could naturally be reversed in successive parliaments – looked less appealing now. One result – most visible in a late piece of writing on juries – was a modification in the tone of his discussion of Norman tyranny and the common law:

> For howsoever men in these days make bold to trample *Magna Charta* under their feet, making sport at the many absurd prerogative and superstitious things therein contained; it is to be noted, that these things are but as a French garb or cloathing, which the Conqueror and his successours, by main strength, forced our fore-fathers to put on: but yet, as an Englishman is to be known from a Frenchman amongst a thousand, though he labor to fashion himself as the most Frenchified Gallant; so are our true English Liberties, contained in Magna Charta, as easy to be differenced from amidst that superstitious and in some measure, tyrannical heap cast upon them, and which that worthy Parliament, in the third year of the late King, culled out to purpose, and reduced into that excellent Law ... the *Petition of Right*, and wherein trials *per* Juries is the principal.[67]

As Dzelzainis has suggested, parliamentarians' newly dismissive attitude to the rights enshrined in the common law may have encouraged the Levellers to reassess its strengths and come to its defence.[68]

This was enabled partly by the flexibility of the legal tradition itself. Common law existed alongside statute, and indeed there was interaction between the two: statute might confirm common law as well as (on some views) being able to abrogate it. When Lilburne and the other Leveller leaders appealed to law as bounding the (arbitrary) powers of any governors, including Parliament, the resilience of a long, customary, unwritten tradition was immensely useful to them; but it was also useful to be able to point to parliamentary confirmations of the customary rights they claimed. Indeed, Magna Carta itself could be seen as one such written confirmation of customary rights. Sometimes it was important to distinguish what was written (and therefore 'known' and 'declared') from the unwritten law, which had the inherent danger of arbitrariness;[69] sometimes to distinguish the 'tenour' or 'equity' from the letter of the law;[70] sometimes to imply that some provisions, even if in some sense 'laws', might not be 'fundamental' ones.[71] The resources of legal thinking itself could thus be exploited – and of course extended – to reconcile the apparent realities of the law with more idealistic interpretations. When Lilburne asserted that 'by the antient, good, just and unrepealed laws of England' parliaments should be held annually, only the fact that parliaments were clearly *not* held annually tells us that 'unrepealed' does not mean 'effectively in force'.[72]

Thus Lilburne did not adopt Norman Yoke theory wholesale once Walwyn had pointed out the error of his ways to him. Rather, he continued to appeal to 'English' law, but with more reservations and caution, and with a greater sense of flexibility about the type of law he was appealing to. He often appealed to the laws of England, and he did not renounce any appeal specifically to the common law; however, when he distinguished statute from common law, he either called on both or came down in favour of statute.[73] The instabilities in Lilburne's account of law and history are nicely summed up in his use of Magna Carta. Accounts of 'ancient constitution' thinking by Weston and Greenberg, and Seaberg's work on the Levellers, suggest that the line between the common law ancient constitution and the Norman yoke could be a thin one: much depended on whether the 'Confessor's Laws' had been maintained through prescription, as well as on the nature of the Norman conquest itself. Magna Carta could be seen as an assertion of ancient rights, an example of prescription; Leveller texts such as *Englands Birthright* perhaps hint at the thesis that Magna Carta and other statutes merely 'declare' the common law when they talk about 'knowne and declared' laws.[74] But when, under pressure from Leveller colleagues, Lilburne did criticize the common law as Norman, Magna Carta could be slotted into the category of statute. He admitted that 'though there may be some veines issuing from former originals, yet the main stream of our Common law, with the practice thereof, flowed out of Normandy'. Clearly he did regard much of the substance of common law, and not just its procedure, as tainted by its Norman origins.[75] However, this did not spell the end of Lilburne's appeals to the rights guaranteed by the law, and he could continue to appeal to exactly the same provisions as he always had – prime among them, Magna Carta. This was because 'in the harshness of my expressions against the Common Law, I put ... a cleare distinction of it, from the Statute Law'. Statute law was also flawed, but contained 'gallant Lawes' such as chapters 28–29 of Magna Carta, the Petition of Right, and the Act abolishing Star Chamber. Magna Carta still, however, fell short of Edward the Confessor's laws 'which the Conquerour rob'd England of'.[76] Although they were here defended as statutes, the excellence of these three measures might easily have been justified by their alleged conformity with the ancient principles of the common law, which they had merely declared. Ultimately, Lilburne's schooling by his colleagues changed his understanding of the history of the law, without dimming his sense that it was one key source of the fundamental liberties of Englishmen. The 'law of England' might not be 'so good, and so exact in every particular, especially in the administrative part of it, as I could, wish it were', Lilburne confessed. Nonetheless, he was still not prepared to abandon it: 'till I can see a better, I for my part will make much of that which we have, as the principall earthly preserver and safeguard of my life, liberty, and property'.[77]

Much of the breadth and ambivalence of Lilburne's view of law would not have been alien to Coke's thinking. He too could emphasize the intent of the law (its 'true sense and sentence') as a crucial principle of interpretation,[78] say that what is against reason is against law ('this is another strong argument in law, *Nihil quod est contra rationem est licitum*'),[79] and assert the importance of at least the penal law being known to those who would be punished under it.[80] Like Lilburne, he could confess a dislike of the law's being in French, and count this among the negative effects of the Norman Conquest: 'we would derive from the Conqueror as little as we could'.[81] He too was ambivalent about the relationship between the common law and parliamentary statute and, like Lilburne, saw principles of interpretation and correction flowing between the two rather than simply in one direction – although clearly Coke's inclination was to assert the superiority of common law over statute, where Lilburne would make the opposite claim.[82]

In spite of their recognition of the problem of the Norman Conquest, then, the Levellers were reluctant to give up the appeal to English law. Instead, they used all the available modes of talking about the law, including the supposed maintenance of pre-Norman rights through prescription and the appeal to statute to back up the force of those rights, alongside looser invocations of the law. But, as we saw in the last chapter, they also drew on natural law arguments in parallel with the appeals to law which I am exploring here.

Of course, this blending of different 'languages of political thought' was not peculiar to the Levellers: parliamentarian writers similarly used arguments from natural law alongside arguments from positive law and the ancient constitution.[83] Indeed, given the long history of natural law ideas, the common law tradition itself had not been untouched by them.[84] For Cromartie, indeed, some common lawyers before the civil war had essentially incorporated the reasoning of natural law into the artificial reason of the law: the common law system was 'natural law applied to English life', and Parker's appeal to *salus populi* was not necessarily an appeal beyond the framework of the law.[85] For the Levellers, similarly, positive law was not a cover for arguments derived from natural law; rather, the two naturally ran alongside each other. Common law included notions of equity and reason (admittedly, an artificial reason[86]), which could go some way to reconciling it with natural law when there was any danger of conflict between the two. Burgess suggests that the common lawyers' logic of equity was reversed in Leveller writing, so that law could be corrected from outside the legal framework rather than from within it.[87] Certainly Lilburne invoked natural reason rather than the artificial reason of the law to correct the defects of positive law.

For Lilburne and the other Leveller authors, reason and the law of nature provided a measure of the adequacy and legitimacy of the laws of England. Thus the freedoms which were given by the law of England were 'very slender and short to what by nature and reason they ought to be'.[88] When English law apparently failed to live up to the requirements of the law of nature, this could prompt a redescription of English law itself. Thus the law of England consisted of all England's existing laws, *providing* that they were 'agreeable to the law Eternall and Naturall'. The *fundamental* law of the land could be described as 'the Perfection of Reason' simply because it was by definition that part of existing law which was in accord with nature and reason.[89] Equitable interpretation meant that law could – and should – be interpreted on the assumption that the law-giver did not intend to enact something which went against reason.[90] At some points Lilburne was prepared to argue that natural and positive law were simply to be appealed to at different times: while common preservation was 'the ouldest Law' and could override normal laws in times of emergency, in safer times one should be satisfied with nothing less than 'the absolute benefit of the Law, and the common justice of *England*'.[91] But, in general, the natural law, when invoked in an apparent clash with the law of England, was used to bring English law into line, and confirm what the fundamentals of English law must really be.

More often, however, Lilburne's appeals to the law of England and the law of nature were so intertwined that he admitted no conflict between the two. Thus he could found the liberties of his countrymen on both positive and natural law: they were 'our natural, rationall, nationall, and legal liberties, and freedoms', 'the rationall, natural, nationall, and legall liberties of my selfe and all the Commons of England'.[92] On a particular procedural point, he might appeal both to 'the light and Law of nature' and to 'the ancient common Law of *England*', finding that the right to plead his own cause was 'the naturall and undoubted right of every individuall Englishmen [*sic*], yea and of every man, upon the face of the Earth'.⁹³ On a couple of occasions Lilburne even went further in his identification of an idealized English law – which he appealed to as if it were real – with the law of nature itself. Here, rather than grounding the specifics of English law in overarching natural and divine law, he put it the other way round. Thus the best elements in the Petition of Right and Magna Carta 'are of universall concernment to all the sons of men, under any just Government in the world'.⁹⁴ As late in his career as his *Apologeticall Narration*, written in exile in 1653, he could still talk about 'all English men or people being all borne free alike, and the Liberties thereof equally entayled to all of them alike', and then go on to subordinate the divine law to this English law: 'And suitable to these most righteous Maximes of the Law of England, are the most glorious and righteous dealings of the Soveraigne Lord of Heaven & Earth.'⁹⁵

'FREE-BORN ENGLISHMEN' AND THE FRANCHISE

We have seen that Lilburne's constant invocation of 'free-born Englishmen' carried a strong political message: Englishmen, simply by birth, had the benefit of a uniform set of liberties and privileges. However, along with these rights went the duty to claim and defend them, and Lilburne's works had a hortatory quality, trying to spur his audience of 'free-born Englishmen' to vindicate their rights. While all Englishmen had these rights, at least unless they had lost them through their own actions, *true* Englishness was also a moral quality against which people should assess their actions.

Lilburne used 'English' as a moral shorthand, declaring himself to be 'a true bred Englishman', 'a true-hearted Englishman', 'Englands Cordiall Freind', 'a true and real-hearted *Englishman*', 'As much an Englishman as ever', 'A *faithful* English-man'.⁹⁶ Sometimes this implicit message was reinforced by a quite explicit use of 'English' or 'Englishman' as a normative term. Thus Prynne's charges against Lilburne were described as 'unsufferable slanders, wicked, bloody and un-English-man-like provocations'.⁹⁷ Similarly, Lilburne's way of praising Wildman's pamphlet *Truths Triumph* was to call it 'his late masculine english peace'.⁹⁸ Lilburne's audience is expected to show the same qualities: he appealed to 'every knowing English eye' and 'every unprejudiced and truly English heart' as the proper judges of the government of the country. In *The Additional Plea* Lilburne proposed to appeal to 'all that have honest, english hearts'.⁹⁹ It was 'old English valour' which was shown by the army's actions at its rendezvous of 4–5 June 1647. London citizens wanting to defend their goods and liberty by not paying tithes must 'play the Englishman'.¹⁰⁰

Lilburne's imagined audience was made up of these 'true hearted', 'true bred' and 'honest' Englishmen. For example, he appealed 'to every true hearted

Englishman that desires a speedie end of these warres';[101] published information for the benefit of 'all true hearted English-men';[102] and addressed his message only to those 'True bred Englishmen, that have a life to lay down, for the defence of your just Liberties and Freedomes'.[103] He recommended books that 'are worth every honest English mans buying' in order to know about government,[104] and wanted to replace monopolizers with 'honest Englishmen ... that love the Fundamentall lawes, and the common and just liberties of the Nation'.[105]

The drive of this language, then, was at inclusivity; but it also required action from its (male) readers. They were supposed to recognize themselves as free-born Englishmen, acknowledge the rights which they were owed, and then work to vindicate and exercise those rights. These rights were not simply passive liberties and protections; they were active rights, involving the exercise of political judgement, particularly in the current struggle to maintain or assert liberties against the encroachments of governors. In spite of Lilburne's impressive popularity and ability to rally people to his support (demonstrated particularly at his two treason trials in 1649 and 1653), it is hard to know how fully those who read his pamphlets and followed his career took this message on board. The usage of the phrase 'free-born Englishmen' was surely boosted by Lilburne's writings, but its subsequent ubiquity cannot be attributed entirely to him, and even where it was adopted from his writing, it does not necessarily demonstrate that his message was fully understood. But at the Putney debates of October–November 1647, we can see Lilburne's language, and the argument implied in it, being clearly made by radical speakers at the Putney debates. As we will see in Chapter 5, this is not necessarily the result of a strong personal influence or active collaboration, though there were contacts between Lilburne and radical army men. The use of Lilburne's arguments here is thus even more striking.

The section of the Putney debates which reveals the influence of Lilburne's writings is the famous debate on the franchise. Henry Ireton argued that some relatively narrow property qualification for the franchise should be retained. The civilians, agitators, and Colonel Rainborough argued instead that all those who lived under a government should put themselves under that government. In their view, that meant that Englishmen were, other things being equal, entitled to the vote. Mendle is rare in taking this theme of the debates seriously, arguing that 'Putney ... was in good measure a debate over who really constituted the English nation'.[106] Nobody, of course, was disputing that the rank and file of the army were English, just as no one was disputing that all Englishmen were free-born. The question was whether English or free-born status were in any way relevant to inclusion in the political nation. Ireton said not. He explicitly argued that, for this purpose, there was no difference between an Englishman and a foreigner: 'the same reason doth extend' to both

The Levellers

cases. For Sexby this claim was simply insulting. Perhaps the angriest speech of the whole debate was his assertion that it was precisely for the English rights which, according to Ireton, were nonexistent that he and his fellow-soldiers had fought: 'Wee have engaged in this Kingdome and ventur'd our lives, and itt was all for this: to recover our birthrights and priviledges as Englishmen, and by the arguments urged there is none.... I wonder wee were soe much deceived.'[107] Sexby's anger was an understandable reaction to Ireton's extraordinary insistence that Englishmen with no fixed property were no more a part of the political nation than 'foreigners' were.

The genesis of the adult male franchise demand itself, as well as its defence at Putney, was linked to Lilburne. He had begun to champion it clearly in 1647, although the unfairness of excluding people 'that by name are free-men of England' from the franchise had already been touched on in his writing on London. The *Case of the Armie* then took up the demand for an adult male franchise in the days before Putney, but as we will see in Chapter 5, it had not been a demand made in the Leveller petitioning by civilians. It is surely no coincidence that the demand was put forward by Lilburne, and welcomed by army men. It meshed very neatly indeed with Lilburne's extension of uniform rights and liberties to all 'free-born Englishmen', and Lilburne's exhortations to free-born Englishmen to fight and claim those rights had an obvious resonance in an army which regarded itself as fighting for Parliament according to its judgement and conscience. The petitioners of January 1648 did indeed claim the franchise on the grounds that it was the 'Birth-right of all English men'. It was, they said, 'the Ancient Liberty of this Nation, that all the Free-born people have freely elected their Representers in Parliament, and their Sheriffs and Justices of the Peace, &c'.[108]

In spite of the natural fit of Lilburne's remaking of English liberties with the franchise demand, however, the case for a near-universal male franchise was usually made in terms of consent theory, even in Lilburne's writing. Thus he declared that it was 'meer vasalage' if a man had 'no vote at all in chusing any Parliament man, and yet must be bound by their Lawes' – exactly the argument that radical speakers were to use at Putney.[109] The third Agreement of the People explicitly based the demand for a much-extended franchise on natural right. When Wildman presented the argument for a radical extension of the franchise in the government of the City of London in 1650, he too moved beyond historical argument to the broader notions of natural right.[110] The franchise seems to be one more example of the congruence of an idealized English birthright of laws with arguments from natural right.

The whole drive of the language of the 'free-born Englishman' was its inclusivity. However, it did encode one obvious exclusion – on the grounds of gender – and it was also bounded by other conditions for the exercise of citizen rights. On gender, Lilburne's language was clearly masculinist; he even used 'masculine' as a term of praise for writings he approved of.[111] He sometimes mentioned women alongside men as being entitled to protection under the law, but clearly women were not the prime examples of English citizen qualities in Lilburne's mind. Ann Hughes has explored the way in which Leveller women – often the wives and relatives of the male leaders – were involved in Leveller campaigning and invoked in Leveller writings, suggesting that the movement depicted itself as a movement of households, with male household heads, and that the sufferings of Leveller women at the hands of the authorities dramatized the threats to households of which the Levellers were complaining.[112] I am less sure that householder status is what resonates as important in Lilburne's language; rather, the moral qualities he demanded from his free-born Englishmen (true-heartedness and the like) crossed over into a type of valour which could be very martial in its colouring. Nonetheless, Leveller women might be able to draw on aspects of Lilburne's language and assert their own rights rather aggressively, as in one of the Leveller women's petitions – although the authorship of these remains unclear.[113]

Other exclusions from the rights of free-born Englishmen were implied by Lilburne's language when he asserted his own rights as someone who had done nothing which might disfranchise him. Certain types of action might forfeit the liberties usually due to the free-born Englishman. The meaning of this was not spelt out, but it seems likely that liberties were forfeited entirely only by those who had acted against the foundations of those liberties. Under the third Agreement of the People, those who sought to undermine the constitution established by the Agreement faced treason charges. Overton, more expansively, explained that 'mankind must be preserved upon the earth, and to this preservation, all the Children of men have an equall title by Birth, none to be deprived thereof, but such as are enemies thereto'. Within his framework of natural law, a version of treason can be committed against the rest of mankind, 'a destruction to humane society'.[114] The Agreements had to confront the dangers of enfranchising those who had fought against Parliament, but the third Agreement excluded royalists from the franchise for ten years, suggesting that liberties could be temporarily forfeited.[115]

The Leveller oeuvre suggests some exclusions which are more difficult to reconcile with Lilburne's inclusive language. It is well known that, at certain points in their career, the Levellers, or people associated with them, were prepared to countenance the exclusion of 'servants' and almstakers from the franchise. However narrowly these categories were defined, they were still exclusions.[116] Lilburne's writing does not, I think, address this problem, and by implication it might be thought to extend the political nation beyond heads of household only. The second, most compromised, Leveller *Agreement* did restrict the franchise to 'House-keepers', and stipulated in detail that they should not be 'servants to, or receiving wages from any particular person', and

111

that, so far from being almstakers, they be contributors to poor relief. Given these detailed restrictions, and the fact that at other points in the third Agreement the words of the second are carried over verbatim, it is perhaps significant that the third Agreement, of 1 May 1649, reverted to the formula of 'all men of the age of one and twenty yeers and upwards' except servants, almstakers, and, for the time being, royalists.[117] The disappearance of the 'householder' requirement seems significant, even though the exclusion of servants remains. This exclusion is in some tension with Lilburne's language, which implies an appeal to *all* English men, potential as well as actual householders. In fact the document which most explicitly applied Lilburne's language to the franchise was *The Case of the Armie*, which gives the vote to 'all the freeborn at the age of 21. yeares and upwards ... excepting those that have or shall deprive themselves of that their freedome'.[118] In Lilburne's writing, as in the initial enthusiasm of the new agents and drafters of the *Case*, establishing the broad principle was the key; concessions could be bargained out later.

CONCLUSION

I have talked about Lilburne's 'free-born Englishman' as a citizen, and shown how the materials of that citizenship were assembled from traditional languages of English law. Pocock suggests that English subjects' traditional rights, properties, and obligations could not in themselves make an individual into 'an active citizen or a political animal'.[119] While it would be wrong to see the Levellers' writings, which are in quite a different idiom, as an early flowering of the classical republicanism of the 1650s (see Chapter 6), Lilburne's remaking of the English materials surely marks one stage in this transformation. As Pocock says, what was already there in England was a set of relatively uncontested ideas about the rights, duties, property, and obligations of individual Englishmen. Citizenship would not consist of this alone: these elements had to be remade, or overlaid, by an idea which could animate these individuals' sense of themselves as citizens in relation to a state. Lilburne's language of the rights and qualities of 'free-born Englishmen' did much to bring that about.

At the Putney debates, while Ireton could not concede to Englishmen any direct connection to the state (meaningful status in the nation could only be achieved via *local* ties of property or status) the radicals had a way of connecting individuals directly with their nation and polity. That this was the key argument of the debates must surely be due to Lilburne's influence. For Lilburne, the content of citizenship could largely be taken as read; what 'liberties and privileges' actually *were* did not need to be spelt out. It was more effective simply to accuse opponents of 'incroaching', 'engrossing', 'invading', or 'usurping' Englishmen's privileges and liberties, as if the content of those liberties was self-evident. The real task facing Lilburne was to make those liberties and privileges into a form of equal citizenship. The content of that citizenship might begin to be articulated under pressure – as it was by others at the Putney debates – but the important thing was to establish that Englishmen, as Englishmen, had political status.

NOTES

1 Contrast G. Burgess, *The Politics of the Ancient Constitution: An Introduction to English Political Thought, 1603–1642* (Basingstoke: Macmillan, 1992) with A. Cromartie, *The Constitutionalist Revolution: An Essay on the History of England, 1450–1642* (Cambridge: Cambridge University Press, 2006).

2 Burgess, *The Politics of the Ancient Constitution*, pp. 90–92; A. Cromartie, 'The constitutionalist revolution: the transformation of political culture in early Stuart England,' *Past & Present* 163 (1999), 120; J. P. Sommerville, *Politics and Ideology in England, 1603–1640* (London: Longman, 1986), p. 237.

3 R. Howell Jr and D. E. Brewster, 'Reconsidering the Levellers: the evidence of the *Moderate*', *Past and Present*, 46 (1970), pp. 68–86, emphasize the diversity and range of Leveller thought; Frank, p. 63 on Lilburne's need for Walwyn as a theoretician; A. Sharp, 'John Lilburne's discourse of law', *Political Science* 40 (1988), p. 19.

4 P. Gregg, *Free-born John: the Biography of John Lilburne* (London: Phoenix Press, 2000 reprint), p. 63.

5 R. C. Johnson et al. (eds), *Commons Debates 1628* (6 vols, New Haven: Yale University Press, 1977–83), III: entries for 23 April to 2 May, for example.

6 John Lilburne, *Coppy of a Letter... to James Ingram and Henry Hopkins* (4 October 1640), p. 4; John Lilburne, *A Copie of a Letter, Written by John Lilburne Leut. Collonell. To Mr. William Prinne Esq.* ([15 January] 1645, pp. 2–3.

7 Wolfe, pp. 265 (January 1648 petition), 374 (petition included in *The Hunting of the Foxes*, 1649) for examples of complaints against being 'subject[ed]' to arbitrary powers.

8 K. Thomas, 'The Levellers and the franchise', in G. E. Aylmer (ed.) *The Interregnum: The Quest for Settlement* (London, 1972), pp. 73–5; P. Wende, '"Liberty" und "property" in der politischen Theorie der Levellers', *Zeitschrift für Historische Forschung* 1 (1974), 147–73; I. Hampsher-Monk, 'The political theory of the Levellers: Putney, property and Professor Macpherson', *Political Studies* 24 (1976), 397–422. C. B. Macpherson, *The Political Theory of Possessive Individualism: Hobbes to Locke* (Oxford: Clarendon Press, 1962), pp. 120–9. Frost, *A Declaration of Some Proceedings*, in H&D, pp. 116–17, and cited in Thomas, p. 75.

9 D. MacCulloch, 'Bondmen under the Tudors', in M. C. Cross, D. M. Loades and J. J. Scarisbrick (eds) *Law and Government under the Tudors: Essays Presented to Sir Geoffrey Elton* (Cambridge: Cambridge University Press, 1988), pp. 91–109.

10 Thomas, 'The Levellers and the franchise', pp. 73–5; D. Sacks, 'Parliament, liberty and the commonweal', in J. H. Hexter (ed.) *Parliament and Liberty* (Stanford: Stanford University Press, 1992), pp. 85, 290n1; Sir Edward Coke, *The Second Part of the Institutes* (1642), p. 45.

11 John Lilburne, *Londons Liberty in Chains* ([October] 1646), pp. 41–3.

The Levellers

12 John Lilburne, *An Impeachment of High Treason against Oliver Cromwell and ... Ireton* ([10 August] 1649), p. 38.

13 Lilburne, *Londons Liberty in Chains*, p. 10.

14 S. Rappaport, *Worlds within Worlds: Structures of Life in Sixteenth-Century London* (Cambridge: Cambridge University Press, 1989), p. 42.

15 Lilburne, *Londons Liberty in Chains*, pp. 38–41.

16 N. Carlin, 'Liberty and fraternities in the English revolution: the politics of London artisans' protests, 1635–1659', *International Review of Social History* 39 (1994), 223–54; A. Houston, '"A way of settlement": the Levellers, monopolies and the public interest', *History of Political Thought* 14 (1993), 381–420, at p. 397.

17 John Lilburne, *The Legall Fundamental Liberties* ([8 June] 1649, first edition), p. 60; he is referring back to his *Innocency and Truth Justified* ([6 January] 1646), pp. 46ff., and to his writings on London.

18 Sir Thomas Smith, *De Republica Anglorum*, ed. Mary Dewar (Cambridge: Cambridge University Press, 1982), pp. 64–77.

19 John Lilburne, *The Copy of a Letter, From Lieutenant Colonell John Lilburne, to a Freind [sic]* ([25 July] 1645), p. 2.

20 Lilburne, *The Grand Plea of Lieut. Col. John Lilburne* ([20 October] 1647), p. 1.

21 Sir Edward Coke, *The First Part of the Institutes* (1639), 129a.

22 John Rastell, *Les Termes de la Ley* (1629 edition), p. 134.

23 John Cowell, *The Interpreter: Or Booke Containing the Signification of Words* (1637 edn), s.v. 'Denizen'.

24 Henry Cockeram, *The English Dictionarie* (1626; 2nd edn).

25 Cowell, *The Interpreter*, s.v. 'Enfranchisement'.

26 Cowell, *The Interpreter*, s.v. 'Villein'.

27 Lilburne, *Innocency and Truth Justified*, p. 67.

28 [Anon], *Englands Birth-Right Justified* ([10 October] 1645), p. 29.

29 Lilburne, *Londons Liberty in Chains*, pp. 52–3.

30 Lilburne, *The Charters of London; or, the Second Part of Londons Liberty in Chaines* ([18 December] 1646), p. 39: reading as in the errata.

31 Wende, '"Liberty" und "property"', pp. 158ff.

32 John Lilburne, *The Juglers Discovered* ([28 September] 1647), p. 12.

33 Lilburne, *The Charters of London*, p. 1.

34 Lilburne, *The Copy of a Letter... to a Freind*, p. 2.

35 Sir Edward Coke, *The Second Part of the Institutes* (1642), p. 56; Lilburne, *Innocency and Truth Justified*, p. 64.

36 Lilburne, *Innocency and Truth Justified*, p. 55.

37 John Lilburne, *The Resolved Mans Resolution* ([30 April] 1647), p. 24.

38 Rastell, *Les Termes de la Ley*, s.v. 'Disabilitie'.

39 Cowell, *The Interpreter*; Rastell, *Les Termes de la Ley*: s.v. terms cited.

40 Lilburne, *The Copy of a Letter... to a Freind*, p. 2.
41 Lilburne, *Innocency and Truth Justified*, p. 16.
42 Lilburne, *Innocency and Truth Justified*, p. 67.
43 Lilburne, *Londons Liberty in Chains*, pp. 71–2.
44 Lilburne, *An Anatomy of the Lords Tyranny* ([6 November] 1646), title page.
45 Lilburne, *The Charters of London*, p. 1.
46 C. Condren, 'Liberty of office and its defence in seventeenth-century political argument', *History of Political Thought* 18 (1997), 460–82, at pp. 470–2.
47 William Prynne, *The Lyar Confounded* ([15 October] 1645), pp. 12, 22.
48 Sharp, 'John Lilburne's discourse of law', p. 33.
49 C. C. Weston, 'England: ancient constitution and common law', in J. H. Burns and M. Goldie (eds) *The Cambridge History of Political Thought, 1450–1700* (Cambridge, 1991), p. 385.
50 Sacks, 'Parliament, liberty, and the commonweal', pp. 93–101; p. 99 quoted.
51 A. Cromartie, 'The constitutionalist revolution: the transformation of political culture in early Stuart England', *Past and Present* 163 (1999), 76–120, at pp. 87–8, 100; G. Burgess, *Absolute Monarchy and the Stuart Constitution* (New Haven: Yale University Press, 1996), pp. 166–71.
52 C. Hill, *Intellectual Origins of the English Revolution Revisited* (Oxford: Clarendon Press, 1997), pp. 224–5; S. White, *Sir Edward Coke and the Grievances of the Commonwealth* (Manchester: Manchester University Press, 1979), p. 226; J. G. A. Pocock, *The Ancient Constitution and the Feudal Law: a Study of English Historical Thought in the Seventeenth Century* (Cambridge: Cambridge University Press, 1957), p. 268; A. Cromartie, *Sir Matthew Hale, 1609–1676: Law, Religion and Natural Philosophy* (Cambridge: Cambridge University Press, 1995), p. 19; J. W. Tubbs, *The Common Law Mind* (Baltimore and London: Johns Hopkins University Press, 2000), pp. 174–5.
53 Burgess, *Absolute Monarchy and the Stuart Constitution*, pp. 200–1; White, *Sir Edward Coke*, pp. 219ff; Cromartie, 'The constitutionalist revolution', pp. 213–16.
54 White, *Sir Edward Coke*, pp. 238–42.
55 Coke, II *Institutes*, p. 47; Sir Edward Coke, *The Third Part of the Institutes* (1644), p. 181. Hill, *Intellectual Origins*, p. 208, citing Wagner's conclusions.
56 Coke, II *Institutes*, p. 47; Wende, '"Liberty" und "Property"', p. 159.
57 Coke, II *Institutes*, p. 63; Cromartie, 'The constitutionalist revolution', pp. 102–3. The quotation from Cicero is given on the title page of Coke, I *Institutes* (1639): 'CICERO. Major haereditas venit unicuiq; nostrum a Jure, & Legibus, quam a Parentibus.'
58 This Coke passage is quoted verbatim in [Anon], *Liberty Vindicated against Slavery* (1646).
59 Coke, II *Institutes*, p. 3. Wende, '"Liberty" und "Property"', p. 159.
60 [Anon], *Liberty Vindicated against Slavery* ([21 August] 1646), p. 1.
61 Coke, II *Institutes*, proem, unpag.
62 Scholars who have suggested that Leveller writers use common law language strategically are G. Burgess, 'Protestant polemic: the Leveller pamphlets', *Parergon* n.s. 11 (1993),

45–67, and G. Burgess, *The Politics of the Ancient Constitution: An Introduction to English Political Thought, 1603–1642* (Basingstoke: Macmillan, 1992), pp. 90–3; Sharp, 'John Lilburne's discourse of law'; Pocock, *The Ancient Constitution and the Feudal Law*, pp. 125–6.

63 For natural law in Leveller writings, see D. Wootton, 'Leveller democracy and the Puritan revolution', in J. H. Burns and M. Goldie (eds) *The Cambridge History of Political Thought, 1450–1700* (Cambridge: Cambridge University Press, 1991), pp. 412–42; I. Hampsher-Monk, 'The political theory of the Levellers: Putney, property and Professor Macpherson', *Political Studies* 24 (1976), 397–422; B. Manning, 'The Levellers and religion', in J. F. McGregor and B. Reay (eds) *Radical Religion in the English Revolution* (Oxford: Oxford University Press, 1984), pp. 65–90; R. Gleissner, 'The Levellers and natural law: the Putney debates of 1647', *Journal of British Studies* 20 (1980–81), 74–89. For historical and legal argumentation in Leveller writings, see R. B. Seaberg 'The Norman Conquest and the common law: the Levellers and the argument from continuity', *Historical Journal* 24 (1981), 791–806, and M. Levy 'Freedom, property and the Levellers', *Western Political Quarterly* 36 (1983), 116–33.

64 *A Remonstrance of Many Thousand Citizens* ([7 July] 1646), p. 3; *An Alarum to the House of Lords* ([31 July] 1646), p. 8.

65 William Walwyn, *Englands Lamentable Slaverie* ([October] 1645), in MMT, pp. 147–8.

66 Pocock, *The Ancient Constitution and the Feudal Law*, pp. 125–7; C. Hill, 'The Norman Yoke', in *Puritanism and Revolution: Studies in Interpretation of the English Revolution of the 17th Century* (London: Secker & Warburg, 1958), pp. 46–111; Q. Skinner, 'History and ideology in the English revolution', *Historical Journal* 8 (1965), 151–78, pp. 161–2 follows this line on the Levellers. J. Greenberg, 'The Confessor's laws and the radical face of the ancient constitution', *English Historical Review* 104 (1989), 611–37, has shown, however, how reverence for the supposed laws of Edward the Confessor was a source of radical versions of history, consistent with denying a complete break at the Conquest. J. P. Sommerville, 'History and theory: the Norman conquest in early Stuart political thought', *Political Studies* 34 (1986), 249–61, has broken down the supposed divide between theoretically minded radicals and historically minded conservatives by arguing that theory often took precedence over history in early Stuart political thought.

67 William Walwyn, *Juries Justified* (1651), in MMT, p. 438.

68 M. Dzelzainis, 'History and ideology: Milton, the Levellers, and the Council of State in 1649', *Huntington Library Quarterly* 68 (2005).

69 John Lilburne, *The Free-Mans Freedome Vindicated* ([16 June] 1646), pp. 3, 7.

70 Lilburne, *The Free-Mans Freedom Vindicated*, p. 10; John Lilburne, 'On the 150th page' in Andrew Sharp, ed., *The English Levellers* (Cambridge: Cambridge University Press, 1998), pp. 3–4.

71 John Lilburne, *The Prisoners Plea for a Habeas Corpus* ([4 April] 1648), unpag.

72 John Lilburne, *The Resolved Mans Resolution* ([30 April] 1647), pp. 19–22.

73 An unqualifiedly positive reference to 'common law' (rather than 'English law'): John Lilburne, *The Lawes Funerall* ([15 May] 1648), p. 9. Both common law and statute appealed to: John Lilburne, *A Defiance to Tyrants* ([28 January] 1648), sig. Av, marginal note; statute superior to common law: John Lilburne, *The Just Mans Justification* ([6 June] 1647), pp. 14–18. John Lilburne, *The Peoples Prerogative* ([17 February] 1648), p. 5 on statute law as granting liberties.

The laws of England and the 'free-born Englishman'

74 *Englands Birth-Right* ([10 October] 1645), p. 3. Weston, 'England: ancient constitution and common law', pp. 379–84; J. R. Greenberg, *The Radical Face of the Ancient Constitution: St Edward's 'Laws' in Early Modern Political Thought* (Cambridge: Cambridge University Press, 2001), pp. 19–32, 226–9; Seaberg 'The Norman Conquest and the common law'.

75 Lilburne, *The Just Mans Justification*, p. 13. Seaberg, 'The Norman Conquest and the common law'.

76 Lilburne, *The Just Mans Justification*, pp. 14–15.

77 John Lilburne, *A Preparative to an Hue and Cry after Sir Arthur Haselrig* ([18 August] 1649), pp. 1–2.

78 Sir Edward Coke, *Le Quart Part des Reportes* (1635), unpag. preface.

79 Coke, I *Institutes*, 97b.

80 Coke, *Le Quart Part des Reportes*, unpag. preface.

81 Sir Edward Coke, *The Third Part of the Institutes* (1644), unpag. proem; I *Institutes* (1639), proem. John Lilburne, *An Impeachment of High Treason*, p. 48.

82 Burgess, *Absolute Monarchy and the Stuart Constitution*, pp. 175–92; Tubbs, *The Common Law Mind*, pp. 154–9, 183–6; Cromartie, 'The constitutionalist revolution', pp. 97–9.

83 Sharp, 'John Lilburne and the Long Parliament's Book of Declarations: a radical's exploitation of the words of authorities', *History of Political Thought* 9 (1988), pp. 19–44, at p. 23; Greenberg, *The Radical Face of the Ancient Constitution*, ch. 5.

84 Robertson, *Religious Foundations of Leveller Democracy*, pp. 61ff. on St German.

85 Cromartie, 'The constitutionalist revolution', pp. 81–2, 86.

86 Tubbs, *The Common Law Mind*, pp. 161–6.

87 Burgess, 'Protestant polemic', pp. 49–59.

88 Lilburne, *The Peoples Prerogative*, p. 5.

89 Lilburne, *Londons Liberty in Chains*, p. 41; John Lilburne, *Rash Oaths Unwarrantable* ([31 May] 1647), p. 28.

90 Lilburne, *The Legall Fundamental Liberties*, p. 54.

91 Lilburne, *The Lawes Funerall*, pp. 4–5.

92 Lilburne, *The Charters of London*, p. 1; Lilburne, *The Juglers Discovered*, p. 5.

93 Lilburne, *The Lawes Funerall*, p. 3.

94 Lilburne, *Rash Oaths Unwarrantable*, p. 28.

95 John Lilburne, *L. Col. John Lilburne his Apologeticall Narration* (Amsterdam, [3 April] 1652), p. 17.

96 Lilburne, *The Just Mans Justification*, p. 16; Lilburne, *The Legall Fundamental Liberties*, p. 22; Lilburne, *Jonahs Cry Out of the Whales Belly* ([26 July] 1647), p. 7; John Lilburne, *To his Honoured Friend, Mr. Cornelius Holland*, reprinted in *An Impeachment of High Treason*, pp. 7, 9; John Lilburne, *A Letter ... to Mr John Price* ([31 March] 1651), p. 12.

97 Lilburne, *The Copy of a Letter... to a Freind*, p. 12.

98 Lilburne, *The Peoples Prerogative*, unpag. proem.

99 John Lilburne, *The Additionall Plea of Lieut. Col. John Lilburne* ([20 October] 1647), p. 24.

100 Lilburne, *The Legall Fundamental Liberties*, in H&D, p. 426; John Lilburne, *As You Were* (Amsterdam, [May] 1652), pp. 14, 13; Lilburne, *A Defiance to Tyrants*, p. 74.

101 John Lilburne, *The Reasons of Lieu Col. Lilbournes Sending his Letter to Mr Prin* ([13 June] 1645), p. 7.

102 Lilburne, *The Peoples Prerogative*, title page.

103 Lilburne, *The Free-mans Freedome Vindicated*, p. 1.

104 Lilburne, *Innocency and Truth Justified*, p. 52. The books are Pym's speech against Strafford, St John's speech for Hampden against ship money, and the judgements of Hutton and Crooks in the ship money case.

105 Lilburne, *Londons Liberty in Chains*, p. 57.

106 M. J. Mendle, 'Putney's pronouns: identity and indemnity in the great debate', in M. Mendle (ed.) *The Putney Debates of 1647* (Cambridge: Cambridge University Press, 2001), p. 125.

107 CP I, pp. 319, 322–3.

108 Wolfe, p. 269 (petition of 18/19 January 1648).

109 Lilburne, *Londons Liberty in Chains*, p. 52.

110 John Wildman, *London's Liberties* ([14 December] 1650).

111 Lilburne, *The Peoples Prerogative*, unpag. proem; *An Impeachment of High Treason*, p. 5; *The Legall Fundamental Liberties*, in H&D, p. 403.

112 A. Hughes, 'Gender and politics in Leveller literature', in S. Amussen and M. Kishlansky, eds., *Political Culture and Cultural Politics in Early Modern England* (Manchester: Manchester University Press, 1995), pp. 162–88.

113 P. Crawford, '"The poorest she": women and citizenship in early modern England', in M. Mendle (ed.) *The Putney Debates of 1647: The Army, the Levellers and the English State* (Cambridge: Cambridge University Press, 2001), pp. 197–218.

114 Richard Overton, *An Appeale from the Degenerate Representative Body the Commons of England Assembled at Westminster: to the Body Represented, the Free People in General* ([17 July] 1647), in Wolfe, p. 178.

115 *An Agreement of the Free People of England* ([1 May] 1649), p. 3.

116 See Macpherson, and the works in response to him, cited above, n. 6; C. Thompson, 'Maximilian Petty and the Putney debate on the franchise', *Past and Present*, 88 (1980), 63–9.

117 Wootton, 'Leveller democracy and the Puritan revolution', pp. 432–3; John Lilburne, *Foundations of Freedom; or an Agreement of the People* ([15 December] 1648), p. 7; Wolfe, p. 342 (Officers' Agreement); *An Agreement of the Free People of England*, p. 3.

118 *The Case of the Armie Truly Stated* (15 October 1647), p. 15. Wootton, 'Leveller democracy and the Puritan revolution', pp. 432–3; and Hughes, 'Gender and politics', both argue for the centrality of household heads to Leveller thinking.

119 J. G. A. Pocock, *The Machiavellian Moment* (Princeton: Princeton University Press, 1975), p. 335.

Chapter 4

Religion, politics, and conscience

In the last chapter we saw how Lilburne's writings created a new conception of citizenship, in the form of the 'free-born Englishman'. Lilburne's writings appealed powerfully to individual readers to consider themselves as free-born Englishmen and to act as such: to stand up for their franchises, liberties, immunities, and privileges as Englishmen, and if necessary to suffer for them as Lilburne himself did. This nexus of ideas was developed through Lilburne's dense, iterative, passionate series of self-publicist writings. But how did these powerfully assertive political ideas relate to the religious thinking of the Leveller movement?

In his early pamphlet *A Worke of the Beast*, Lilburne asserted his identity, claimed his rights, and urged his readers to vindicate their identity through their righteous actions, just as he did in his later political works. Here, however, the identity which Lilburne took upon himself and urged upon his readers was a religious one. He claimed his rights not on the basis of his membership of the nation, but as a member of Christ's kingdom: 'I being one of his [God's] chosen ones, did claim my share and interest [in God's promises to his people]'. Rather than motivating and judging his readers through the ideal of the 'free-born Englishman', he would judge whether someone was 'a faithfull Subject, of Christs Kingdome' (according to whether they refused to take the High Commission oath), and set out what he and his audience must do 'If that we will true Subjects bee, unto our Saviours Law'. The emphasis on the action required of the godly was matched by an emphasis on the need for people to search out the truth for themselves, rather than take anything on trust – a characteristic Lilburnian and Leveller theme. Familiar, again, from his later political writings, is Lilburne's utterly characteristic refusal to accept that his individual action was illegitimate. He agreed that ministers *should* take the lead in the service of God, but refused to accept that it was a sign of 'singularitie and pride, and selfe ends' when a 'private man' such as himself

The Levellers

acted to remedy the cowardice and passivity of ministers. In fact, anyone, of whatever rank, was positively 'bound' to act for Christ. Similar accusations of self-interest, pride, and irresponsible individualism were of course levelled at Lilburne's later, Leveller, writings and actions.[1]

What should we conclude from this striking transplantation of a fully developed set of notions and emphases from the religious to the political sphere? Does it perhaps confirm a common perception that the Levellers' interests shifted fundamentally from an early concern with religion to a more secular agenda? Reading the pamphlet in this way, we might emphasize the apparent incompatibility of an exclusive, elect identity as a subject of God (in Lilburne's strongly separatist, Calvinist theology at the time) with his strongly inclusive, universalising conception of the 'free-born Englishman' as he subsequently developed it. Or, rather than a decisive shift from one world-view to another, should we see a continuity of concerns from religious to political matters, a common thinking which informed both sides of Lilburne's and the Levellers' thought? On this reading, we might see the identities of true Christian and free-born Englishman as mapped onto each other, producing compatible or even identical demands on the individual's conscience.

The relationship between the Levellers' religious and political thought has been much discussed and much disputed. Freedom of conscience in matters of religion was one of the Levellers' earliest and most consistent demands; it was central to the Leveller movement. Indeed, Davis and Russell-Jones have both argued that freedom of conscience was the Levellers' primary concern, and that political and legal accountability were added to the Leveller programme because they were crucial in the defence of religious liberty.[2] Given the early advocacy of freedom of conscience by the future Leveller leaders, the case is chronologically plausible. Certainly there were parliamentarians who valued, and fought for, civil liberties and law largely because they saw them as a fence against ecclesiastical tyranny. Many at the start of the civil war took the view that, as the Protestant church in England was established by law, it was to be defended by defending against any incursion on the law. They interpreted the dubiously legal actions of Charles I's regime, with its prominent churchmen, as undermining the law in preparation for imposing popery on the church. The Levellers might have had such arguments in mind as they tried to conceptualize legal modes of protection not for one uniform Protestant church, but for the more fundamental right of individual freedom of conscience.

The contrary case has also been made – that religious liberty, for the Levellers, was a prerequisite for political liberty.[3] Certainly, some arguments for liberty of conscience, and ones which the Levellers were happy to use, did emphasize the secular benefits of a tolerationist society; Sirluck classified the Levellers as predominantly 'secular' in their tolerationist reasoning, in contrast with more religiously driven tolerationists.[4] In a time of violent religious division across Europe, and wars with religious dimensions waged across the three kingdoms, there was a strong argument that peace itself depended on toleration. Similarly, within a nation, civil peace and the inclusion of all within citizenship – if that was a primary commitment of the Levellers – was dependent on eliminating religious discrimination in the civil sphere.

Clearly the Levellers' religious commitments were as important as their political ones, and in this chapter I will argue that their conceptualization of liberty of conscience as a natural and inalienable right places it in the same framework as the more secular rights which they also defended. This does not make either religious or secular matters logically prior in their thought, although both types of rights are ultimately derived from duties to God. Rather, it raises the question of how closely related the principles of the Levellers' religious and political thought were to each other. Woodhouse influentially claimed that – in spite of a separation between the spheres of nature and grace – democratic principles were imported into politics by analogy from the gathered congregations with which the Levellers were familiar, and that the idea of a religious covenant was translated into the political notion of the Agreement of the People.[5] Robertson, while abandoning Woodhouse's exact mechanisms for this, agreed that congregational experiences, and a sense of spiritual worth in spite of lowliness, influenced the Levellers in their democratic thought – particularly as, unlike Woodhouse, he emphasized the scope in Leveller theology for a belief in general salvation.[6] In the light of modern work, we can comfortably abandon some of the baggage of past scholarship. The attempts which have been made to demonstrate that concepts or devices in Leveller political thought were largely derived from their religious thought and experience now seem, whatever their attractions, rather redundant. There is simply no need to go hunting in covenant theology or congregational practice for Leveller political ideas of equality and 'democracy', or for a prototype of the Agreement of the People. The contractarian and voluntarist elements of parliamentarian political thought, and the extension of natural rights thinking into justification for political action in extreme circumstances by the people themselves, render hypothetical religious sources for such ideas in the Levellers' writings redundant. Parliamentarian thinking, whether tolerationist or not, is a viable source for all the structural elements of Leveller political thought.[7]

It is still worth asking, however, how fully entwined religion and politics were in Leveller thought. If the spheres of nature and grace are conceived of as radically separate, and Leveller tolerationism is seen as reproducing that separation by simply removing any spiritual matters from the purview of the state, then we might expect the principles operative in religion and in politics to be entirely different. Secular politics might still be valued in its own right, even when set against the course of spiritual history which might soon overwhelm it,[8] but there would be no necessary consonance between politics and religion. However, as I have already suggested in the case of Lilburne's language of religion and politics, there do seem to be strong resonances between the two realms in Leveller thought; in Lilburne's case, the parallelism even overrides the obvious disjunction between the elect and the whole body of the nation. The less than Calvinist theology of the other Leveller leaders makes this a less pressing problem, and we will see that while some formal distinction between the realms of nature and grace can be found in Leveller thought, the two realms could often be assimilated through a sense of divine reason and God's purposes in nature. Ultimately, then, it is not surprising that similar principles – such as the adequacy of even ordinary understandings to discern fundamental truths – should apply across religion and politics, although we may still be startled by Walwyn's willingness to list 'freeing a Common wealth from all Tyrants' among the actions which marked out true Christians.[9]

THE LEVELLERS IN RELIGIOUS CONTEXT

The Long Parliament, which fought the civil war, also dismantled the pre-war Church of England. The political uncertainties of war and its aftermath were mirrored by the suspension and fragmentation of religious authority, too. By the time a scheme of settlement had been worked out by the Presbyterian-dominated Westminster Assembly, it already had violent enemies among the Independent congregations and the sects which had flourished, at least in London, in the early years of the civil war.

The Levellers were deeply rooted in this sectarian world. The open flowering of gathered churches and sects was an effect of war, but the roots of this nonconformity reached back to the pre-war years.[10] Calvinist predestinarian theology could encourage the withdrawal, or at least semi-separatism, of those who considered themselves to be the elect and sought to worship within the true, voluntary churches of the saints. Lilburne was committed from the time of his first imprisonment in 1638 to just such a separatist theology; in the 1640s he attended Edmund Rosier's separatist church.[11] Overton signed the confession of faith of a congregation in exile in the Low Countries, probably in the late 1630s or early 1640s; in the 1640s he was associated with Lambe's General Baptist congregation in London.[12] Walwyn used to be seen as a more outwardly conformist man, whose sympathy for the sects came from a disposition to be a 'seeker', rather than from any reluctance to participate in his own parish church.[13] He remained an active member of his own parish church of St James Garlickhythe, and of its vestry, into the early 1640s, but on moving fails to appear in the records of his new parish. Como persuasively suggests that Walwyn's rhetorical stance as a friend but no member of the sects may have masked a more active sectarian allegiance from this point.[14]

All three of the main Leveller authors, then, were immersed in the sectarian world of London, and it is indisputable that the activities and fortunes of the Leveller movement were bound up with their success or failure in rallying these congregations. Many other participants in the Leveller movement were active members of such congregations.[15] The congregations also provided opportunities for the circulation and subscription of petitions, that key Leveller strategy.[16] Nonetheless, although the relationship with the sectarian congregations was fertile, it was also troubled, and eventually it broke down.[17] Perhaps it is even surprising that there was so much support among the sects for a programme which increasingly emphasized the natural laws which should govern political life, alongside the key demand for freedom of conscience: for some sectarians, the things of this world did not deserve such positive and systematic consideration. Indeed, even freedom of conscience could be interpreted in differing ways, and not all who desired some freedom for their own worship would be as willing to grant it to others.

Of course those who separated from the national church had only formed part of the charged religious atmosphere of the 1630s. Others of puritan spirituality waged their battles from within the church, protesting particularly against the 'lordliness' and tyranny of the Laudian bishops. Both Lilburne and Overton became enthusiastic participants in the broader campaign against the prelates and their supposed popery. Lilburne was prosecuted in 1638 for his activities in smuggling Bastwick's anti-episcopal works from the Netherlands. His defiant demeanour and his gift for righteous martyrdom – no doubt influenced by his reading of Foxe's *Book of Martyrs* – were displayed when he underwent his punishment. Subjected to whipping, the pillory, and his first imprisonment, he used the occasion as an opportunity to publicize his message and his plight, both in the pillory (if his own account is to be believed) and in print.[18] Lilburne was released from prison once the Long Parliament met, his case supported by Oliver Cromwell.[19] Overton's earliest signed works in 1642 focussed gleefully on the downfall of the Laudian hierarchy, mocking the Laudian church for its popery.[20] Naturally, a hatred for the Laudian bishops and the activities of Star Chamber and High Commission was shared across the puritan spectrum, and future tolerationists formed only part of this spectrum. It seems likely that these early attitudes to the bishops fed into the Leveller leaders' later political thinking as much as into their religious thinking. Although at the time the anti-Laudians emphasized their loyalty to the king, accusing the bishops of usurping his *jure divino* status, the critique of lordliness and arbitrary power which they developed was politically resonant later in the 1640s.

The movement of ideas in the 1640s was swift, and, freed of effective church or state control, puritan religiosity proved to be extremely fissiparous. While the core of the movement retained its Calvinist severity, at the fringes more open and even mystical strains of religious expression developed. It must be significant that the key leaders and writers of the Leveller movement were drawn towards these anti-predestinarian beliefs, and even towards more seriously heterodox theologies. Walwyn developed an 'antinomian' theology of salvation which emphasized 'free justification by Christ alone' rather than the rigours of the Old Testament Law; in his personal faith antinomian 'free grace' was transformed into a theology of universal salvation.[21] Walwyn emphasized the simplicity of this true religion, and its availability to any intellect; and he drew accusations of atheism and heresy by initiating questing and clearly disconcerting conversations in which he might question the truth of scripture or the doctrine of the Trinity.

Overton, as a General Baptist, believed in free grace, accepted or rejected by individuals. This generous soteriology was accompanied by unorthodox 'mortalist' views which circulated among General Baptists but never became an accepted doctrine.[22] Overton's anonymous tract on *Mans Mortallitie* was published twice, in 1644 and, in a revised edition, in 1655, testifying to the stability of his heretical views over the period of the Leveller movement.[23] The implications of his account were far-reaching: the view of mortalists as 'soul-sleepers' who believed in the death of the soul with the body until Resurrection entirely fails to do justice to his theology here. As Overton explained, he believed that man was 'a Compound wholy mortall', denying 'that common distinction between *Soule and Body*'.[24] Spirit could not be divorced from matter, but was a property which matter could possess in greater or lesser degrees. As McDowell suggests, Overton's position is more fully understood as 'vitalism' rather than mortalism, and his sense that human flesh could become rational and spiritual or, when drained of spirit, beastly and degenerate, explains Overton's oscillation between optimism and despair about human nature.[25] We know little of John Wildman's religious beliefs, and although he attracted accusations of unorthodoxy, these may partly be the common coin of anti-radical discourse in the period. There are hints of Independent connections, but also of a willingness to associate with Catholics, which would be unusual in a puritan milieu. Some of his closest associates – including Henry Marten and Henry Neville – were noted for their apparent irreverence and their distrust of religious enthusiasm, and Burnet saw Wildman as a deist, although such views may have developed later in life.[26]

Lilburne seems at first sight the most orthodox puritan of the Leveller leaders, with an early commitment to Calvinist theology and the separation of the elect. By his death in 1657, however, Lilburne had become a Quaker. The new faith's mystical reliance on the indwelling light was a radical challenge to predestinarian theories of salvation, to the status of the Bible, and even to the necessity of knowledge of Christ.[27] We do not know what theological path Lilburne took in his years of Leveller activity, between his early separatist writings and his conversion to Quakerism in 1655.[28] But the religiosity of his early pamphlets quickly became subsumed in the political concerns of the emerging Leveller movement, and Lilburne's chosen audience was to be all free-born Englishmen, not just the spiritually elect. It is possible that Lilburne's theology had shifted substantially well before he became a Quaker, although some have seen markers of his original theology persisting in his writings until 1647 or even 1649.[29]

However unorthodox the Leveller leaders' theology was, we should be wary of interpreting it as irreligious, radically sceptical, or reductively rationalist. The Levellers' secular thought did not necessarily arise from a secularizing mindset. Walwyn and Overton's heterodoxies remained fully Christian: Walwyn's faith was based around 'that *unum necessarium*, that pearle in the field, free justification by Christ alone', the discovery of which had allowed him to jettison the distractions and anxieties of Calvinist, clergy-dominated orthodoxy; Overton's universe of matter imbued with spirit still found room for the physical location of Christ after his ascension, in the sun.[30] Walwyn's defence of his belief in scripture – admittedly, offered under pressure of criticism – seems more 'fideist' than deist: scripture simply had within it an 'irresistible perswasive power', whose operation was not reducible to human reasoning.[31] Scripture was self-authenticating, and faith was based on a type of revelation in the working of the scripture on the believer, although the age of direct revelation through prophecy was past.[32] For Walwyn, religious truths 'could never have beene perceived by the light of nature and reason' and thus required people to be freely convinced in faith rather than subject to compulsion.[33] Wildman's comments in the Whitehall debates about the limits of the 'light of nature' in matters of religion may similarly have been intended to throw religious matters back onto revelation and faith rather than pure reason, and not to question whether 'there is a God'.[34] Lilburne, who started his career with the zeal of the religious martyr, and ended it as one of the spiritual vanguard in the mystical Quaker movement, cannot have been a sceptic or religious rationalist at any point in his journey.

Spiritual knowledge and the search for salvation could not be reduced simply to human, secular reasoning; but for the Levellers, reason was not merely human and secular. When Woodhouse discussed the relationship between the Levellers' religious and political ideas, he struggled to find a mode of connection between them, in spite of his argument that the Levellers were committed to a disjunction between the spheres of nature and grace, and, hence, of politics and religion. His argument for this 'principle of separation' had many strengths: it could explain why the Levellers excluded the civil magistrate from exercising any restraint or compulsion in matters of religion; it could also enable us to see a separatist like Lilburne as fully committed to the 'saints' in religious terms, while inclusive and egalitarian in political terms; and, in support of more recent revisionist views, it might suggest that the Levellers' religious liberty could be purely instrumental – a means to the achievement of religious truth – even while their political liberty was valued in itself.[35] Of course, the nature–grace divide might also imply the devaluing of the realm of nature in comparison with the spiritual, and the civil war period could provide numerous examples of puritan rhetoric denigrating anything 'worldly', 'fleshly', or 'carnal' in comparison with what was spiritual and of Christ. This is not a language which we find in the Levellers, and it is their positive view of nature which has led people to question Woodhouse's account of the 'principle of separation' between grace and nature.[36]

For the Levellers, 'nature' had higher purposes than merely to keep humans under control while their spiritual salvation or damnation was worked out; in itself, it expressed something of the divine order for the world. What there is of a split between nature and grace for the Levellers – and it has been compellingly argued by Russell-Jones that this separation is needed to make sense of Leveller thought – is a logical distinction rather than a gaping chasm between sinful nature and divine grace.[37] There is a positive divine order – and human potential – embedded in natural law. Perhaps one should make some exception for Lilburne, whose God 'is circumscribed, governed, and limited by no rules, but doth all things meerly and onely by his soveraign will, and unlimited good pleasure', but, in general, Davis is right to argue that the Levellers' God is more law abiding and less arbitrary than the providential God of most puritans.[38]

The question, then, is not so much about the split between nature and grace as about the Leveller conception of nature itself. We have already seen in Chapter 1 that the Levellers displayed an optimism about human reason, arguing that, at least through the reparative work of Christ, it was capable of instituting modes of government which approximated to a prelapsarian ideal of consent and benevolence. The realm of nature, and the human reason with which the divine purposes of nature were discerned, was not corrupted beyond repair by the Fall. Overton, rhapsodizing about reason at the start of his *Appeale*, entered into a striking discussion of the relationship between reason, God, and the world, which might be interpreted as narrowing the gap between the natural and the divine. 'God is not a God of irrationality, and madnesse, or tyranny'; therefore 'neither *Morality* nor *Divinity* amongst *Men* can or may transgresse the limits of *right reason*'. Overton elaborated on this assimilation of the moral and the divine through their shared reasonableness: reason

> is graduall in its *Quantity*, but one in its *Quality*; severall are its *Degrees*, but its *perfection* and fulnesse is *only* in *God*, and its several *Branches* and *Degrees* are only communicable, and derivated from *Him*, as severall *Beames* and *Degrees* of *heat* from the *Body* of the *Sunne*, yet *all heat*; so in *Reason* there are different degrees, as, from *Morality* to *Divinity* ... yet *all one* and the *same* in *nature*, the difference only lying in the degree of the thing.

Religion, politics, and conscience

Like many of Overton's more energetically abstract passages, this is not easy to interpret, but it clearly suggests that morality, the merely natural laws of behaviour which apply to all humankind, is a product of exactly the same reason as (Christian) divinity itself, except in a different degree. Indeed, Overton argues that in 'all our Actions' we are judged by right reason, and by that we are 'justified or condemned'. Is this the language of earthly judgements, or of salvation and damnation? It is hard to tell; perhaps the spheres of nature and of grace really are different in degree rather than in kind. Overton's view here is, of course, an unusual one, and the whole paragraph, with its comparison to the beams of the sun and its near-identification of reason with God, is marked by a rather mystical or perhaps neostoic tone.[39]

We should read these views in the light of Overton's philosophy in *Mans Mortallitie*. There he argued quite explicitly that the concept of a 'soul', as distinct from the body, was unjustified by either scripture or reason. This makes it extremely unlikely that Overton assumed a sharp division between natural and spiritual life. To insist, heretically, on such a total integration of all aspects of humanity that it was not even appropriate to speak of the 'soul' at all, let alone to think that the fates of the soul and the body might be different, was surely to deny the existence of two utterly separate spheres in which spiritual and natural life were lived. Furthermore, Overton provided an explicit discussion of the 'naturall Faculties [which] make [man] in his kind more excellent than the Beasts'. This rationality which grew with the growing person was not the 'soul' in any conventional sense, as it did not even develop until after infancy and did not live on beyond the person. But Overton did not try to rescue a specifically spiritual faculty within human beings. Rationality was left as the highest faculty, characterizing human nature (at least, at its best); both religious and secular truths must, then, be apprehended through human rationality. Indeed, in his section of the *Picture of the Councel of State*, Overton revealed that he had drafted a work 'wherein I endeavoured the probation of a God, a Creation, a State of Innocencie, a Fall, a Resurrection, a Restorer, a Day of Judgment, &c. barely from the consideration of things visible and created'. Human reason did not compete with religion; rather, as Overton's intended title spelt out, God's will was revealed through the world as well as through scripture, with no contradiction between the two.[40]

Walwyn more explicitly contrasted nature and reason with the more spiritual means by which divine truths were known by individuals. Nonetheless, the Holy Spirit did not bypass human rationality but, rather, acted upon it; Walwyn's knowledge of God came not from 'natural argument or reason' but from 'an unexpressible power, that in a forcible manner constraines my understanding'.[41] However, Walwyn attributed a similarly mysterious intrinsic power to the truth itself, whether secular or divine; and both secular and religious knowledge could operate through people's natural faculties: 'Men are not born with the knowledge of this [religious truth] more then of any other thing; it must therefore either be infused by God, or begoten in us by discourse and examination as other things are.'[42]

THE LEVELLER THEORY OF LIBERTY OF CONSCIENCE IN RELIGION

Freedom of religious conscience was a central Leveller concern from the embryonic stages of the movement onwards. Scholars in the first half of the twentieth century, fleshing out a picture of a genuinely 'puritan revolution', did not find this problematic: naturally the greatest advocates of political liberty would also advocate liberty in the religious sphere which had generated the revolutionary spirit in the first place. W. K. Jordan and Ernest Sirluck classified Leveller tolerationists with 'rationalists and sceptics' and 'secular' tolerationists respectively, revealing volumes about their Whiggish assumptions both about the nature of this thought and about its intellectual legacy.[43] However, revisionist scholarship on early modern ideas about liberty of religious conscience has challenged any easy assumptions that early modern toleration might be the forerunner of modern toleration in its motivations and assumptions.

Blair Worden and J. C. Davis agree that the overriding aim of almost all advocates of religious toleration was ultimately religious unity and religious truth.[44] Richard Tuck has argued that thinkers who tended to scepticism might be more, rather than less, likely to think that peace should be ensured by enforced conformity in religion.[45] Ultimately, it was the devout, the committed, the aligned, who had the motivation to urge toleration; the sceptical or lukewarm could live without it. In the phrase 'liberty of conscience', it is conscience rather than liberty which is key for these scholars. This suggests that any comfortable alignment between liberty in politics and in religion should be questioned: liberty in religion was instrumental; it was not an end in itself. Woodhouse's pairing of 'puritanism and liberty' has been energetically debunked.[46]

In the light of all this, it is a brave scholar who argues now that religious liberty and the toleration of diversity were ends in themselves for most mid-seventeenth-century tolerationists. However, John Coffey has argued not the minimal case that religious toleration overspilled its instrumental aims and became an end in itself, but the stronger case that for some radical tolerationists their religion positively required them to be advocates of a 'multi-faith society'. Modelling themselves not on the Old Testament religious nation of Israel but on the teaching of Christ and the early church, they believed that the true church would be an embattled minority without state sanction or the support of the civil magistrate. As Coffey points out, such a view of the church had deep roots in puritan tradition, and this novel belief that it required full toleration – even of non-Christians – therefore emerged not from the (possibly Arminian) fringes of puritan tradition but from its (Calvinist) heart.[47]

Coffey's work thus provides one model of freedom of conscience which makes it more positive and meaningful in its own right than Davis and Worden concede, and more open to the toleration not just of the sincere and reasonably orthodox Protestant conscience but of error, of other Christian churches, and even, possibly, of non-Christian or heretical views. Others besides Coffey have seen the Levellers as rejecting the Old Testament model of a religious polity, in favour of a voluntary church on the New Testament model, and Lilburne spelt out the theory in his early writings.[48] Certainly, too, the Levellers rejected religious coercion on the grounds that it was popish persecution: like Milton, Overton and Lilburne traced a direct line from the Church of Rome to the Church of England, and hence to the new presbyters.[49] Coffey's picture of a tolerationism based on the requirements of true Christianity rings true for the Levellers. There are other angles, too, from which we can rebuild a more positive view of the Levellers' thinking on liberty of conscience. There were elements in Leveller thought which render Worden and Davis's very instrumental accounts of religious liberty less directly applicable to Leveller thinkers than to other advocates of liberty of conscience. Such factors might include Walwyn and Overton's generous views about potentially universal salvation; an antiformalist requirement that true religion not be bounded by conformity to a single set of practices; and the Levellers' greater faith in human rationality, and in divine benignity in the world, than that of their more providentialist fellow puritans.[50]

Leveller arguments for freedom of conscience were not born of a radical scepticism about the existence of religious truth. Much of the Levellers' discourse about religion and liberty of conscience was about the conditions under which religious truth could be discovered, grow, and spread. Persecution militated against the spread of truth, because it was always possible that 'he who is in errour, may be the constrainer of him who is in the truth'.[51] Toleration, on the other hand, allowed the intrinsic power of the truth to act on people's understandings. Truth would triumph, almost mechanically, once ideas were in free circulation.[52] That free circulation was seen at work not in obscurantist sermons by university-educated ministers, but in lay preaching and in personal discussion.[53] In secular as in religious matters, Walwyn valued 'the giving, and hearing, and debating of reason'.[54] The Levellers' faith in the power of truth to make its own way if unobstructed was matched by a faith in people's capacities to grasp the truth, whatever their status or even education. Walwyn pointed out that 'He that bade us try all things, and hold fast that which was good, did suppose that men have faculties and abilities wherewithall to try all things, or else the counsell had beene given in vaine.'[55]

The Levellers

While the existence of truth, and its fundamental power, were at the root of Walwyn's arguments for religious toleration, the scepticism of Montaigne and Charron influenced his belief that knowledge could not be attained with certainty. Even so – assuming that the attribution of *The Compassionate Samaritane* to Walwyn is correct – he wistfully left open the possibility of religious unity's finally being achieved in this world simply through the force of truth:

> All times have produced men of severall wayes, and I beleive no man thinkes there will be an agreement of judgement as longe as this World lasts: If ever there be, in all probability it must proceed from the power and efficacie of Truth, not from constraint.[56]

The impossibility of anyone – persecutor or persecuted – being able to vindicate the absolute truth of their beliefs in this world underpinned Walwyn's tolerationism. As McDowell points out, it was views like these which led the French sceptics towards a pragmatic conformity; Walwyn instead found that their insights led him to 'an optimistic conception of the moral dynamism of uncertainty and the self-sufficiency of grace vouchsafed as reason'.[57]

What was the Levellers' attitude to the differences of judgement which would persist in this world? Were they merely signs of human insufficiency, reflecting the limited scope of human reason to apprehend divine truth? Or did they exemplify a positive freedom and autonomy of judgement which might contribute to the discovery of truth? J. C. Davis has argued that the 'liberty' of 'liberty of conscience' was simply the liberty to submit oneself unconditionally to God: a liberty which was self-denying, a repudiation of 'will' or 'wilfulness'.[58] Yet Leveller and other accounts of freedom of conscience display a far more positive sense of God's purposes in allowing humans to have conscientious disagreement. In spite of God's role as the source of any individual's conscientious understanding, people's consciences were still very meaningfully their own. The phrasing of the *Remonstrance of Many Thousand Citizens* is telling here: conscience determines 'what ... in our owne particular understandings, wee approve to be just'. The first Agreement of the People, in a clause which drew on the wording of the *Remonstrance*, stated that people were bound to obey 'what *our Consciences dictate* to be the mind of God'.[59] The mind of God was inaccessible except through individual consciences; and furthermore, as the army radical John Jubbes put it in his version of an Agreement of the People, God gave 'to every one a various and different Spirit' which was not subject to anyone else's control.[60] Clearly, for some tolerationists in this period, individual conscience was to be protected because that variety of insight was part of God's will for humanity.

The Levellers thus emphasized the importance of everyone, from the lowest to the highest, taking responsibility for their own views. For Walwyn, Romans 14 became a key text enjoining 'liberty of conscience'.[61] He tended to juxtapose verse 23 – 'whatsoever is not of faith is sin' – with verse 5: 'Let every man be fully persuaded in his own mind'. Because conscience cannot be coerced without sin, 'every one of us ought to be fully assured in our owne mindes' on matters of the worship of God.[62] His justification for liberty of conscience was thus deeply religious, but did not require the annihilation of self in the service of God, so much as the strenuous exercise of each person's 'own mind' in trying to apprehend religious truth. *The Power of Love* stressed the point that when the Apostle instructs us to try all things, ''tis your self must do it, you are not to trust to the authority of any man'.[63] *Tolleration Justified* again urged people to 'be their own men, and make use of their own understandings in the search and beleif of things', rather than trust to the vaunted certainties of the London ministers; the people should remember that 'God hath not given them understandings for nothing; the submission of the mind is the most ignoble slavery'.[64] As McDowell points out, the exercise of individual capacities in matters of faith was even more important to Overton than to the other Levellers, as he believed that it was the individual's actions in life which could rob them of the salvation which God offered to all.[65]

The exercise of conscience and judgement was enjoined in political as well as religious matters. Thus impressment was to be outlawed, 'every mans Conscience being to be satisfied in the justness of that cause wherein he hazards his own life, or may destroy an others'.[66] Thomas Prince, responding to slights on his independent stature as a Leveller activist, emphasized that his participation in individual Leveller activities was always dependent on his having been 'convinced, and satisfied in my owne understanding in the justnesse of it'.[67] But the Levellers' emphasis on people's exercise of their own understandings brought in another layer of thought about people's autonomy and self-assertion: people were to make the effort to understand *themselves*. Overton lamented that the people had become 'ignorant of themselves' and lost the capacity to understand 'their own naturall immunities, and strength too, wherewith God by nature hath inriched them'.[68] In Overton, this self-understanding was related to his view of human nature as dependent on the spiritual refinement of the flesh; self-understanding was both a marker and a requirement of this. For the other Levellers, self-understanding might be rather more mundane. Walwyn protested against Henry Robinson's challenge to trial by jury: 'Mr. Robinson is troubled, the plain people should be put upon occasions to understand themselves in any measure.' This self-understanding largely consisted in the people becoming less 'ignorant of the laws of the land'.[69] More generally, Walwyn asserted that the learning of foreign tongues was unnecessary to him, since 'my care is rightly to understand my self in my native language'.[70] These types of self-understanding could line up neatly with the self-understanding which Lilburne required of his audience of free-born Englishmen. For the Levellers, they should also enable people to be

The Levellers

aware of duties towards God and one's fellow citizens, and of the rights which sometimes had to be asserted in order to fulfil those duties.

CHURCH AND STATE IN LEVELLER THOUGHT

The Levellers' mature theory of toleration argued that the civil magistrate had no power over people in matters of religion: civil powers could not set up coercive church structures or enforce attendance, and they could not punish people for peaceable religious expression. The Leveller movement as a whole certainly took a stricter line on the role of the magistrate than did some other tolerationists. In December 1648, at the Whitehall debates, Leveller leaders attempted to secure army agreement for a draft Agreement of the People as a preliminary to action against the king. As Polizzotto has shown, all the debaters were happy to deny the magistrate compulsive power (the power to force people into conformity); what was debated was the magistrate's exercise of restrictive power (the power to restrain people from some types of religion which could be seen as blasphemous, disorderly, or heretical). Independents had a tendency to defend the magistrate's restrictive power, hoping that the civil powers would thus help to throw down false religion.[71] The Levellers denied the magistrate either kind of power, and this was the position they upheld at Whitehall.[72] This strict separation meant that church membership was entirely voluntary, and the Levellers were correspondingly committed to the abolition of tithes, which were a compulsory system of taxation supporting the clergy of the established national church. This, too, put the Levellers at the radical end of the spectrum, and indeed was the only demand the Levellers made which might genuinely be seen as a threat to existing property rights. In keeping with their defensiveness on this point, the Levellers proposed provisions for impropriators to be compensated when an alternative to tithes was put in place.[73]

The Levellers' hardline denial of real religious power to the magistrate is sometimes described as a complete separation of church and state. This, I think, is rather misleading, particularly if it suggests a version of the Lutheran 'two kingdoms' theory. In the separatist tract *Light for the Ignorant*, which Lilburne recommended in his early career as a puritan martyr, the theory of entirely separate 'states' or 'governments' was indeed set out. The author distinguished between three states: the civil state, the true ecclesiastical state (the voluntary congregations of the saints), and the false ecclesiastical state (Rome and its branches, including the coercive national church in England). In *An Answer to Nine Arguments*, Lilburne followed this line in his description of the *'politike Kingdom* or *Body'* of a true church, formed by the *'uniting, joyning* or *combining* of a *company of Beleivers* together amongst themselves' and promising obedience to 'Christ *their only and alone head and King'.*[74] This allegiance did not seem to conflict with obedience to the king in civil matters, and indeed Lilburne protested that he spoke only of God, not of 'temporall state matters, with which I have nothing to doe and say unto'.[75]

A strict view of the 'two kingdoms' theory would seem to imply that there were two legitimate governments, independent of each other, in the temporal and ecclesiastical spheres, both of which could exercise authority over their subjects. This, of course, was not a view restricted to separatists: it was also associated with the anti-tolerationist clericalism of strict Presbyterianism, precisely the enemy against which the Levellers' tolerationist works took aim. It is therefore not surprising to see the Leveller writers criticizing any vision of the role of the ministry which seemed to give them potentially tyrannical power. Indeed, the pretensions of presbyters seemed to follow on directly from the *jure divino* claims of the Laudian bishops. The struggle against the bishops naturally roused puritans' suspicions of the tyranny of the clergy (and indeed, their usurpation on civil matters). When the Parliament seemed to offer a remedy against this tyranny, some were prepared to trust religious control to it, or at least glorified its struggle against the Laudian bishops in ways which did not suggest a great concern to keep the civil magistrate out of religious concerns. The concern with clerical tyranny naturally continued, as the Presbyterian dominance of the Westminster Assembly issued in a modified Presbyterian model for England. Overton's *Certaine Articles*, appended to his *Appeale* in July 1647, asked that tithes should be replaced by (voluntary) contributions for the maintenance of ministers 'for the benefit of the Subject, and his freedome therein, for prevention of the Lordlinesse, in and the Commotions, oppressions and tyrannies, that might happen by the Clergy'.[76] Yet the Levellers chose not to remedy such problems by placing powers of religious government in the civil magistrate, even while they strove to make such magistrates legitimate and accountable.

Did this mean that they had to accept the authority of parallel religious structures? There were ways in which they might have been able to do so while minimizing the danger of a religious tyranny. If membership of churches – national or sectarian – was voluntary, the discipline exercised over members of those churches was less absolute. Davis has pointed to the harsh discipline of some of the separated churches, but Lilburne and the separatist tract he recommended depicted them in ways which mitigated the danger of human arbitrariness.[77] The only absolute ruler in this religious sphere was Christ. The voluntary congregations of the visible church gathered in consenting ways, and congregations regulated not only their members, but also their ministers. *A Light for the Ignorant* emphasized that the true church had far fewer officers than the false, had no national or provincial institutions, and that its officers 'have not onely there authority from the particular congregation, but do originally and naturally arise out of the same'. What was more, those

The Levellers

gathered congregations retained the 'liberty' and 'power' to act autonomously, unlike the unfortunate, coerced subjects of the false ecclesiastical estate.[78] If this was Lilburne's vision too, the government of the true churches might be not only benign, but a striking analogue of benign consensual government in the secular realm.

But this notion of separate but parallel spiritual and civil spheres with their own structures of authority was challenged in Leveller thought, particularly by Walwyn. *The Compassionate Samaritane* launched a specific attack on the clergy's self-interested promotion of a parallel ecclesiastical government alongside the civil government, arguing that 'two Governments in one Common-wealth hath ever been, and will ever prove inconsistent with the peoples safety'. Sirluck interpreted this as expressing an Erastian trust in the control of the civil magistrate over religion, but Walwyn's point was rather different. The tract in fact argued that 'one sort of Government which we call the Civill' either was or might be made sufficient to fulfil all the purposes of government: promoting virtue, restraining vice, and protecting property. Moral government was thus transferred into the civil sphere, but there was no hint that specifically religious control was to be exercised by Parliament.[79] A strikingly similar formulation of the point appears in one of Walwyn's signed tracts against Thomas Edwards. Edwards, says Walwyn, 'must needs know, that, only things naturall and rationall are properly subject unto government'. Things supernatural or divine, by contrast, 'are not liable to any compulsive government'.[80] For Walwyn, all government was, by definition, civil. It was this type of thought which determined the framing of the 'reserve' against the magistrate's power in religion.

From another angle, too, it seems inadequate to see the Leveller position as the advocacy of a complete separation of church and state. In spite of their radical restrictions on the role of the magistrate, the Levellers quite consistently allowed for a national church to be provided for by the state, provided it was not 'compulsive'. The first two Agreements of the People, and the petition of 11 September 1648, allowed for some form of public worship to be provided at the discretion of the Representative; the third Agreement assumed the survival of a national, parochial church without explicitly giving the Representative any role in it.[81] The significance of this Erastian but non-compulsive church in Leveller thought is hard to pin down. It was advocated both by Lilburne, in spite of his separatism, and by Walwyn, in spite of his objection to the application of any form of government to matters of religion. It was acceptable to them both simply because it was to be non-compulsive. For Walwyn that appears to mean that it is not an example of 'government'; for Lilburne it is not an example of the state impinging on church government. Indeed, Lilburne's first contribution to the toleration debate in 1645 accepted '*the Parliaments setting up a S[t]ate-Government for such a Church as they shall thinke fit, to make the generality of the Land members of*.[82] Lilburne in at least one of his early writings admitted that salvation was possible without entering one of the true separate churches, even though separation was God's command;[83] for him a non-compulsive national church government would not be a branch of the false ecclesiastical state characterized, among other things, by its coercion.

In the third Agreement of the People we see a further evolution in the proposed national church: its ministers were to be elected by their congregations, on the same franchise as elections to the Representative.[84] The national church would be knitted into the system of local and national citizenship which applied to the whole nation. Of course, with such a system of election, the church would effectively be congregational. Whether those who chose to be members of it would be subject to censure or discipline within their congregations was not spelt out, although Leveller principles would dictate that on points of conscience this would not be acceptable. If they were subject to discipline on other points of behaviour, the election of ministers should ensure that this power was not exercised in an arbitrary way. With a parish 'electorate' identical to the electors of the Representative, indeed, the nearest body to a general assembly of the national church would be the Representative itself. Walwyn's principle that two competing governments should be avoided finally brought even the non-compulsive oversight of the national church back under the civil power.

It seems, then, that the Levellers' principle of liberty of conscience did not spring from a desire for an absolute separation of religious affairs from the state, although Lilburne's separatist thinking may have contributed to the complete prohibition on the civil magistrate's exercising religious power over any individual. The Levellers' emphasis on restricting the civil magistrate from interference in religion was no doubt also the result of bitter experience in the 1640s as it became clear that Parliament was not going to be the guarantor of religious liberty that some had hoped. In many ways, however, the Levellers' insistence that the magistrate could not exercise certain powers in religion was simply parallel with the other restrictions on the government's power which the Levellers wanted to guarantee. As I will argue below, certain principles ran across the Levellers' attitude to religion and to politics in ways which challenge the revisionist notion that religious liberty was not an analogue of political liberty.

Liberty of conscience was to be provided for in order to allow people to seek and achieve their salvation in the realm of grace. It was also treated by the Levellers as a natural, inalienable right. If we look at this right alongside its political analogues – as Leveller writers sometimes did – we may be able to understand more about the structure of such rights and the relationship between religious and political life in Leveller thought.

The Levellers

Freedom of conscience took a prominent place in the Agreements of the People. The first Agreement, in 1647, undoubtedly emanated from an attempt to create an army–civilian alliance and cannot be attributed solely to civilian Leveller creators (see Chapter 5). However, the subsequent history of attempts to settle the nation by such an Agreement, and the wording of the 1647 conscience clause itself, reveal that the treatment of freedom of conscience in the first Agreement was aligned with civilian and Leveller concerns more than with army ones.[85] The Agreements were characterized by the innovative device of specified 'reserves', areas where the civil magistrate was prohibited from exercising any power. In the 1647 Agreement, in Lilburne's *Foundations of Freedom* (his preferred version of the Agreement crafted in late 1648), and in the Levellers' third Agreement, of 1 May 1649, the first area reserved from the power of the magistrate was religion. By contrast, the 'Officers' Agreement' approved by the army for presentation to Parliament in January 1649 removed the issue of religion from the 'reserves' entirely, and discussed it under a separate heading.

The Levellers' concept of reserved powers, most crisply set out in the Agreements but implied in much of their writing, was derived from the natural law tradition used by parliamentarian propagandists. As we saw in Chapter 1, consent theorists preferred to argue that certain powers were reserved from the king in the original contract, rather than to admit that Parliament was reclaiming these powers from the king. Parker stated that in the original contract the people had reserved some things to themselves in Parliament, and some out of Parliament. These things reserved out of Parliament, the ancestors of the Levellers' reserves, are likely to have been the very minimal but crucial rights of individual self-defence. Self-preservation was conventionally seen as the prime law of nature, and self-defence was thus entailed as a duty. With the Levellers' development of this theory into the 'reserves' against the magistrate's power, this duty is just on the cusp of being transformed into a right.

The Levellers' development of this theory seems to have taken liberty of conscience as its prime and test case. Nonetheless, it was presented on its first appearance as being the instantiation of a broader (and perhaps conventional) principle. In *A Helpe to the Right Understanding* in February 1645, Walwyn wrote:

> That the people of a Nation in chusing of a Parliament cannot confer more then that power which was justly in themselves: the plain rule being this: That which a man may not voluntarily binde himselfe to doe, or to forbear to doe, without sinne: That he cannot entrust or refer unto the ordering of any other: Whatsoever (be it Parliament, Generall Councels, or Nationall Assemblies:) ... therefore no man can refer matters of Religion to any others regulation.[86]

This combines the principle of constituent authority (stating that the power which Parliament exercises over people is simply the people's own transferred power) with the requirement to preserve oneself from moral self-destruction through sin.

A strikingly similar pattern of thought turned up in the justification for guaranteeing freedom of conscience in the *Remonstrance of Many Thousand Citizens* in 1646, the wording of which was echoed in the first Agreement of the People in 1647. Walwyn's words in 1645 prefigured the *Remonstrance* in arguing that the restraint of conscience was not a power which anyone could (rightly) exercise over *themselves*. The *Remonstrance*, addressing Parliament, expounded precisely the same point:

> Yee may propose what Forme yee conceive best, and most available for Information and well-being of the Nation, and may perswade and invite thereunto, but compell, yee cannot justly; for ye have no Power from Us so to doe, nor could you have; for wee could not confer a Power that was not in our selves, there being none of us, that can without wilfull sinne, binde our selves to worship God after any other way, then what (to a tittle,) in our owne particular understandings, wee approve to be just.[87]

The verbal resemblance between this and the first reserve in the first Agreement is striking, although the expression of the argument is more compressed:

> That matters of Religion, and the wayes of Gods Worship, are not at all intrusted by us to any humane power, because therein wee cannot remit or exceed a tittle of what our Consciences dictate to be the mind of God, without wilfull sinne: neverthelesse the publike way of instructing the Nation (so it be not compulsive) is referred to their discretion.[88]

A consistent Leveller argument, perhaps linked by Walwyn's involvement, runs through these three texts.

Was this argument novel? Frank finds Walwyn's *Helpe to the Right Understanding* unoriginal, comparing it with the writings of early seventeenth-century agitators for freedom of conscience and with the more recent writing of Henry Robinson and Roger Williams in the same cause.[89] Thomas Helwys in 1612 did indeed argue that no power but God's could be exercised over the people in divine matters. However, for Helwys it was God, rather than the people, who both gave the king all his earthly power and 'reserved to himself' all power in things not of this earth.[90] Robinson and Williams both argued in quite different tones – Robinson in a mode of pragmatic and pacific empiricism; Williams on a biblical basis, which picked apart any scriptural claims a civil magistrate might use to support the notion that he had spiritual power, but did not discuss the processes by which modern magistrates might be constituted in their power by the people.[91] The linking of liberty of conscience to the theory of popularly constituted political authority is a move which is characteristic of the Levellers.

The argument made by Walwyn is systematic, interesting, and political; it also begs the question. The premise on which it rests is simple: *if* the magistrate has any power over the people, that power must derive from the people. For the Levellers, this was a universal principle, which applied just as much to religious as to secular powers. There was no natural human hierarchy in matters of religion, just as there was no natural human hierarchy in political authority: any authority of one person over another would have to be created by consent, using the original power of the person consenting to be governed. As we saw in Chapter 1, this theory of constituent authority was not universal among parliamentarian theorists; and it was seriously tendentious to apply it to religious authority. For many, it would have been axiomatic that authority in religion was granted by God, not by humans. Designation theory might cater better to this perception, arguing that whatever role human consent played in the selection of magistrates, their powers were given to them directly by God. By stating that any just power held by magistrates must come from the people, the Levellers suggested that, by definition, the magistrate's power was purely civil.

On the Levellers' terms, though, the argument was not that simple, and the mechanism used is suggestive of further links between civil and religious issues. Walwyn's argument was at one level the necessary corollary of the theory of constituent power: people cannot hand over to their governors powers which they do not possess in the first place. But Walwyn and Overton both elaborated on this notion of the people's original power. It was not specified as a collective power inhering in the people as a whole, but very specifically as individuals' power. While other theorists of political consent might argue about whether people in the state of nature were able to execute justice on each other, and while Hobbes gave people in the state of nature complete (and therefore competing) rights over each other, for the Levellers there were no powers over other people in the state of nature.[92] If there had been such powers, the premise that authority depended on consent would have been undermined. The powers which people originally held and could transmit to their governors were powers *over themselves* as individuals. We have already seen in Chapter 2 the language of majesty and sovereignty which Lilburne and Overton applied to individuals in the state of nature, and suggested that this should be seen as a sovereignty over the self as well as over nature.

The logic of reserved powers was also expressed in terms of power over the self, but in this case, these powers were reserved precisely because they could *not* be legitimately exercised even over the self. A person could not bind herself to go against her conscience in matters of religion; she therefore could not transfer to anyone else the power to overrule her conscientious religious decisions. The Leveller theory thus focussed on individual powers, combined with the individual's conscience. I argued earlier in the chapter that conscience, for the Levellers, was a part of each person's particular and different apprehension of God's will, rather than a neutral and instrumental channel for God's communication with humanity. Thus, even though the free exercise of conscience was defined through the individual's lack of power over her own conscience, it could still be framed as one of the things 'reserved by the represented to themselves'.[93] And since a person's conscience could not be ruled by anyone else, the effect was, indeed, that in religious life everyone should determine their own actions, according to their consciences.

What is more, this paradoxical 'reservation' by the people of a power which they did not in fact possess was not just a feature of the reserve on religion. Richard Overton claimed that natural and, consequently, political freedom consisted in a kind of self-ownership (although still one given by God).[94] Because of this natural 'selfe propriety' the only legitimate political power was that voluntarily alienated by individuals to the magistrate; also because of this self-propriety it was impossible for individuals to hand over powers which would threaten their self-preservation. Exactly as in the case of conscience, people could not hand over these powers, precisely because they did not in fact (rightly) have them over themselves: 'for as by nature, no man may abuse, beat, torment, or afflict himselfe; so by nature, no man may give that power to another, seeing he may not doe it himselfe'.[95] In other words, self-ownership actually seems – however illogical it may appear – to *generate* the claim that certain things are not so much inalienable rights as powers which we simply don't have, even over ourselves. Somehow, our most basic and inalienable self-propriety seems to *consist* in not having these powers to give away. In religion, we are forced to own our consciences and not give them away; in politics, we are forced to own our basic physical security and political freedom and not give it away.

The 'reserves' in the Agreements of the People expressed what might be thought of as natural and inalienable rights, but these rights were also duties. They resemble rights in that they are possessed by and claimable by individuals; furthermore, particularly in the case of conscience, they protect a sphere of genuine individuality and selfhood. That assertion of individual rights which in Lilburne's writing was most often articulated in more mundane legal language was here reached by other means. Those rights, however, were also duties to God, reflecting the fact that in religion people were directly subject to the power of God, and in politics they were 'mediately' 'by the hand of nature' ruled by and beholden to God.[96] And yet for the Levellers, this relationship with God inspired not just humility but also, on the human plane, self-assertion. Even Leveller women were able to exploit this. Katherine Chidley, a religious separatist writer who was later to coordinate Leveller women's petitions in Lilburne's cause, was claiming as early as 1641 that an unbelieving husband had no 'authority ... over the conscience if his beleeving wife', in spite of his 'bodily and civill' authority over her.[97] The boldest of the women's petitions claimed the right to petition on the grounds that the women had 'an interest in Christ, equal unto men, as also ... a proportionable share in the Freedoms of this Common-wealth'.[98] Leveller claims for freedom of conscience, and for other rights which could not be alienated to governors, did depend, ultimately, on God's ownership of his human creation. But submission to God enabled, even required, autonomy and self-assertion against the claims of other human beings, even those in authority.

Duties to God and individuals' rights against their governors were mutually reinforcing, and they applied both to politics and to matters of religious conscience. This does not undermine the basic distinction between the spheres of nature and grace: the life of a human society expressing the natural order as given 'mediately' by God was different from the spiritual life of an individual oriented towards eternal salvation. Nor does the discussion of freedom of conscience as a right against the magistrate imply that a secular notion of rights is logically prior to religious freedom in Leveller thought; it simply suggests that inalienable rights may be spiritual as much as civil. In religion, as in political life, individuals had original, natural freedoms and rights; only some of these could be traded away by mechanisms of consent. We might even interpret the Levellers' national but voluntary church as the religious analogue of government by consent. As with the government of the polity, original natural rights are not abrogated by subsequent arrangements, if those arrangements are legitimate; rather, government protects inalienable natural rights by withdrawing from any attempt to exercise power in those areas.

Leveller politics was remarkably inclusive. As we have seen, Lilburne strove to render the 'birthright' of the English law uniform, and to make it into the bearer of uniform political status for all 'free-born Englishmen'. But at the beginning of this chapter we saw Lilburne in his earlier writings calling on God's elect in much the same rallying spirit as we see in his subsequent appeals to his fellow countrymen. How did the particularities of religious allegiance relate to the universal aspirations of Leveller politics?

Walwyn and, to some extent, Overton had a generous soteriology which might minimize this problem, but as we have seen, it is hard to tell whether Lilburne came to share such views during the lifetime of the Leveller movement, and it is certain that much of the Levellers' following in London was drawn from sectarian congregations with more orthodox Calvinist doctrine. The Levellers' advocacy of toleration was one strategy for reconciling the interests of the people of God with the good of the nation as a whole. The Levellers denied that uniformity in religion was necessary for the unity of the state; like some other tolerationists, they preferred to argue that civil peace could be secured only by a broad extension of liberty of conscience.[99] In secular matters, the Levellers held a deep suspicion of political and judicial enclaves embedded within the body politic and in tension with the public good.[100] However, in religion they sought not so much a uniform authority as a uniform lack of authority, which could encompass the differing allegiances of many of the sects, as well as those who were content to remain in a purified national church. They were also prepared to defend the sects against the charge that they were divisive and a threat to the public good. Overton made 'Mr Publike-Good', a member of the Grand Inquest in *The Araignement of Mr Persecution*, a spokesman for the rebuttal of such charges. This gave him the opportunity to stress, as the Leveller authors often did during the first civil war, the contribution of the sects to the war effort, and their supposedly superior commitment to the common good. It was not sectarians, but rather the principle of persecution itself, which threatened the unity of the nation:

> this Fellow, Persecution, diverteth the publique good from the Generality to this or that Sort, to this or that prevailing Faction: so that where, or in what State soever he is Predominate, there is an impossibility of an equall enjoyment of the publique good, but even the better sort, such as stand for the good of others as well as their owne, and have hazarded their lives for the publique good against the common Enemy, as Anabaptists, Brownists &c are by him deprived of the publique liberty ...[101]

At this time, before the war was even over, the sects appeared to the future Leveller leaders as a vanguard acting for the public good as well as for true religion. Perhaps, indeed, when Lilburne appealed to free-born Englishmen there was a similar sense that only a minority would heed the call, at least at first. As we saw in Chapter 2, the search for viable institutional representatives of the political nation could be fraught: hence, in 1647, the attempts by some to transfer that role from Parliament to the army. The sects, perhaps, had played a similar role at some points, as actors for the *true* nation.

Leveller praise for the sects was not to last for ever. Murray Tolmie has argued that a sometimes uncomfortable alliance between the Levellers and sectarian supporters broke down decisively at the time of the regicide.[102] The Levellers' former allies and supporters in the sects wrote some of the most stinging and damaging attacks on the Levellers after this breakdown occurred. Walwyn (if the text is rightly attributed to him) retaliated in his critique of the sectarian churches, *The Vanitie of the present churches*, and a major plank in his attack was precisely the divisiveness and intolerance of these churches; Walwyn and Lilburne both endorsed the argument of the tract.[103] The sects had ceased to contribute to the public good and had fulfilled the anti-tolerationists' predictions that they could cause nothing but division.

Toleration was not a complete solution to the problem of religious allegiance and the public good. While peaceable religious expression was apparently universally protected in Leveller proposals, this was not enough to render people of all religions equal in citizenship. The third Agreement stipulated that no one was to be barred from office on the grounds of religious belief, 'excepting such as maintain the Popes (or other forraign) Supremacy.'[104] While this was framed as a secular complaint, and had not been included as a proviso in other Leveller documents, anti-Catholic attitudes were visible in Lilburne's version of the second Agreement too, where the magistrate was allowed to provide public worship as long as it was not 'expresse Popery'.[105] Nonetheless, the Levellers were prepared to extend toleration much further than were many sectarian colleagues; and often saw persecution, rather than Catholicism, as the root cause of troubles and bloodshed across Europe and in the three kingdoms. Overton's catalogue of the blood shed by persecution across Europe included the Irish rebellion alongside Protestant resistance, with no suggestion that it differed morally:

> What occasioned the *revolt* of the *Germaine Princes*, from the *House* of *Austrea*, of the *Netherlanders* from the King of *Spaine*, the *bloody Massacry* in *France*? And amongst our selves, what occasioned the *rising* of the *Scots*, the *Rebellion* in *Ireland*, and those *bloody divisions* in *England*, but this divelish Spirit of binding the conscience?[106]

Walwyn was circumspect about making such statements in print, but Thomas Edwards and the authors of *Walwins Wiles* both accused him of sympathizing with the political aims of the Irish rebels ('the very same with our cause here', ridding themselves of their oppressors), and Edwards reported him as asking 'why should not they enjoy the liberty of their Consciences?'[107] Durston notes that Walwyn preferred to ignore than to refute that charge in his *Just Defence*.[108] Any argument that most of the Leveller-fomented resistance to the Irish campaign in 1648–49 was inspired by such altruistic motives is surely overly charitable, but Walwyn's reported sympathies here resonate with his tolerationist stance.[109]

The wide, but not untroubled, reach of Leveller tolerationism reflects a mixture of attitudes and motives. The radical tolerationists described by Coffey would happily live alongside Jews, Muslims and Catholics, while potentially maintaining a Calvinist theology of election which might give them little regard even for the religious seriousness of some of their fellow Protestants. On the other hand, some of the Leveller leaders, at least, were more theologically generous, as well as being systematically antiformalist, and their tolerationism may have had more room for a positive spiritual respect for those who did not share their religion. While even Catholics might be extended such respect in some cases – Walwyn's reading of continental Catholic authors is notable – the Catholic Church might also still represent the origin and exemplar of the persecution and clericalism which the Levellers so profoundly rejected.

CONCLUSION

Older views of the Levellers tended to place them either as secularist, rationalist thinkers who were proponents of liberty of conscience for humane reasons and to ensure the functioning of a civil society divorced from religion; or as 'Christian democrats' whose Christianity amounted to little more than the secularized ethical system of 'practical Christianity'. Revisionists challenged such views, emphasizing the primacy of religious motivation in the political struggles of the civil war, and making the Levellers' commitment to liberty of religious conscience a primary and genuinely religiously motivated one, which might leave their political thought as a mere appendix. More recently we have begun to refine our understanding of the Levellers' personal religious views, and we can now better appreciate the aspects of Leveller religion which led some scholars to call them rationalist, but which we can now understand as irreducibly Christian, however unorthodox. This, in turn, enables us to steer a path through some of the old debates about the relationship between Leveller religion and politics. Christian salvation and political life did take place within the different spheres of nature and grace, but Overton, at least, began to identify the divine with reason; and the Leveller authors had a very positive conception of God's purposes operating through nature. Thus the realms of grace and nature could come closer together, both seeking the fulfilment of God's purposes for humankind, in this world and the next.

Those divine purposes for humans included individuals' autonomy in the expression of religious conscience, and in political life whose decisions, of course, were also made in accord with conscience. To fulfil God's purposes, people often had to assert their own rights against others (particularly their own governors), and that was the case in matters both of religion and of secular well-being. This fundamental sense of conscientious action as a duty to God, but also as a vehicle for the expression of rights, was something which the Levellers had in common with the New Model Army. In the next chapter I will examine the development of the army as a political force, and its relationship with the incipient Leveller movement.

NOTES

1 John Lilburne, *A Worke of the Beast* (1638), cited from Lilburne, *The Christian Mans Trial* (1641; E181/7), pp. 4, 13, 31, 16–17, 23.

2 J. C. Davis, 'The Levellers and Christianity', in B. Manning (ed.) *Politics, Religion and the English Civil War* (London: Edward Arnold, 1973), pp. 247–8; I. Russell-Jones, 'The relationship between theology and politics in the writings of John Lilburne, Richard Overton and William Walwyn' (DPhil dissertation, University of Oxford, 1987).

3 B. Manning, 'The Levellers and religion', in J. F. McGregor and B. Reay (ed.) *Radical Religion in the English Revolution* (Oxford: Oxford University Press, 1984), esp. p. 82.

4 E. Sirluck, 'Introduction', in E. Sirluck (ed.) *The Complete Prose Works of John Milton, Vol II: 1643–1648* (New Haven: Yale University Press, 1959), pp. 78ff.

5 Woodhouse, pp. 84–6, 74–6; Vallance has more recently modified the account of covenant in the Agreement, suggesting that this was transmitted to the Levellers through the army: E. Vallance, *Revolutionary England and the National Covenant* (Woodbridge: Boydell and Brewer, 2005), ch. 6.

6. D. B. Robertson, *The Religious Foundations of Leveller Democracy* (New York: Columbia University Press, 1951), p. 15, ch. 2.

7. D. Wootton, 'From rebellion to revolution: the crisis of the winter of 1642–3 and the origins of civil war radicalism', *English Historical Review* 105 (1990), 668.

8. B. J. Gibbons, 'Richard Overton and the secularism of the interregnum radicals', *The Seventeenth Century* 10:1 (1995), 68–70.

9. Manning, 'The Levellers and religion', esp. p. 82; A. L. Morton, 'A still and soft voice', in *The World of the Ranters: Religious Radicalism in the English Revolution* (London: Lawrence & Wishart, 1970), p. 148.

10. D. R. Como, *Blown by the Spirit: Puritanism and the Emergence of an Antinomian Underground in Pre-Civil-War England* (Stanford: Stanford University Press, 2004), pp. 445–56; M. Tolmie, *The Triumph of the Saints: The Separate Churches of London, 1616–1649* (Cambridge: Cambridge University Press, 1977), chs 1–4.

11. Tolmie, *The Triumph of the Saints*, pp. 36–7, 66; [Anon.], *A Light for the Ignorant* (Amsterdam, 1638), pp. 9–13: a tract recommended in John Lilburne, *The Poore Mans Cry* (1639), p. 14, and possibly in *An Answer to Nine Arguments* (1645), p. 29 (although the title is misremembered); Lilburne, *An Answer to Nine Arguments*, pp. 37–8; Lilburne, *Come Out Of Her My People* (1639).

12. Gibbons, 'Richard Overton and the secularism of the interregnum radicals', pp. 64–5; N. McDowell, *The English Radical Imagination: Culture, Religion and Revolution, 1630–1660* (Oxford: Oxford University Press, 2003), p. 52; Tolmie, *The Triumph of the Saints*, pp. 76, 82; D. R. Adams, 'Religion and reason in the thought of Richard Overton, the Leveller' (PhD dissertation, University of Cambridge, 2003).

13. Thomas Edwards, *Gangraena: or A Catalogue And Discovery Of Many Of The Errours, Heresies, Blasphemies And Pernicious Practices Of The Sectaries Of This Time* (1646; Part 1), p. 96.

14. D. R. Como, 'An unattributed pamphlet by William Walwyn: new light on the prehistory of the Leveller movement', *Huntington Library Quarterly* 69:3 (2006), 357–8; MMT, p. 2; Tolmie, *The Triumph of the Saints*, pp. 145–6.

15. See Tolmie, *The Triumph of the Saints*, esp. ch. 7. Among the most prominent individuals in Leveller activities are the separatist bookseller William Larner; Thomas Prince, a parochial Independent; and the separatist Samuel Chidley.

16. Tolmie, *The Triumph of the Saints*, p. 153; I. Gentles, 'London Levellers in the English revolution: the Chidleys and their circle', *Journal of Ecclesiastical History* 29 (1978), 292.

17. Tolmie, *The Triumph of the Saints*, pp. 49, 149–53, 170–2, 176–87.

18. Lilburne, *A Worke of the Beast, The Poore Mans Cry, The Christian Mans Triall* (1641).

19. M. A. Gibb, *John Lilburne the Leveller: A Christian Democrat* (London: Lindsay Drummond, 1947), p. 77.

20. Richard Overton, *Articles of High Treason Exhibited Against Cheap-side Crosse* ([January] 1642); Richard Overton, *New Lambeth Fayre* ([March] 1642).

21. MMT, pp. 395–6; Como, *Blown by the Spirit*, pp. 445–56; Como, 'An unattributed pamphlet', 359–60; McDowell, *The English Radical Imagination*, pp. 75, 82 n. 80.

22. Tolmie, *The Triumph of the Saints*, p. 82; N. T. Burns, *Christian Mortalism from Tyndale to Milton* (Cambridge, Mass.: Harvard University Press, 1972), pp. 126–32.

23 [Overton], *Mans Mortallitie, or a treatise wherein 'tis proved* ([19 January] 1644; E.29/16; unsigned; false Amsterdam imprint); [Overton], *Man Wholly Mortal* (1655; Wing O629A; second edition of *Mans Mortallitie*, signed R.O.). On the attribution of the work to Richard Overton, see P. Zagorin, 'The authorship of *Mans Mortallitie*', in his *The English Revolution: Politics, Events, Ideas* (Aldershot: Ashgate, 1998), pp. 155–9.

24 [Overton], *Mans Mortallitie*, title page.

25 McDowell, *The English Radical Imagination*, pp. 59–60, 65–7.

26 M. P. Ashley, *John Wildman, Plotter and Postmaster. A Study of the English Republican Movement in the Seventeenth Century* (London: Jonathan Cape, 1947), pp. 11–12, regards him as an 'agnostic'; pp. 17, 72 on Catholics. Richard L. Greaves, *ODNB* s.v. 'Wildman', on Independency.

27 T. A. Davies, *The Quakers in English Society, 1655–1725* (New York: Clarendon Press, 2000), pp. 15–17.

28 Gibb, *John Lilburne*, pp. 331–4.

29 W. Lamont, 'Pamphleteering, the Protestant consensus and the English revolution', in R. C. Richardson and G. M. Ridden (eds) *Freedom and the English Revolution: Essays in History and Literature* (Manchester: Manchester University Press, 1986), pp. 83–4; Russell-Jones, 'The relationship between theology and politics', p. 13, sees Lilburne as retaining his Calvinist theology in 1645–47; pp. 236–43 on changes in his theology; N. Carlin, 'The Levellers and the conquest of Ireland in 1649', *Historical Journal* 30:2 (1987), 297, points to Lilburne's support for the reconquest of Ireland in 1649: Lilburne, *An Impeachment of High Treason*, pp. 4, 8.

30 MMT, p. 398; [Overton], *Mans Mortallitie* (1643), p. 33; McDowell, *The English Radical Imagination*, p. 58; Gibbons, 'Richard Overton'; Tolmie, *The Triumph of the Saints*, p. 82.

31 MMT, p. 271; Russell-Jones, 'The relationship between theology and politics', pp. 130–3; 138; L. Mulligan, 'The religious roots of William Walwyn's radicalism', *Journal of Religious History*, 12 (1982), 163–7.

32 McDowell, *The English Radical Imagination*, pp. 84–5.

33 Walwyn, *A Prediction of Mr. Edwards his Conversion*, in MMT, p. 229.

34 CP 2.121.

35 Woodhouse, pp. 84ff. Woodhouse draws the first two of the three conclusions mentioned here.

36 Davis, 'The Levellers and Christianity', p. 227.

37 Adams, 'Religion and reason in the thought of Richard Overton', pp. 236–42 argues that while Lilburne did sometimes assimilate divine and natural law, Overton preserved the distinction fairly consistently; Russell-Jones, 'The relationship between theology and politics' points out that linguistic slippage over 'natural law' and 'divine law' was common, and not restricted to radicals. Manning, 'The Levellers and religion', pp. 78–92.

38 John Lilburne, *The Free-mans Freedom Vindicated* ([16 June] 1646), p. 11; J. C. Davis, 'Religion and the struggle for freedom in the English revolution', *Historical Journal* 35:3 (1992), 527.

39 Richard Overton, *An Appeale from the Degenerate Representative Body the Commons of England Assembled at Westminster: to the Body Represented, the Free People in General* ([17 July] 1647), p. 2.

40 *The Picture of the Councel of State* (1649) [signed by John Lilburne, Thomas Prince, and Richard Overton], p. 28 (H&D p. 216): Overton's intended title was *Gods Word Confirmed by his Works*; Russell-Jones, 'The relationship between theology and politics', pp. 186–93.

41 MMT, p. 271; cf. MMT, p. 178.

42 MMT, p. 238.

43 W. K. Jordan, *The Development of Religious Toleration in England*, 4 vols (London: Allen and Unwin, 1932–56), vol. 4, pp. 180–96; E. Sirluck, 'Introduction', p. 79. 'Secular' indicates that these writers' call for toleration was motivated more by politics than by religion, rather than that they had no religious concerns. Indeed, Jordan and Sirluck share each other's assumptions, Jordan describing the growth of a tolerationist 'lay spirit', and Sirluck discerning in the Levellers and Henry Robinson 'a relativistic attitude towards differences of faith which hints of skepticism'.

44 B. Worden, 'Toleration and the Cromwellian Protectorate', in W. J. Sheils (ed.) *Persecution and Toleration*, (Oxford: Basil Blackwell, 1984), pp. 199–233; Davis, 'Religion and the struggle for freedom'.

45 R. Tuck, 'Scepticism and toleration in the seventeenth century', in S. Mendus (ed.) *Justifying Toleration: Conceptual and Historical Perspectives* (Cambridge: Cambridge University Press, 1988), pp. 21–35.

46 W. Lamont, 'Puritanism, liberty and the Putney debates', in M. Mendle (ed.) *The Putney Debates of 1647: The Army, the Levellers and the English State* (Cambridge: Cambridge University Press, 2001), pp. 241–55.

47 J. Coffey, 'Puritanism and liberty revisited: the case for toleration in the English revolution', *Historical Journal* 41:4 (1998), 961–85.

48 D. Wootton, 'Leveller democracy and the Puritan revolution', in J. H. Burns and M. Goldie (eds) *The Cambridge History of Political Thought 1450–1700* (Cambridge: Cambridge University Press, 1991), p. 439; Lilburne, *An Answer to Nine Arguments*, pp. 37ff.; Lilburne, *Come Out Of Her My People*, p. 27.

49 Richard Overton, *The Araignement of Mr. Persecution* ([8 April] 1645), p. 1; John Lilburne, *A Copie of a Letter, Written by John Lilburne Leut. Collonell. To Mr. William Prinne* ([15 January] 1645), p. 3; cf. John Milton, *Areopagitica*, in E. Sirluck (ed.) *Complete Prose Works of John Milton*, vol. 2, pp. 501–5, 539–41 on the genealogy of licensing of printing; John Milton, 'On the New Forcers of Conscience under the Long Parliament', in J. Carey (ed.) *John Milton, Complete Shorter Poems* (London and New York: Longman, 1981), pp. 293–6; E. Sirluck, 'Introduction', pp. 89–91.

50 Davis, 'Religion and the struggle for freedom', pp. 527–8; Worden, 'Toleration and the Cromwellian Protectorate', pp. 207–8.

51 [Walwyn], *The Compassionate Samaritane*, MMT, p. 104; cf. Overton, *The Araignement of Mr. Persecution*, p. 24.

52 MMT, p. 371 (*The Fountain of Slaunder*), on the power of truth; R. Foxley, '"The wildernesse of tropes and figures": figuring rhetoric in Leveller pamphlets', *The Seventeenth Century* 21:2 (2006), 270–86.

53 Richard Overton, *A Sacred Decretall* ([31 May] 1645), p. 6; Richard Overton, *Divine Observations upon the London Ministers Letter against Toleration* ([24 January] 1646), pp. 11–12.

54 MMT, p. 372 (*The Fountaine of Slaunder*); cf. MMT, pp. 320, 330 (*The Vanitie of the Present Churches*), advocating 'conferences, and mutuall debates, one with another (the best way

for attaining a right understanding)' over 'long set speeches' as means for achieving religious truth. This tract is unsigned, and although Walwyn twice mentioned it approvingly (MMT, p. 21), his authorship is not certain.

55 MMT, p. 108 (*The Compassionate Samaritane*); a similar faith in the capacities of the lowliest for conscientious understanding is expressed in signed works by Walwyn: MMT, pp. 258; 440–1.

56 MMT, p. 116. For the attribution to Walwyn, see Haller, *Tracts on Liberty in the Puritan Revolution, 1638–1647*, 3 vols (New York: Columbia University Press,1934), vol. 1, pp. 123–5; MMT, pp. 97–9; these arguments are plausible but not conclusive.

57 McDowell, *The English Radical Imagination*, p. 83, criticizing Mulligan's account of Walwyn's religion.

58 Davis, 'Religion and the struggle for freedom', pp. 515–19; cf. J. C. Davis, 'Living with the living God: radical religion and the English revolution', in C. Durston and J. Maltby (eds) *Religion in Revolutionary England* (Manchester: Manchester University Press, 2006), pp. 19–41.

59 *A Remonstrance of Many Thousand Citizens* (1646), p. 12; *An Agreement* (1647), p. 4 (my emphasis).

60 [John Jubbes], *Several Proposals for Peace & Freedom, by an Agreement of the People* (1648), p. 8.

61 MMT, p. 211.

62 MMT, p. 225; cf. p. 114.

63 MMT, p. 81. *The Power of Love* is an unsigned tract attributed to Walwyn by Haller, *Tracts on Liberty*, vol. I, p. 123 and MMT on the basis of its characteristic themes.

64 MMT, p. 163.

65 McDowell, *The English Radical Imagination*, pp. 59–60, 65.

66 *An Agreement of the Free People of England* (1 May 1649), p. 5.

67 Thomas Prince, *The Silken Independents Snare Broken* ([20 June] 1649), p. 9.

68 Richard Overton, *A Defiance Against All Arbitrary Usurpations* ([9 September] 1646), p. 2; McDowell, *The English Radical Imagination*, pp. 65–7.

69 MMT, p. 439.

70 MMT, pp. 397–8.

71 E. Sirluck, 'Introduction', p. 67.

72 C. Polizzotto, 'Liberty of conscience and the Whitehall debates of 1648–9', *Journal of Ecclesiastical History* 26 (1975), 69–82.

73 *To the Right Honourable the Commons of England, in Parliament Assembled* (11 September 1648), item 16; John Lilburne, *Foundations of Freedom; or An Agreement of the People* ([15 December] 1648), p. 14; *An Agreement of the Free People of England*, p. 6.

74 Lilburne, *An Answer to Nine Arguments*, p. 24.

75 Lilburne, *A Worke of the Beast*, pp. 15–16; Lilburne, *Come Out Of Her My People*, p. 25: his defence concerns his words in the pillory.

76 Overton, *An Appeale*, p. 37; see also p. 36, where any legislation compelling people to hear the Book of Common Prayer, or 'other Popish Rits, and Ceremonies' is to be

abolished; this article is under the heading 'Articles concerning the Lawes, and corruptions thereof, with other publique Grievances', and makes no mention of the argument that the magistrate should not be involved in religious affairs – popery is the issue here.

77 Coffey, 'Puritanism and liberty revisited', p. 981; Davis, 'Religion and the struggle for freedom', p. 512.

78 Lilburne, *An Answer to Nine Arguments*, p. 24; [Anon.], *A Light for the Ignorant*, pp. 8, 13–16.

79 E. Sirluck, 'Introduction', pp. 85–6; MMT, pp. 107–8.

80 MMT, p. 229: *A Prediction of Master Edwards his Conversion and Recantation*.

81 *An Agreement of the People*, p. 4; *To the Right Honourable the Commons of England, in Parliament Assembled*, item 4; Lilburne, *Foundations of Freedom*, p. 11; *An Agreement of the Free People of England*, p. 6.

82 Lilburne, *A Copie of a Letter, ... To Mr. William Prinne*, p. 7; E. Sirluck, 'Introduction', pp. 89–90.

83 Lilburne, *An Answer to Nine Arguments*, p. 35.

84 *An Agreement of the Free People of England* (1649), p. 6.

85 See my chapter in P. Baker and E. Vernon (eds) *The Agreements of the People, the Levellers and the Constitutional Crisis of the English Revolution* (Basingstoke: Palgrave Macmillan, forthcoming 2012).

86 MMT, p. 136.

87 *A Remonstrance of Many Thousand Citizens* (1646), p. 11.

88 *An Agreement of the People* (1647), p. 4.

89 Frank, p. 48.

90 Thomas Helwys, *A Shorte Declaration of the Mistery of Iniquity* (Amsterdam[?], 1612: STC 13056), p. 41.

91 Henry Robinson, *Liberty of Conscience* (1644); Roger Williams, *The Bloudy Tenent, of Persecution* (1644), e.g. pp. 71, 73.

92 See John Locke, *Two Treatises of Government*, ed. P. Laslett (Cambridge: Cambridge University Press, 1988), pp. 271–3, for the contrasting view that individuals in the state of nature must have the power to punish others for violations of the law of nature. The Levellers simply did not discuss the problem of where the magistrate's power to punish came from if individuals in nature had no such power. All their formulations suggest that the powers exercised by the magistrate were those which people could exercise over themselves; perhaps the notion of self-punishment would not have seemed incoherent to them. A person could not bind herself to go against her conscience in religion; but she might well bind herself to submit to appropriate punishment if she violated the law of nature.

93 *An Agreement of the People*, p. 4.

94 Richard Overton, *An Arrow Against All Tyrants And Tyrany* (1646), p. 3; see above, ch. 2.

95 Overton, *An Arrow*, p. 4.

96 Overton, *An Arrow*, pp. 3–4.

97 Gentles, 'London Levellers in the English revolution', p. 284.

98 'To the Supreme Authority of England, the Commons Assembled in Parliament, the Humble Petition of Divers Well-affected Women' (5 May 1649), in *The Moderate*, 43, Tuesday 1–Tuesday 8 May 1649.

99 E. Sirluck, 'Introduction', pp. 76–92.

100 A. C. Houston, 'A way of settlement: the Levellers, monopolies and the public interest', *History of Political Thought* 14 (1993), 381–420.

101 Overton, *The Araignement of Mr. Persecution*, p. 5.

102 Tolmie, *The Triumph of the Saints*, chs. 7–8.

103 MMT, p. 308.

104 *An Agreement of the Free People of England*, p. 7.

105 Lilburne, *Foundations of Freedom*, p. 11.

106 Overton, *The Araignement of Mr. Persecution*, p. 12.

107 H&D, p. 310; Edwards, *Gangraena*, II, p. 27. It may be significant that Rutherford attributed such views to 'sundry Antinomians': C. Hill, *The World Turned Upside Down: Radical Ideas during the English Revolution* (Harmondsworth: Penguin, 1975), p. 337.

108 C. Durston, '"Let Ireland be quiet": opposition in England to the Cromwellian conquest of Ireland', *History Workshop Journal* 21 (1986), 110.

109 T. C. Pease, *The Leveller Movement Movement* (Gloucester, Mass.: Peter Smith, 1965; originally published in 1916), p. 300; Brailsford, pp. 496–510; Carlin, 'The Levellers and the conquest of Ireland in 1649'.

Chapter 5

Levellers and the army: England's freedom, soldiers' rights

Over the course of the 1640s the parliamentarian coalition fragmented. The Leveller leaders played their parts in that play of faction, and had links, and for a long time backers, among the Independent group. The activities of the Leveller movement were one manifestation of the extension of parliamentarian politics beyond Parliament itself; but from 1647 a much more powerful extra-parliamentary political force mobilized: the New Model Army. Associated from its foundation with the Independent side of the parliamentarian movement, the army now found itself one of the chief obstacles to the newly dominant Presbyterians in their search for a speedy settlement with Charles I.[1] When it came under threat of disbandment, the army resisted the orders of Parliament and pledged with their senior officers that they would not disband until certain conditions – political as well as professional – had been met. The army's overt politicization dated from the spring of 1647, but from that point onwards its history was punctuated by episodes of intervention in politics. In 1647 the army seized the king from Parliament's control and acted as a leader and channel for alternative negotiations with him through the 'Heads of the Proposals', demanded the removal of the hostile 'eleven members' from Parliament, and occupied London to reverse a counter-revolution. In 1648–49 it engineered Pride's Purge and the campaign which resulted in the trial and execution of Charles I. Even beyond the regicide it continued to exert political pressure on the regimes of the interregnum, and could intervene when it, or its leaders, lost patience.

But of course the New Model Army was a complex political organism. The direction and form of its interventions into politics were determined by a complicated mixture of pressures from within the army and decisions by its leaders. This was never more true than in 1647, when the innovation of the 'General Council of the Army' temporarily allowed representation to soldier and officer 'agitators' from each regiment alongside the grandees in the decision making of the army.² This was the context of the famous Putney debates of the autumn, in which civilian spokesmen and officer and soldier agitators debated army policy and constitutional settlement with the general officers of the army. But even after the system of agitators had been dissolved, the body of the army could exert informal influence, and the grandees had to steer but also negotiate with the views which were present within the ranks. During the life of the Leveller movement the views of soldiers and officers were often in contact or in dialogue with Leveller demands, not just – in much-disputed ways – in 1647 before and at the Putney debates, but again on the eve of regicide, including at the Whitehall debates, and again in army mutinies as the Commonwealth regime was establishing itself in 1649. The interplay between Leveller ideas and the thinking of the more radical elements within the army was not always harmonious, and neither army nor Leveller radicalism were monolithic or unchanging. But they were certainly interacting elements in the debates which went on, from 1647 to the regicide and beyond, at the most extreme end of the parliamentarian spectrum. In this chapter I will take up the question of the political character of the New Model Army and look again at the relationship of the army to the Levellers and to Leveller thought. I will start by examining the relationship between civilian/Leveller radicals and the army over the whole period from 1647 to 1649, arguing that the Levellers and army need to be placed within a spectrum of shifting views and alliances at the radical end of the parliamentarian spectrum; I will then look at the ways in which army thought on political action and citizenship could be a platform for Leveller ideas; and finally, I will consider the constitutional thought of the army and the Levellers.

THE RADICAL SPECTRUM: LEVELLERS AND THE ARMY, 1647–49

The Putney debates have formed a pivotal and climactic point in the story of the political unleashing of the army in 1647, ever since their publication by C. H. Firth from the rediscovered Clarke papers in 1891. The New Model Army came under a concerted political attack from the Presbyterians in Parliament in the spring of 1647. Measures for the disbandment of some of Parliament's forces, and the sending of others to Ireland, were transparently skewed by considerations of political expediency rather than a simple response to military and strategic needs.³ The Scots had left, the king was in Parliament's hands, and the Presbyterian majority intended to restore him on their terms rather than the army's. The Presbyterians' fears about the political character of the army were amply borne out when their disbandment proposals were resisted by an organized campaign which explicitly asserted the army's status as a political body rather than as mere hired men, and led to army men seizing the king

The Levellers

and negotiating with him directly. Through the spring and early summer, the majority of the army that chose to resist disbandment and the Irish service developed an impressive unity, with the army's most senior officers making common cause with grievances originally expressed through agitation in the ranks. That concerted resistance was expressed through a *Solemne Engagement* on 5 June 1647,[4] a covenant of the soldiers with their officers not to divide or disband until their grievances were addressed, which gave representation to the soldiery and officers of each regiment alongside the senior officers in the General Council of the Army. The army's *A Declaration or Representation* which followed on 14 June set out the army's broad political aims.[5]

By the time of the famous Putney debates in October and November 1647 that army unity was under threat if not actually shattered. Two documents, the *Case of the Armie truly stated*, and *An Agreement of the People*, were at the heart of the discussion, offering differing, but radical, challenges to the mode and terms of settlement proposed through the army leadership in the 'Heads of the Proposals' offered to the king. Where did these challenges come from? From 1647 onwards, the suspicion has circulated that it was external agents who fomented a distinctive strain of uncontainable radicalism within the army. The 'Levellers' acquired that nickname precisely in the wake of Putney, when the reification of these disturbing influences was most useful to their enemies.[6] These claims of external, civilian, Leveller involvement, however, were multiply convenient: civilian Levellers had an interest in claiming involvement with events in the army and support there for their aims; the grandees had an interest in saying that the threats to army unity were in some way 'external'; Presbyterians and royalists had an even greater interest in raising the spectre of a levelling army. This story of Leveller intrusion is helped along by the fact that, at Putney, the General Council of the Army was joined by civilian guests – Wildman and Petty. Moreover, both the *Case of the Armie* and the *Agreement of the People* were presented in the names not of the original 'agitators' but of the 'new agents', who had appeared in some cavalry regiments by the end of September, in the wake of Leveller literature castigating the backsliding of the original agitators, and who were never officially incorporated into the General Council of the Army.[7] This story, then, bolsters the now traditional association between the Levellers and the Putney debates,[8] but also separates Leveller and army thought rather neatly, leaving the army able to shake off the threat of radicalism after the debates of the General Council of the Army were suspended and the agitators were sent back to their regiments, before the failed mutiny at Ware. Some of the older revisionist work effectively drew on these stories of unwelcome intrusion by civilian radicals in the affairs of the army to argue against the notion that the army had become a hotbed of Leveller radicalism, asserting instead that the Levellers made a rather cynical and opportunist attempt to capitalize on army discontents which were fundamentally professional rather than political, and that this attempt failed.[9]

The roots of the confrontations at the Putney debates, however, lie deeper within the New Model Army's history in 1647 than this story allows. The New Model Army was hardly 'one Lilburne throughout', but it underwent its own processes of politicization and radicalization in 1647, which yielded currents of radical thought within the army which were to be resilient presences over the year leading up to the regicide and beyond.[10] The autonomy of that army thought has been stressed by Kishlansky in his exploration of army ideology, shearing it away from any supposed Leveller roots.[11] More recent revisionist work has built on that by moving away even from the claim that there was significant Leveller input at Putney: if one wave of interpretation rescued the original agitators from Leveller influence, leaving only the 'new agents' contaminated, further waves have swept the new agents, the *Case of the Armie*, and even the *Agreement of the People* beyond the Leveller sphere.[12] Two important insights have emerged from this work. Firstly – while it may not have been the intention of all the 'revisionist' historiography to suggest this – army ideology needs to be looked at on its own terms, and any radical elements in it need not have been intruded from outside. Secondly, especially in more recent work, the army's interaction with civilians has been reinterpreted, giving us a broader sense of the 'radical' end of the Independent political tendency. For some historians, elements of this radical tendency were only on the verge of coalescing into the recognizable movement which would become known as the Levellers, and the process was catalysed by Putney, rather than leading into it.[13] In the light of the petitioning campaign of the spring of 1647, the pre-existing cooperation between the core Leveller leaders, and the growing consistency of concerns and demands in the sequence of joint and individual works associated with the Leveller leaders, this scepticism about the movement seems exaggerated. The reminder that Leveller radicals operated within a larger spectrum of radical parliamentarianism, however, is important, and the relationship between Leveller radicalism, army radicalism, and a broader radical sentiment is examined later in the chapter through the newsbooks of 1648–49.

None of the attempts in the literature to slice a clean line between one set of texts and people and another (whether those are 'Leveller', 'Independent' or 'army') is entirely convincing. Both at the level of written ideas and at the level of personnel, the threads which connect these three groups are too tangled to undo. It is certainly true that relationships between these groups might change, but so too might their thinking at particular points. Thus, when Lilburne was pushing monarchical solutions later in 1647, army radicals might still have been looking back to January's *Regall Tyrannie Discovered* to support their anti-monarchism, whether or not they were aware of Lilburne's changed emphasis. Connections may still run through texts and speeches, in spite of disagreement between individuals on particular issues at particular times. As I will discuss below, ideas about parliamentary reform also ran in unpredictable ways between Leveller writing and documents such as the *Case of the Armie* and the *Agreement of the People* which were produced in or for an army context. For all these reasons – plus of course the problems of patchy evidence – a study of the personal links of Levellers with army men is far from the whole story of the relationship between the Levellers and the army. But it is part of the story, and I will look at some of these links before resuming the story of the Levellers' relationship with the army.

Such civilian–army links were not confined to the lower levels of the army. Indeed, it is clear that the army leadership was in 'cautious dialogue' with Leveller ideas in 1647.[14] Some of those ideas made their way into an easily recognizable list of Leveller demands included in the 'Heads of the Proposals' for the Parliament's future consideration, covering issues such as monopolies, tithes, and legal reform.[15] The inclusion of these ideas was almost certainly the result of personal contacts between civilians and the army leadership in the period of the drafting of the 'Heads'. William Walwyn, John Wildman, and Maximilian Petty all visited army headquarters at this time; Walwyn also visited Cromwell at his house in Drury Lane.[16] The question is what interests they were sent, or invited, to represent there. The designation 'Leveller' was not yet in use. Walwyn had written (anonymously) for Lilburne; he had quite possibly had a hand in the *Remonstrance of Many Thousand Citizens* printed by Overton; he had almost certainly orchestrated the Large Petition and its subsequent petitions in the spring of 1647. It may be that he was more publicly identified with a particular group of City Independents than with an identifiable Leveller movement – though he complained that 'most of the uppermost Independents stood aloof' during the tribulations of the petitioning campaign.[17] Wildman, Petty, and Walwyn were all listed in a cipher key, probably from the autumn of 1647, used by Henry Marten (who was later to employ Petty and Wildman), and the omission of the imprisoned Lilburne and Overton has been remarked on as a sign that they were marginal to this Independent network during 1647.[18] The distance between Walwyn's Independent grouping and the imprisoned Lilburne and Overton at this time should not be exaggerated, however: the Large Petition's second demand – after the removal of any negative voice over the Commons' legislative authority – was justice for any (unnamed, but easily identifiable) commoners unjustly imprisoned by any authority whatsoever; and Lilburne followed the fate of the petitions and their presenters closely, even proprietorially.[19] The 1646 *Remonstrance of Many Thousand Citizens*, printed if not authored by Overton, fed directly into the *Agreement of the People* in 1647 in its wording on the issue of freedom of conscience. That does not prove that 'Levellers' wrote the *Agreement of the People* as an expression of a Leveller programme. But, at the very least, it shows that the Independent alliance, identified by Baker and Vernon as crucial in the generation of the *Agreement*, already had links with Overton in 1646 and was still drawing on ideas from that time in 1647. Whatever their other connections, those who formed the core of the Leveller movement were already a group with personal connections and recognizably consistent demands.

However sympathetic Walwyn's Independent associates seemed to some in the army leadership, divisions did open up between them, echoing the earlier scepticism of Lilburne and Overton about the army leadership. By the time of the Putney debates, Petty was claiming that even when the 'Heads' were being debated he had already dissented from their position on the negative voice of the king and the House of Lords. This view had been strengthened by hearing the views of an emerging 'companie of men that doe stand uppe for the power of the House of Commons', although Petty himself was at the time 'much unknowne to any of them'.[20] If Wildman had been an interlocutor of the army leadership, rather than of the agitators, on his earlier visits to headquarters, he too was speaking for a rather different group by the time of the debates at the end of October.[21] Even Walwyn's relationship with the grandees fell away in the wake of their rejection of his militia proposals, which may have been backed by the agitators; his advocacy of unity in the army was conditional, as he himself explained, on its being unity in the right cause.[22]

Civilian radicals, including Levellers, were thus talking to the army leadership and having some impact; but they were also bringing pressure to bear in ways which were not always welcome, and making links with other constituencies within the army as well. On the army side, the extent to which particular figures active in the politicization of 1647, in the Putney debates, or in mutiny and unrest at Ware and beyond might have been in contact with civilian radicals or influenced by Leveller thought is much disputed. Thomas Rainborough's memorable and passionate speeches at Putney have made him central to the modern legend of Putney; by the time of his death in 1648 he clearly had a similarly totemic contemporary status as a radical figurehead for army men. In revisionist historiography his views and, indeed, character have come under attack, with the implication that his relationship with any political movement must have been unstable at best.[23] Certainly his keen sense of slights to his own honour, and his feud with Cromwell, fed into the passion with which he engaged in some of the political events of 1647, but it would be reductive to suggest that this cancels out or explains his radical views and the appeal they doubtless had for both some soldiers and civilians. He did also have some contacts with civilian radicals. He was included in Marten's cipher key along with Walwyn, Wildman, and Petty.[24] In the midst of the Putney debates he visited Lilburne in the Tower, although whether there was any prior personal acquaintance is unclear, and the uncharacteristically royalist sentiments Rainborough expressed could have been a strategic appeal to Lilburne and his current royalist associates in the Tower.[25] Rainborough continued his contumacious stance at Putney in his actions at Corkbush field, but was reconciled to the senior officers in December. Perhaps unaware of this, Wildman remarked on the army leaders' poor treatment of 'that gallant Patriot *Rainsbrough*' in his *Putney Projects*.[26] Whether or not those who had made common cause with Rainborough at Putney were disappointed in his return to the fold, his future career was still followed with enthusiasm by the radical, army-focussed newsbooks.[27] His funeral, and the calls for vengeance which followed his death at the hands of royalists and which fed into the campaign for justice on Charles I, are a classic case of the exploitation of a radical reputation which ran across army and civilian interests.[28]

Edward Sexby, another passionate if less prolific speaker at Putney, has also attracted historiographical controversy. Sexby was one of the original 'agitators' who emerged in the cavalry regiments, but later was listed among the 'new agents' too, and introduced the civilian visitors, Wildman and Petty, at the Putney debates. However, his assumed centrality to the army agitation has been questioned, as have been his links to civilian Levellers. Difficulties of attribution make Sexby's place in these events even harder to trace: Morrill and Baker have posited Sexby as the author of the *Case of the Armie*; Norris has challenged the attribution of certain agitator documents to Sexby; Mendle has credited him with one of the texts printed on the Hills-Harris Oxford press for the army in 1647.[29] The evidence of the royalist Dyve's letter-book suggests that Lilburne saw Sexby as a figure in the army whose influence might be important if he could be brought to work for some kind of royal settlement, but this is clearly very ambivalent as evidence of genuine Leveller links.[30] In addition, Lilburne had clearly targeted Sexby as a key player, whether or not he knew him personally, and sent him copies of his self-justificatory works, both in print and perhaps in manuscript, which he hoped Sexby would make use of to further his cause in the army.[31] By the time of Putney, then, Sexby was a significant figure in army agitation, and his role among the new agents places him towards the radical edge of army opinion. We know that the agitators did actively manage contacts with civilian radicals in London, but exactly who these civilian contacts were is less clear, and we cannot pin down Sexby as the intermediary.

Similarly, with other army men involved in radical activity or outspoken in the political contexts of 1647 and beyond, simple alignment with 'Leveller' positions is often impossible to determine. Major Alexander Tulidah is a rare example of an army man (although his military background before July 1647 is obscure) who was clearly active both in the civilian radical movement – imprisoned for his support of the Large Petition in March 1647 – and in the politicization of the army, urging a march on London in the General Council of the Army at Reading.³² According to Dyve, John Reynolds and Francis White, as well as Sexby, were picked out by Lilburne as men who could take army opinion with them. Although both men, like Rainborough, made their peace with the grandees in December 1647, Reynolds was involved in renewed army agitation for an Agreement of the People in April 1648, and White continued to express sympathy with some Leveller aims even while justifying his role in the suppression of the Burford mutiny in 1649.³³ William Bray was arrested for his involvement in mutiny in 1647, was one of the few officers to continue backing the Leveller cause in 1649, and was still campaigning for the 'good old cause' in 1659.³⁴ Conversely, civilian Levellers could appropriate and endorse the reputations of army radicals. White was praised as 'a constant man to his promises and principles' in *The second part of Englands New-chaines discovered*.³⁵ William Thompson – a mutineer of dubious repute – was later bailed out of prison by Lilburne, who probably drafted *Englands Freedome, Souldiers Rights* on his behalf.³⁶ Robert Lockyer, like Rainborough a 'martyr' whose funeral became a spectacular demonstration for the radical cause, was linked to the Leveller cause in death. *The Army's Martyr*, in at least one edition, had a letter from Lilburne and Overton to Fairfax protesting at Lockyer's court-martialling attached to it, and emphasized his principled attachment to the army's cause, in spite of the less noble mutiny for which he died.³⁷

None of this solves the question of whether there was a large amount of genuine support for Leveller ideas in the army. Clearly Lilburne and Overton lobbied the army, Lilburne with some sense at least of precisely whom to target. In August he sent his pleas to 'his much honoured friends the Councell of Adjutators'; in July the agitators had already represented to Fairfax 'the sadd Condition of divers persons with whom wee have a fellow feeling', most notably Lilburne.³⁸ Nonetheless, such broad potential alliances did not necessarily lead to active or constant collaborations, and the strands of army and civilian radicalism continued to divide on certain issues. Collaboration clearly also waxed and waned according to circumstance: in April 1648 Overton was wondering whether to forge an alliance with the agents of the soldiers, so any links made in 1647 were perhaps insubstantial or impermanent.³⁹ However, even if direct attempts at collaboration were one sided or limited, aspects of the Levellers' incipient programme and thinking did make some impact on the army. Indeed, the much-quoted reports by contemporaries of the influence of Lilburne in the army seem to be comments on the influence of his writings, rather than personal contacts.⁴⁰

In short, the exact alignments of the radical speakers at the recorded Putney debates in October and November 1647 cannot be precisely pinned down. The politicization of the army had its own internal course and logic, but the agitators also deliberately maintained links with civilian allies (though it is not clear who they were), and certainly showed some regard for the imprisoned Leveller leaders. Lilburne and Overton, for their part, wanted to capitalize on the army unrest, and had some knowledge of key figures in the army agitation to target. Later in the chapter we will see how civilian and army radical thought interacted, without ever merging completely; in Chapter 3 I showed how Lilburne's discourse of the rights of 'free-born Englishmen' gave the radical speakers at Putney the tools to answer Henry Ireton's argument for a limited franchise. These speakers defended aspects of the *Agreement of the People* at length, asserting that the army's more moderate engagements did not need to be adhered to if considerations of the people's safety and well-being outweighed them; supporting the extension of the franchise to all Englishmen, on grounds of natural law, as long as they had not forfeited that 'birthright'; and disputing the wisdom of restoring the king. The radical momentum was retained even in the committees which followed the recorded debates, and only crushed by the swift dispersal of the agitators back to their regiments, and the putting down of attempted mutiny at Ware. The *Agreement of the People* became the badge of that mutiny, and civilian Levellers supported the mutiny.[41] The Agreement itself, as I will show, was a distillation of fundamental principles designed to render civilian and army demands compatible. It may have had army origins, but it was taken up and promoted in an energetic campaign by the civilian radicals who were now named Levellers; and their further 'Agreements of the People' were similarly designed to appeal to army support. The Putney debates and the promotion of the Agreement marked not the end but the beginning of a potentially fertile alliance between civilian Levellers and army radicals.

This reverses the picture painted by the standard revisionist historiography. For historians such as Kishlansky, the period following the Putney debates proved the superficiality and weakness of army–Leveller links in 1647. Once the army grandees decided to close down the discussions of the General Council and its committees, from 8 November, agitators went meekly back to their regiments.[42] Revisionists point to the weakness of the gestures of mutiny at Ware; even historians who accept the seriousness of the mutiny itself also emphasize the 'vociferous loyalty' of the majority who were not involved in the mutiny.[43] Fairfax's *Remonstrance* reunited the rank and file behind the army leadership, and various radical officers accepted the chance to make their peace with the army leadership in December.[44]

Yet, if the Levellers and the army did approach Putney 'from opposite directions', as Kishlansky claims,[45] why did they keep converging for so long afterwards? Gentles finds himself struggling to explain 'the revived radical consciousness within four months of the dramatic reconciliation at headquarters in December 1647'.[46] In April 1648 agitation in the army for a Leveller Agreement of the People was deemed threatening enough for Captain Reynolds to be cashiered for leading it.[47] This was the moment at which Overton revealingly asked the parliamentarian astrologer, William Lilly, 'whether by joining with the Agents of the private soldiery of the Army' he would have success in achieving 'Comon right and freedome' for England.[48] Later in the year the campaign for justice on the king drew on Leveller as well as army support, and the army leadership courted – or at least temporized with – the Leveller leaders, inviting them to the Council of Officers to agree the second Agreement of the People. Once the regicide was accomplished, the Levellers were disowned and the second version of the Agreement was dropped. But Leveller and army dissatisfaction with the new regime again fused, producing the mutinies crushed at Banbury and Burford in May 1649, which have become the conventional terminus of accounts of the Leveller movement. Even after that, a mutiny of Leveller-inspired character broke out again in Oxford in September. Gentles emphasizes the seriousness of the threat to the regime posed by these mutinies: the number of men involved in the three mutinies was over 2,500; the failure of the mutineers to act together rather than in these separate episodes may have been what enabled them to be suppressed relatively easily.[49]

The revisionist story about Putney and its aftermath cannot easily account for these continuing connections. They can, however, be better understood if we reject an excessively simplistic reading of the moments when the army leadership acted, apparently successfully, against radical currents inside and outside the army. It may seem that this relatively successful action by the grandees is an index of the insignificance of the Levellers or of extremists within the army's ranks. However, such moments of conflict should not be read as punctuating an untroubled, relatively conservative grandee hegemony over the army: rather, the times of reduced conflict were often a sign that the grandees had had to move towards the more radical positions espoused by many of those they commanded. At such times, Leveller radicalism might become less visible, because it had been co-opted into a broader stream in which its distinctive features might be lost, in spite of the energy it contributed.

Applying these thoughts to the aftermath of the Putney debates and the Ware mutiny, we may see the apparent reassertion of grandee control over the army, and rejection of outside Leveller influences, in a rather different light. In the spring and summer of 1647, the shared threat from the political Presbyterians produced a radicalism in the army which the grandees eventually allied themselves with, and which opened up possibilities for Leveller alliances too. But by the autumn the army leadership's ability and willingness to negotiate directly with the king had sown suspicion among both army and civilian radicals. After Putney, Charles's flight paved the way for the second civil war, exposing any hope of a benign, army-backed restoration as hollow, and leaving the grandees who had so recently courted him both exposed and humiliated. Unity was restored not so much by the exclusion of external disruption or the evaporation of internal radicalism, but by a partial return of the army leadership to a closer rapprochement with army radicalism after it had been pulled astray by its vain hopes of settlement with Charles.

The new-found willingness of the army leadership to bypass the king made it crucial for it to repudiate the more dangerous and disruptive strands of radicalism, and there was a genuine crackdown. But conversely, its fear of the potential of Leveller radicalism to disrupt the army and political life made it all the more important for it to conciliate potential Leveller support both inside and outside the army. Fairfax's *Remonstrance* uniting the army in the wake of Putney railed against disruptive external influences on the army, but it was deliberately conciliatory towards radical, if not specifically Leveller, constitutional thinking.[50] At the start of 1648 the grandees, as part of the 'middle group', were supporting more fiery radical MPs in the Vote of No Addresses, and Cromwell was making overtures to the republicans Ludlow and Marten; simultaneously, Lilburne was imprisoned (for the first time at the instigation of the Independents), partly for trying to make trouble between Cromwell and Marten with a slanderous story which emphasized the ideological distance between the republican Marten and Cromwell as a recent courter of the King.[51] Cromwell was trying to slice up the radical spectrum one way; Lilburne another.

These polemically different interpretations of the radical spectrum were to shift again over the following year and a half. One way of tracing them from the inside is through the pages of the radical newsbooks the *Moderate* (July 1648–September 1649) and John Harris's shorter-lived *Mercurius Militaris* (October–November 1648, with a revival possibly also by Harris in April–May 1649).[52] The *Moderate* has been read as a 'Leveller' publication and examined for the light it may shed on the nature of the Leveller movement – an enterprise which has led historians to conclude either that the 'Levellers, far from being a unified party with an agreed programme, were a complex, and, in many ways, unhappy alliance of malcontents',[53] or that the *Moderate* itself strayed from its allegiance to the 'party' on certain issues or at certain times.[54] In my reading, the *Moderate*, like *Mercurius Militaris*, most often voiced an army-inflected type of radicalism, rather than one which was straightforwardly 'Leveller' in its preoccupations. But the newsbook also had a compendious character: it included the words of correspondents (presumably army men in most cases) stationed around the country; printed and reprinted petitions, pamphlets and other material, including much associated with the Levellers; and editorialized in its own voice – although the editor or editors are unknown.[55] All of this means that in the *Moderate*, in particular, we may well be able to see some of the subtle negotiations which went on between different strands of radical opinion.

The *Moderate* began publication in July 1648, in the midst of the second civil war. As Underdown explains, by this stage a rift had opened up in the

Levellers and the army

Independent alliance which had, in January, secured the Vote of No Addresses, rejecting negotiation with the king. The defection of most middle-group MPs to line up with the Presbyterians in support of a settlement with the king left the army leadership exposed, stranded between the commitment to a treaty with a king whom they were again about to fight, on the one hand, and the radicalism of their own men, committed to the Vote of No Addresses, on the other.[56] The army leadership's behaviour, whatever its hopes of compromise and of rebuilding the Independent alliance, was from now on, as in early 1647, strongly swayed by the need to keep the army together and, as the year progressed, this resulted in increasing rapprochement with Leveller ideas.

The *Moderate* itself gave space to both Leveller and army figures, with approving comment on both Lilburne and Colonel Rainborough.[57] It also strategically resisted any temptation to push the perspective of such radicals in a way which would undermine Cromwell at a time when he was under concerted political attack from the Presbyterians. Lilburne himself refused to repay his Presbyterian liberators by continuing his own attack on Cromwell or joining Major Huntington's.[58] The *Moderate* similarly rejected such attempts to divide the army leadership from the radical cause. It defended Cromwell from Major Huntington's accusations by referring to 'the privity and consent of the whole Army' in its actions of 1647, a comment which also invoked the power of an earlier period when the grandees had united themselves with the radicalism of the army.[59] Both civilian and army radicals recognized that, with renewed civil war, Presbyterian dominance, and overwhelming hostility to the army itself, they needed Cromwell on their side; but they also hoped that their loyalty would be rewarded. As politics became ever more polarized in the autumn of 1648, it seemed for a while that their hopes were met.

According to Ian Gentles, the 'autumn of 1648 would witness the forging of that alliance so ardently sought by the Levellers in 1647 but thwarted by the army high command'. This was a process in which Cromwell and Ireton themselves played a role, and the signs of it could be read in both Leveller and army documents.[60] The Levellers' petition of 11 September 1648 praised the 'wonderfull victories which God hath blessed the Army withall' and included pay and indemnity for the soldiers in its list of demands.[61] This totemic petition became a checklist of the civilian Levellers' demands, often referred back to, but it also attracted almost immediate army support, and became one focus for an army-based petitioning campaign.[62] The army petitioners read the 11 September petition as a rallying cry against the treaty and for the trial of the king, as much as for its more characteristic Leveller proposals for what should follow.[63] Lilburne implied that the army's *Remonstrance* of 16 November reached its final balance between demands for justice on the king and Leveller proposals (including an Agreement of the People and support for the 11 September petition) only as a result of Leveller intervention.[64] The White-

The Levellers

hall debates on the new draft Agreement of the People again revealed tensions between the Levellers and the army leadership, although Lilburne's Leveller colleagues did not join him in condemning and abandoning the collaboration prematurely. Indeed, junior army officers offered as much opposition to Ireton's position as Lilburne did, and on some of the same issues.[65]

It is hard to read the exact character of radical intentions in the months which led up to the regicide. The Levellers published very little; the army leadership fluctuated in its commitment to settlement by an Agreement of the People, although it displayed some of its commitments in the process of negotiating it. *The Moderate* became a vociferous opponent of any treaty with the king and a great proponent of justice on him, but only once it had printed the Levellers' 11 September petition. It pushed hard for a radical interpretation of the army's November *Remonstrance* and supported Pride's Purge as a matter of 'much necessity, and no lesse Iustice'.[66] This attitude to what Goodwin was to call 'might and right well met' was characteristic of the army-aligned radical politics of the newsbook.[67] Existing law was a product of the Norman Yoke, and constitutional legitimacy was a delusion; 'all the Laws of this Land, and most part of the earth, are Tyrannical and Arbitrary, being made and maintained by the sword'. Even when Magna Carta was seen as a law of freedom rather than condemned as 'Arbitrary', it only supported the appeal to the sword: it had been 'gained by the sword, against the Kings or Tyrants of this Nation'.[68] Even parliaments were covers for Norman power.[69] The *Moderate*'s anti-monarchical and tyrannicidal arguments were rooted in a dismissal of the status quo which valorized the sword and the saints as means to political ends, even as it urged the adoption of an Agreement of the People.[70]

The *Moderate* celebrated the impending regicide with a characteristically aggressive biblicism, quoting Psalm 149: 'Let the High Praises of God be in the Mouth of all his Saints, and a two-edged Sword in their hand, to execute vengeance upon the Heathen ... To binde their Kings with chains'.[71] But the period after the regicide brought wariness and growing alarm. There were some signs of the potential split between constitutionalist and providentialist radicalism: the *Moderate* lamented the Rump's Declaration to maintain the fundamental laws as a continuation of 'the Normand slavery', in stark contrast to the Levellers' assertion (reported in the paper itself) that they 'never fought to destroy the known Laws of the Land' which protected them from the 'Arbitrary Wills of men'.[72] But the *Moderate*'s concern to maintain the radical direction of politics meant that it was distanced from the cheerleading of those whose blandly brutal de facto writings defended the new regime. Under the threat of betrayal of the revolution, less legitimist political thinkers could make common cause with the Levellers' objections against the new regime.

The Leveller leaders had been rather quiet over the period from Whitehall to regicide and on into February 1649. Two key publications during the period before the king's trial indicated something of their fears, and of their attitude to Pride's Purge. *A Plea for Common Right and Freedom*, dated 28 December and signed by a roster of supporters of the 11 September petition, including Lilburne and Overton, and the petition of 19 January 1649, also in the name of the supporters of the 11 September petition, both hinted at the 'extraordinary means' which had been used to purge the House. *A Plea* even referred to it as 'breaking all Authoritie'. Both expressed fear of domination by military power, urging army reform and urgently opposing the enforcement of censorship by the army. And yet both maintained a certain tact and perhaps ambivalence, still hoping that events would turn out well. *A Plea* urged the army to display its 'Affection to the Common wealth, as, being that without which your extraordinary proceedings, in overturning all the visible supream authority of the Nation, can never be justified before God or man'. The authors claimed, at least, that the army might yet prove to be the liberator of the nation. The January petitioners again kept their options open on Pride's Purge: the army had removed 'that major part' which had 'degenerat[ed] from the true Interest of the people', leaving the 'minor part' of whom better could, theoretically, be expected – even if the first signs were not promising.[73]

From this tact – and indeed from the willingness of Wildman, and initially Walwyn, to maintain that quietism into the post-regicide period – we might well suspect that before condemning outright the constitutional ruptures of Pride's Purge and the kangaroo court set up to try Charles I, the Levellers were waiting to see which way the new regime would go. The Agreement of the People was still on the table in a form which would have been preferable to many alternatives: the officers' version was presented to Parliament on 20 January. Had it been adopted, even with a retrospective subscription process, perhaps the Levellers, in spite of their subsequent protests, could have been persuaded that many of their major aims had been met. Indeed, even in *Englands New Chains Discovered*, his condemnation of the new regime, Lilburne conceded that 'those extraordinary courses that have of late bin taken' could never be justified 'unless they end in just liberty, and an equal Government'. He did not explicitly say that he had been waiting to see if they would, but it seems possible.[74]

When Lilburne broke the silence in February with *Englands New Chains Discovered*, speaking for the 11 September petitioners, it was in response to the accumulating signs that the new regime had resolved on reaction, rather than the extension of the revolution. The *Moderate* had graduated from enigmatic hints at such forebodings to documenting these signs too. It had already printed a Leveller petition condemning the exclusion of the anti-trinitarian John Fry from the House of Commons, an incident which formed part of Lilburne's indictment of the new regime.[75] Concern that there might still be some future for the monarchy and the House of Lords was another shared apprehension.[76] But the most interesting focus of both the *Moderate*'s and the Levellers' indignation was the new Council of State. Ian Gentles finds Lilburne's condemnation of the officers' intrusion of such a Council into their version of the Agreement 'irrational', but Lilburne went into print on this point only once the composition and powers of the Rump's Council of State had begun to stir serious concern among radicals.[77] A week before Lilburne presented *Englands New Chains* to Parliament, the *Moderate* had printed the list of the appointees to the Council, commenting pointedly on the inclusion of Lords and those who had opposed or failed to cooperate with the trial of the king.[78] Lilburne's objections to the roster of councillors overlapped with those of the *Moderate*, although they were not identical, Lilburne protesting against the inclusion of army commanders and former Star Chamber judges. Lilburne gestured towards the broader radical objections too, though, reminding the Rump that most of its councillors were 'such as have refused to approve of your Votes and proceedings, concerning the King and Lords': a surprising objection, given that part of his own indictment of the Rump was its creation of the High Court of Justice.[79] The *Moderate* also expressed concern about the Council of State's secrecy and powers in the same week that Lilburne took up the issue in *Englands New Chains*.[80] The *Moderate*'s army-oriented radicalism overlapped with Leveller concerns about the direction of the revolution, even though any Leveller endorsement of the regicide was far more wary and conditional. The paper continued to report on the fortunes of the Levellers and to print their works.

Ian Gentles has suggested that, in the months leading up to the Levellers' third Agreement of the People on 1 May 1649 and the abortive mutinies which followed it, opinion in the higher ranks of the army swung decisively away from the Leveller cause. At Whitehall, officers had been divided; by the time of Burford, the Leveller leaders' rash vituperation of the grandees in print had burnt any bridges.[81] The *Moderate*, while consistently radical, had always been cautious about challenging the army leadership (unlike the short-lived *Mercurius Militaris*, also aimed at an army radical audience).[82] We might thus expect the paper to support Gentles' argument here, but it does not. The paper grew increasingly uneasy about the stirrings of active unrest, with its (army?) correspondents round the country reporting on it with some ambivalence or hostility,[83] and did not endorse the mutinies.[84] But it continued to report on the Leveller leaders themselves with approval, in spite of the character of their writings; and while it cautiously omitted to print the *Agreement of the People*, it dropped heavy hints of its continued support for 'Leveller' doctrines even in the wake of the mutiny's defeat: 'but have a care of that, because its one of the Levellers Tenets'.[85] On the evidence of the *Moderate*, support for the Leveller programme in the army did not wither away in the aftermath of Burford, and some might still be significant supporters who had not thrown themselves into mutiny.

Worden argues that after the defeat of the Levellers, even some who had formerly been associated with them readily abandoned that allegiance in favour of conciliation. In the *Moderate* we do indeed find a striking emphasis on conciliation in this last phase of its existence, but it is not the mainstream conciliation between Independents and Presbyterians which Worden depicts.[86] Rather, while refusing to endorse Leveller violence, the *Moderate* sought to bind together the radical cause, and urged those of the Independent interest in power to win the compliance of radicals by acknowledging the force of their principles – even principles now labelled as 'Leveller'. Rather than simply crushing the Levellers by force, the authorities should 'conquer their Reasons and Understandings';[87] and indeed, the paper continued to follow the fortunes of Lilburne and the other Leveller leaders closely, right up to its demise at around the time of the Oxford mutiny in September 1649, shortly before Lilburne's trial at the Guildhall secured another blaze of publicity for the supposedly extinct cause. Reading these last issues of the *Moderate* does not suggest either an easy and clean suppression of Levelling, or a sudden loss of Leveller influence in the army. The Leveller leaders, and principles identified by the tag 'Leveller', continued to be dear to the army radical interest, which the *Moderate* served well beyond Burford.

CITIZENS AND SOLDIERS IN ARMY AND LEVELLER THOUGHT

One of the revisionist lines of attack on the traditional narrative of the 'Leveller' Putney debates is that Leveller and army interests could never coalesce. On this argument, the Levellers' demands on behalf of the civilian population were incompatible with the maintenance of a standing army and the burdens which went with it. Conversely, the chief engines of the army's politicization were the 'bread and butter' issues of arrears and indemnity – of interest only to soldiers; they did not meaningfully identify themselves with the civilian population.[88] For Kishlansky, 'the army and the Levellers arrived at [Putney] from opposite directions'.[89] However, as we will see, Kishlansky's own observations about the political context of 1647 suggest that the division between soldier and civilian was not so cut and dried. In this section I will discuss the soldiers' understanding of themselves as both army men and Englishmen, arguing that this double identification is the key to much of the radical rhetoric of the army from 1647 onwards, and that it offered significant scope for the adoption of Leveller ideas; and I will examine the civilian Levellers' attitudes to army identity and its relationship to national politics.

The politicization of the army was not just in the service of the soldiers' pay, arrears, and indemnity. It is true that those concerns animated the earliest signs of resistance, but the soldiers' fury was partly sparked by the perception that the attack on them was politically motivated. What is more, their demands for better treatment revolved round a complex sense of their own identity. Ian Gentles has remarked on the army's 'sense of separateness from the rest of society'.[90] Certainly their identity as soldiers and as an army was important, but they were keen to distinguish themselves from other armies as much as from civilians. The 14 June 1647 *Declaration* based the army's right to intervene on the fact that

> we were not a meer mercinary Army, hired to serve any Arbitrary power of a State, but called forth and conjured by the severall Declarations of Parliament, to the defence of our owne and the peoples just Rights and Liberties; and so we tooke up Armes in judgement and conscience to those ends, and have so continued them ...[91]

The claim to conscientious action – the condition Walwyn was to set for legitimate participation in war[92] – meant that their identity as conscientious people was logically prior to their status as an army. They had become an army because of their judgement about what the nation's liberties required. This generated a consistent yoking together of 'our owne and the peoples' interests in the army and agitator texts. This does not, I think, indicate a deep disjunction between the army's own interests and their perception of civilians' interests; rather, the sense is that the soldiers had acquired interests as an army which lay alongside their own, broader interests as Englishmen concerned with their liberties. The army did not have to struggle to identify with the rights of Englishmen: they were their own rights, and it was for those rights that they had fought in the first place.

The army's rights as Englishmen were directly impugned in the 'Declaration of Dislike' which Parliament passed in response to the stirrings of the army petition in March 1647. Those who continued to promote the petition were to be 'looked upon, and proceeded against, as Enemies to the State, and Disturbers of the Public Peace'.[93] Both agitator and official army documents naturally protested against this slight. Thus the 'Second Apologie' asserted that the soldiers had fought 'to free this our Native Land and Nation from all Tyrannie and Opressions whatsoever', and protested that it was 'cordiall freinds' to the army, Parliament, and the nation's liberties who had been branded 'enemies to the State and Kingdome'.[94] According to the army 'Remonstrance' of 23 June, the effect of the 'Declaration of Dislike' had been 'to destroy all just freedome either of Souldiers or Subjects'.[95] By denying to the soldiers the subject's right of petitioning, the 'Declaration of Dislike' played a key part in transforming a demand for the redress of material grievances into an assertion of political rights. For Kishlansky, this brought the army into a coincidental and temporary alignment with the Levellers, whose Large Petition and petitioners were treated with similar contempt, but I would argue that this realization of citizen status did not produce such limited or temporary effects.[96]

Levellers and the army

What was more, the army were facing disbandment. This prompted them to think very urgently about how they could secure indemnity for their actions, and also about their status as soldiers and as citizens, as Kishlansky, again, has argued.[97] In the *Solemne Engagement* of 5 June, the army declared that they needed security:

> that we our selves (when disbanded, and in the condition of private men) or other the free-borne people of *England* (to whom the consequence of our Case doth equally extend) shall not remaine subject to the like oppression, injury or abuse, as in the Premisses hath been attempted and put upon us while an Army by the same men's continuance in the same credit & power.[98]

The army's growing sense of themselves as Englishmen among other Englishmen, whether soldier or civilian, was spurred by the very urgent realization that they would soon lose any special protections they could expect while part of an army. As it was put ten days later in the army's *A Declaration or Representation*, the other 'free-born people of England' would be 'in the same condition with us', at least after army disbandment.[99] So the soldiers would soon be individual civilians themselves; and their ill-treatment even when they had the protection of the army suggested to them that the plight of civilians who were up against the will of the authorities must be hopeless indeed.[100] By the time of the Putney debates themselves, the immediacy of this threat had receded: in the spring of 1647 a standing army of 6,400 men had been proposed by Parliament; by September it was to be of 26,400.[101] In the period of the army's rapid polarization in the weeks before Putney the language of identification with the interests of all Englishmen apparently lost its force for some in the army, leaving the radicals helplessly appealing back to the documents of the early summer, when it had been the common coin of the army's politicization.

The timing and nature of army politicization has been disputed in the historiography, as has the extent to which any underlying political awareness in the ranks before 1647 need be assumed.[102] It is indisputable that the army became politicized in that it resisted the orders of its political masters in a deliberate and concerted fashion, and (even leaving aside the 'Heads of the Proposals') set out minimal conditions of political reform that needed to be met. If, however, even those political reforms were simply a means to an end – the achievement and protection of the soldiers' arrears and indemnity – this politicization may still be seen as shallow.[103] For Kishlansky, the army ideology which developed as a response to material grievances and fears in 1647 and was expressed in official declarations comprised three unifying elements: the belief that all Englishmen had birthrights and liberties; the status of Parliament as the location of civil authority; and the priority of the public good over private interest.[104] These elements, of course, could be unifying because they were broadly conceived. What the birthrights and liberties were which *all* Englishmen had, and which were limited to men of property, was an issue to be hotly debated at Putney; the army could uphold the authority of the institution of Parliament without ruling out the need to purge it, and could differ on how to reform it; these commitments did not even definitively settle the question of whether the king should be restored. Such broad beliefs offered multiple possible alliances, and resonated with aspects of the political language of various groups. The details of the political thought emerging in army circles will be discussed below; here I simply want to note that the broad principles picked out by Kishlansky were powerful ones, and could act as the vehicle for deep, but also contested, politicization. Most importantly, Kishlansky's first and third principles generated the assertion that the army, whether as a corporate body or as individuals, could and indeed must act politically, for the common good, to safeguard their rights as Englishmen.

It is easy to point to the material circumstances which prompted politicization, and to the preponderance of practical demands in early statements from the soldiery as well as the army as a whole.[105] However, the early emergence of demands made for and as subjects, and the army's endorsement of political aims in its official declarations, are also enormously important, perhaps more so for not being Leveller in character. It was from within the army that these modes of thinking emerged, and they formed a basis for the development of a more contested politics within the army, and for possible civilian alliances. Both printed and manuscript documents dating from the emergence of the 'agitators' in April–May declared a determination to vindicate 'the just Rights and liberties of the Subjects' and the 'ends of our taking up Armes' against the 'heavier yoakes or servitude' which may yet be imposed by potential 'Tyrants'.[106] Older scholarship saw such documents as evidence of the importation of political demands into the army by an agitator organization directly influenced by the Levellers; more recent and army-focussed work convincingly points to the lack of signature Leveller demands and rejects the notion of direct Leveller links.[107] Officers, including those to be active as officer-agitators, also expressed eloquently the hope that 'by being Soldiers we have not lost the capacity of Subjects, nor divested ourselves thereby of our Interest in the Common-wealth; that in purchasing the Freedoms of our Brethren, we have not lost our own'.[108] The early agitators set themselves to 'Persuade the Generall Officers not to depart from the Army untill these stormes be overblowne'.[109] They had remarkable success in this goal, and the upshot was the forging of the declarations of the whole army already quoted, in which the soldiers claimed their status as conscientious Englishmen.[110]

By the time of Putney, however, the nature and direction of the army's politicization were sharply contested. Divisions had opened up over immediate political tactics in July, when agitators pressed for the army to march on London. Nonetheless, the 'Heads of the Proposals' offered to the king were accepted for debate by the General Council of the Army without evident rancour.[111] Accusations of backsliding in the army – and on the part of the agitators as well as grandees – were already being made by civilian Levellers, but the discontents were to become more severe following the army's arrival in London; the failure to release Lilburne from prison, as well as the pursuing of a relatively generous settlement with the king, became increasingly unignorable sore points with the civilian radicals.[112] Whether prompted by dissent from inside the army or outside, and whatever the level of authority they may have had, the 'new agents' emerged in and expressed this increasing atmosphere of distrust. At the same time, the army leadership in the wake of the army's reversal of the London counter-revolution seemed to have retreated from the assertion of the army's political identity, issuing documents which returned explicitly to 'the Desires of the Army in relation to themselves as Souldiers'.[113]

For the grandees' critics, inside and outside the army, to allow that rights as soldiers and as commoners could be talked about separately was in itself a retreat from the implicit message of the army's political declarations of the summer. The new agents' *Case of the Armie Truly Stated* took the increasingly voluble radical critique of the army's direction to the army leadership itself. While the document as a whole may have been intended to be constructive, and it was accepted for discussion in spite of the unclear status of the new agents, it did accuse the senior officers of failing to hold to the principles of the army's earlier declarations. Morrill and Baker have argued that the *Case* – except for two 'intruded' sections covering civilian concerns – is focalized from the point of view of the soldiers, 'a document by and for an army'. I do not want to dispute the army genesis of the *Case*'s thought, but the new agents explicitly rejected the 'prioritisation of the army's self-interests' which Morrill and Baker find in the document, if that prioritization was to be at the expense of the claims of the soldiers as citizens.[114] Thus, speaking of the 14 June Declaration, the *Case* says:

> it was declared that they proceeded upon the principles of right and freedome, and upon the law of nature and Nations,: [sic] But the strength of the endeavours of many hath been, and are now, spent to perswade the Soldiers and Agitators, that they stand as Soldiers only to serve the State, and may not as free Commons claime their right and freedome as due to them, as those ends for which they have hazzarded their lives, and that the ground of their refusing to disband, was only the want of Arrears and Indempnitie.[115]

The explicit argument of the *Case* was that the army's engagements had *bound* them to consider themselves as citizens acting for the general good, rather than for their specific interest as soldiers. By refusing to act on the basis of 'the law of nature and nations' which the *Declaration* had appealed to (in a passage which Wildman was to expound again in the debates which ensued), the army 'now strip themselves of the interest of English men'.[116] This argument of the

Case was picked up at Putney by the radical spokesmen, and fed directly into the passion with which they defended the expansion of the franchise.[117]

This was not only the argument of the *Case*. It had no place in the pared-down constitutional proposals of the *Agreement of the People*, but the new agent or Leveller writings analysing the betrayals of the army leadership made much of their alleged reversion to purely army grievances. Overton was already explicitly defending the army council's right to speak 'not only as *Soldiers* for the good and safety of the Army; but as *Commoners*, for the peace, freedome, and liberty of the Kingdome' in August;[118] as time went on, the accusation that the army leadership was going back on this sharpened. The new agents, defending the *Case* against its detractors, declared: 'As for refusing to stand as *Englishmen* for our Nations freedom, and perswading the Souldiers and Agitators, that they stood as Souldiers onely: we suppose such arguings have been too publike at the head Quarters, for any to have the face to denye it.'[119] Wildman picked up the theme in his *Putney Projects* in December, suggesting that the retreat from political commitment had started as early as the end of June, and castigating Cromwell and Ireton's claims 'that it was proper for them to act only in their own spheares, as Soldiers', as an insult to 'our gallant heroick English-men' in the army.[120] Indeed, this was an issue which persisted into a later phase of army activism, with the author of *The Hunting of the Foxes* in 1649 directly citing the *Case* on this issue, and objecting to a judgement that soldiers must not petition: 'while you are souldiers, you (in their account) are no Free-men, neither have an equal right in the Common-wealth with other of your fellow-members therein'.[121]

The *Agreement of the People* itself, a document closely linked to the *Case of the Armie*, took up the question of army–civilian relations in a different but forthright way. The *Agreement* was tendered to 'all the free COMMONS of ENGLAND' for their concurrence through subscription. But it is not drafted in the voice of the whole people; rather, it is drafted in the voice of the well-affected, and refers to the cause's 'Enemies' and to the large number of 'our Country-men' who have opposed it. The authors' or subscribers' 'late labours and hazards' are evidence of their sincere struggle for just freedom.[122] This viewpoint might well be subscribed by well-affected civilians, and clearly was designed to be, but it is more easily read as the voice of the soldiers themselves. That impression is reinforced by the separate letters to the new agents' 'fellow-Commoners' and 'Fellow Souldiers' accompanying the text. The *Agreement*, far from being a social contract of individuals to reconstitute a polity, here appears, rather tellingly, as an agreement *between* the army and the people. The army's motives for seeking 'this Agreement *with* the people' are explained both to the soldiers and to the commoners.[123] The soldiers are urged that for indemnity and security from impressment, they need to seek 'a mutuall Agreement between the people & you'; this Agreement, which will secure the nation's

'Rights and Freedomes' for the benefit of both soldiers and commoners, will then result in 'so firm an union ... between the people and you, that neither any homebred or forraigne Enemies will dare to disturb our happy peace'.[124] Significantly, *A Cal to all the Souldiers* on 29 October supported both the *Case* and the *Agreement*, presenting the *Case* as the paper proposed to solve army issues internally, and then finally urging the soldiers to 'joyne and be one with [the people] in heart and hand, with all possible speede in some substantiall and firme AGREMENT', before moving on to present in a newly titled and paginated section of the pamphlet a message to the army from a civilian perspective.[125] Obviously, this vision of an 'Agreement' *between* the army and the people acknowledges, implicitly, that harmony between army and people is not found but has to be created. This is to be done by establishing 'the certaine Rules of equall Government', which will protect both parties from their 'Oppressors' and enable them to see their interests as conjoint.[126] This was an audacious proposal for a treaty not between king and Parliament – the parties which had fought the civil war – but between army and people. And yet it did not presuppose the maintenance of the army for the future; rather, it was designed to bring the army's and people's interests into a close enough alignment that both soldiers and ex-soldiers would be secured from political malice, alongside their fellow commoners.

Historians have seen powerful inhibitors to a Leveller–army alliance on the Leveller as well as the army side. Morrill argues that the resolution of the army's grievances of pay and indemnity provisions was fundamentally incompatible with Leveller aims to decentralize power; Schwoerer has placed the Levellers in an emerging tradition of hostility to standing armies, which tallies with the view of other historians that the Levellers must have been hostile to the maintenance of the New Model Army as a burdensome standing force in peacetime.[127] In this section I will examine the Levellers' attitude to and relationship to the army, exploring the ways in which the Levellers could conceive positively of the army as a body of conscientious citizens. As we saw in the last section, the coupling of soldier and civilian demands, and the claim to conscientious action, became a crucial feature of the army's declarations, and these aspects were crucial in Leveller appeals to these documents.

The Levellers were naturally well aware of the political importance of the army at a time of Presbyterian dominance in Parliament. Gradually, in the process of abandoning hope for the current House of Commons, Lilburne and Overton began to direct their attention to the army, and to seek the support of the private soldiers against their officers. By the autumn, they were encouraging mutiny. What is less clear is the Levellers' underlying attitude to the army itself and to military issues.

Lilburne himself, of course, had fought for Parliament and attached full political value to that fact: 'I have been in the field with my sword in my hand,

The Levellers

to venter my life and my blood (against Tyrants) for the preservation of my Freedome.'[128] When reporting news to the House of Commons from Fairfax's army in 1645, Lilburne showed full awareness of the fact that the pay and provisioning of the troops was critical to the political cause as well as the war effort: *'the readiest way to make the people yours, is to inable the Souldiers to pay their quarters'*.[129] By 1647, of course, the army's burdens on the people were just as severe, and victory seemed to have rendered them unnecessary. Surely any support the Levellers offered for the New Model Army at this point was the product of political expediency rather than an endorsement of any continuing role for the army?

The lack of support for a standing army in peacetime need not have been a bar to Leveller sympathy with the New Model Army in 1647, as the army and its agitators professed that once their grievances were settled, they would be happy to disband.[130] This was spelt out in the *Case of the Armie* (in a section which has been characterized as voicing military rather than civilian demands) in a way which may well have been acceptable to civilian Levellers. Once the army's demands have been met,

> then the Armes may be disposed into the hands of the faithfull well affected of the Nation, which may be so formed into a military posture, as to be ready on all occasions of service, and as many of the forces that are kept in constant pay, as shall not be absolutely necessary for the preservation and safety of the people, may be as speedily as possible disbanded, that they may not be a burthen to the Nation.[131]

This not only promised disbandment of paid standing forces (admittedly allowing for a judgement about security), but proposed a militia of the well-affected, a suggestion which might tally very well with Leveller attitudes to the army. In a sense, this was simply a return to a pre-war system of local militias, but with a political qualification imposed in the light of the polarized post-war situation. The Levellers, however, might have understood such a proposal in a fuller sense as an expression of conscientious citizenship. Indeed, a similar proposal had already surfaced in the civilian radical movement, and had proved unacceptable (reasonably enough, in the judgement of historians) to the army leadership. Walwyn had been the spokesman of the proposal that the Tower and Southwark be guarded by a citizen militia, a proposal which Fairfax rejected.[132] In the third Agreement of the People, in May 1649, the Levellers proposed that armed forces were to be raised strictly by local divisions, and officered by men elected locally; only the general officers were to be appointed by Parliament.[133] Wildman was to express similar views in more specifically republican terms in the 1650s, opposing 'mercenary' armies in favour of the people being 'masters of their own Arms' and acting for the good of the nation. Strikingly, one of the works in which he advocated these views was written in the name of three colonels in the New Model Army, and in its opposition to 'mercenary' service it cited the army's own *A Declaration or Representation* of 14

June 1647. While in 1653 Wildman did advocate the disbandment of the army, and the 1654 petition of the colonels again protested against a standing army on the grounds that under the Lord Protector it was likely to become mercenary, there evidently was some scope to argue, on the basis of the New Model's own engagements, that it was a force which might be justified through its conscientious status.[34]

However, in 1647, as later, the army's claim to legitimacy through being an army ruled by conscience and fighting on principle was one which would only convince Levellers if certain conditions were met. Just as Lilburne both addressed his readers as freeborn Englishmen and urged them to become worthy of that designation, the Levellers addressed the army as a conscientious army partly as a hortatory strategy. This involved urging upon the army certain interpretations of the commitments they had made. For the Leveller authors, freedom from impressment was a crucial prerequisite for a conscientious army; in documents endorsed by the army and its leadership, freedom from impressment might be a more pragmatic demand restricted to certain contexts.[35] The Levellers put great weight on their own interpretation of the army's *Solemne engagement*, with its provision for the representation of soldier and officer agitators on the General Council of the Army. As Woolrych stresses, the Levellers' view that the agitator system had suspended the traditional command structure of the army was not justified either by the text of the *Solemne engagement* or by the agitators' interpretation of it at the time.[36] But it enabled the Leveller authors to appeal in a stratified way to the lower ranks of the army for action, expressing their fear that it was the army's (senior) officers who were betraying the radical cause, and it meshed with Leveller theories of political representation and the exercise of conscience. According to Lilburne, the army, discharged of its obedience to the political authorities, was now 'dissolved into the originall law of Nature', and in acting for their own safety according to natural law, the soldiers each 'ought freely to have their vote, to chuse the transactors of their affaires', as otherwise they could not be bound by such supposedly collective decisions.[37] Overton defended the full General Council of the Army against a perceived threat that the soldier-agitators would be discontinued, arguing that the army was the 'Body naturall' and the Council the 'Body representative', which needed to maintain 'true representation' rather than shrinking to an officer-only body which 'would become only *Representors of themselves* not of the *Body of the Army*'. This neatly paralleled Overton's thought about the representativeness of the House of Commons as opposed to the House of Lords, who represented only themselves. He also stressed that wisdom was to be found as much in the soldiery as among the officers and protested against their consciences being bound up in 'a blinde ignorant, and implicite faith'.[38] These arguments picked up the army's declarations about the soldiers' right to speak as Englishmen and, as the situation became more polarized, the Levellers started to argue that soldiers should be subject only to the same jurisdiction as any other free-born Englishman, martial law not being applicable, given the supposed dissolution of the army as a hierarchical polity.[139] It also became possible to argue that the General Council of the Army was only one expression of the electoral power of the soldiery, and that they should also choose new officers for themselves.[140] This theme was developed in the crisis of 1648–49 and its aftermath, with Leveller documents expressing concern about whether army officers were sufficiently independent in December 1648, and demanding in the third Agreement of the People that all officers be locally elected.[141] Clearly, these arguments were incitements to, or defences of, mutiny; equally clearly, Leveller thought offered a framework within which these claims could be made as a matter of principle.

To a certain extent these Leveller interpretations meshed with the army's own radical interpretations of its position. The army, however, insisted that there was no incompatibility between speaking as soldiers and as Englishmen; for the Levellers, the latter status appeared to have dissolved the former. Among army men, it was William Thompson – his words almost certainly ghost-written by Lilburne – and the 'new agents' who came closest to taking up the Leveller mode of argument. Even so, the agents defending the *Case of the Armie* argued that they were justified in acting without their officers on the grounds of the parliamentarian arguments cited in the army's *A Declaration or Representation* of 14 June (that authority lay in the office rather than the persons, and therefore that resisting the persons in case of necessity was no resistance of authority). They did not say that army authority had been dissolved and could be remade by the soldiers.[142]

On the face of it, another Leveller line of argument, suggesting that the army remained as the only institution which could lead the English people, given the defection of Parliament, seems to be at odds with the Levellers' desire to dissolve the distinctive structure of the army into a body of free-born Englishmen whose interests were identical with the rest of the (well-affected) population. Overton's *Appeale* was directed 'in especiall' to Fairfax and to the officers and soldiers under his command, although perhaps in its wording it appealed to them as individuals rather than as a corporate army. Nonetheless, Overton argued that with regal and parliamentary power forfeit, the army was the only *'formall and visible Head* that is left unto the people for protection and deliverance'. But the army was not a substitute for the representative body; rather it was the *'naturall Head* of the *Body naturall* of the people at this present', and needed to act, in accordance with its own *Solemne engagement* to defend the good of commoners such as Overton.[143] In appealing to the army, Overton was simply focusing and directing his appeal to the people to that part of the people which was able and had bound itself to give leadership for the good of the whole. If they failed in that duty, they would 'instate the people in a just capacity of *Insurrection* against you', and the chain of appeal really would have reached its final link in the people in general.[44]

From 1647 the army stressed their rights as Englishmen in ways which strongly recalled, and were certainly compatible with, Lilburne's discourse of the citizenship of free-born Englishmen. This gave the army a position from which to intervene politically; and it gave the Levellers a platform for grafting their thought onto army radicalism and trying to steer army radicals towards their own political programmes. The relationship between radical thought in civilian circles and as it developed in the army is not straightforward, but through an examination of constitutional proposals put forward in both civilian and army contexts, we can begin to trace the lines of influence and the potential for alliance.

THE CONSTITUTIONAL THOUGHT OF THE ARMY AND THE LEVELLERS

The Putney debates have become iconic, largely due to the radicals' eloquence in the debate on widening the franchise: according to Rainborough, 'the poorest he that is in England' had the right to consent to his government, 'as well as the richest he'. This demand is profoundly resonant in the light of more recent struggles for the vote, and the twentieth-century triumph of democracy as a global ideal, if not as a universal practice. But it was far from being the most central plank of the emerging Leveller programme – although Lilburne had articulated it and it did draw strength from central Leveller principles – and, as we have seen, the status of the Putney debates as a 'Leveller' event is very doubtful. This raises the question of the relationship between the constitutional thought emerging in army radical circles and that expounded by the civilian Leveller writers. As we will see in this section, in 1647 and beyond, army radical thought was distinctive, but was influenced by and interwoven with Leveller thought as well as the official proposals of the army; both the *Case of the Armie* and the first Agreement of the People contain elements of both.

The removal of the 'negative voice' (the veto power in legislation) of the king and the House of Lords was perhaps the most distinctive and consistent Leveller demand by 1647. This was articulated as the key demand of the Large Petition orchestrated by Walwyn in the spring, and reiterated in the demands appended to Overton's *Appeale* in July; it drew on the theme of the arbitrary power of the king and Lords, which had by 1647 become well established in the writings of the Leveller leaders. Its prominence in the minimalist programme of the Agreement of the People was a clear contribution to the army's debates from the agenda being articulated by civilian radicals including both Walwyn and Overton. Not only that, but the authors of the *Case of the Armie* also endorsed the campaign for the removal of the king's negative voice, and did so on strikingly army-related grounds, suggesting that elements of the Leveller programme could have traction for army radicals precisely on the 'bread and butter' issues which might seem less politicized. According to the authors of the *Case* – and contrary to the opportunist royalist arguments of men such as David Jenkins – indemnity for the parliamentarian soldiers depended on the removal of the king's negative voice.[145] Rather than the king's fiat being the only secure basis for indemnity, the word of a king given 'under restraint' in negotiations with the army was void.[146] The *Case* was taking on the 'Heads of the Proposals' directly: the 'Heads' provided for a parliamentary act of indemnity under a king restored with his veto power intact. The civilian radicals' demand for the removal of the king's negative voice offered a solution to this problem which army radicals were happy to take up.

Annual parliaments were advocated in *Englands Birth-right justified* in 1645, were part of the programme set out in the *Remonstrance of Many Thousand Citizens* in 1646, and had become a relatively consistent Leveller demand. The *Remonstrance* had argued strongly for 'our free choice of a Parliament once every yeer, fresh and fresh for a continuall Parliament', and when parliamentary terms did come under consideration, we might expect the Levellers to bring out that proposal again.[147] Lilburne, in his *Resolved Mans Resolution* and *Rash Oaths Unwarrantable*, again demanded elections 'once every yeare without faile'.[148] However, both the *Case of the Armie* and *An Agreement of the People* demanded only biennial parliaments – as in the army's 'Heads of the Proposals' put to the king. Nonetheless, the pressure of Leveller thought may perhaps be seen in the accompanying letter commending the Agreement to the English people, which did refer to the demand for parliaments every year.[149] Indeed, a demand for fixed-length annual parliaments is also found among army papers in the 'Heads of demaunds to be made to the Parliament' in early May 1647, although the issue was not then debated within the army, and whether the author was a soldier or a civilian is unclear.[150] Even after 1647, demands for biennial as opposed to annual parliaments continued to distinguish some, mostly army, documents from those of the Levellers. The 'New Engagements' related to army radical agitation for an Agreement of the People in the spring of 1648 specified biennial parliaments.[151] The Leveller petition of 11 September 1648 demanded annual parliaments, whereas the 'Officers' Agreement' presented to Parliament in January 1649 wanted biennial ones.[152] It is perhaps a sign of the attempt at Leveller–army conciliation between these dates that the army's 'Remonstrance' of 16 November allowed for parliaments to be either 'Annuall, or Bienniall'; while Lilburne's version of the second Agreement, his *Foundations of Freedom*, did not specify the frequency of parliaments.[153] In their defiant third Agreement the Levellers returned to their insistence on annual parliaments.[154]

Leveller proposals for the frequent succession of parliaments included other details in which we might be able to track some civilian radical influence. The *Remonstrance of Many Thousand Citizens* in 1646 had specified that election meetings should take place 'upon one certaine day in *November* yeerly throughout the Land in the Places accustomed' and that electors should simply turn up, with 'no summons to be expected.' This was followed by the manuscript 'Heads of demaunds', which suggested an annual day of election 'without issuing forth of Writts'; along with the document's insistence on the primacy of 'the peoples Sovereign Power', this confirms Gentles' impression of 'unmistakeable' Leveller influence in a document which was at least targeted at army counsels.[55] In spite of the *Case of the Armie*'s adherence to the army proposal for biennial rather than annual parliaments, it followed the Leveller mechanism, enshrining in its 'law paramount' that 'the people shall of course meet without any warrants or writs once in every two yeares upon an appointed day in their respective Countyes'.[56] The 'Heads of the Proposals', by contrast, intended to use the complex chain of responsibility set out in the 1641 Triennial Act to ensure that writs were issued, allowing spontaneous electoral assemblies only if every other link in the chain were to fail.[57]

The Levellers' developing thought on consent and representation might be thought to have led naturally to an argument for adult (male) suffrage, but for a long time their focus on recalling the existing House of Commons to its trust militated against that. Putting too much emphasis on the very imperfect mechanisms by which the supreme House of Commons was constituted out of the sovereign power inherent in the people would have been impolitic and counter-productive. Some issues of principle over the representativeness of the House were raised in Lilburne's 1646 collaborative pamphlet, *London's Liberty in Chains*. The logic of Lilburne's argument here pushed against the property franchise qualification: those without a 40-shilling freehold 'shall have no vote at all in chusing any Parliament man, and yet must be bound by their Lawes, which is meer vasalage'. Yet his argument here was ostensibly against the outrageous disproportion in representation in the Commons caused by the existence of so many 'decayed' boroughs, and his solution was to proportion the number of MPs to the rates paid.[58] This was a demand which made its way into the body of the 'Heads of the Proposals': to make the House of Commons 'an equall Representative of the whole' by proportioning representation to the rates paid, or 'according to some other rule of equallity or proportion'.[59] The potential for this mode of argument to bleed into an argument for 'equal' representation for all men subject to the law is almost as present in the grandees' 'Heads of the Proposals' as it is in Lilburne's tract on London, but Lilburne, in *The Charters of London*, followed up his argument in *London's Liberty* with a much more suggestive comment, arguing (as Rainborough was to do at Putney) that 'the poorest that lives, hath as true a right to give a vote, as well as the richest and greatest'.[160] Ireton was both to anticipate and to block this extension of the argument for 'equal' representation at the Putney debates.[161]

Lilburne returned to the demand for manhood suffrage in 1647. While the civilian petitioners of the spring, addressing the House of Commons itself, tactfully refrained from questioning its right to sit or its principles of election, Lilburne and Overton had already mounted their direct attack on the sitting Parliament in the form of their 'appeal to the people'. They could now begin to articulate reasons for the failure of the Parliament to represent the people; and in appealing to the army as the natural head of the commoners, the offer of manhood suffrage might be particularly useful. In *Rash Oaths Unwarrantable*, Lilburne urged that each county should divide itself into 'Divisions, Hundreds or Weapontacks' where the people could conveniently meet to vote. In this way 'every free man of *England*, as well poore as rich' who was subject to law would be able to vote: 'it being a maxim in nature, that no man justly can be bound without his own consent'.[162]

Lilburne had made this demand for manhood suffrage in May; in October a more systematic version of it appeared in the *Case of the Armie*. Morrill and Baker have argued quite rightly that the *Case of the Armie* is to be read as an army document rather than a transcript in an army context of Leveller demands, and while they see Leveller 'intrusions' into the text, these do not include the electoral and franchise arrangements.[163] But here, as elsewhere, it is not so easy to draw a sharp line between 'army' and 'civilian' or 'Leveller' forms of radicalism. The authors of the *Case* sought the franchise for 'all the freeborn at the age of 21. yeares and upwards ... excepting those that have or shall deprive themselves of that their freedome, either for some yeares, or wholly by delinquency' – not just for all *soldiers* who had fought on the right side.[164] Lilburne's influence on both the thought and the phrasing of this demand seems strong.

The *Agreement of the People*, of course, stepped back from the explicit demand for manhood suffrage, instead subtly altering the emphasis of the 'Heads of the Proposals' by proposing to remedy the unequal distribution of electors in their counties, cities, and boroughs by proportioning them 'according to the number of the Inhabitants' – rather than according to the rates paid.[165] In spite of its tact, though, this followed Lilburne's logic in *Rash Oaths*, where population was linked to adult male suffrage. Ireton swiftly unmasked it as a claim to manhood suffrage, and those speaking in its favour did not dissent from that proposition, although some were prepared to modify it slightly in the course of the debates.[166] The debates and decisions in committee at Putney reveal a fusion of Leveller and army radical thought on the franchise. The radical speakers at Putney drew unmistakably on Lilburne's logic and language in their arguments for a franchise for Englishmen and their outraged rejection of Ireton's argument that some Englishmen deserved no more 'birthright' than foreigners in England (see Chapter 3). But the victory that they won in committee on 30 October compromised on those issues of most concern to civilian radicals: the final decision about the extent of the franchise was to be left to the current Parliament (rather than specified by a non-parliamentary Agreement), but as a minimum must include 'all freeborne Englishmen, or persons made free denizons of England' who had served Parliament in the war or voluntarily assisted it with money, plate, horse, or arms. There is some discomfort in the meeting of Lilburne's inclusive language of free-born Englishmen and the soldiery's vindication of their particular rights through their claim to that English status, but Lilburne's language was still in circulation and won the soldiers a temporary victory; indeed the agitators claimed that they had secured a vote for civilians' rights of election too, although no record of this survives.[167] By the aftermath of Ware, the army leadership was confident enough to go back on any such guarantee. Fairfax's *Remonstrance ... and Declaration ... for the Future Uniting of the Army* maintained the army's demands for the 'freedome and equality of Elections', but promised only to make the House representative of 'the People that are to elect'.[168] By the time of Leveller–army rapprochement in 1648–49, it was possible to reach a compromise position on an adult male franchise excluding certain categories of men by social and economic status, and the Levellers' third Agreement did not modify this much, although it added a gloss justifying a broad franchise by 'natural right'.[169]

Other aspects of the status of Parliament could also cause controversy within the radical spectrum, potentially opening up divisions between army and civilian reformers. Certainly there were some divergent tendencies. Army men remained more willing to vest absolute authority in Parliament, even if they had to purge parliaments to make them worthy to exercise it. Thus the civilian Leveller leaders developed an argument that MPs should not be excluded from their seats except through some process of consent by their electors; the *Case of the Armie*, on the other hand, was happy to let the House itself be responsible for calling to account all erring 'officers', although the removal of MPs was not specifically discussed.[170] In the winter of 1648–49, a more definite division can be seen between the Officers' Agreement, which made the Commons the locus of ultimate appeal, and Lilburne's *Foundations of Freedom*, which was careful not to grant such power.[171] The army's *Remonstrance* explicitly gave the future parliament 'extraordinary' and 'arbitrary' power and stated that its decisions were binding and 'conclusive' to the people, while offering rather token reserves from their power in comparison to the Agreements of the People.[172]

Some have seen potential divisions between Leveller and army approaches to the renewal of Parliament, arguing that the army were more willing to support

The Levellers

purges of Parliament – as with the Eleven Members and demands for further purges in 1647, and more famously with Pride's Purge in December 1648 – rather than the dissolution of Parliament.[73] Willingness to purge Parliament suggests a pragmatic willingness to sacrifice legitimacy of process to political ends. Dissolution, on the other hand, could be justified if it was thought that Parliament had forfeited its trust by its actions, and advocating it might thus be a sign of a greater concern with the legitimacy of political authority. However, both Levellers and army men tended to veil their intentions towards Parliament, and it is hard to make the case that there was any very systematic difference between them. When Lilburne and Overton appealed from the House of Commons to the people in 1647, they did not spell out whether the rising of the people was supposed to unseat or merely pressure Parliament. The agitators who pressed the grandees at Reading in July for a swift march on London were similarly unexplicit about their motives, implying that they simply wanted to restore the incentive for the Parliament to comply with their list of demands (which included the release of Lilburne and his colleagues). At the Reading debates, the radicals urged the importance of the placing of power in the right hands, while Ireton argued that force could not be used to change the locus of power until the principles on which that power was to be exercised had been clarified. (Ireton was to present his 'Heads of the Proposals' for a settlement with the king the next day.) This debate about the placing and displacing of power perhaps originated in the question of the London militia, as well as the agitators' demands for a march on London; it became a debate about the future of the Parliament itself.[74]

Both Levellers and army radicals sought the exclusion of MPs in the course of 1647, and never clearly demanded anything other than a voluntary dissolution of Parliament.[75] Morrill and Baker imply that the Levellers' commitment to an Agreement of the People went hand in hand with a desire for an 'immediate' dissolution of Parliament, in contrast to the (army) *Case*'s more 'orderly' transition of power.[76] This argument founders on the fact that the *Agreement of the People* explicitly stated the date on which it required Parliament to dissolve: 30 September 1648, nearly a year in the future.[77] The *Agreement* – a document which emerged from an army context, attempted to unite army radical and civilian concerns, and was taken up by a systematic Leveller campaign – on the face of it planned quite carefully for a significant period of transition.

Later tensions about legitimacy, processes, and modes of transition focussed around Pride's Purge. According to their retrospective accounts, the Levellers objected strongly to any precipitate attack on Parliament in preparation for the trial of Charles I, while army men argued with their civilian allies about whether to purge or dissolve Parliament. However, while Lilburne did pay at least lip-service to the question of legitimacy and due process in his account of the Levellers' objections, it is clear that his main concern – understandably – was the danger that would face England if hasty action by the army against both Parliament and king left power entirely in the hands of the grandees.[78] Certainly there were army radicals who cheered on the foundation of the Commonwealth, by whatever means it was achieved – they were given a voice in the *Moderate*, as we have already seen. But we have also already seen that purge and regicide did not mark a decisive break between the Levellers and all those who had supported these 'extraordinary' measures: those who found themselves dissatisfied with the compromises of the new regime could still turn to the civilian Levellers for alternatives.

The future of the monarchy was the great constitutional question facing the army in 1647. Civilian Leveller authors had become increasingly strident on this, with *Regall Tyrannie Discovered* published anonymously in January 1647. In the texts which the Levellers did acknowledge as their own, they insisted on ending the veto power of the king, leaving little room for him to be anything other than an executive 'officer' under the authority of the Representative. By contrast, it has been argued that the shared political culture of the army tended to monarchism, and even that army radicals at this time expressed a distinct strain of 'royalism'.[79] Certainly the language of the 'kingdom' and of 'subjects' is far more prominent in the army documents than in Leveller texts, where, as we have seen, Lilburne replaced 'subjects' with 'free-born Englishmen'. The army grandees entered into negotiation with Charles I on the basis of the 'Heads of the Proposals', and offered him restoration with 'safety, Honour and freedome'.[80] Army radicals, as well as the grandees, had reason to hope that a settlement with the king might be more favourable to army concerns than a settlement on Parliament's terms. Even once the question of the king became a breaker of counsels within the army itself, it has been argued, it did not cleanly divide junior, anti-monarchical radicals from conservative grandees.[81]

Of course, Leveller anti-monarchism was itself far from complete, in 1647 and later. Lilburne was in dialogue with royalists in prison in 1647, and he associated with royalists while banished in the Low Countries in the early 1650s. Some of the plotting against Cromwell undertaken by former Levellers in the 1650s was done in association with royalists (see Chapter 6). But we should be wary of denominating any such willingness to restore the king as 'royalism', except in the most minimal sense.[82] In 1647 a monarchical settlement was still by far the most likely outcome, and the struggle was for the terms of that settlement. In a Leveller version the king would have no negative voice and, as we have seen, the authors of the *Case of the Armie*, as well as the *Agreement*, took up that demand. For all Lilburne's 'royalist' connections in 1647, there is no reason to think that he reneged on that condition, though he may well have soft-pedalled it for Sir Lewis Dyve's benefit. Both Leveller and army speculation about restoring the king must be read alongside other statements about monarchy and the king from the same groups; in both cases, pragmatism rather than royalism was visible.

One division which may have opened up was between those who were more alarmed by the person of the king – Charles I himself – and those who were more concerned about monarchical power. A plausible case has been made that, from the time of Putney, under the influence of Charles's duplicity in his negotiations with the grandees, Cromwell was already deeply hostile to Charles I and was awaiting the time when God would pull him down, while remaining in conviction a 'monarchist'.[183] In contrast, other contemporaries might argue that a restoration of Charles I was perfectly safe if he had no negative voice, or alternatively that any end to kingship need not imply the personal destruction of the king. The Levellers' ostensible position, and that of the *Case of the Armie* and the *Agreement of the People*, was that the king could be restored as long as he had no negative voice; William Allen insisted at Putney that this remained the view of the majority of those backing the *Case*.[184] The Levellers went on to object – at least retrospectively – to the king's trial and execution. Francis White, an army officer whose relationship with the radicals within the army was unstable, both objected to negotiations with the king in 1647 and objected to the execution of the king in 1649 because 'it is not so much the person that can hurt us, as the power that is made up in the Kingly office by this corrupt constitution'.[185]

In practice, of course, the views on the future of the monarchy which radicals reached from 1647 to 1649 were a mixture of principled reflection on monarchy, reaction against the reign of Charles I himself, and often providential interpretation too. The most clear-sighted expounders of principles of government by consent were equally capable of personal hostility to the king. John Wildman, as well as Thomas Harrison, was already calling Charles I a man of blood in 1647, a reference which clearly suggested execution.[186] The Levellers' *Regall Tyranny Discovered* condemned the tendency of the institution towards tyranny by narrating the sins of monarchs since the Norman conquest, culminating in the supreme tyranny of Charles I. In the run-up to the regicide, the radical army press, too, was both urging punishment on Charles for the blood he had spilt, and ridiculing the claims of hereditary monarchy while exalting the possibilities of republican regimes like '*Venice, Holland, Switzerland*'.[187] Indeed, even the army's official *Remonstrance* of November 1648 seemed to echo John Harris's discussion of the rights of kings in *Mercurius Militaris* the previous month, where the various possible sources of kingly authority were discussed (and mocked) in turn, and the lack of proof of divine designation was acidly commented on.[188]

Another set of distinctions cut across these debates about the personal future of Charles I, or the Stuart monarchy, as opposed to hereditary monarchy, or any monarchy at all. This is the spectrum of types of monarchy, which we might break down as follows: an absolute monarchy; a limited but not accountable monarchy; a limited monarchy which could be held accountable by its lesser magistrates or subjects; a politically powerless monarchy retaining the privileges of monarchical rank; and a powerless monarchy without privileges. The speakers at Putney were debating these two sets of variables at once, adding to the difficulties of an imperfect record. There were strong voices against restoration at Putney, and they won a short-lived victory in committee when Rainborough secured the sending of a letter to Parliament on 5 November opposing further addresses to the king.[189] But the same speakers also pushed the question of what level of monarchical role could be safely restored, partly, no doubt, as a strategy for exposing the dangers of any restoration generous enough for Charles I to accept. The king's negative voice was somewhat inconsistently handled by Ireton, but the radicals solidly rejected it, and Ireton was prepared to move as far as compromise proposals suggested in committee. The Agreement went beyond the *Case of the Armie* in giving all the 'marks of sovereignty' to the Representative, but in the debates this seems to have been rolled up in the question of the negative voice, with Ireton suggesting that without a negative voice the king and Lords would have no power at all.[190] He proposed at least to rescue certain privileges for the king and Lords, allowing them to exempt themselves from the Commons' laws where their persons and personal estates were affected.[191] This was strongly rejected by Wildman, and was an attack on the principle of equal subjection to the laws laid down by the Agreement and maintained in subsequent campaigning by civilian Levellers.

In short, both civilian and army radicals placed strict limits on the power of any restored king and were unanimous in doing so, while the grandees still felt that the king legitimately held some privileges which must be preserved. There were divisions among the radicals, though: for some, the necessary restrictions on the king's power would guarantee safety; for others, they were so extensive that they almost rendered any restoration meaningless and unnecessary, and so essential that any compromise made restoration hazardous in the extreme.

CONCLUSION

In this chapter we have followed the complicated relationship between the radicalism of civilian Levellers and that of army men. The army certainly were one audience for Leveller ideas, but they fused them with their own and the two streams never completely merged. The soldiers' politicization was deeply driven by their sense of themselves as Englishmen, as well as their grievances as soldiers. The mutineers at Ware appeared on the field with 'Englands Freedome, Souldiers Rights' written on the copies of the *Agreement of the People* in their hats.'⁹² This was a perfect slogan for those who saw those two causes as deeply intertwined, and it explains why the combination of civilian and army radical interests continued to be powerful up to the regicide and beyond.

NOTES

1 For the army's broad alignment with 'war party' or Independent interests at its founding and before 1647, see Gentles, pp. 7–20, 140–1; Woolrych, pp. 14–15; as against M. A. Kishlansky, *The Rise of the New Model Army* (Cambridge: Cambridge University Press, 1979), pp. 19–45; M. A. Kishlansky, 'The case of the army truly stated: the creation of the New Model Army', *Past and Present* 81 (1978), 51–74.

2 Woolrych, *Soldiers and Statesmen* traces the lifespan of the General Council of the Army, including rank-and-file agitators as well as officer-agitators, to a relatively brief period from Reading in July through to Putney in early November 1647.

3 Woolrych, pp. 27–30; Gentles, pp.151–2.

4 *A Solemne Engagement of the Army* (5 June 1647), reprinted in AD, pp. 23–7.

5 *A Declaration or Representation from his Excellency Sir Thomas Fairfax, and the Army under his Command* (14 June 1647), reprinted in AD, pp. 36–46.

6 B. Worden, 'The Levellers in history and memory, c.1660–1960', in M. Mendle (ed.) *The Putney Debates of 1647: The Army, the Levellers and the English State* (Cambridge: Cambridge University Press, 2001), pp. 280–2; while the first recorded uses of the term are by royalists, there may be truth in the Levellers' own claim that it was the generals who invented it.

7 Gentles, p. 199; Woolrych, pp. 203–11.

8 For an example of the cultural transmission of some of these ideas, see C. Churchill, *Light Shining in Buckinghamshire* (London: Nick Hern Books, 1996), e.g. p. 23, where Thomas Rainborough introduces himself as 'a Leveller'; a more recent example is G. Robertson and P. Baker, *The Putney Debates: The Levellers* (London: Verso, 2007).

9 J. S. Morrill, 'The army revolt of 1647', in A. C. Duke and C. A. Tamse (eds) *Britain and the Netherlands: Vol. VI, Law and Society* (The Hague: 1977), pp. 54–78; Kishlansky, 'The case of the army', p. 74; M. A. Kishlansky, 'Ideology and politics in the parliamentary armies, 1645–9', in J. Morrill (ed.) *Reactions to the English Civil War* (London: Macmillan, 1982), pp. 163–83; M. A. Kishlansky, 'The army and the Levellers: the roads to Putney', *Historical Journal* 22:4 (1979), 795–824.

10 Woolrych, p. 63: royalist newswriter, 19 April 1647.

11 Kishlansky, 'Ideology and politics'.

12 Gentles, pp. 162, 175–6, 197–202; Woolrych, pp. 203–6; J. S. Morrill and P. Baker, 'The case of the armie truly re-stated', in M. Mendle (ed.) *The Putney Debates Revisted* (Cambridge: Cambridge University Press, 2001), 103–24; E. Vernon and P. Baker, 'What was the first Agreement of the People?', *Historical Journal* 53 (2010), 39–60.

13 See especially Vernon and Baker, 'What was the first Agreement of the People?'; compare J. Peacey, 'John Lilburne and the Long Parliament', *Historical Journal*, 43:3 (2000), 625–46 for an earlier period.

14 Woolrych, p. 164 on the 'Heads of the Proposals'.

15 AD, pp. 118–20. Brailsford, p. 245, remarks that this list of desired reforms in the 'Heads' adopted 'nearly every item' of the Levellers' programme.

16 W. Walwyn, *Walwyn's Just Defence*, MMT, pp. 391–3; Clarke MSS, vol. 41, fol. 167; CP 1.351. Morrill and Baker, 'The case of the armie', pp. 119–20 for a discussion of the possible links between the three men.

17 MMT, p. 390.

18 Vernon and Baker, 'What was the first Agreement of the People?', p. 45 and note; *ODNB*, s.v. 'Petty, Maximilian'.

19 MMT, p. 283; John Lilburne, *Rash Oaths Unwarrantable* ([31 May] 1647).

20 CP 1.351.

21 Wildman's proposals on the London militia, presented at army headquarters, had agitator links: Morrill and Baker, 'The case of the armie', p. 120; CP 1.356–7 suggests he was present at debates on the 'Heads of the Proposals'.

22 MMT, pp. 386, 392–3; Woolrych, pp. 190–1; John Lilburne, *The Second Part of Englands New-Chaines Discovered* ([24 March] 1649), pp. 4–5, where the initiative is attributed to 'the Agitators, friends of *London, Southwark*, and the places adjacent'.

23 A. Woolrych, 'Putney revisited: political debate in the New Model Army in 1647', in C. Jones, M. Newitt and S. Roberts (eds) *Politics and People in Revolutionary England: Essays in Honour of Ivan Roots* (Oxford: Blackwell, 1996), pp. 110–12; Woolrych, *Soldiers and Statesmen*, pp. 196–7; p. 204; Gentles, pp. 205–6; M. A. Kishlansky, 'Consensus politics and the structure of debate at Putney', *Journal of British Studies* 20 (1981), 55.

24 Vernon and Baker, 'What was the first Agreement of the People?', p. 45 and note.

25 Sir Lewis Dyve, 'The Tower of London letter-book of Sir Lewis Dyve, 1646–7', ed. H. G. Tibbutt, *Bedfordshire Historical Record Society*, 38 (1958), pp. 95–6; W. Jones, *Thomas Rainborowe (c.1610–1648): Civil War Seaman, Siegemaster and Radical* (Woodbridge: Boydell and Brewer, 2005), pp. 47–50, 83–4; Gentles, pp. 207–8. Rainborough visited Lilburne on Sunday 31 October; Gentles concludes that he must also have visited him when in London on 28–29 October, and sees his vehement speeches at Putney on 29 October as 'perhaps ... a result' of this – purely hypothetical – meeting.

26 John Wildman, *Putney Projects* ([30 December] 1647), p. [45].

27 *The Moderate*, no. 6, 15–22 August 1648; *Mercurius Militaris*, no. 2, [24 October] 1648, p. 16.

28 Jones, *Thomas Rainborowe*, pp. 126, 131–6.

29 M. A. Norris, 'Edward Sexby, John Reynolds and Edmund Chillenden: agitators, "Sectarian Grandees" and the relations of the New Model Army with London in the spring of 1647', *Historical Research* 76: 191 (2003), 30–53; Morrill and Baker, 'The case of the armie'. Woolrych's account sees Sexby as the active Leveller link between the old agitators, the civilian Levellers, and the new agents, e.g. *Soldiers and Statesmen*, pp. 203–4. M. Mendle, 'Putney's pronouns: identity and indemnity in the great debate', in M. Mendle (ed.) *The Putney Debates Revisited* (Cambridge: Cambridge University Press, 2001), pp. 129–30, on *The Grand Informer*.

30 Dyve, 'Tower of London letter-book', p. 92, where Lilburne is reported to want the king to reassure Captain Reynolds, Major White, and the agitator 'Saxby' that their fears about a restoration are groundless.

The Levellers

31 John Lilburne, *The Just Mans Justification*, second edition ([28 September] 1647), p. 26; John Lilburne, *The Juglers Discovered* ([28 September] 1647), pp. 1–2. Morrill and Baker, 'The case of the armie', p. 117, note only one of these passages, and offer what seems to me an absurd explanation for Sexby's possession of Lilburne's books.

32 MMT, pp. 29, 277, 288–90; *CP* 1.204; Kishlansky, *The Rise of the New Model Army*, p. 261; Gentles, p. 152: from July 1647 Tulidah was adjutant-general of the New Model horse for a few months; Woolrych, p. 64 n. 22.

33 Dyve, 'Tower of London letter-book', p. 92; Francis White, *A True Relation of the Proceedings in the Businesse of Burford* ([27 September] 1649), pp. 8, 12–13; Gentles, pp. 245, 320, 332–3, 341–6.

34 Gentles, pp. 221–4, 229, 320; R. Mayers, *1659: The Crisis of the Commonwealth* (Woodbridge: Royal Historical Society, 2004), pp. 211, 224.

35 C. H. Firth and G. Davies, *The Regimental History of Cromwell's Army*, 2 vols paginated as one (Oxford: Clarendon Press, 1940), pp. 326–9.

36 Firth and Davies, *Regimental History*, pp. 221–2; Woolrych, p. 293.

37 *The Army's Martyr* ([7 May] 1649), pp. 6, 11–12. Gentles, pp. 326–9 on Lockyer's mutiny, death, and funeral.

38 Lilburne, *The Just Mans Justification*, with letter to the adjutators dated 27 August; Clarke MSS, vol. 41, fol. 164v: paper of 6 July 1647.

39 D. R. Adams, 'Religion and reason in the thought of Richard Overton, the Leveller' (PhD dissertation, University of Cambridge, 2003), p. 130; *ODNB*, s.v. 'Overton, Richard', 'Lilly, William'.

40 Richard Baxter, *Reliquiae Baxterianae* (1696), p. 53, speaks explicitly of the circulation of pamphlets by Overton and Lilburne. Woolrych, p. 63 suggests that this is 'suspect' as first-hand testimony, since Baxter's army chaplaincy finished in July 1646, but Baxter specifically mentions Overton's Marpriest tracts, published in 1645; Lilburne had also published plenty of autobiographical material by this time. Woolrych, p. 63, on the two references in royalist newsletters in April 1647; one of these says 'Lilburne's books are quoted by them as statute-law'.

41 Gentles, p. 223; I. Gentles, 'London Levellers in the English revolution: the Chidleys and their circle', *Journal of Ecclesiastical History* 29 (1978), p. 291.

42 *CP* 1.413–14, 416, 441–2; Gentles, pp. 217–20; Woolrych, pp. 254–67.

43 Morrill, 'The army revolt of 1647', in A. C. Duke and C. A. Tamse, *Britain and the Netherlands: Vol. VI, Law and Society* (The Hague, 1977), pp. 72–3; M. A. Kishlansky, 'What happened at Ware?', *Historical Journal*, 25 (1982) 827–39; Woolrych, pp. 283–6.

44 Major Francis White and Colonel Rainborough both apologized, White for his words at Putney and Rainborough for his actions at Ware: White was readmitted to the General Council and Rainborough was allowed to take up his sea command, which had been frozen by a narrow vote of the Commons after Fairfax had reported on his behaviour. Leniency was also shown to Bray and others who were court-martialled, and evidently to Cobbett. (Woolrych, pp. 298–9; Firth and Davies, *Regimental History*, p. 326; E. Peacock, 'Notes on the life of Thomas Rainborowe', *Archaeologia* 46 (1881), 27–8.)

45 Kishlansky, 'The army and the Levellers', p. 796.

46 Gentles, p. 244. He suggests that the soldiers were feeling 'disgruntlement' because

many of their close friends had been demobilized, but does not attempt to explain the connection between this and radical ideology.

47 Gentles, p. 245; *The Armies Petition: Or a New Engagement* (1648, received by Thomason on 3 May), p. 5 demanded an Agreement; *A New Engagement, or, Manifesto* (1648, received by Thomason 3 August), presented the same demands from a civilian perspective. See P. Baker and E. Vernon (eds) *The Agreements of the People, the Levellers and the Constitutional Crisis of the English Revolution* (Basingstoke: Palgrave Macmillan, forthcoming 2012) for further consideration of the place of these 'New Engagements' in the history of the Agreements of the People.

48 Adams, 'Religion and reason in the thought of Richard Overton, the Leveller', p. 130; *ODNB*, s.v. 'Overton, Richard', 'Lilly, William'.

49 Gentles, pp. 345–6; Firth and Davies, *Regimental History*, p. 378.

50 Gentles, p. 224, and P. Baker, '"A despicable contemptible generation of men"? Cromwell and the Levellers', in P. Little (ed.) *Oliver Cromwell: New Perspectives* (Basingstoke: Palgrave Macmillan, 2009), p. 105, both see Leveller influence.

51 David Underdown, *Pride's Purge: Politics in the Puritan Revolution* (Oxford: Oxford University Press, 1971), pp. 87–90; Baker, '"A despicable contemptible generation of men?"', p. 106.

52 J. Raymond, *The Invention of the Newspaper: English Newsbooks, 1641–1649* (Oxford: Clarendon Press, 1996), p. 68; on Harris's links with Leveller and army radicals, see M. Heinemann. 'Popular drama and Leveller style: Richard Overton and John Harris', in M. Cornforth (ed.) *Rebels and Their Causes: Essays in Honour of A. L. Morton* (London: Lawrence and Wishart, 1978), pp. 84–5; Woolrych, p. 133.

53 R. Howell Jr and D. E. Brewster, 'Reconsidering the Levellers: the evidence of the *Moderate*', *Past and Present*, 46 (1970), p. 70.

54 Howell and Brewster, 'Reconsidering the Levellers', argues that the *Moderate* diverged from the Leveller party line post-Putney of excluding servants from the franchise; and from the Leveller party line from January 1649 of compromising on religious toleration for Catholics and Anglicans. Whether the Levellers' own views were as systematic as the authors claim is unclear. J. Diethe, 'The Moderate: politics and allegiances of a revolutionary newspaper', *History of Political Thought*, 4 (1983), 247–79 argues that the *Moderate* supported Jubbes's alternative proposals in preference to the Leveller *Agreement* of 1 May 1649.

55 Authorship of the newsbook is uncertain, but some contemporaries assumed that it was by Gilbert Mabbott (see *Moderate* no. 12, 26 September–3 October 1648, unpag., for a denial of this authorship), and there is circumstantial evidence in favour of this. Some have suspected help from another Leveller/radical writer in some of the more eloquent editorials. Frances Henderson in her ODNB biography of Mabbott doubts his editorship.

56 Underdown, *Pride's Purge*, pp. 90–7.

57 *Moderate*, no. 6, 15–22 August 1648, p. 34.

58 P. Gregg, *Free-Born John: A Biography of John Lilburne* (London: Phoenix Press, 2000 reprint), pp. 245–7; Baker, '"A despicable contemptible generation of men?"', p. 107.

59 *Moderate*, no. 4, 1–8 August 1648, unpag.

60 Gentles, pp. 266–7, 283.

The Levellers

61 *To the Right Honourable the Commons of England in Parliament Assembled* (11 September 1648; 669.f.13/16).

62 Gentles, pp. 267–8.

63 Of the army petitions between 11 September and the issuing of the army's own *Remonstrance* the next month (Gentles, p. 515 n.10), few explicitly include demands drawn from the 11 September petition, most focusing generally on the demand for justice on offenders, including the king, and rejection of a dangerous treaty, and more specifically on the immediate problems of army pay and free quarter (for example, *Severall Petitions Presented to his Excellency the Lord Fairfax* (1648, E.474/5), pp. 3–4, p. 6). *A Petition from Severall Regiments of the Army* (1648, E.470/32), pp. 4–6, is rare in not only invoking the petition of 11 September but also including its demands for the clarification of the extent of the supreme power and that parliaments in future should meet without writ or summons; significantly, this petition also calls for an investigation into the murder of Rainborough. Among the later army petitions supporting the 'Leveller programme' in Gentles' view, explicit commitment to the constitutional details and priorities of Leveller thought is again rare: for example, *The Declarations and Humble Representations of the Officers and Souldiers* (1648; E.475/24) includes the rejection of 'Negative Voyces... against the Peoples Freedom and just Liberty' (p. 4), but such specific statements are rare in this document, and even more so in some of the other petitions.

64 John Lilburne, *The Legal Fundamental Liberties* (1649, 2nd edn; E.567/1), pp. 34–5; Gentles, pp. 273–4; Frank, p. 172.

65 Gentles, pp. 287–94.

66 *Moderate*, no. 22, 5–12 December 1648, unpag.; cf. the celebratory letters in the following issue: *Moderate*, no. 23, 12–19 December 1648.

67 John Goodwin, *Might and Right Well Met* (2 January 1649).

68 *Moderate*, no. 17, 31 October–7 November 1648, pp. 137–8.

69 *Moderate*, no. 38, 27 March–3 April 1649, p. 385.

70 *Moderate*, no. 39, 3–10 April 1649, p. 397.

71 *Moderate*, no. 29, 23–30 January 1649, p. 273. The paper had commended Hugh Peter's sermon on this text, preached to the High Court of Justice. Hugh Peter's differences with the Levellers after the regicide are apparent in Lilburne's account of a meeting with him in May 1649, with Peter commending the sword (and saying all laws came from the sword), and Lilburne the established law: John Lilburne, *A Discourse Betwixt Lieutenant Colonel John Lilburn ... and Mr Hugh Peter* ([29 May] 1649), pp. 2–5.

72 *Moderate*, no. 32, 13–20 February 1649, p. 315; *Moderate*, no. 38, 27 March–3 April 1649, unpag.

73 John Lilburne et al., *A Plea for Common Right and Freedom* ([28 December] 1648), p. 6; *To the Right Honourable, the Supreme Authority of this Nation, the Commons of England in Parliament Assembled*, 19 January 1649, in Wolfe, p. 329.

74 John Lilburne, *Englands New Chains Discovered* (26 February 1649), sig. A3v.

75 *Moderate*, no. 30, 23–30 January 1649, unpag.; Lilburne, *Englands New Chains Discovered*, sig. A3v; *ODNB*, s.v. 'John Fry', on Thomas Prince's presentation of the petition for Fry.

76 Lilburne, *Englands New Chains*, sig. A2; *The Moderate*, no. 30, 30 January–6 February 1649, p. 285 and unpag. (debates of 2 and 5 February); *The Moderate*, no. 31, 6–13 February, p. 298.

77 I. Gentles, 'The Agreements of the People and their political contexts, 1647–1649', in M. Mendle (ed.) *The Putney Debates of 1647: The Army, the Levellers, and the English State* (Cambridge: Cambridge University Press, 2001), p. 168.

78 *The Moderate*, no. 32, 13–20 February 1649, p. 312.

79 Lilburne, *Englands New Chains*, sig. A4v.

80 *The Moderate*, no. 33, 20–27 February 1649, p. 330.

81 Gentles, pp. 319–20.

82 Two issues of *Mercurius Militaris* in April–May 1649 are extant (no. 1, 17–24 April 1649, E551/13; no. 3, undated, E554/13); they continued the acid commentary on the grandees provided in John Harris's *Mercurius Militaris* from October–November 1648. Gentles is wrong to suggest that the character of the *Moderate* changed at this point, and the assumption that this was due to the end of Mabbott's editorship, coinciding with a challenge to his role as licenser, is speculative in any case: Gentles, p. 325; Raymond, *The Invention of the Newspaper*, p. 71 on the mention of the *Moderate* in the challenge to Mabbott as a licenser.

83 *The Moderate*, no. 42, 24 April–1 May 1649, unpag. (from Haverford, 27 April); *The Moderate*, no. 43, 1–8 May 1649, unpag. (Oxfordshire and Barnstaple); Gregg, *Free-born John*, p. 282.

84 *The Moderate*, no. 44, 8–15 May 1649, unpag. (Sussex, 9 May).

85 *The Moderate*, no. 45, 15–22 May 1649, unpag. The *Moderate* never explicitly endorsed any Agreement proposals which were clearly not the Officers' Agreement, apart from John Jubbes's proposals under that name; however, they often left it tactically open as to which version of the Agreement they were arguing for, as in this issue (45), where they referred to what was set out in the 'agrements [sic, plural] of the people'.

86 Blair Worden, *The Rump Parliament* (Cambridge: Cambridge University Press, 1973), pp. 195–9.

87 *The Moderate*, no. 53, 10–17 July 1649, p. 605; cf the paper by 'J. P.' in issue 51.

88 Morrill, 'The army revolt of 1647', *passim*; Gentles, p. 201.

89 Kishlansky, 'The army and the Levellers', p. 796.

90 Gentles, p. 105.

91 AD, p. 39.

92 Walwyn, *The Bloody Project*, in MMT, pp. 294ff.

93 LJ, ix, 111: 30 March 1647; CJ, v, 127–31: 27–30 March 1647.

94 AD, p. 9.

95 AD, p. 60.

96 Kishlansky, 'The army and the Levellers', pp. 796–805.

97 Kishlansky, 'Ideology and politics'; Kishlansky, *The Rise of the New Model Army*, pp. 180–1, 197–200.

98 AD, p. [26].

99 AD, p. 40.

100 AD, pp. 11, 40.

The Levellers

101 Woolrych, 'Putney revisited', p. 106.
102 Kishlansky, 'The army and the Levellers', p. 797; Woolrych, pp. 19–20 argues for some politicization before spring 1647.
103 Morrill, 'The army revolt of 1647'; J. S. Morrill, 'Mutiny and discontent in English provincial armies, 1645–1647', *Past and Present*, 56 (1972), 49–74.
104 Kishlansky, 'Ideology and politics', p. 170.
105 Austin Woolrych, 'Putney revisited', p. 100; Kishlansky, *The Rise of the New Model Army*, pp. 180–1; Woolrych, pp. 75–86; Gentles, p. 149.
106 The first 'Apologie', 28 April, signed by 'Commissioners' of eight cavalry regiments, including Edward Sexby, William Allen, and Nicholas Lockyer: *AD*, p. 8; *CP* 1.23, anonymous 'Advertisements for the managing of the Councells of the Army'. 'A Second Apologie' takes up similar themes: *AD*, pp. 9–11.
107 Frank, pp. 121–2; Woolrych, pp. 64–5.
108 Woolrych, p. 54.
109 *CP* 1.23.
110 Gentles, pp. 174–5 on the sponsoring of the agitators' activities by the army.
111 *CP* 1.170–175 gives the agitators' *Representation* setting out the reasons for the desired march to London; 176–214 gives the Reading debates on the possible march to London, and the introduction of the 'Heads' into the debate; 214–16 is a newsletter reporting the agitators' acquiescence in the decisions taken at Reading. Woolrych, pp. 156–62.
112 Woolrych, pp. 147, 164.
113 *AD*, p. 160.
114 Morrill and Baker, 'The case of the armie', pp. 106–7, 112.
115 *The Case of the Armie Truly Stated* (15 October 1647), p. 5.
116 *The Case of the Armie*, p. 7; *CP* 1.260.
117 *CP* 1.320, 322–3, 353.
118 Richard Overton, *Eighteene Reasons Propounded to the Soldiers of the Body of the Army* ([13 August] 1647), p. 3.
119 *Two Letters from the Agents of the five Regiments of Horse* ([28 October] 1647), p. 6.
120 Wildman, *Putney Projects*, pp. 9, 46.
121 *The Hunting of the Foxes* ([21 March] 1649), pp. 3, 9.
122 *An Agreement of the People* (1647), title page; p. 1.
123 *An Agreement of the People* (1647), pp. 13, 9 (emphasis added); cf. also *A Copy of a Letter Sent by the Agents of Severall Regiments... to All the Souldiers in the Said Armie*, 11 November 1647, E413.18, sig. A: '*a mutuall agreement* between the people and you'.
124 *An Agreement of the People for a Firme and Present Peace* (1647), pp. 11–12.
125 John Wildman, *A Cal to All the Souldiers* ([29 October] 1647), p. 8 [mispaginated 7].
126 *An Agreement of the People* ([3 November] 1647), pp. 12–13.
127 Morrill, 'The Army Revolt of 1647'; L. G. Schwoerer, *No Standing Armies! The Antiarmy Ideology in Seventeenth-Century England* (Baltimore and London: Johns Hopkins University Press, 1974), pp. 51–4.

128 John Lilburne, *The Copy of a Letter, From Lieutenant Colonell John Lilburne, to a Freind [sic]* (1645), p. 2.

129 John Lilburne, *A More Full Relation of the Great Battell ... Made in the House of COMMONS by Lieut: Col: Lilbourne* ([16 July] 1645), pp. 7–[8]. That Leveller support for soldiers in expression of their grievances was not completely determined by expedience is suggested by Samuel Chidley's continuing activities in the 1650s on behalf of disbanded soldiers seeking their arrears – although, as Gentles points out, he may have had his own interests at heart as well (Gentles, 'London Levellers in the English revolution', pp. 299, 304).

130 *CP* 1.24: the original agitators envisaged the keeping up of a minimal force of cavalry and the disbandment of the rest of the army; *Solemne Engagement: AD*, p. 26; Woolrych, p. 97.

131 *The Case of the Armie*, pp. 19–20.

132 Woolrych, p. 190; *MMT*, p. 386.

133 *An Agreement of the Free People of England* (1 May 1649), p. 7.

134 *To his Highness the Lord Protector, &c. and our General, The Humble Petition of Several Colonels of the Army* (1654); John Wildman, *The Leveller: or, the Principles and Maxims Concerning Government and Religion, which are Asserted by those that are Commonly Called, Levellers* ([16 February] 1659), pp. 8–9; John Wildman, *A Mite to the Treasury* (1653), p. 15–16; Schwoerer, 'No Standing Armies!', pp. 51–6, 60–1, 68.

135 See my chapter in Baker, P. and Vernon, E. (eds), *The Agreements of the People, the Levellers and the Constitutional Crisis of the English Revolution* (Basingstoke: Palgrave Macmillan, forthcoming 2012).

136 Woolrych, pp. 118–20.

137 John Lilburne, *Jonah's Cry* (1647), postscript, p. 13, dated 16 July 1647.

138 Overton, *Eighteene Reasons*, pp. 1, 4–5, 7.

139 'A Defence for the honest Nownsubstantive Soldiers', February 1647, in John Lilburne, *The Peoples Prerogative* ([17 February] 1648), pp. 42, 44; *Englands Freedome, Souldiers Rights* ([14 December] 1647), also reprinted in *The Peoples Prerogative*, pp. 45–6, 51.

140 Wildman, *A Cal to All the Souldiers*, second pagination, p. 7.

141 Lilburne et al., *A Plea for Common-Right and Freedom* ([28 December] 1648), p. 5; *An Agreement of the Free People of England*, p. 7.

142 *Two Letters from the Agents*, pp. 2–3.

143 Overton, *An Appeale from the Degenerate Representative Body the Commons of England Assembled at Westminster: to the Body Represented, the Free People in General* ([17 July] 1647), title page and pp. 27–9.

144 Overton, *An Appeale*, title page and p. 29.

145 David Jenkins, *An Apology for the Army* (1647), pp. 5, 10; David Jenkins, *The Armies Indemnity* ([31 May] 1647).

146 *The Case of the Armie Truly Stated*, pp. 6, 12.

147 *A Remonstrance of Many Thousand Citizens* (1646), pp. 19–20; the demand had already been made in *Englands Birth-Right Justified* ([10 October] 1645).

148 John Lilburne, *The Resolved Mans Resolution* ([30 April 1647), pp. 19, 22; Lilburne, *Rash Oaths Unwarrantable*, p. 50.

The Levellers

149 *The Case of the Armie*, p. 15; *An Agreement of the People*, pp. 3, 9.

150 Clarke MSS, vol. 41, fols 18–18v; Woolrych, p. 69 suggests Wildman or Captain Francis White as possible authors.

151 *The Armies Petition*, p. 4; *A New Engagement*; Woolrych, pp. 326–7, sees the 'New Engagement' as a minor episode sparked only by proximity to London; this detail, however, suggests that there was a noticeable element of army thought rather than just civilian radical influence here.

152 *To the Right Honourable the Commons of England in Parliament Assembled*, article 2; *An Agreement Prepared for the People of England* (20 January 1649), p. 16.

153 *A Remonstrance of his Excellency... and of the Generall Councell of Officers* (18 November 1648), p. 66; John Lilburne, *Foundations of Freedom; or an Agreement of the People* ([15 December] 1648).

154 *An Agreement of the Free People of England*, p. 4.

155 *A Remonstrance of Many Thousand Citizens*, p. 20; Clarke MSS, vol. 41, fol. 18v; Gentles, p. 161.

156 *The Case of the Armie*, p. 15.

157 AD, p. 112.

158 John Lilburne, *Londons Liberty in Chains* ([October] 1646), pp. 53–4; this part of the tract is authored by Lilburne.

159 AD, p. 113; S. R. Gardiner (ed.), *The Constitutional Documents of the Puritan Revolution, 1625–1660*, 3rd edn (Oxford: Clarendon Press, 1906), p. 317. The 'or' is not in the original text but does seem to be implied. Less specifically, the army's *A Declaration or Representation* of 14 June, in an edition apparently printed at Cambridge, spoke of redistributing seats so as to 'render the Parliament a more equal Representative of the whole' (H&D, pp. 60–1, 51).

160 John Lilburne, *The Charters of London; or, the Second Part of Londons Liberty in Chaines* ([18 December] 1646), p. 4.

161 CP 1.299.

162 Lilburne, *Rash Oaths Unwarrantable*, p. 50.

163 Morrill and Baker, 'The case of the armie', p. 113.

164 *The Case of the Armie*, p. 15.

165 *An Agreement of the People*, p. 2.

166 CP 1.299–301; A. L. Morton, 'Leveller democracy – fact or myth?', in his *The World of the Ranters: Religious Radicalism in the English Revolution* (London: Lawrence & Wishart, 1970), pp. 204–5.

167 CP 1.365–6; *A Letter Sent from several Agitators of the Army to their Respective Regiments* (1647), p. 4; Woolrych, pp. 243–4.

168 *Remonstrance from His Excellency Sir Thomas Fairfax ... and Declaration ... for the Future Uniting of the Army* (15 November 1647), unpag.; Gentles, p. 224; Woolrych, pp. 287–8.

169 Lilburne, *Foundations of Freedom*, pp. 7–8; *An Agreement Prepared for the People of England*, pp. 16-[17]; *An Agreement of the Free People of England*, p. 3.

170 *Remonstrance of Many Thousand Citizens*, p. 20; Overton, *An Appeale*, pp. 32–3; *The Case*

of the Armie, p. 15; Morrill and Baker, 'The case of the armie', p. 113 contrasts the *Case* with the Levellers on this point.

171 *An Agreement Prepared for the People of England*, p. 22; Lilburne, *Foundations of Freedom*, pp. 10–11.

172 *A Remonstrance of his Excellency*, pp. 15–16, 66–7.

173 Morrill and Baker, 'The case of the armie', p. 116; Kishlansky, 'Ideology and politics', pp. 174–6.

174 *CP* 1.179–82, 192–207.

175 Woolrych, p. 148; H. Shaw, *The Levellers* (London: Longman, 1968), p. 95.

176 Morrill and Baker, 'The case of the armie', p. 114.

177 *An Agreement of the People*, pp. 2–3.

178 Lilburne, *Legal Fundamental Liberties*, pp. 33–8, 43–4.

179 Kishlansky, 'Ideology and politics', p. 173; Mendle, 'Putney's pronouns'.

180 *AD*, p. 147.

181 J. Morrill and P. Baker, 'Oliver Cromwell, the regicide and the sons of Zeruiah', in J. Peacey (ed.) *The Regicides and the Execution of Charles I* (Basingstoke: Palgrave, 2001), p. 18.

182 J. McElligott, *Royalism, Print and Censorship in Revolutionary England* (Woodbridge: Boydell Press, 2007), p. 6.

183 Morrill and Baker, 'Oliver Cromwell'.

184 *CP* 1.377.

185 Francis White, *The Copy of a Letter Sent to his Excellencie Sir Thomas Fairfax* ([11 November] 1647), pp. 5–6; Francis White, *The Copies of Severall Letters Contrary to the Opinion of the Present Powers* ([20 March] 1649), p. 4.

186 Wildman, *A Cal to All the Souldiers*, p. 5; *CP* 1.417; P. Crawford, 'Charles Stuart, that man of blood', *Journal of British Studies* 16 (1977), 41–61; Morrill and Baker, 'Oliver Cromwell', pp. 19, 22.

187 *Moderate*, no. 20, 21–28 November 1648, unpag.

188 *Mercurius Militaris* no. 2, 10–17 October 1648, pp. 13–14; *A Remonstrance of His Excellency*, p. 48.

189 *CP* 1.440–41.

190 *An Agreement of the People*, pp. 3–4; *CP* 1.391.

191 *CP* 1.403.

192 *Englands Freedome, Souldiers Rights* is the title of a document purportedly by William Thompson; if it is by him, he had a remarkable capacity to write in Lilburne's style, and it seems likely, as Wolfe conjectures (p. 242) that it is by Lilburne himself. (Reprinted in Wolfe, pp. 248–58.) The slogan had been written on the outside of the copies of the *Agreement of the People* which mutineers wore in their hats at Ware (Gentles, p. 223). The pairing of notions had come up in *Two Letters From the Agents*, p. 4: the new agents urged the soldiers 'to insist speedily upon the souldiers Rights, Englands freedomes, to be secured and setled'.

Chapter 6

Levellers into republicans?

On 19 May 1649 the regime which emerged from purge and regicide finally declared itself to be a 'Commonwealth and Free State'.[1] There was an almost uncannily neat divide between the end of Levelling and the beginning of an official republic. The army mutineers had been cornered at Burford only a few days before this official declaration; seven days after it, on 26 May 1649, the Long Parliament voted that a national day of thanksgiving should be held 'for Publick Thanksgiving to Almighty God, for his great Mercy vouchsafed to this whole Commonwealth, by the Success he hath given to the Parliament Forces, in timely suppressing the late Insurrection and Rebellion'.[2]

In spite of the decisiveness with which the regime marked these two turning-points, little was genuinely settled. The celebratory bonfires which greeted John Lilburne's acquittal in his treason trial at the Guildhall in October revealed that the Levellers had not lost their cultural power overnight. Equally, those who welcomed the advent of the 'Commonwealth and Free State' had still to engage in a lengthy struggle, aborted rather than resolved at the Restoration, to determine exactly what that might mean. What criteria did a government have to fulfil for the nation to qualify as a commonwealth and free state? Could the rule of the Rump Parliament, or of a Nominated Assembly, or of a Protector with his council and parliaments, ever qualify? What foundations would enable an English republic to endure and flourish?

Answers to these questions in the 1650s were increasingly framed in a classical republican mode, but the Leveller thought of the 1640s had already offered some answers to them in a rather different language, and contemporaries as well as historians have seen continuities between Levelling and republicanism. Cromwell, at the end of his first Parliament in January 1655, referred to 'that party of men, called Levellers, and who call themselves Commonwealthsmen'.[3] In the autumn of the next year, Cromwell warned darkly that 'There is a generation of men in this nation that cry up nothing but righteousness, and justice, and liberty; and these are diversified in several sects and sorts of men', who, Cromwell was keen to point out, had been consorting, if not with cavaliers, certainly with rogues. He went on to specify one of these 'sects' more specifically: 'And that Levelling party hath some access lately that goes under a finer name or notion. I think they would be called Commonwealthsmen, who perhaps have reason little enough. And it is strange that men of fortune and great estates should join with such a people.'[4] For Cromwell, 1650s republicanism was a continuation of 1640s Levelling, but also a transformation of it – if only because the self-styled 'commonwealthsmen' of the 1650s had greater intellectual and social pretensions.

Cromwell, of course, is not the only person to have seen continuities between the Levellers of the 1640s and the republicans, or 'Commonwealthsmen', of the 1650s.[5] Jonathan Scott's *Commonwealth Principles* takes it as axiomatic that the Levellers were republicans and that their history and thought should be taken as continuous with that of the canonical 1650s republican writers, speaking of the 'emergence of republicanism from civil war radicalism, and that of the Levellers in particular'; Scott's emphasis on Nedham's role in this process follows Blair Worden's work, arguing that 'Though the Levellers were defeated in 1649, Nedham's [*Mercurius Politicus*] editorials resumed the Leveller program and gave it a classical dimension.'[6] Nigel Smith and Joad Raymond have argued for the importance of John Streater as an exemplar of a popular republicanism in the 1650s which was, in important senses, a continuation of 1640s Levellerism.[7] For Brailsford, 'After 1653 [Lilburne's second trial] the mass of the Levellers is merged in a republican opposition which blends the most incongruous elements – Grandees like Sir Harry Vane and Sir Arthur Haslerig, a group of Anabaptist colonels, and the intellectuals whom Harrington inspired.'[8] S. D. Glover's work contains two different but interesting suggestions about the relationship between 1640s Levelling and 1650s republicanism: firstly, that there was a continuity between the arguments of the Levellers in the 1640s and the republican arguments which they themselves were associated with in the 1650s; and secondly, that 'The "classical republicanism" of theorists of the 1650s [particularly referring to Nedham] may in fact have been formulated, at least in part, in response to a more representative and popular republicanism advocated by the Levellers in the previous decade.'[9] As Glover recognizes, 'there was nothing inherently egalitarian or democratic about republicanism', and the relationship between Levellers and (other) republicans was not necessarily simple.[10] These tensions, as well as possible continuities, are my focus in this chapter.

The classical republicanism of the 1650s was a complex phenomenon, with authors who wrote for the regime often balanced on a knife-edge between critique and propaganda, and those who wrote against the regime often framing devastating criticisms of it as helpful suggestions for further development.

The Levellers

Not only were the republican writers of these years not always in agreement with each other; given the need to keep up with, and perhaps defend, changes of constitutional form, together with changes in personal fortune and political context, they might well change their own positions between one publication and another. There is no monolithic English republicanism against which we can assess the reception of Leveller thought in the 1650s; rather, the legacy of the Levellers became intertwined with the internal disputes and uncomfortable compromises of republican writing. Accordingly, there is no simple answer to the question of Leveller influence in republicanism; rather, there are congruities and tensions which were thrown into relief according to context in the shifting debates of the 1650s.

NETWORKS AND CONNECTIONS

There is prima facie evidence of potential continuities in the links which we can see between Leveller and republican personnel. In the 1640s, Henry Marten and Marchamont Nedham both appear to have had moments of alliance with Leveller activists, although the stability and intellectual depth of these is hard to trace.[11] In spite of his mixed success in appealing to Marten in the 1640s, Lilburne again wrote to Marten from his exile in the Low Countries in the 1650s, presumably choosing him as the most sympathetic member of the Council of State.[12] Nedham is implicated in some Leveller-associated pamphlets from 1645 to 46 which we will consider below. In the 1650s, some former Levellers were certainly involved in republican thinking and plotting, although those who were most central to the Leveller project in the 1640s were not always those who engaged most directly and keenly with classical republicanism in the 1650s. John Lilburne, the great figurehead of the Levellers in his public presentation, did indeed show an (entirely novel) interest in the language of classical republicanism and the works of Machiavelli in the 1650s (he confessed to Henry Marten that before embarking on this reading he had not known why his friend had called him 'Noble Cato').[13] As we will see, Lilburne is a case study in the very selective assimilation of classical ideals. Lilburne also tactically cited the republic's own propagandists, John Milton and Marchamont Nedham, against their masters, much as he had used Parliament's *Book of Declarations* against it throughout the 1640s. As with the parliamentary declarations, Lilburne was able to detect genuinely shared principles of love of country in Milton's writing, and of frequently elected parliaments in Nedham's, but it took selective reading, and he used his texts to hint at courses of action which might be far from the overt intention of the authors cited.[14] Richard Overton's dealings in the 1650s are obscure and possibly shady, and no works can be certainly attributed to him, but he does seem to have been involved in some anti-government activity.[15] William Walwyn's name was invoked by radicals in a couple of documents in the 1650s, but this seems to have been a projection from his earlier activities, as does the Council of State's apparently unexecuted order for his imprisonment in 1653; he intervened in public life only to state views on jury trial and on freedom of trade, but 'neither took nor was suspected of taking any action hostile to the Commonwealth'.[16] The central Leveller figures, then, did not slip directly into republican activity; Lilburne, indeed, was more known for cavalier than republican links, although in the 1650s the two were not incompatible. The most prominent Leveller-linked figures who did play a central role in the republicanism of the 1650s were John Wildman (an agent of Henry Marten, a member of Harrington's Rota and the host of the precursor meetings at Nonsuch House) and Edward Sexby (the presumed author of *Killing Noe Murder*, which advocated the tyrannicide of Cromwell).[17] Sexby's links with the Levellers in the events of 1647 have, of course, been much disputed.

In spite of these links, though, republicans of the 1650s might be prepared to attack the Levellers and their ideas. The Levellers and their allies posed a serious threat to the Commonwealth in its first months. That threat was countered not just by Fairfax and Cromwell leading their troops to Burford to quell their mutinous colleagues, but also by the propagandists of the new regime. Among those called on were John Milton and Marchamont Nedham, now canonical authors in the roll-call of 1650s republican writers. While Milton never completed the work against the Levellers commissioned from him, Nedham devoted one chapter of his *Case of the Commonwealth* (1650) to an excoriating attack on Leveller principles. John Hall, seen by some scholars as a notably republican writer, wrote commissioned propaganda which attacked John Lilburne alongside the populist republican John Streater, although these works were part of his anonymous output.[18] Other republicans could also express disapproval of the Levellers: Henry Marten set out a florid preamble to a case against the Levellers in an unfinished manuscript of uncertain date, although he did not get as far as explaining the grounds of his objections.[19]

Pay and political expediency were powerful forces, of course, and there is suspicion that some republicans may have felt real sympathy for Leveller objectives even while employed by the regime which denigrated them. Milton's failure to fulfil his commission against the Levellers has been the subject of much scholarly discussion, with controversy over the possibility that he might have had significant enough sympathies with the Levellers to hold him back from writing against them until the need to counter them was past.[20] Nedham, in spite of his apparently enthusiastic inclusion of Levellers among the misguided opponents of the regime in his *Case of the Commonwealth*, omitted the material on the Levellers from the series of editorials he recycled from this work for *Mercurius Politicus*. Again, it has been suggested that a degree of sympathy for Leveller aims lay behind this decision, particularly given that the *Case* was written as Nedham's 'job application' to his future employers and thus needed to toe the line.[21] When republican authors were either covertly or overtly writing against the regime, consonances with Leveller thought might emerge much more clearly. Nedham's further series of *Mercurius Politicus* editorials have been described by Blair Worden as fusing 'the Leveller vision of Lilburne and Richard Overton to the republican one of Machiavelli'.[22] John Streater's provocative and entirely oppositional republican writing was initially prompted by his opposition to the dismissal of the Rump Parliament in 1653 and the political developments which followed; he not only incorporated Leveller arguments about political consent into his classical republicanism, but also spoke up for John Lilburne himself; an opponent tellingly described Streater's 'Party' as 'Levellers'.[23]

CLASSICAL 'LANGUAGES' AND REPUBLICAN THOUGHT

There are reasons beyond the vagaries of personnel and propaganda in the 1650s to problematize the continuity of Levelling into 1650s republicanism. A recognizably distinct classical republican language, which had barely impinged on Leveller circles at all in the 1640s, began to circulate widely in the 1650s. If there was continuity of political impulses between Levelling and 1650s republicanism, therefore, it was accompanied by a significant shift in political language, and presumably in thought, and we will need to ask ourselves why a new language was necessary, or available, in the England of the 1650s, which the Levellers had not exploited in the 1640s.

The study of republicanism is bedevilled by the flexibility of the term, and the aim of this chapter is characterize the thought of various strands of republicanism in relation to aspects of Leveller thought, rather than to pronounce on whether Leveller thought was inherently 'republican', or republican thought 'Leveller'. Evidently, if republicanism is defined simply by anti-monarchism, the sometimes very explicit anti-monarchism of the Levellers' position might qualify them on these technical grounds, whatever the broader texture of their constitutional thought or their political discourse. But of course, the key question of the 1650s was precisely the question of what, beyond anti-monarchism, constituted a true commonwealth. Lilburne himself explained the issue when interrogated by Prideaux shortly before his 1649 trial: this (Rump) Parliament, without a renewal of its trust, had not been mandated by the people 'to set up new Constitutions, and to alter the Government of the Nation from a Kingdom to a Common-wealth'. When Prideaux retorted that Lilburne surely had in the past thought a commonwealth preferable to a king, Lilburne agreed, but explained that that commonwealth had to be properly constituted, with bounds and limitations, with annually elected, accountable magistrates; not what he called the 'name' of a commonwealth, imposed by the sword, and 'absolutely arbitrary'.²⁴ The distinction between the 'name' of a commonwealth and the thing itself became something of a trope for republican critics of the new regime. Lilburne repeated in 1653 that the English people had been 'free (never since they were about 4 years ago declared a free people) in nothing else but bare name'.²⁵ In the same year Wildman asked whether the people were to be satisfied with 'the names onely of those good words, *Common-wealth, free-State, free people* ... if the things themselves are denied'.²⁶ Marchamont Nedham, having in his original propaganda for the regime defended a minimal version of a 'free state' defined almost entirely by its freedom from monarchy, later came to assert that the supposed liberty of merely living in a non-monarchical state was empty: merely expelling the 'name King' from Rome had not achieved liberty; once the 'thing King' was expelled too, with the assertion and expansion of plebeian rights: 'Now, and never till now, could they be said to be a *free state* and *Commonwealth*, though long before declared so'.²⁷

For at least some Levellers, however, the necessary fleshing out of the principles behind anti-monarchical politics could lead to less-than-republican conclusions. Lilburne went on to explain to Prideaux that even a king – suitably bounded – would be preferable to the arbitrary mock-commonwealth of the Rump.²⁸ Hans-Christoph Schröder has argued that the logic of the Levellers' thought was driven by individual rights and distrust of *any* power, not just monarchy; while they may have furthered the revolution which came about, their own principles did not involve an insistence on republican constitutional forms for their own sake.²⁹ Indeed, royalist links compete with republican ones in the historiography of former Levellers in the 1650s, and royalists and republicans might conspire together against a regime which pleased neither of them.³⁰

More substantial types of republicanism can be delineated through attention to their language and sources, as well as their treatment of more detailed constitutional arrangements or their commitment to fuller ideas about citizenship and virtue. When the republican tradition is discussed by historians, it is often a specifically classical republican or civic humanist tradition that is at issue. The reception of this tradition in England has been quite variously understood. While there is no doubt that the classically informed culture of Renaissance humanism had penetrated English learned culture, and education more broadly, it is less clear whether a participatory civic ideology necessarily accompanied this. Between the wide availability of classical materials and the less ample evidence of meaningfully and robustly classical republican theorizing about politics in the earlier seventeenth century there has been scope for much scholarly disagreement. While Pocock had influentially argued that the English adoption of Machiavellian thinking was late and rather difficult, other strands in the scholarship of Elizabethan and early Stuart England have suggested that the civic humanist impulses of the early sixteenth century were not completely blotted out or transformed into a less idealistic discourse by the later years of the century.[31] Although common-law constitutionalist and natural-law contractualist understandings have dominated interpretation of early Stuart political discourse, Quentin Skinner has detected a 'neo-Roman' concept of liberty infusing these early Stuart debates.[32] S. D. Glover's work has emphasized the availability of classical works in translation, and of translations of Machiavelli, in his argument that classical republican thought of a plebeian kind did make its mark on the Levellers' thought in the 1640s.[33] Nonetheless, it remains very possible to maintain that political discourse before the civil war, and even in the 1640s, was relatively little touched by classical republican argument. Many scholars of English republicanism see a step change in the usage of classical republican sources and argument after the regicide, and that proves to be largely borne out by a study of the Levellers' writing.

Earlier chapters have explored the Levellers' use of natural-law contractualist and common-law arguments in their writing of the 1640s. These were the structural elements in Leveller political argument, and they were not elaborated with any very overt reference to the tropes or sources of classical humanism. Where authority was sought and cited – particularly, of course, in Lilburne's over-stuffed margins – it tended to be the authority of English legal history and, more opportunistically, Parliament's own declarations and propaganda, rather than of classical authors or ancient history. Yet it is possible to see both Overton and Walwyn as humanists, if perhaps in idiosyncratic ways, and Leveller authors certainly shared some of the classical knowledge which was central to early modern educational and learned culture. Overton's university education left him comfortable with Latin and with the use and parody of certain kinds of academic language, and his heretical work *Mans Mortallitie* in its two published versions referred to an array of classical, patristic, and more modern authorities, although his citations may not all be at first hand.[34] John Wildman may, like Overton, have studied at Cambridge.[35] Walwyn's lack of the classical languages did not prevent him from reading extensively in translation and defending the value of 'humane authors' such as Thucydides, Plutarch, Seneca and Lucian.[36] Like Walwyn, whose love of classical literature was based on English translations, and who has been characterized as a 'vernacular humanist',[37] Overton was opposed not to humanist ideals of learning and education, but to their perversion into a system of privilege. As McDowell remarks, 'In his emphasis on the pedagogical efficacy of persuasion and argument and on the democratizing role of education in enabling human beings to understand themselves and their God-given freedoms, the Leveller Overton was the true heir of the humanist ideal.'[38] Lilburne, in the 1640s, was certainly the least classically minded of the Leveller authors, but in the others we might expect some aspects of their reading to colour their political thinking, perhaps lending their radical politics a classical republican flavour.

To what extent, then, was the potential for classicizing republican language realized in Leveller writings of the 1640s? The language of liberty and slavery was certainly present, and it is certainly arguable that the use of these terms in political discourse was owing to the penetration of English political discourse by ideas of classical origin. To a certain extent, when 'liberties' became 'liberty' this may have been under the influence of a more abstract classical conception of liberty. One aspect of that notion has been described by Quentin Skinner under the label of 'neo-Roman liberty', in which liberty as non-dependence, rather than any mere de facto enjoyment of freedom of action, is the standard required for an adequate politics.[39] Leveller authors, including Lilburne, were keen to push this point home, partly through the theatrical presentation of Lilburne's case as, potentially, 'every man's case': others might, like Lilburne, find that their liberties were continued on sufferance rather than guaranteed to them. Government under such conditions was 'arbitrary', whereas the government of laws rather than of men would guarantee (neo-Roman) liberty. Arbitrary government was, in effect, a form of slavery for those subject to it, and tyranny for those exercising it. This whole nexus of ideas undoubtedly has a classical foundation.[40]

Classical though these ideas were, however, they tended to appear in the writing of the 1640s in a pared-down form, stripped of overt references to classical sources and exempla. On the rare occasion when a classical source was invoked, it could be used to reinforce a perspective based on England's law and constitutional arrangements, rather than expressing an influx of distinctively Roman or republican ideals, as in *Liberty Vindicated Against Slavery*, where Cicero was cited only to back up Magna Carta.[41] Overt citations of classical material were rare in any case, the exception which proves the rule being a pair of pamphlets supporting Lilburne's cause: *England's Miserie, and Remedie*, from 1645; and *Vox Plebis*, from 1646, a pamphlet which Lilburne himself recommended.[42] Both Nedham and Marten, among others, have been suggested as possible authors of these texts, although the most convincing evidence points to Nedham.[43] Even in these pamphlets, classical material underwent some striking accommodations and adaptations to fit it to the Leveller cause, and these pamphlets are very atypical of the movement. Only in a few places in the more mainstream Leveller oeuvre of the 1640s does an attentive reader pick up faint resonances of a rounded classical republican world-view.

Classical and republican ideas did not just explicate the external conditions under which liberty could be said to be enjoyed; they also emphasized the internal dimensions of liberty and slavery. Here, too, we may see some consonant concerns in Leveller writings, even if not directly expressed in classical language. Leveller authors were certainly concerned to combat the psychology of servility. I have argued that John Lilburne's famous catchphrase of the 'free-born Englishman' was used by him to connote, and promote, an active participation of the individual in the defence of liberties guaranteed by the law of the land.[44] This, I think, had the potential to converge with a republican account of the nature and importance of citizenship, and Lilburne presented it in terms which were strongly ethically coloured, again offering parallels to the ethical – and masculine – aspects of republican citizenship. His ideal Englishmen were 'true-hearted' and 'honest', and Englishness was associated with masculinity and valour. In spite of all this, there is very little sign of any classical republican account of psychology underlying this in Lilburne's writing – no sense that the free-born Englishman was engaged in any struggle of reason with the passions, and no use of the language of virtue. In Overton's *Appeale from the Degenerate Representative Body* a more complex mixture of sources animated this idea of the English people's duty to defend their rights against a Parliament grown tyrannical. 'Reason' is much more prominent in Overton's writing, and he appealed to it in his readers, much as Lilburne appealed to their English honesty: 'no rationall man can gainesay it'; 'can any reasonable man conclude ...?'[45] He urged his readers not to 'sit still and yeeld up your selves, as contented slaves', and linked the Englishness so prominent in Lilburne's rhetoric with a kind of biblical republicanism in a rather Miltonic way: 'For shame never let an English spirit be taxed with that dishonour; you have *Othniells*, *Ehuds*, *Baraks*, and *Gideons*, before you, even a mighty and puissant vertuous Army'.[46]

The *Remonstrance of Many Thousand Citizens* from 1646 made bold arguments against the 'intollerable incon[v]eniences of having a *Kingly Government*' and urged the House of Commons to abolish monarchy.[47] It drew on English history and the Norman Yoke rather than any argument about the inherent superiority of republics or citation of classical examples, but in spite of this it was one of the few Leveller tracts to flesh out the idea of the relationship between kingship or tyranny and servility in a republican way. It condemned 'Courtly ... behaviour' in governors, and 'Arristocraticall Government over the People in the State', and offered models of an unhealthily servile people, but also, significantly, of a robustly civic people.[48] The English had become servile as princes had cannily perpetuated the Norman enslavement 'by giving ease and wealth unto the People, but withall, corrupting their understanding, by infusing false principles [about government] ...; and also using all means to corrupt and vitiate the manners of the youth, and ... Gentry'.[49] The Dutch, on the other hand, were able to provide for their military needs without impressment because of their republican government, and the consequent public spirit of the men who would serve. England should copy 'the *Hollanders* our provident Neighbours', which is done simply by ensuring 'that all sorts of men might find comfort and contentment in your Government'. The author quickly presses home the Dutch moral:

> And if yee would in many things follow their good example, and make this Nation a *State*, free from the Oppression of *Kings*, and the corruptions of the Court, and shew love to the People in the Constitution of your Government, the affection of the People, would satisfie all common and publike Occasions ...[50]

In the absence of explicit classical humanist argumentation (and even the rather republican elements discussed here are dispersed among rather different kinds of material and argumentation), and with the contemporary example of the Dutch rather than any historical republics foregrounded, the type of 'republicanism' this recalls most strongly is the strain of oppositional writing represented by Thomas Scott in the 1620s.[51]

Leveller use of the language of tyranny occasionally became freighted with the full classical overtones of the word. Overton integrated Ciceronian argument and language about the nature of tyranny into his argument in *An Appeale* that 'the resistance of Tyrants is no resistance of Magistrates, except it be of such so nominally; but really and essentially monsters and pests of humanity'. Like Cicero, he used the idea that the social body may 'prune, amputate and cut of [sic] the corrupt putrified Members', and expanded on the idea of the community defined simply by its 'humanity and humane civility', excluding only 'the unnaturall and the inhumane'.[52] It is hard to believe that Overton did not have the well-known passage from the third book of *De Officiis* at least at the back of his mind as he wove these ideas through a few consecutive pages of his own tract. Overton's denunciation of such 'Monsters in nature and humanity' ends suggestively with a paragraph appealing to 'every rationall honest Common-wealths man' to endeavour their 'extirpation'.[53] Here we have a key Leveller of the 1640s already adopting the label of 'commonwealthsman' in the way that Cromwell saw former Levellers doing in the 1650s. Even the *Appeale*, however, was structured around the 'radicall principle[s] in Nature' – the dominant Leveller language of natural law – and the discussion of tyranny took its place in a work which used resistance theory far more than classical republican sources. A fully classicizing work on tyranny from a 'Leveller' pen did not emerge until *Killing Noe Murder* appeared in 1657, attributed to Edward Sexby.

The Levellers' use of consent as a key mechanism and legitimation for political power also found some classical resonances. The authors of *Regall Tyrannie Discovered* offered an interesting account of a community where people 'live in mutuall society one amongst another in *nature and reason*', in which 'all the particulars or individuals knit and joyned together by mutuall consent and agreement, becomes a *Sovereign Lord* and *King*'.[54] On the face of it, this is a passage about the natural law (here equated both with reason and with the law of God), but it also recalls Ciceronian notions of political community. The reference to Cato which follows may suggest that classical ideas were indeed informing the author's account of natural law at this point.

England's Miserie and *Vox Plebis*, the two early classicizing works possibly by Marchamont Nedham, derived from classical works – sometimes at second hand – a suitably Leveller insistence on a fundamental popular sovereignty. The mediating role of Buchanan's political thought and Walter Raleigh's history in these references is evidence for the currency of such interpretations of classical thought in the early modern period. Buchanan's fusion of Calvinist resistance theory with classical materials had yielded a dialogue which was notoriously extreme in its espousal of popular power and resistance against abuse of power,[55] and Raleigh's *History of the World* (written in the Tower of London) also had a reputation for its harsh words for princes.[56] *Englands Miserie* mentioned Buchanan as a source of the view that supreme power was in the people, before going on to invoke the Roman example.[57] Both tracts used material on C. Flaminius from Raleigh's *History*, although only in the second was it attributed to Raleigh rather than (impossibly) to Livy. It was indeed Raleigh's own analysis of Flaminius's political thought – 'understanding the Majesty of Rome to be wholly in the people, and no otherwise in the Senate, then by way of delegacy, or grand Commission' – which attracted our author.[58] *England's Miserie, and Remedie* quoted too from Pliny's *Panegyricus* – an uncomfortable text for a republican, but one which evidently offered quotable statements of the republican values to which the Emperor Trajan graciously paid lip-service – to assert the principle of consent in government.[59] Such themes are perhaps not those which we would most associate with ancient political thought, but clearly there was precedent in the early modern period for using classical materials to illustrate them. Nevertheless, putting these tracts in the context of the whole Leveller output, it is clear that while classical examples might add authority to the case for popular power and consent, they were the least common way of making those points, for which other political vocabularies were quite adequate and perhaps more forceful for most of the Levellers' readers.

In other ways, too, Leveller ideas seem uncomfortably cast into classical form in these tracts. A very English emphasis on private property and individual liberty (and one which pervades Leveller thought) pulls against or has to be harmonized with the republican emphasis on the fortune of the whole state throughout *Vox Plebis*. Having set up the story of the 'publike liberty' of the Romans being defended by the tribunes against the nobles, the author then moved on to define 'the liberty [of] the people of this Commonwealth' as consisting of three things: liberty of conscience, liberty of the person, and liberty of estate.[60] The importance placed on individual rights was backed up by the discussion of Magna Carta; that on property by the topical objection to 'those ravenous Committees'.[61] But classical material as well as modern was ransacked in support of private property rights in the compendium of examples of rebellions ancient and modern brought about by excessive financial exactions on the people.[62] Sometimes Machiavelli was flatly contradicted: for our author it was a 'Maxime of all oppressing States ... *to maintain the publick, wealthy, and the particular poore*' – the opposite of Machiavelli's advice.[63] The tension between the common wealth (as republicans might see it) and private property seems too deep for an easy assimilation of one set of values to the other – and it was clearly the more individualistic notions of English political and legal discourse which won out.

Vox Plebis is evidence of a parallel tension between a republican view of law as shaping the morality of the governed and the republic as a whole, and the very different view of law which we see in the English material.[64] Again, rather than envisaging republican law-making which might re-found a state and create new generations of good citizens, our author adapted Machiavelli to suggest that the maintenance of existing law was paramount: instead of Machiavelli's comment, in Dacres's version, about good education proceeding from 'good laws', *Vox Plebis* had it springing from 'the due observance of setled lawes'.[65] Even the praise of 'free states' was tailored to a less republican and more individualistic political culture: the author argued, following Dacres's Machiavelli (but tellingly altering the singular 'liberty' to 'liberties') that 'Common-wealths have never been much amplified, neither in dominion nor riches, *unlesse only during their Liberties*'. In Machiavelli, the meaning was quite clear and was amplified by the examples of Athens after the fall of the Pisistratids and Rome after it got rid of its kings.[66] In *Vox Plebis* the author ignored these examples and went on to argue, in a way entirely within the bounds of an English monarchical system, that those who governed the 'Kingdome' should make sure they ruled over 'free Subjects' and not 'Vassals'.[67] Machiavelli's English translator, Dacres, had himself objected to Machiavelli's argument at this point in a lengthy note; the altered direction in which our author took this passage perhaps suggests that English discomfort with such a radical Machiavellianism persisted.[68]

John Lilburne's own adoption of some of the resources of the republican tradition in the 1650s was similarly limited and compromised. According to Nigel Smith, by the time of his *L. Colonel John Lilburne Revived* in 1653 we see Lilburne, in spite of his slightly 'blundering' use of his new reading, 'convert partial into fully-fledged republicanism' with an anti-tyrannical emphasis.[69] Lilburne certainly acquired his republican veneer slowly, and he used it to feed two aspects of his own political personality – his furious rejection of the supposed dishonesty and betrayal of his enemies, the potentates of the new regime, and his sense of the heroic project of the people's assertion of their liberty.

The Levellers

Lilburne read Machiavelli for the first time in the 1650s, and found the *Prince* – perhaps the only work he read[70] – a tract for the times, useful 'in corrupt times & places' as a guide to the machinations which the enemies of freedom (in this case, Cromwell) would employ. Lilburne referred twice to chapter 18 of *The Prince*, '*In what manner Princes ought to keep their words*', where Machiavelli commended integrity but commented on the lack of it in successful men and went on to elaborate on the skills of the lion and the fox.[71] In reading Machiavelli in this way, Lilburne was partly following the lead given by Edward Dacres, the English translator of Machiavelli. Lilburne lifted a couple of exculpatory phrases from Dacres's preface to his translation of *The Prince*: Dacres told the sceptical reader that 'thou shalt find him [Machiavelli] much practisd by those that condemne him', and Lilburne followed that account in explaining that he found Machiavelli useful 'to help me clearly to see through all the disguised deceits of my potent, politick, and powerfull adversaries'.[72] Lilburne also drew historical lessons from the collapse of the Roman republic: the murderous and self-interested cooperation of the second triumvirate against any former friends who were 'lovers of the liberties & freedoms of Rome' reminded him of the cooperation of Lambert, Harrison, and Cromwell.[73] Indeed, having emphasized only a page earlier that human rationality entitled mankind to choose their own governments according to moral principles, Lilburne reverted to the material of classical history to warn of the brutish nature of men if unchecked, which he attributed to the effects of the Fall, and exemplified by citing Sulla, Marius, and Catiline.[74] The cynicism of an author – Machiavelli – whom Lilburne recognized as republican, and the materials of classical history, were here being used to fathom statecraft and condemn tyranny and the ambitions of military men, rather than to develop a more positive vision of republican life. What is more, Lilburne's tendency to figure 1650s England as the dying days of the Roman republic suggests an odd nostalgia for the old regime, one which Lilburne openly expressed in the same pamphlet. In retrospect, government by consent had been enjoyed 'in England in great measure under the establishment of Kings'; 'with all its imperfections' it had nevertheless been 'in the constitution of it, the best, rationalest, and for the people of England most securest [sic] of declared and setled Governments now extant in the whole world'.[75]

Lilburne's engagement with republican and classical writing certainly had a more positive side too. Lilburne added to Dacres's more condemnatory comments his own understanding that Machiavelli was forced by circumstance to adopt some 'unhandsome disguises' and was in fact 'one of the most wisest, judicious & true lovers of his country of Italies liberties and freedomes, and generally of the good of mankind that ever I read of'.[76] Lilburne found in classical histories examples, with which he was quick to identify, of men fighting 'to set at libertie and freedome their neighbours', as Lilburne was doing from the Netherlands.[77] Classical history could offer inspirational examples of the people's own power to assert their rights and liberties. Lilburne's use of classical material was designed to reinforce the message of popular sovereignty, and to show how unstoppable the people could be when they chose to exercise it. He promised to instruct 'the people of England' in how to gain 'the reall exercise of their declared rightfull supreme power', partly by producing

> Presidents from the practise of the people in the Ancient & most famous Commonwealth of Rome, and the Ancient Grecian Common-wealths of Athens, Corinth, Thebes, &c. how they practised their supreme power upon many occasions, even upon the greatest Generalls, Patricians, Noblemen, Senatours, or Parliament-men they had.[78]

The struggle to achieve liberty was crucial; but there is little sense of Lilburne's moving beyond that to any definition of republican government or liberty which differed from his Leveller views.[79] Lilburne pasted a thin layer of classical exempla – heroes or bogeymen – onto his characteristic Leveller concerns.

It would, of course, be foolish to expect English republicanism to adopt classical or Machiavellian principles wholesale. Undoubtedly many of the English republicans adapted their republican discourse to local concerns and assimilated it to English political culture. For example, Worden finds Nedham's Machiavellianism 'diluted' by traditional English concerns with consent and with the protection of individual liberty and property; Rahe comments on an adaptation in which the positive role played by tumults in Machiavelli's version of Rome could be played by elections in England.[80] The question is how uncomfortable such appropriations and assimilations were. In this section I have suggested that even where the Leveller programme adopted a classical republican guise, this tended to be a little superficial. In the remaining two sections of this chapter, I will consider whether classical republicanism in the 1650s was capable of expressing deeper consonances with Leveller thought.

POPULARITY AND ANTI-POPULISM

The hallmark of Leveller thought was its populism. Not only was Leveller theory pervaded by the persistence of equal natural rights which must shape political life, but the Levellers' practice of popular politics through print, petitioning, and the crowd became notorious. Leveller populism evidently meshed with some republican notions of active citizenship, but republicans were often quite as concerned as others to repudiate the potentially uncontrollable involvement of the mass of the people. Given the consistency with which critiques of the Levellers were couched in anti-populist terms, often of a very alarmist kind, this republican caution also made for a difficult adoption of Leveller ideas into republican language.

The Levellers

One meeting between Leveller populism and a classical republican language occurred in the *Vox Plebis* pamphlets of 1645–46 which we have already seen. Glover has pointed out that they displayed a version of republicanism which was particularly 'plebeian'; it is striking that they also made little attempt to pacify fears about plebeian politics. The argument for a fundamental popular sovereignty and government based on consent was the core idea supported by the pamphlets' classicizing citations, but it was set out in ways which emphasized the impossibility of controlling a dissatisfied people. *Englands Miserie, and Remedie* included a dictum from Livy to support the contention that 'it is not credible that either people or person, in any outward condition under which they mourne, sigh, or groane, will continue any longer therein, then they have occasion of good termes to be delivered'.[81] A genuinely Machiavellian theme which characterizes both *Vox Plebis* and *England's Miserie* is the mutability of states and the concern with the conditions of their survival. In both works, this concern was used to create a sense of threat hanging over the oppressors of England: 'for every State governed by fantasticall and Arbitrary power, must needs be floting, inconstant, and subject to change'.[82] Machiavelli's emphasis on the positive value of tumult or conflict between the orders was used to reinforce this point; in this Englished version, however, the emphasis was less on the relations between the orders than on the relation between the people and their governors, which might not necessarily be understood in terms of social distinction. That emphasis on strife meshed neatly with the radical ancient constitutionalism of the English tradition, emphasized too in Leveller writing: the author asks us to consider 'the proceedings of our Ancestors, in the Acquisition and defence of their just liberties, and the continuall vigilance of them in making and ordaining good Lawes for their necessary preservation'.[83] Maintaining the emphasis on productive political strife, the pamphlets discussed the controversial figures C. Flaminius and Camillus in positive terms, not following the spirit of the more censorious treatments of them by Roman and Renaissance historians. Indeed, our author noticeably adjusted the tone of the material on Flaminius which he took from Walter Raleigh's *History of the World*. Raleigh's own attitude to Flaminius was ambivalent, seeing him as the first to have found out the increasingly common route to power by 'court[ing] the Multitude'. The author of *Vox Plebis* doctored the quotation so that Flaminius 'assisted' rather than 'courted' the multitude, and added a phrase all of his own (still in italics as if part of the quotation): Flaminius did not just help the people 'in reforming their disorders' as in Raleigh, but also in 'vindicating the publike liberty of his Countrey'.[84] All in all, the author of *Englands Miserie* and *Vox Plebis* invoked classical material in a way which was strikingly plebeian but hardly benign; it echoed the more threatening Leveller demands that their readers agitate for their liberties, rather than offering any way of envisaging a functioning order for a popularly governed state.

Levellers into republicans?

When it came to mapping out an actual constitutional order for a republic, Leveller proposals were more difficult to adopt than we might expect. The major obstacle to accommodating Leveller thought within a republican tradition was the spectre of 'democracy'. As we have seen, the Levellers strenuously avoided the classical language of constitutional forms in setting out their political vision, even though they might have done so without characterizing it as a simple, unrestrained democracy. They could have claimed that there might be a 'mixed' or aristocratic element in the administration of government by officials, even though the election of a unicameral legislature made sovereignty itself unmixed and democratic. They could have emphasized that they were not seeking a direct democracy – often seen as the most dangerous type, and one which civil war propagandists could condemn as 'cantoning and folkmoots' – but a more restrained representative democracy, in which the wisdom of experienced elected representatives of good social standing might moderate any tendency to fickleness or folly in the mass of the people. The fact that the Levellers chose to avoid this constitutional language altogether suggests two things. Firstly, it was extremely important to them to avoid conceding that what they were suggesting was any kind of constitutional innovation; they were, in their own rhetoric, simply defending the essential character of the English constitution as it existed, rather than proposing blueprints for a new system. Secondly, the danger of their views being seen as democratic was great, and the opportunities for minimizing their democratic character were not necessarily strong. Discussing the constitution in explicit terms might have forced the Levellers into being more specific than they wished to be about the composition of the electorate or the purely subordinate and official character of anyone with a role in government (including king or Lords) who was not an elected representative. A unicameral sovereign legislature elected on a broad franchise was a constitution which, defined by the location of sovereignty, *was* essentially democratic; and this was something which it would be profoundly unwise to concede.

Opponents of the Levellers, however, had no hesitation in framing Leveller views in these terms. Anti-democratic attitudes were widely shared in early modern culture; the expression of them was not limited to one end of the political spectrum, and they were articulated by republicans and royalists alike. The Presbyterian heresiographer Thomas Edwards accused 'sectaries', including the Levellers, of rejecting monarchy and aristocracy in favour of a 'democracie' which was entirely unlimited:

> they make it noe other then an Anarchie, making all alike, confounding of all rancks and orders, reducing all to Adams time and condition and devolving all power upon the state Universall and promiscuos [sic] multitude, whom they make the Creator and Destroyer of Kings, Parliaments and all Magistrates at there meere pleasure, without tying them to any rule, or bounding them by any lawes.

The Levellers

For Edwards, the Levellers' representative system of government, as expressed in Overton's pamphlets, had the effect of 'setting up the body of the common people, as the Soveraigne Lord and King; denying King and Lords any power, and the House of Commons any further then the peoples Deputies, and at the pleasure of and will of the people'. It was this ultimate reduction of all government to the will of the people, which Edwards interpreted as fundamentally unmediated by any restraining influence, which made Leveller thought democratic.[85]

Accusations of democratic leanings were perhaps not surprising coming from royalists or from Presbyterians, but anti-democratic thought held a key place in the republican tradition too. Not only did the various strands of the republican tradition draw on ancient Greek and Roman materials which were suffused with arguments against 'extreme' democracy; such arguments were rooted in the same accounts of human psychology and ethics which often underpinned republican accounts of virtuous government (including self-government); and, of course, republican constitutional forms might be more likely to attract the slur of democracy, so republicans might take pains to defend themselves by co-opting anti-democratic argument. In this light it becomes more understandable that republicans were happy to deploy such arguments against Levellers when writing against them.

Nedham did explicitly place Leveller populism under the heading of democracy. Indeed, he took the term 'levelling' and brought it into direct relationship with the vocabulary of democracy. The Levellers' 1649 Agreement of the People urged, according to Nedham, a *'Popular Form, or a Government by the People'*, and the equality of right in choosing and being chosen to the Representative, regardless of birth, quality or wealth, was a form of 'levelling'. From here he asserted 'that this Term of *Levelling* is equivalent with *Aristotle*'s 'ισονομια, which is translated *aequalitas Juris*'. He then summed up his sense of what the Leveller proposal was explicitly in terms of democracy: 'Such a *Democratick*, or *Popular Forme*, that puts the whole multitude into an equall exercise of the *Supreme Authority*, under pretence of maintaining *Liberty*.'[86] The vocabulary was developed more, though not necessarily very systematically, later in Nedham's chapter: 'meer popularity' translated 'regimen democraticum', or, in Greek, δημοκρατια ακρατος (unmixed democracy), but it also received a more idiosyncratic gloss: *'a meer Popular State* (or Levelling popularity)'.[87] For Nedham, all of these descriptions or translations of democracy were a very different thing from the *'Free State'* which he himself was defending; one of the things that was wrong with a democracy was that it would destroy a free state, especially a new and vulnerable one.[88] What is striking about all this is how far removed it is from the language of the document it supposedly draws from, *An Agreement of the People*. Essentially, Nedham extrapolated from 'people' to 'popular form', understood as 'democracy', but even the phrase

'Government by the People' which Nedham used to sum it up did not appear in the Levellers' Agreement.

Nedham's identification of the Levellers with democrats, even though it had no basis in their own vocabulary, may have been reasonable as an assessment of their thought. But his tendentious purpose in labelling them as democrats is clear from his decision to ignore the distinction drawn by one of his major sources, Christoph Besold's *Synopsis Politicae Doctrinae*, between direct democracy and the mere election and correction of magistrates. Besold labelled direct democracy 'libera democratia', and it was this form, rather than the more stable 'democratia adstricta', to which he attached the notion of isonomia (Nedham's 'levelling') and the ills of demagoguery.[89] But Nedham spoke simply of democracy as 'meer popularity', making no such distinction. Even though the system proposed in the Levellers' Agreement was an electoral one, Nedham warned that the annual elections proposed by the Levellers would descend into violence, due to 'those prodigious multitudes' who would be allowed to elect: partly, no doubt, a fear grounded in real-life election disturbances, but perhaps partly a transference of the fears of the potential chaos of direct democracy to the indirect model.[90]

These identifications enabled the full panoply of anti-democratic arguments to be used against the Levellers. The anti-democratic tradition saw democracy as a political system in which the disordered self-seeking psychology of the rabble, where reason could not command the passions and virtue was impossible, was transferred to the state as a whole. The democratic polity would not be ordered by reason, but would simply seek to fulfil the worst impulses of its people – often understood as the impulses of its lowliest people. It would not promote virtue but actively punish the virtuous, as the popular electorate would give office only to those who promised to indulge their whims. Consequently, the whole value system of a democracy became perverted, with the fine-sounding democratic watchwords of 'liberty' and 'equality' in fact signifying disordered licence and a refusal to acknowledge merit. This all offered abundant reasons for republicans to doubt the wisdom of apparently populist schemes, favouring instead more truly 'aristocratic' regimes which could institute virtue and the rule of reason; and it offered abundant rhetorical resources for attacking Leveller appeals to liberty and equality.

Nedham followed this tradition to the letter in his attack on the Levellers. His low opinion of the capacities of the multitude for reason and virtue formed the basis of his critique. Nedham cited classical sources in arguing that 'the multitude is so Brutish, that ... they are ever in the extreames of kindness or Cruelty; being void of Reason, and hurried on with an unbridled violence in all their Actions'.[91] This inconstancy, in his view, infected the Levelling movement as a whole, making them 'giddy and rapid in their Motions'.[92] The Levellers' writings had urged 'free-born Englishmen' to know their own capacities and to assert their own equal birthrights, but Nedham, by contrast, criticized the multitude as 'self-opinionated' individuals filled with a deluded sense of their 'equall Interest and power'.[93] The Levellers' claims for liberty, too, suddenly appeared suspect in the framework of republican anti-democratic thought. Republicans did, of course, rally round the idea of liberty, but they felt that populist ideas of liberty misunderstood it as licence, the simple ability to live as one likes rather than as one should. These ideas acquired a particular edge in England after the regicide, as they enabled many republican propagandists to explain how it was that the people could show the apparent zeal to fight for liberty from tyranny, but then prove incapable of the type of self-government which might produce real, lasting liberty. If the people had been pursuing the wrong kind of liberty, they could not be entrusted with exercising the right kind, and in pursuit of their whims might indeed plunge the nation back into tyranny, even the return of the Stuarts. Thus for Nedham, democracy, which brought the whole multitude into government 'under pretence of maintaining *Liberty*', was in fact 'the greatest enemy of *Liberty*'; the irrational multitude in fact scorned all sacred and civil matters in their pursuit of 'that their *Liberty*, which *Clapmarius* calls a most dissolute *licentiousnesse*, or a licence to doe even what they list'.[94]

This all meant that there were two ways in which democracy, according to the anti-democratic tradition, led not to liberty but to tyranny. Firstly, the licentious rule of the lowest of the people might itself be a tyranny; Nedham quoted several sources, ancient and modern, to this effect, including, pointedly in the context of 1650, Guicciardini's warning about the licentious tyranny into which a newly liberated people may break out.[95] Even more pointedly, the people's proneness to be gulled by anyone promising excessive liberty meant that a democracy could very easily tip over into a tyranny – even, as Nedham did not hesitate to point out, the tyranny of 'those out of whose hands [liberty] was first recovered'.[96] This popular desire not of true liberty but of licence could thus lead to the thwarting of the people's interests in the long run; but in the meantime it resulted in bad government. Nedham stressed that, in democracies, the people would only choose the *'lowest of the People'* for office, as being 'like to satisfie them in all their phren'tick humours'. The people were ultimately seeking indulgence from their governors, not direction or order; at elections they would reject 'such as they have found averse to their licentious waies, as Enemies of Liberty'.[97] Nedham expanded at length on the trope that democracies were in the habit of expelling their best men. The correlate of this, of course, was that leaders arose who flattered and indulged the people, but always with the intention of serving their own interests in the end.

Nedham was the republican writer who most directly turned these arguments against the Levellers, but anti-populist attitudes were widely shared among republican writers in the 1650s. Milton's complex attitude to the potential and weaknesses of the people more often than not led him to believe that only the few 'Worthies' could defend England's newly won liberty 'amidst the throng and noises of Vulgar and irrational men'.[98] Circumstances, of course, might seem to suggest that the 'image-doting rabble' really could not be trusted not to revert to the idols of kingship;[99] blocking the participation of royalists in any future elections was a concern of the regime echoed by its republican propagandists. The royalist complexion which the activities of some former Levellers took on during the 1650s might have supported the view that populism would come full circle to a renewal of kingly tyranny. An 'aristocratic' republicanism of the few could seem the best option for circumstances like these, especially for those, like Milton and Vane, who melded that conception with a religious understanding of the godly few. Other republicans, such as Harrington and his followers, might seek to protect the commonwealth from the more dangerous inclinations of the people by circumscribing their involvement in government with complex mechanisms and counterbalances. While republicans and Levellers might in theory share an optimism about the potential of human nature for citizenship in a well-constructed participatory political system, in the 1650s holding to that vision and rejecting more restrictive republican visions was hard.[100]

In spite of these difficulties, Marchamont Nedham and John Streater have been identified as republicans from the 1650s who used classical republican language and argument to support a more populist republican programme. Nedham, as we have seen, had written vehemently against the Levellers in his *Case of the Commonwealth*; but there are also good reasons for linking him to the *Vox Plebis* pamphlets from the 1640s with their threatening classical exempla of popular unrest. Although Nedham's career as a political writer and propagandist continued to twist and turn with the exigencies of the changing political landscape in the 1650s, there were times when his supposed propaganda was clearly a critique, if a sly one, of current political arrangements. In this new mode, many of his earlier strictures on the Levellers were so pointedly overturned that he almost seemed to be pointing at his own inconsistencies, and the poles of his former anti-populist arguments were reversed to support his new demand for government by successive elected assemblies. Naturally, when Nedham is apparently criticizing rather than defending his paymasters we may suspect that the views he expresses are more fully his own. Yet even now the nature of Nedham's populism was complicated, and the extent of it could be strikingly limited. While there are good reasons for seeing his condemnatory chapter on the Levellers as something of an 'outlier' even in Nedham's rather jagged recorded political course, he did not simply abandon his anti-democratic arguments.

Nedham's Machiavellian republicanism was in many ways more populist than a republican theory had any need to be, what with his praise of Athens and of the tumults which secured the people's liberties at Rome.[101] In this new phase of his republican career, it was suddenly the people who had the most accurate understanding of what liberty was; the people were less luxurious and less ambitious than kings and grandees; worth and virtue were best rewarded under a system of regular popular election: in short, 'Temperance, Vertue, and Freedom ... flourished under the government of the people' in Rome.[102] Nedham appears to be deliberately rehabilitating popular government from all the criticisms which he himself had applied to it. But the anti-democratic caution did not disappear: he reconciled the belief that the people had to be the guardians of their own liberty with the republican exaltation of virtue and discipline simply by defining the 'people' in a deliberately limited way. Nedham's grand statements about the role of the people were accompanied by strictures that the people were not 'the confused promiscuous body of the People' (let alone delinquents).[103] Indeed, while he sometimes talked of the people electing their assemblies, he could even go so far as to say that the 'people' were not the electors but only those actually chosen as representatives; and his mantra was that the people *in* successive assemblies were the best keepers of their own liberties.[104] Following the anti-democratic tradition, he was careful to deny that freedom was simply the ability to do as one liked; and to stress, by speaking of the 'Discipline and Freedom both together' to be found in republican Rome, that liberty was not licence;[105] again, in an anti-democratic trope, he emphasized that free commonweals promoted 'not an equality (which were irrational and odious) but an equability of condition among all the Members'.[106]

For all this traditional anti-democratic colouring to Nedham's republicanism, his populism was striking. The core of it lay in his belief that only the people could be trusted to defend their own interests. Nedham's attraction to interest theory persisted through many changes of political allegiance; to cite the title of one of his own tracts, published in 1659, he believed that 'Interest will not Lie'. Nedham was thus one of the popularizers of the notion of interest as a 'social force' divorced from questions of right.[107] This approach does not sit easily with the republican language of discipline, temperance and virtue which appears in his more enthusiastically republican editorials. But perhaps it does explain how his populism could be simultaneously so emphatic and so distrustful of the people themselves, so violent (his Machiavellian endorsement of tumult was striking, even if he saw it transformed into English terms) and so conservative. What mattered for preserving the liberty of a state was not so much the people's judgements or their moral character (which Nedham would not necessarily judge positively), but simply their innate tendency to seek their own interests. If that was harnessed through a political system which had a central place for the expression of the people's will, their genuine interest in freedom ought to prevail. Of course, people were not necessarily the best judges of their interest – they had to be 'so wise as to understand [their] own Concernment'. Many of Nedham's works were meant to clarify to the relevant audience where their interest lay in the current political circumstances – it being, he explained, important that people should not 'be seduced from a right understanding of their Interest'.[108] However, the notion that interest could not lie began to hint at the almost mechanical power that the people's interest, however dimly they sensed it, might exert on political events. Indeed, for Nedham it was partly the weakness of character of the 'vulgar' which made their appreciation of their liberty and power so forceful: he appealed not to the people's reason but to their passions – their 'jealousy' in particular – to defend freedom.[109] Even though the government of the people – 'the successive revolution of Authority by their consent' – was what protected the state against tyranny, the sentiments of the 'greater part' of the people themselves, the 'Rabble of mankind', were prejudiced in favour of tyranny, either because of its 'outward splendor' or because they saw something in it for themselves.[110] In the editorial where he did – for once – talk about free states as fostering the 'use of that Reason and understanding God hath given' to men, he swiftly added a catch-all note that 'when we mention *the People*, observe all along, that we doe not mean the confused promiscuos body of the People'.[111] Where the mass of the people was concerned, it was not reason so much as the bare experience of liberty after tyranny – 'the possibilities or enjoyments of the present' – which taught them 'that their main Interest and Concernment consists in Liberty'; their reaction was more emotional than rational: they 'become ... extreamly affected with it' and revenge themselves on any who threaten it.[112]

Streater's populism was much fuller than Nedham's, and it resonated deeply with Leveller ideals. He therefore offers a fascinating case study of the ways in which the non-classically expressed priorities of the Levellers could be brought within a discourse which included many of the elements of classical republicanism and was often framed through the use of classical texts and examples. For Streater, as for the Levellers, the people's safeguarding of their own liberty operated through the collective exercise of individuals' political judgement. Streater directly addressed the people as readers, asking them to develop their knowledge and exercise their reason; Nedham, even at his most populist, had analysed the people and attributed their 'jealousy' of their liberty to their suggestible nature and uncontrollable emotions.

Streater's populism was made more resilient by the persistence of concepts of rights – reminiscent of Leveller notions – into his republican language. Thus he urged in 1653 that 'the *Common-wealth* be engaged to elect a new Representative according to their undeniable Rights'; the plural suggests that the commonwealth was understood as a composite of individuals, with individual rights of election.[113] Indeed, he urged his readers to recognize that 'since Monarchy is destroyed, thou hast a perfect equalitie, in respect of thy Rights and Priviledges'.[114] Streater, writing in the post-regicide context, was able to pronounce as a new fact the uniformity of rights which Lilburne had read into English law. These equal individual rights were underpinned by a notion of fundamentally equal capacities, again recalling the Levellers' emphasis on the adequacy of individuals' reason. Streater specifically rejected the idea that 'common capacities' were not sufficient to consider matters of 'publick concernment'; in fact 'every Member of the Common-wealth, of right and in duty, ought to watch to their Liberty, and prevent Absoluteness in persons of great Trust'.[115] Unlike Nedham, Streater attempted to resist on principle the idea that there were mysteries of state which the generality of the people could not concern themselves with.[116] As with the Levellers, though, there was still a sense of an ongoing process of education of the people in their political rights, a project most urgent in these dangerous times, and one which Streater's own writing overtly intended to promote:

> Reader, Here thou art guided to know thy self, to know others; Their Power and thy Liberty. There is no one thing under Heaven the cause of misery by the assumed Lording of Usurpers, but *Thy not knowing thy Liberties and Rights.*[117]

We have already seen the Levellers' similar concern that the people 'understand themselves'; a reflexive politics of self-government by consent required political knowledge to be reflexive too. To govern themselves – even through governors – the people must know themselves; and that knowledge should fortify them to act for their own rights with a justified sense of entitlement.

It would be possible to frame the distinction between Streater's and Nedham's populisms as a distinction between older and newer forms of republicanism: Streater's a republicanism which relies on the moral and intellectual qualities of the citizens for its robustness; Nedham's a more Machiavellian 'modern' republicanism based on analysing human behaviour rather than trying to change it.[118] But what is striking is that Streater resisted the course taken by many of the more traditional republican theorists, particularly easy in the context of the 1650s, of falling back on an aristocracy of virtue, however defined, rather than attributing sufficient moral capacity and rationality to the people.

MECHANISMS AND PRINCIPLES

The Levellers' populist thought was the greatest determinant of the political system they proposed. A unicameral representative, exercising the powers of the people who had directly elected it, was the only legitimate institutional sovereign. Responding to dangers to the liberty of individuals' persons and consciences, the Levellers sought protection, ever more urgently, in the people's capacity to know and protect their own rights and liberties. The

Levellers' struggle against arbitrary power and oppression ultimately depended on two simple mechanisms: the reservation of powers, and the regular and frequent succession of elections. The reserved powers were simply powers which were not to be exercised by any of the arms of government, including the Representative, because in curious ways they both belonged only to the people themselves, and belonged to no one. There was little mechanism for protecting these reserved powers, except for enshrining them in an Agreement of the People whose popular subscription would validate it, and hoping that the popular legitimacy of Parliament would prevent it from encroaching on them, and the people themselves would be able to call to account any who attempted it. This would be done through fresh elections, and the mechanism of election extended, by the time of the third Agreement of the People in May 1649, to any public officers who might be in danger of infringing the people's rights: local officials, juries, army officers, and parish ministers as well as the members of the sovereign representative.[119] While the Levellers never quite lost faith in the power of laws to bind rulers as well as ruled, and particularly the fundamental law embodied in the Agreement of the People, ultimately it was only the action of the people through election and re-election which offered any institutional means to protect these laws from violation by the members of the sovereign representative.

Election was a mechanism which republican authors could also embrace, but the ambivalent attitudes towards the people which we have already examined could make this problematic, leading either to limitations on election or to a belief that a single elected body could form only part of an adequate republican constitution. Indeed, the exigencies of the early period of the republic might make even propagandists of a republican bent seek for definitions of 'Commonwealth and Free State' which did not require free electoral politics, let alone any popular subscription to the new regime, as envisaged by the Agreement of the People. Nedham spent many early issues of *Mercurius Politicus* defending the legitimacy of the Rump Parliament against 'that Chimaera which they call the Universall consent of the People'.[120] The glorious free state which he defended in the *Case of the Commonwealth* was defined purely by its freedom from 'regall Tyranny'.[121] John Hall in 1653 protested against Streater's criticism of the Nominated Assembly, retorting that 'I cannot apprehend, that the Liberties of the people consist so much in electing their Governours, as in being well governed.'[122]

But an insistence on electoral politics was to return to 1650s republicanism. Streater queried whether an oligarchic arrangement could count as the 'Gove[r]nment of a Common Wealth, when the Common Wealth is excluded from the liberty of making a choice of persons to govern?'[123] He derived similar messages from the history of Rome and from Aristotle's idea of ruling and being ruled in turn, insisting that election of governors – preferably annual –

was the mark of a 'Free-People'. He went on to give examples of contemporary republics where this might be observed.[124] All of this resonated with Streater's Leveller-like emphasis on the people's own judgements, as well as being given a classical republican colouring.

Nedham, with his rather different mode of populism, also reverted to a plea for electoral politics as the key to creating and maintaining a genuinely free state. While it may have been the people's passions as much as their judgements which made election useful in Nedham's view, for both Nedham and Streater election had a role partly as the mechanism which could ensure rotation.

The Levellers' increasing concern about the corruption of rulers had led them to emphasize rotation too. The requirement that elected rulers 'be in a capacity to tast of subjection, as well as rule' had been one of the features commending the first Agreement of the People in 1647, although it fell short of the full republican notion that people should rule and be ruled in turn, which was ultimately derived from Aristotle's discussion of citizenship.[125] In the Levellers' version, not everyone could express their citizenship through ruling as a member of the Representative, but every member of the Representative must experience periods outside government, when they would be subject to the laws which they had made. In the 1649 Agreement, a new representative was to be chosen every year, and former members were only free to be elected again after one annual session had intervened.[126] Republican schemes of the interregnum echoed this concern for succession and rotation, similarly intended to minimize the danger of those in power becoming corrupt and forming factions. Nedham, writing under the Rump, urged that liberty would never be preserved by a 'standing power' but only by a constant succession of assemblies of the people, this succession preventing corruption.[127] Streater, in 1653, described the arrangements of republican Rome in terms which echoed the Levellers' demands, emphasizing the annual election of military as well as civil officers.[128] Perhaps it is symptomatic of John Streater's closeness to certain aspects of Leveller thought that he came to emphasize time-limits on office so strongly. Scholars have found it odd that he should present an idealized picture of the aristocratic republic of Ragusa (modern Dubrovnik) in a tract which professed to defend democratic government, but his overriding concern was that no magistrate should be able to stay more than a year in power. His run-down of the councillors and magistrates of Ragusa and their varying time-limits, with no one serving more than a year, the Rector serving only one month, and even night-watchmen swapping at midnight so that no one could both close the city gates at night and open them the next morning, was a perfect illustration of this. 'By this often changing of Officers, they preserve themselves', he declared; 'This is the true Embleme of a Free-State.'[129] Streater did not attempt to align the complicated conciliar and electoral systems of Ragusa with the popular government by election which he had recommended in the general part of the pamphlet; indeed, he commented that the Ragusan system of government was modelled on that of Venice, which he had mentioned as an aristocracy rather than a popular government. Like the Levellers, Streater put great faith in the people's self-government; this meant that, like them, he also had to emphasize frequent rotation of authority as one of the only possible mechanisms for limiting this legitimately; and Ragusa, undemocratic though it was, exemplified this rotation. For Streater, perhaps, the ancient notion of citizenship as ruling and being ruled in turn came closer to being reclaimed in its full symmetry than it did in the Leveller expressions of it. He commended Lycurgus' concern that his 'Citizens' should 'every one ... be as able to rule, as those that are chosen to rule', and explained that even though not every one in England would in fact rule, there was at least 'a possibility for every one that can arrive to Credit by his Parts, to be Chosen and Elected for the Next Representative'.[130]

Streater, of course, was one of the printers of Harrington's *Oceana*, and rotation of office was a republican principle which could extend far beyond those who were committed to very popular forms of republicanism. Harrington's description of the intricate 'revolutions' of Oceana's councils and their fit with the 'rotation' of the Senate, which 'being always changing, is forever the same', as it cannot 'instagnate', is enough to make a reader dizzy.[131] For Harrington, however, these rotations did not go with a meaningfully popular electoral system, but were part of a labyrinthine mechanism which made 'democracy' and representation safe for a commonwealth by stripping them of any meaningful link with the actual judgements of the people.[132]

For the Levellers, the sovereignty of a uniformly, directly elected single-chamber representative was the only safeguard against the tyranny of unaccountable, unelected rulers such as the king and the House of Lords had been. They were therefore not able to countenance any division of sovereignty (except perhaps the difficult division between the people themselves and their representatives). The notion of a separation of powers could not have any place in Leveller thought if it implied any division of sovereignty. Executive powers might be deputed to officers – even a 'king' as a mere chief officer – but those officers would always be appointed by the Representative and answerable to the Representative and, through that, the people. But for many republican authors, the people as a single undivided mass, and a single sovereign body of representatives directly elected by that people, could not provide sufficient safeguard against corruption and tyranny, or even sufficient guarantee of competent government.

The rejection of unicameral sovereignty was, of course, most pronounced in Harrington's political theory, with its crucial division between a Senate which proposed legislation and a popular chamber which merely voted for or against it. Harrington's influence spread among his circle of associates: John Wildman's thought showed early influence from Harrington when he wrote in 1653 that consideration should be given to 'how many of those chosen [to the Representative] shall have power to debate, and how many to Enact'.[33] In 1659, Wildman's exposition of 'Leveller' principles still included Harrington's stipulation that while legislation should be made by none but the people's successively elected deputies, those should be divided into 'Senators' who were to debate proposals, and a wider 'great assembly of the Peoples Deputies' who were to decide on them.[34] But other more popular and more pragmatic republicans than Harrington and his associates might also be uneasy with the idea of unicameral sovereignty; few of the models for republican government, in the ancient or early modern worlds, were so unmixed, and the disappointments of the Rump might foster this unease. Worden has even suggested that Nedham's praise for the popular institutions which limited the power of the Senate at Rome was a disguised plea for mixed government in England, rather than the populist statement it seems.[35] Even for those, such as Streater and – at least overtly – Nedham, who advocated sovereign single-chamber parliaments kept uncorrupt by successive elections, there was the temptation of inserting a more independent executive than the Levellers' fears might have tolerated.[36]

CONCLUSION

The Levellers were subtly at odds with both old and new forms of republicanism. Any emphasis on an aristocracy of virtue, or even on the glory of the state, sat uneasily with the fundamental Leveller emphasis on the equal rights of individuals and the necessary sovereignty exercised by a popularly elected representative. On the other hand, a newer and more Tacitean republicanism inclining towards interest theory, such as is often discernible in Nedham's writings, was more cynical, and at times more inclined to a brutal de-factoist justification of existing powers, than Leveller optimism about citizenship and legitimism about government could be comfortable with. The harnessing and taming of interest, whether in Nedham or in Harrington and his disciples, often seemed to mean the channelling of the people's irrational but reliably self-interested passions. This might exclude rather than encourage any reasoned, self-conscious exercise of citizenship on the people's part.

John Streater's synthesis offers a more optimistic story about the potential marriage of Levelling and classical republicanism. His was a genuinely classical republicanism which relied on the moral and intellectual qualities of the citizens for its robustness. That mode of republicanism was often committed to the anti-democratic principle which Paul Rahe has called 'differential moral and political rationality', i.e., an essentializing elitism, but Streater

Levellers into republicans?

was able to construct a version of it which kept but generalized its idealistic hopes for human reason and virtue. He resisted the course taken by many republican theorists, and particularly easy in the context of the 1650s, of falling back on an aristocracy of virtue, however defined, rather than attributing sufficient moral capacity and rationality to the people. Just as the Levellers, however despairing and disillusioned, always fell back on the remedy of *more* election, *more* representation, *more* popular power, so Streater maintained a faith that elective politics must always provide the answer, and that it must do so not through a cynical mechanism of interest-satisfaction, but through a meaningful engagement by citizens with their politics. In Streater's case, indeed, this belief led him to break through the taboos of both Levellers and republicans and state directly that 'Democracy ... is the most Natural, and best sort of all Governments.'[137]

NOTES

1 19 May 1649: S. R. Gardiner, *The Constitutional Documents of the Puritan Revolution: 1625–60*, 3rd edn (Oxford: Clarendon Press, 1906), p. 388; *A Declaration of the Parliament of England, Expressing the Grounds of their Late Proceedings, and of Setling the Present Government in a Way of a Free State* (22 March 1649; E.548[12]) justified the foundation of the commonwealth but offered no blueprint for the constitutional future.

2 *CJ*, vi, 217–18 (26 May 1649).

3 Oliver Cromwell, speech of 22 January 1655: I. A. Roots (ed.), *Speeches of Oliver Cromwell* (London: J. M. Dent, 1989), p. 65. This 'party' had been in correspondence with cavaliers.

4 Oliver Cromwell, speech of 17 September 1656: Roots (ed.), *Speeches*, p. 89. Cromwell was, again, discussing radicals associated with cavaliers in Penruddock's rising of March 1655; these included John Wildman, arrested along with his *Declaration of the Free and Well-Affected People of England now in Armes against the Tyrant Oliver Cromwell Esq.* (1655), which expressed the fear that the rebels would be branded 'arbitrary Cavileeres, Levellers' and the like. It retains language which is more Leveller-like than classical republican, relying on honest Englishmen and appealing to Magna Carta; perhaps it could be read as having royalist constitutionalist overtones too. M. Ashley, *John Wildman: Plotter and Postmaster: A Study of the English Republican Movement in the Seventeenth Century* (London: Jonathan Cape, 1947), pp. 90–2.

5 The term 'commonwealthsmen' is sometimes used to refer to a particular republican faction in the 1650s; I am here using it to refer to all who fall within the republican spectrum.

6 J. Scott, *Commonwealth Principles: Republican Writing of the English Revolution* (Cambridge: Cambridge University Press, 2004), p. 241; B. Worden, 'Marchamont Nedham and the beginnings of English republicanism, 1649–1656', in D. Wootton (ed.) *Republicanism, Liberty, and Commercial Society, 1649–1776* (Stanford: Stanford University Press, 1994), p. 66. Scott cites Leveller writing on his 'republican' themes throughout the book, although he does particularly pick out the sequence of pamphlets which he associates with Nedham and which I will discuss below.

7 N. Smith, 'Popular republicanism in the 1650s: John Streater's "heroick mechanicks"',

in D. Armitage, A. Himy and Q. Skinner (eds) *Milton and Republicanism* (Cambridge: Cambridge University Press, 1995), pp. 137–55; J. Raymond, 'John Streater and the Grand Politick Informer', *Historical Journal* 41:2 (1998), 567–74.

8 Brailsford, p. 627.

9 S. D. Glover, 'The classical plebeians: radical republicanism and the origins of Leveller thought' (PhD dissertation, University of Cambridge, 1994), pp. 175–82, quotation at p. 216.

10 S. D. Glover, 'The Putney debates: popular versus elitist republicanism', *Past and Present* 164 (1999), 80.

11 See S. Barber, *Regicide and Republicanism: Politics and Ethics in the English Revolution, 1646–1659* (Edinburgh: Edinburgh University Press, 1998), ch. 2; on Marten's sympathies and links with Lilburne, see J. Peacey, 'John Lilburne and the Long Parliament', *Historical Journal*, 43:3 (2000), 633, 638–43. Lilburne's references to and published correspondence with Marten from 1647 reveal a strained and disillusioned relationship: John Lilburne, *The Oppressed Mans Oppressions Declared* ([30 January] 1647), pp. 36–7; John Lilburne, *Rash Oaths Unwarrantable* ([31 May] 1647); John Lilburne, *Two Letters, the one from Lievtenant Colonell John Lilbourne to Colonel Henry Marten* (July 1647); John Lilburne, *Jonahs Cry out of the Whales Belly* ([26 July] 1647), p. 16 (letter of July 1647); John Lilburne, *Two Letters Writ By Lieut. Col. John Lilburne ... to Col Henry Martin* (13 and 15 September 1647). On Nedham as a Leveller ally in 1640s, Peacey, 'John Lilburne and the Long Parliament', pp. 628–9, 640; B. Worden, '"Wit in a Roundhead": the dilemma of Marchamont Nedham', in S. D. Amussen and M. A. Kishlansky (eds) *Political Culture and Cultural Politics in Early Modern England: Essays Presented to David Underdown* (Manchester: Manchester University Press, 1995), pp. 320–1; especially citing John Lilburne, *An Answer to Nine Arguments* (1645), which has a preface by 'M. N.' which Worden attributes to Nedham. Scott, *Commonwealth Principles*, pp. 83–4, and B. Worden, *Literature and Politics in Cromwellian England: John Milton, Andrew Marvell, Marchamont Nedham* (Oxford: Oxford University Press, 2007), p. 42 n. 53, cite repetition from *Vox Plebis* (1646) into later works securely attributed to Nedham, to support the cooperation of Nedham with the Levellers; p. 147 n. 24 suggests that John Wildman, *The Lawes Subversion* ([6 March] 1648) also had input from Nedham, even during his royalist phase. Of course, during this royalist period Nedham attacked the Levellers too: 'Mercurius Pragmaticus' [Marchamont Nedham], *The Levellers Levell'd* ([3 December] 1647) associated Independents and Levellers with regicide, democracy, and a threat to private property. M. Dzelzainis, 'History and ideology: Milton, the Levellers, and the Council of State in 1649', *Huntington Library Quarterly* 68 (2005), p. 281, links Marten, Wildman, Overton, and Nedham in talking about a Leveller-linked common-law fightback against Parliament's absolutism in the 1640s.

12 BL Add. MSS 71533, f. 8. John Lilburne: Letter to [Henry Marten] as member of the Council of State; 'Bridges' [Bruges], 8 September 1652; a further letter to Marten from Bruges is reprinted in John Lilburne, *L. Colonel John Lilburne Revived* (1653), pp. 10–23.

13 Lilburne, *L. Colonel John Lilburne Revived*, p. 23.

14 John Lilburne, *As You Were* (Amsterdam, [May] 1652), pp. 16, 29; N. Smith, *Literature and Revolution in England, 1640–1660* (New Haven and London: Yale University Press, 1994), p. 150, reads the reference to Milton more straightforwardly as praise of a fellow 'embattled Machiavellian'.

15 ODNB. While Overton shows up as linked to Wildman and Sexby in some anti-government activity, his interactions with Thurloe suggest that he may have been a double agent.

16 MMT, pp. 43–6, quotation at p. 44.

17 MMT, p. 45; Barber, *Regicide and Republicanism*, p. 12 with note; S. Barber, *A Revolutionary Rogue: Henry Marten and the English Republic* (Stroud: Sutton, 2000); Ashley, *John Wildman*. Wildman also became an agent of Thurloe's: D. Underdown, *Royalist Conspiracy in England* (New Haven: Yale University Press, 1960), p. 192. Another army Leveller who can be traced into 1650s republicanism is William Bray, whose activities involved writing a 'Leveller' tract in 1659: MMT, p. 46.

18 Hall was appointed to help in the 1649 prosecution of Lilburne: *CSPD* 1649–50, p. 314; [John Hall], *Stop to the Mad Multitude* (1653) attacks Streater and also Lilburne, in the public eye at the time of his 1653 trial. J. Raymond, *ODNB* s.v. 'Hall, John'; D. Norbrook, *Writing the English Republic: Poetry, Rhetoric, and Politics, 1627–1660* (Cambridge: Cambridge University Press, 1999), p. 217; pp. 212–21 on Hall's most 'republican' phase; on Hall's developing political thought, and some of its more Hobbesian manifestations, J. Peacey, 'Nibbling at Leviathan: politics and theory in England in the 1650s', *Huntington Library Quarterly* 61 (2000), 241–57.

19 BL Add. MSS 71532, ff. 14, 14v. Marten, Tract against the Levellers (undated). It is unclear whether this manuscript is pre- or post-regicide.

20 Dzelzainis, 'History and ideology', pp. 275–6 on the scholarly debate; passim on the differing ideologies of Levellers and Milton.

21 P. A. Rahe, *Against Throne and Altar: Machiavelli and Political Theory under the English Republic* (Cambridge: Cambridge University Press, 2008), pp. 233–5. P. A. Knachel, 'Introduction', in Marchamont Nedham, *The Case of the Commonwealth of England, Stated*, ed. P. A. Knachel (Charlottesville: Folger Shakespeare Library, University Press of Virginia, 1969), p. xxxvi offers more pragmatic reasons for the omission: the lapsing of the Leveller threat in the intervening period, and the more popular audience which Nedham could expect in the newsbooks, which might have been alienated by his anti-populist arguments.

22 Worden, 'Marchamont Nedham and the beginnings of English republicanism', p. 66.

23 [John Streater], *A Further Continuance of the Grand Politick Informer* [Thomason: 31 October 1653], pp. 41–2; [John Hall], *Stop to the Mad Multitude*, p. 20.

24 John Lilburne, *Strength out of Weaknesse* ([19 October] 1649), p. 12.

25 John Lilburne, *The Upright Mans Vindication* ([1 August] 1653), p. 6; cf. also p. 12, 'a nominal free State, or Commonwealth'.

26 John Wildman, *A Mite to the Treasury* (1653), p. 6.

27 *Mercurius Politicus* 72 (16–23 October 1651), p. 1143; 73 (23–30 October 1651), p. 1157.

28 Lilburne, *Strength out of Weaknesse* (1649), p. 12.

29 H.-C. Schröder, 'Die Levellers und das Problem der Republik in der englischen Revolution', *Geschichte und Gesellschaft* 10:4 (1984), 461–97.

30 Underdown, *Royalist Conspiracy in England*, pp. 123–4, 192–4, for genuine evidence of Leveller-royalist links; ibid., 24–5 less reliable rumours of this in 1649 were inflated by the authorities.

31 P. Collinson, 'The Monarchical Republic of Queen Elizabeth I', *Bulletin of the John Rylands University Library of Manchester* 69:2 (1987), 394–424, and discussion of these issues in J. F. McDiarmid (ed.), *The Monarchical Republic of Early Modern England: Essays in Response to Patrick Collinson* (Aldershot: Ashgate, 2007). Markku Peltonen's

case for the continuing importance of classical humanist vocabulary, including republican ideas, in politics from the later Elizabethan period through to the eve of the civil war is strong but cautious, recognizing the dominance of juristic discourses of politics, and acknowledging that some elements of the republican tradition were muted in their transition into the later sixteenth century, or from continental into English versions: M. Peltonen, *Classical Humanism and Republicanism in English Political Thought, 1570–1640* (Cambridge: Cambridge University Press, 1995), ch. 1; pp. 47ff; on Jacobean and Caroline England Peltonen acknowledges the importance of juristic discourse as a dominant alternative to humanist notions: chs. 3, 6. The importance of notions of citizenship is a theme taken up by M. Goldie, 'The unacknowledged republic: office-holding in early modern England', in T. Harris (ed.) *The Politics of the Excluded, c. 1500–1800* (Basingstoke: Palgrave, 2001), pp. 153–94; P. Withington, *The Politics of Commonwealth: Citizens and Freemen in Early Modern England* (Cambridge: Cambridge University Press, 2005) discusses these issues in relation to the civic culture of towns.

32 Q. Skinner, 'Classical liberty and the coming of the English civil war', in Q. Skinner and M. van Gelderen (eds) *Republicanism: A Shared European Heritage*, 2 vols (Cambridge: Cambridge University Press, 2002), vol. 2, 97–118; for a critique see J. P. Sommerville, 'English and Roman liberty in the monarchical republic of early Stuart England', in J. F. McDiarmid (ed.) *The Monarchical Republic of Early Modern England: Essays in Response to Patrick Collinson* (Aldershot: Ashgate, 2007), 206–16.

33 Glover, 'The classical plebeians'; Glover, 'The Putney debates'.

34 Richard Overton, *Mans Mortallitie, or a treatise wherein 'tis proved* ([19 January] 1644; Richard Overton, *Man Wholly Mortal* (1655). Ancient authorities mentioned include Aristotle, Ovid, Pliny the Elder; later authors include Nemesius and Tertullian, and modern authors include Ambroise Paré.

35 J. Venn and J. A. Venn, *Alumni Cantabrigienses: A Biographical List of All Known Students, Graduates, and Holders of Office at the University of Cambridge, from the earliest times to 1900*, 2 parts in 10 vols (Cambridge: Cambridge University Press, 1922–54), IV.408.

36 MMT, pp. 4–5.

37 A. L. Morton, 'A still and soft voice', in his *The World of the Ranters: Religious Radicalism in the English Revolution* (London: Lawrence & Wishart, 1970), p. 158.

38 N. McDowell, *The English Radical Imagination: Culture, Religion, and Revolution, 1630–1660* (Oxford: Oxford University Press, 2003), p. 72.

39 Q. Skinner, *Liberty before Liberalism* (Cambridge: Cambridge University Press, 1998).

40 The terminology of 'arbitrary' power does seem to have come into English in the later sixteenth century and the *Oxford English Dictionary*'s examples of some senses of the word do suggest that the 1640s was a key period for its adoption. 'Tyranny' is a word which came into English earlier but does seem to be strongly associated with classical examples.

41 *Liberty Vindicated Against Slavery* ([21 August] 1646), p. 9.

42 Lilburne, *The Oppressed Mans Oppressions Declared*, pp. 2–4, 14.

43 The suggested attributions, for *England's Miserie* and/or *Vox Plebis*, are: John Wildman (Glover, 'The Putney debates' 63–71; Frank p. 61 n. 40 attributes *England's Miserie* to Wildman); Marchamont Nedham (Worden, '"Wit in a Roundhead"', pp. 320–1; Scott, *Commonwealth Principles*, p. 84 n., noting reused if not identical material in Nedham's later writings; Barber, *Regicide and Republicanism*, p. 41); Henry Marten (Frank, p. 98);

Levellers into republicans?

Overton (D. M. Wolfe, *Milton in the Puritan Revolution* (New York: Thomas Nelson & Sons, 1941), pp. 480–1); Sexby (D. Wootton, *Divine Right and Democracy* (London: Penguin Books, 1986), pp. 53–4, with particular reference to *England's Miserie, and Remedie*). Glover attributes the introductory sections of two other pamphlets to the same author: *London's Liberty in Chains Discovered* (1646); *The Charters of London* (1646).

44 R. Foxley, 'John Lilburne and the citizenship of "free-born Englishmen"', *Historical Journal* 47:4 (2004), 849–74, and chapter 3 above.

45 Overton, *An Appeale from the Degenerate Representative Body the Commons of England Assembled at Westminster: to the Body Represented, the Free People in General* ([17 July] 1647), pp. 8, [10] (Wolfe, pp. 172, 173). Overton deliberately structures this work around key 'principles of reason', i.e., laws of nature, so this invocation of his readers' reason may be particularly heightened here.

46 Overton, *An Appeale*, p. [9]: Wolfe, p. 173.

47 *A Remonstrance of Many Thousand Citizens* ([7 July] 1646), p. 6.

48 *A Remonstrance*, pp. 16, 12.

49 *A Remonstrance*, p. 4.

50 *A Remonstrance*, p. 16.

51 For a classical humanist reading of Scott, see Peltonen, *Classical humanism and republicanism*, ch. 5.

52 Overton, *An Appeale*, pp. [22]–[24] (page numbers missing): Wolfe, pp. 178–81. Cicero, *De Officiis*, 3.6.32; cf. Cicero, *De Re Publica*, 2.26.48, but this text was not directly available to early modern readers.

53 Overton, *An Appeale*, p. 26: Wolfe, p. 183.

54 *Regall Tyrannie Discovered* ([6 January] 1647), p. 11.

55 Buchanan, George, *A Dialogue on the Law of Kingship among the Scots: A Critical Edition and Translation of George Buchanan's De Iure Regni Apud Scotos Dialogus*, ed. R. A. Mason (Aldershot: Ashgate, 2004), 'Introduction', lvii–lxiii. It is striking that Nedham's *Mercurius Britanicus* invoked Buchanan in its final editorial before it was forced out of publication in 1646, arguing that the man (Charles I) who had tried to rob the commons of their liberties was thereby a tyrant; he did not, however, spell out in this editorial what, according to Buchanan, should be done to tyrants. *Mercurius Britanicus* no. 130, 11–18 May 1646, E.337[24], p. 1111; Worden, '"Wit in a Roundhead"', p. 316; Norbrook, *Writing the English Republic*, p. 150.

56 *ODNB*, s.v. 'Ralegh, Sir Walter'.

57 *England's Miserie, and Remedie* ([14 September] 1645), p. 3.

58 *England's Miserie, and Remedie*, p. 4; *Vox Plebis* ([19 November] 1646), p. 68. The Raleigh passage is not derived from Livy (the 'Decade 5' cited in *England's Miserie* for this passage is a misleading reference; Livy's material on Flaminius is in Book 20 – which does not survive – and books 21 and 22); Raleigh's comment follows on from his account of an incident recorded in Polybius.

59 *England's Miserie, and Remedie*, p. 6.

60 *Vox Plebis*, pp. 3–4.

61 *Vox Plebis*, p. 62.

The Levellers

62 *Vox Plebis*, pp. 64–66: the list is supposed to show '[h]ow many flourishing States have been ruined by the Avarice, Pride, Cruelty, and non-observance of the lawes by the Governours', but in almost all the examples given, this cruelty and illegality is expressed through financial exploitation.

63 *Vox Plebis*, p. 63.

64 *Vox Plebis*, pp. 1, 12 (law as 'our defensive *Charter of Liberty*').

65 *Vox Plebis*, p. 1; Niccolò Machiavelli, *Machiavels Discourses upon the first Decade of T. Livius*, trans. E[dward] D[acres] (1636), p. 21.

66 Machiavelli, *Discorsi*, 2.2. Machiavelli, *Machiavels Discourses*, p. 260.

67 *Vox Plebis*, p. 67.

68 Machiavelli, *Machiavels Discourses*, pp. 261–2.

69 Smith, *Literature and Revolution*, pp. 149–50.

70 F. Raab, *The English Face of Machiavelli: A Changing Interpretation 1500–1700* (London: Routledge and Kegan Paul, 1964), p. 173.

71 John Lilburne, *The Upright Mans Vindication* ([1 August] 1653), p. 7; John Lilburne, *A Defensive Declaration* (1653), p. 6.

72 Lilburne, *The Upright Mans Vindication*, p. 7; Niccolò Machiavelli, *Nicholas Machiavel's Prince*, trans. E[dward] D[acres] (1640), 'The Epistle to the Reader' (unpag.)

73 Lilburne, *The Upright Mans Vindication*, p. 9, citing Livy and Plutarch as sources. Livy, *The Romane historie written by T. Livius of Padua*, trans. Philemon Holland (1600), p. 1260, Florus' epitome of Book CXX; Plutarch, *The Lives of the Noble Grecians and Romanes Compared Together by ... Plutarke*, trans. Thomas North (1579), life of M. Antonius, p. 978.

74 Lilburne, *The Upright Mans Vindication*, pp. 12–13.

75 Lilburne, *The Upright Mans Vindication*, p. 12.

76 Lilburne, *The Upright Mans Vindication*, p. 7.

77 Lilburne, *L. Colonel John Lilburne Revived*, p. 12. For the various classical leaders, see pp. 13–23.

78 Lilburne, *L. Colonel John Lilburne Revived*, p. 9.

79 Lilburne, *L. Colonel John Lilburne Revived*, pp. 12–13, hints at some more substantial ideals of republican liberty: Pericles opposing aristocratic or oligarchic government in Samos; Lycurgus's Sparta; but these hints are barely developed.

80 Worden, 'Marchamont Nedham and the beginnings of English republicanism', pp. 69–70; Rahe, *Against Throne and Altar*, p. 237.

81 *England's Miserie, and Remedie*, p. 6.

82 *England's Miserie, and Remedie*, p. 3.

83 *Vox Plebis*, p. 4

84 Sir Walter Raleigh, *History of the World* (1621 edition), book 5, p. 357; *Vox Plebis*, p. 68.

85 Thomas Edwards, *The Third Part of Gangraena* (1646), preface (unpag.), p. 149.

86 Nedham, *Case of the Commonwealth*, pp. 70–1.

87 Nedham, *Case of the Commonwealth*, pp. 72, 73, 75.

Levellers into republicans?

88 Nedham, *Case of the Commonwealth*, pp. 72–3.
89 Christoph Besold, *Synopsis Politicae Doctrinae* (1648, 6th edn), cap. 8 'De Democratia', Section 4, and sections 5ff. on 'libera democratia' and 10ff. on 'democratia adstricta'; pp. 125–9.
90 Nedham, *Case of the Commonwealth*, p. 74.
91 Nedham, *Case of the Commonwealth*, p. 71.
92 Nedham, *Case of the Commonwealth*, p. 69.
93 Nedham, *Case of the Commonwealth*, p. 74.
94 Nedham, *Case of the Commonwealth*, p. 71.
95 Nedham, *Case of the Commonwealth*, p. 72.
96 Nedham, *Case of the Commonwealth*, p. 73.
97 Nedham, *Case of the Commonwealth*, p. 74.
98 John Milton, 'The Tenure of Kings and Magistrates and Eikonoklastes', in M. Hughes (ed.) *Complete Prose Works of John Milton*, vol. 3 (New Haven and London: Yale University Press, 1962) p. 192; S. Achinstein, *Milton and the Revolutionary Reader* (Princeton: Princeton University Press, 1994).
99 Milton, 'Eikonoklastes', in M. Hughes (ed.) *Complete Prose Works*, vol 3, p. 601; K. M. Sharpe, '"An image doting rabble": the failure of republican culture in seventeenth-century England', in K. M. Sharpe and S. N. Zwicker (eds) *Refiguring Revolutions: Aesthetics and Politics from the English Revolution to the Romantic Revolution* (Berkeley and London: University of California Press, 1998), 25–56.
100 Leveller authors were optimistic about the potential of reason and conscience in all men, a theological optimism which Worden suggests was shared by many republicans who were, at best, unorthodox puritans: Worden, 'Marchamont Nedham and the beginnings of English republicanism', p. 47.
101 Athens: *Mercurius Politicus* 73 (23–30 October 1651), p.1158; tumults at Rome: *Mercurius Politicus* 70 (2–9 October 1651), p. 1111; *Mercurius Politicus* 71 (9–16 October 1651), pp. 1125–7; *Mercurius Politicus* 72 (16–23 October 1651), p. 1143. This emphasis on the people's strength is very reminiscent of the *Vox Plebis* pamphlets of 1645–46 in which Nedham was probably involved.
102 Ambition: *Mercurius Politicus* 77 (20–27 November 1651), p. 1222; luxury contrasted with Roman temperance, virtue and freedom: *Mercurius Politicus* 84 (8–15 January 1652), pp. 1333–8; worth and virtue: *Mercurius Politicus* 82 (25 December 1651–1 January 1652), p. 1303; liberty: *Mercurius Politicus* 83 (1–8 January 1652), p. 1319.
103 'People' as well-affected, excluding delinquents: *Mercurius Politicus* 74 (30 October–6 November 1651), pp. 1174–5; 'confused promiscuous body': *Mercurius Politicus* 87 (29 January–5 February 1652), p. 1385.
104 *Mercurius Politicus* 77 (20–27 November 1651), pp. 1221–3; *Mercurius Politicus* 78 (27 November–4 December 1651), p. 1237.
105 True freedom: *Mercurius Politicus* 69 (25 September–2 October 1651), p. 1095; Discipline and freedom: *Mercurius Politicus* 84 (8–15 January 1652), p. 1335.
106 This appears to mean, however, that no excessively prominent individuals are allowed, and no nobility may arise: not equality as proportional equality. *Mercurius Politicus* 88 (5–12 February 1652), p. 1393.

107 Nedham referred to the writing of the duc de Rohan in one of his earlier editorials: *Mercurius Politicus* 39 (27 February–6 March 1651), p. 623. Rohan's *A Treatise of the Interest of the Princes and States of Christendome* appeared in two English editions in 1640 and 1641; Gunn points out that no English work made use of the notion of the 'interest of England' until this translation appeared. Rohan's work included different notions of 'interest', including implicitly the self-regarding interests of private individuals, although this meaning was only explicitly discussed in a work not translated until 1660: J. A. W. Gunn, *Politics and the Public Interest in the Seventeenth Century* (London: Routledge & Kegan Paul, 1969), pp. 36–8, 43–4 on Nedham, quotation at p. 43.

108 Marchamont Nedham, *Interest Will not Lie. Or, a View of England's True Interest* (1659), p. 3. This work aims to satisfy all parties, except the 'Papist', that it is in their interests to resist a Stuart restoration. Nedham's *Case of the Commonwealth* had made a similar case for the interest of various groups in submitting to the new regime in 1650; and, on the opposite side, his *Case of the Kingdom* in 1647 had used the same method. B. Worden, '"Wit in a Roundhead"', pp. 317–19 on Nedham's concept of 'interest'.

109 *Mercurius Politicus* 71 (9–16 October 1651), p. 1126.

110 *Mercurius Politicus* 91 (26 February–4 March 1652), p. 1442.

111 *Mercurius Politicus* 87 (29 January–5 February 1652), pp. 1383, 1385.

112 *Mercurius Politicus* 83 (1–8 January 1652), pp. 1319–20.

113 John Streater, *Secret Reasons of State* (1659), p. 5.

114 John Streater, *A Glympse of that Jewel, Judicial, Just, Preserving Libertie* (1653), sig. A2.

115 Streater, *A Glympse*, sig. A2v.

116 Streater argued that '*Romes* power began to decline, when the power and secret reasons of State were assumed by few, or one person.' He conceded that some expertise was necessary to government, but provided only for twelve legal, political and military experts to form an on-going council (exempt from annual re-election) which would be purely advisory, with no executive or judicial powers at all. *A Glympse*, pp. 1, 14.

117 Streater, *A Glympse*, sig. A2v.

118 Rahe, *Against Throne and Altar*, pp. 179–243, sees Nedham's republicanism as Machiavellian, and Machiavellian republicanism as of a distinctively 'modern' kind. The most obvious exemplar of an 'ancient' republicanism of virtue in the 1650s is John Milton, who was often tempted towards the model of 'differential moral and political rationality' which Rahe sees as characteristic of the ancient rather than the modern republican mind-set.

119 *An Agreement of the Free People of England* (1 May 1649) pp. 6–7. The representative retained the power to appoint the general officers of the army.

120 *Mercurius Politicus* 30 (26 December 1650–2 January 1651), p. 487.

121 Nedham, *Case of the Commonwealth*, p. 83.

122 Hall, *A Stop to the Mad Multitude*, p. 16.

123 Streater, *Secret Reasons of State*, pp. 5–6.

124 Streater, *A Glympse*, p. 1; [Streater, John], *Observations Historical, Political, and Philosophical*, no. 2 (11–19 April 1654), pp. 9ff.

125 *An Agreement of the People for a Firme and Present Peace* ([3 November] 1647), p. 8.

126 *An Agreement of the Free People of England*, pp. 3–4.

127 *Mercurius Politicus* 73 (23–30 October 1651), p.1157; *Mercurius Politicus* 78 (27 November–4 December 1651), p. 1237.

128 Streater, *A Glympse*, p. 1.

129 John Streater, *Government Described* (1659), pp. 4, 6–8; quotation at p. 8.

130 Streater, *A Glympse*, A2v; Streater, *Government Described* (1659), p. 5.

131 James Harrington, *The Commonwealth of Oceana and A System of Politics*, ed. J. G. A. Pocock (Cambridge: Cambridge University Press, 1992), pp. 122–3, 144–5; J. Scott, 'The rapture of motion: James Harrington's republicanism', in N. Phillipson and Q. Skinner (eds) *Political Discourse in Early Modern Britain* (Cambridge: Cambridge University Press, 1993), 139–63.

132 H. M. Höpfl, *ODNB* s.v. 'Harrington, James'.

133 Wildman, *A Mite to the Treasury*, p. 5.

134 [John Wildman], *The Leveller: or, the Principles and Maxims Concerning Government and Religion, which are Asserted by those that are Commonly Called, Levellers* ([16 February] 1659), pp. 6–7.

135 Worden, 'Marchamont Nedham and the beginnings of English republicanism', pp. 67–8.

136 Nedham's judgement that uniting the legislative and executive power was an 'inlet to tyranny' was perhaps tendentious, forming part of his republicanizing rationalization for the provisions of the Instrument of Government: Nedham, *A True State of the Case of the Commonwealth* (1654), p. 10; however, his endorsement of a kind of Areopagus which could handle mysteries of state was less compromised. [Streater], *Observations Historical, Political, and Philosophical*, no. 4 (25 April–2 May 1654), p. 28.

137 Streater, *Government Described*, p. 4.

Conclusion

The Levellers, by 1649, were a force worth defeating. The defeat of the army mutineers was one branch of the new regime's suppression of radical dissent in the spring of 1649. The arrest of the Leveller leaders Lilburne, Walwyn, Overton, and Prince was another. It was Lilburne who had launched the attack on the new regime in the first part of *Englands New Chains Discovered*, but this challenge to the new regime was issued in the name of '*a part of the People*', who were '*the Presenters, Promoters, and Approvers of the Large Petition of* September 11. 1648', and drafted by Lilburne '*and divers other Citizens of London, and Borough of Southwark*'.[1] *The Second Part of Englands New-Chaines Discovered* appealed to any reader who agreed with its contents 'to subscribe it, and bring in their Subscriptions to the Presenters and Approvers of the foresaid Petition of the 11 of Sept.'[2] This perfectly illustrates the nature of the Leveller movement. It had a recognizable core, who could define themselves as a group; it united round particular statements of principle and assessments of events at particular points; it reached out beyond the core to those who were prepared to agree; it required an action of subscription from them which might be seen not just as a contribution to the cause but as an alliance, if a temporary one, with the movement; and it operated through a mixture of publicity and personal and local knowledge. A reader of the pamphlet had to know where to go to find the promoters of the petition – but the authors could be confident that some readers, obtaining the pamphlet from some sources, would be able to do this. It was also a movement with leaders, however unofficially the Leveller authors assumed this role, and however variable it was over time. When the authorities – disturbed, as Frank points out, as much by the threat of collective and organized action implied in the request for subscriptions as by the content of the text – acted to quell this opposition, they did so by taking four men into custody.[3] Walwyn was not saved from arrest by his retreat from political activity; the authorities clearly thought of him as an important figure at the core of Leveller organization alongside Lilburne, Overton, and the less prominent Thomas Prince. The Leveller movement was an enterprise in which thinking, writing, and publishing by the more prominent figures helped to orchestrate the activities of a much larger group of people. But that popular activity, formalized in petitioning, subscribing, and public shows of numerical strength, both reflected the nature of the Leveller leaders' political thought and contributed to it.

Conclusion

The warring parties of the civil war had actively mobilized people to act on behalf of one side or the other, whether in arms or not. The propaganda which increasingly extended its reach through the literate population – and perhaps, indirectly, beyond it – was a casuistical literature, aimed at people's consciences. The Levellers came to a strong belief in the fundamental equality and potential adequacy of people's – or men's – political capacities, which were ultimately rooted in the gifts given to humans by God and nature, including conscience itself, and certain natural rights which were inalienable, and which the Levellers tended to assume people had the judgement and capacity to defend. These capacities were exercised in the participatory politics which the Leveller movement itself engaged in and pioneered, and they would be reflected too in the role of the people in authorizing a settlement by their subscription to an Agreement of the People, and in their role as the (enormously widened) electorate which would constantly refresh the government by its choice of national representatives and local officials. While Leveller authors certainly accepted that people might falter in their understandings, they were never resigned to this, and their writings often aimed to rally the people to understand and defend their rights. Human corruption and weakness was more often castigated in governors than in the governed: the real radicalism of the Levellers lay in their consistent and even growing willingness to trust to the judgements of the people to correct the faults of their governors, rather than the other way round. Few of the republicans of the 1650s shared that faith.

The Levellers' genuine populism could set them at odds with the other groups who drove the radicalization of the revolution in the 1640s. The English revolution, like many since, ran an increasingly divisive course, until control was eventually seized by a minority. A coup within the parliamentarian side resulted in the trial and execution of the king and the founding of a shortlived republic. The Levellers were certainly implicated in that story. From the start of the war the Leveller leaders were aligned with the 'war party' and then the political Independents, who pushed for a full victory in the war which would enable Parliament to drive a hard bargain with the king. The political thought developed by the Independents would eventually be deployed in support of the regicide, while their former parliamentarian allies, the Presbyterian theorists, could not countenance the elimination of the king from the constitution. Leveller thought in its essentials derived from this Independent thought, which placed political power originally in the people and which drew the conclusion that the people's only direct representatives were elected MPs; the Levellers spelt out more forthrightly the conclusion that they need not necessarily entrust any of their power to a king.

The Levellers' thought was not merely a logical development of Independent thought, however. The Independent thinkers based their arguments on populist premises, but they did not draw populist conclusions: the people's power was transferred irrevocably to their governors, and the acts of the Parliament were the people's own acts, against which they had no recourse. The Levellers' appeal to the people had more in common with some writers within the Presbyterian strand of parliamentarian thought, who allowed more space, in extreme circumstances, for the people's consciences to be involved in decisive action for the safety of the people.

The same dynamic may be discernible in some cases in the Levellers' interactions with the sects and the army. Leveller populism might not mesh well with the exclusivity of the saints and the demands of providence, which led some sectarian congregations to accept the revolution of 1649 in spite of the lack of popular endorsement or due process (the foundation of Leveller objections). For the Levellers, the sects were a key constituency, but the overthrow of one constitution and the establishment of another could not be justified simply by God's providence. The fact that the Levellers wanted a popularly subscribed Agreement of the People to ground the new constitution was a signal of their positive valuation of the people, and of secular reason as well as religious conscience. Again, the men of the New Model Army, along with the Levellers, were instrumental in the campaign which led to the death of Charles I. For some of the army men, there was great appeal in the Levellers' sweeping depiction of the rights of free-born Englishmen, and the army radicals' thinking on the franchise in 1647 certainly chimed with the arguments developed by Lilburne. Some of the army men were to rise for an Agreement of the People in 1649. Many, however, were happy to validate the regicide on grounds which were both less constitutionalist and less populist: the power of the sword was the foundation of government, and popular agreement was not required for legitimacy.

Of course the Levellers did not necessarily explore the limits of their populism: they could concede exclusions of various kinds from their vision of a political nation of equal individuals; and they often either spoke a masculine language of citizenship, or spoke in more general terms, but did not spell out the place of women in relation to the political nation. And of course, the Leveller position was itself a radical one, embraced only by a minority. But to see the Levellers as just one more radical minority bent on imposing their view on a reluctant nation would be to miss the sincerity of the Levellers' belief in the means of popular mobilization and political consent, and the ends of the people's knowledge and defence of their own liberties.

The Levellers both drew on and contributed to the radicalization of parliamentarian thought. Naturally, they spoke in the same 'languages' as those around them, invoking natural law and natural rights, the liberties and privileges protected by law, and the claims of religious conscience. Some of their parliamentarian colleagues moved in similar directions as the war ended and the period of public campaigning by the Levellers began. Henry Marten's long-standing hostility to the king was incorporated into a more definite tendency in Parliament with Chaloner's 'speech out of doors' in 1646, and the monarchy was already the target of strong attacks by army men in 1647. George Wither and others developed a radical reading of the implications of parliamentary representation, particularly from 1645, asserting the authority of the electors over those elected to serve them. Supporters of the army could justify their resistance to parliamentary orders in 1647 on the same grounds as the Levellers' appeal to the people in the same year. But the Levellers produced a unique synthesis and development of these different strands of parliamentarian thought, and embodied this thought in the actions of a collective political movement.

The legacy of the Levellers is disputed, and it seems fair to say that it has been fragmented and discontinuous. The immediate legacy of the Levellers was in the most populist republican writing of the 1650s. But at the Restoration, the Levellers became one potent symbol of the overthrow of the social order which – in some people's eyes – had threatened to follow the civil wars and the cutting off of the king's head. Evidently, 'Levelling' carried connotations of a threat to property, which the Levellers themselves had taken care to repudiate when they were in defensive mode. But beyond that, the political levelling which was central to Leveller thought, and to their political practice on the streets, also posed a threat to social hierarchy and the power of the propertied political elite. It was natural for accusations of 'Levelling' or 'Lilburneism' to be thrown at those – like the activists for Exclusion in 1679–81 – who might seem to be reviving Leveller methods or Leveller aims.[4] The fear of Levelling was one of the revolution's most obvious legacies, and those dubbed 'Levellers' played a part in that.

Did the radicals themselves look back to the Levellers' ideas and example? Scattered examples of the reprinting of Leveller texts over the next two centuries suggest that the memory – of Lilburne particularly – still had some force.[5] The immediate influence of the Levellers in the next generation of radicals and resistance theorists in the Restoration is hard to calculate; personal connections or continuities have been established more easily than any clear intellectual or political legacy. Before the end of the century, new political crises pushed John Locke and others to explore again the theory of resistance to abused political power. Although some have tried, Locke has proved hard to enlist as a disciple of the Levellers, seeming better placed within longer traditions of natural rights and resistance theory, which enabled him to construct a theory which was, in important respects, much more conservative.[6]

The Levellers participated in the creation of a type of public politics which haunted the memory of the later seventeenth century, and which did not disappear at the Restoration. The civil wars and the Levellers' role certainly had a legacy in political culture. But the difficulty of tracing the Levellers' ideas into the later seventeenth century should remind us how remarkable those ideas were. While other parliamentarians and later authors produced superficially similar arguments about resistance, the Levellers' arguments drew on a deep sense of the underlying sovereignty of the people. Power came originally from the people – and from the self-propriety and rights which God and nature had given to individuals – and power often rested in the hands of the people again, even in a polity which had not dissolved itself and reverted to the state of nature. While others, of a republican or Hobbesian bent, might trust the people to act for their own self-preservation out of an almost mechanistic 'interest', the Levellers spoke constantly not of people's interests, but of their judgements and consciences, rights and liberties. The people should subscribe to the fundamental settlements of the Agreements of the People, or vote, or give their verdict in a trial, by their own judgements and consciences, just as they should trust to no one else's judgement about the path to salvation. ''Tis your self must do it', wrote Walwyn, and that applied in politics as much as in religion.[7] If the people would only understand themselves and their liberties, political life would be both healed and transformed.

NOTES

1 John Lilburne, *Englands New Chains Discovered* (26 February 1649), sig. A.

2 John Lilburne, *The Second Part of Englands New-Chaines Discovered* ([24 March] 1649), first title page (Wing L2180; two versions of title page in same tract).

3 Frank, p. 195.

4 T. Harris, 'The Leveller legacy: from the Restoration to the Exclusion Crisis', in M. Mendle (ed.) *The Putney Debates of 1647: The Army, the Levellers and the English State* (Cambridge: Cambridge University Press, 2001), p. 234; B. Worden, 'The Levellers in history and memory, c.1660–1960' in M. Mendle (ed.) *The Putney Debates*, pp. 256–82, doubts how specific reference to the Levellers is in later condemnations of 'Levelling'.

5 F. K. Donnelly, 'Levellerism in eighteenth and early nineteenth-century England', *Albion* 22:2 (1988), 261–9.

6 R. Ashcraft, *Revolutionary Politics and Locke's Two Treatises of Government* (Princeton: Princeton University Press, 1986), notes associations between radical whigs and references to Levellers, e.g., at pp. 249, 347. Arguments against situating Locke within a Leveller legacy are made by J. Marshall, *John Locke: Resistance, Religion and Responsibility*, Cambridge Studies in Early Modern British History (Cambridge: Cambridge University Press, 1994), pp. 171, 262–4, 270–1; G. E. Aylmer, 'Locke no Leveller', in I. Gentles, J. Morrill and B. Worden (eds) *Soldiers, Writers and Statesmen of the English Revolution* (Cambridge: Cambridge University Press, 1998), pp. 304–22.

7 MMT, p. 81.

Bibliography

PRIMARY SOURCES

Manuscripts

British Library
Additional MSS 71532, 71533 (Henry Marten papers).

Worcester College, Oxford
Clarke MSS 41 (consulted in Harvester microfilm edition, ed. G. E. Aylmer, 1979).

Printed primary sources

The place of publication of all pre-1700 works is London unless otherwise indicated.
All classmarks/catalogue numbers in this bibliography are Thomason Tracts (E- or 669.f.-, as in Fortescue's catalogue), unless otherwise stated.
Dates in square brackets are Thomason's.

Anonymous, pseudonymous, and multi-authored works (alphabetically by title)

An Agreement of the Free People of England (1 May 1649; E.552/23) [signed by J. Lilburne, W. Walwyn, T. Prince, R. Overton: the 'Third Agreement'].
An Agreement of the People for a Firme and Present Peace ([3 November] 1647; E.412/21).
An Agreement Prepared for the People of England (20 January 1649; Wing A783A) [The 'Officers' Agreement'].
An Alarum to the House of Lords ([31 July] 1646; E.346/8).
The Armies Petition: Or a New Engagement ([3 May] 1648; E.438/1).
The Army's Martyr ([7 May] 1649; E.554/6).
The Case of the Armie Truly Stated (15 October 1647; E.411/9).
A Declaration of the Parliament of England, Expressing the Grounds of their Late Proceedings, and of Setling the Present Government in a Way of a Free State (22 March 1649; E.548/12).
The Declarations and Humble Representations of the Officers and Souldiers (1648; E.475/24).
The Engagement Vindicated & Explained, or the Reasons upon which Leiut. [sic] Col. John Lilburne, Tooke the Engagement (22 January 1650; E.590/4).
Englands Birth-Right Justified ([10 October] 1645; E.304/17).
Englands Freedome, Souldiers Rights ([14 December] 1647; E.419/23).
England's Miserie, and Remedie ([14] September 1645; E.302/5).
An Exact Collection of all Remonstrances, Declarations, Votes, Orders, Ordinances, Proclamations, Petitions, Messages, Answers, and Other Remarkable Passages betweene the Kings most Excellent Majesty, and his High Court of Parliament (1643; part 2, E.243/1).

Bibliography

The Hunting of the Foxes ([21 March] 1649; E.548/7).
A Letter Sent from Several Agitators of the Army to their Respective Regiments (1647; E.414/8).
Liberty Vindicated against Slavery ([21 August] 1646; E.351/2).
A Light for the Ignorant (Amsterdam, 1638).
Mercurius Britanicus. Newsbook, various editions, 1645–46.
Mercurius Militaris or the Army's Scout. Newsbook, various editions, 1648–49.
Mercurius Politicus. Newsbook, various editions, 1650–52.
The Moderate. Newsbook, various editions, 1648–49.
A New Engagement, or, Manifesto ([3 August] 1648; 669.f.12/97).
The Out-Cryes of Oppressed Commons ([28 February] 1647; E.378/13).
An Outcry of the Youngmen and Apprentices of London ([29 August] 1649; E.572/13).
A Pearle in a Dounghill ([30 June] 1646; E.342/5).
A Petition from Severall Regiments of the Army (1648; E.470/32).
Regall Tyrannie Discovered ([6 January] 1647; E.370/12).
A Remonstrance from His Excellency Sir Thomas Fairfax ... and Declaration ... for the Future Uniting of the Army (15 November 1647; E.414/14).
A Remonstrance of His Excellency... and of the Generall Councell of Officers (18 November 1648; E.473/11).
A Remonstrance of Many Thousand Citizens ([7 July] 1646; E.343/11).
Remonstrans Redivivus: Or, an Accompt of the Remonstrance and Petition, Formerly Presented by Divers Citizens of London, to the View of Many (25 July 1643, E.61/21).
Severall Petitions Presented to his Excellency the Lord Fairfax (1648; E.474/5).
To His Highness the Lord Protector, &c. and Our General, The Humble Petition of Several Colonels of the Army (1654).
To the Right Honourable the Commons of England in Parliament Assembled (11 September 1648; 669.f.13/16).
Touching the Fundamentall Lawes, or Politique Constitution of this Kingdome, the Kings Negative Voice, and the Power of Parliaments ([24 February] 1643; E.90/21).
Two Letters from the Agents of the five Regiments of Horse ([28 October] 1647; E.412/6).
Vox Plebis ([19 November] 1646; E.362/20).

Attributed works

Augustine, *The City of God against the Pagans*, ed. R. W. Dyson (Cambridge, Cambridge University Press, 1998).
Ball, William, *Tractatus de Jure Regnandi, & Regni* (1645).
Baxter, Richard, *Reliquiae Baxterianae* (1696).
Besold, Christoph, *Synopsis Politicae Doctrinae*, 6th edn (Amsterdam, 1648).
Bowles, Edward, *Plaine English, or, a Discourse Concerning the Accommodation, the Armie, the Association* (1643; E.84/42).
Buchanan, George, *A Dialogue on the Law of Kingship among the Scots: A Critical Edition and Translation of George Buchanan's De Iure Regni Apud Scotos Dialogus*, ed. R. A. Mason (Aldershot: Ashgate, 2004).
Burroughs, Jeremiah, *The Glorious Name of God, the Lord of Hosts ... with a Post-Script, Briefly Answering a Late Treatise by Henry Ferne* (1643).
Chaloner, Thomas, *An Answer to the Scotch Papers* (1646).

Cockeram, Henry, *The English Dictionarie* (2nd edn, 1626; Pollard & Redgrave 5462).
Coke, Sir Edward, *Le Quart Part des Reportes* (1635).
Coke, Sir Edward, *The First Part of the Institutes* (1639).
Coke, Sir Edward, *The Second Part of the Institutes* (1642).
Coke, Sir Edward, *The Third Part of the Institutes* (1644).
Cowell, John, *The Interpreter: Or Booke Containing the Signification of Words* (1637 edn; Pollard & Redgrave 5901).
Dyve, Sir Lewis, *The Tower of London Letter-book of Sir Lewis Dyve, 1646–7*, Bedfordshire Historical Record Society, No. 38 (1958), ed. H. G. Tibbutt.
Edwards, Thomas, *Gangraena: or A Catalogue And Discovery Of Many Of The Errours, Heresies, Blasphemies And Pernicious Practices Of The Sectaries Of This Time* (1646; 3 parts).
Ferne, Henry, *The Resolving of Conscience* (Cambridge, 1642).
Goodwin, John, *Anti-Cavalierisme, or, Truth Pleading As well the Necessity, as the Lawfulness of this present War* (1642).
Goodwin, John, *The Army, Harmlesse* (1647) [not signed].
Goodwin, John, *Might and Right Well Met* (2 January 1649).
[Hall, John], *Stop to the Mad Multitude* (1653).
Harrington, James, *The Commonwealth of Oceana and A System of Politics*, ed. J. G. A. Pocock (Cambridge: Cambridge University Press, 1992).
Helwys, Thomas, *A Shorte Declaration of the Mistery of Iniquity* (Amsterdam[?], 1612: STC 13056).
[Herle, Charles], *A Fuller Answer to a Treatise Written by Doctor Ferne, Entituled, The Resolving of Conscience* ([29 December] 1642; E.244[27]).
Hobbes, Thomas, *Leviathan*, ed. R. Tuck (Cambridge: Cambridge University Press, 1996).
Hooker, Richard, *Of the Laws of Ecclesiastical Polity: Preface, Book I, Book VIII*, ed. A. S. McGrade, Cambridge Texts in the History of Political Thought (Cambridge: Cambridge University Press, 1989).
Hunton, Philip, *A Treatise of Monarchie* (1643; E.103/15).
Jenkins, David, *An Apology for the Army* (1647).
Jenkins, David, *The Armies Indempnity* ([31 May] 1647; E.390/10).
[Jubbes, John], *Several Proposals for Peace & Freedom, by an Agreement of the People* (1648; E.477/18).
Lilburne, John, *Lilburne, A Worke of the Beast* (1638), cited from Lilburne, *The Christian Mans Trial* (1641; E.181/7).
Lilburne, John, *Come Out Of Her My People* (1639).
Lilburne, John, *The Poore Mans Cry* (1639; Pollard & Redgrave 15598).
Lilburne, John, *The Christian Mans Triall* (1641).
Lilburne, John, *Coppy of a Letter ... to James Ingram and Henry Hopkins, Wardens of the Fleet* (4 October 1640; Pollard & Redgrave 15597).
Lilburne, John, *An Answer to Nine Arguments* (1645).
Lilburne, John, *A Copie of a Letter, Written by John Lilburne Leut. Collonell. To Mr. William Prinne* ([15 January] 1645; E.24/22).
Lilburne, John, *The Reasons of Lieu. Col. Lilbournes sending his Letter to Mr Prin* ([13 June] 1645; E.288/12).

Bibliography

Lilburne, John, *The Copy of a Letter, From Lieutenant Colonell John Lilburne, to a Freind [sic]* ([25 July] 1645; E.296/5).
Lilburne, John, *A More Full Relation of the Great Battell... Made in the House of Commons by Lieut: Col: Lilbourne* ([16 July] 1645; E.293/3).
Lilburne, John, *Innocency and Truth Justified* ([6 January] 1646; E.314/21).
Lilburne, John, *The Just Mans Justification* ([6 June] 1646; E.340/12; second edition [28 September] 1647: E.407/26).
Lilburne, John, *The Free-mans Freedom Vindicated* ([16 June] 1646; E.341/12).
Lilburne, John, *Londons Liberty in Chains* ([October] 1646; E.359/17) [part by another author].
Lilburne, John, *An Anatomy of the Lords Tyranny* ([6 November] 1646; E.362/6).
Lilburne, John, *The Charters of London; or, the Second Part of Londons Liberty in Chaines* ([18 December] 1646; E.356/12).
Lilburne, John, *The Oppressed Mans Oppressions Declared* ([30 January] 1647; E.373/1).
Lilburne, John, *The Resolved Mans Resolution* ([30 April] 1647; E.387/4).
Lilburne, John, *Rash Oaths Unwarrantable* ([31 May] 1647; E.393/39).
Lilburne, John, *Two Letters, the One from Lieutenant Colonell John Lilbourne to Colonel Henry Marten* (July 1647).
Lilburne, John, *Jonah's Cry out of the Whales Belly* ([26 July] 1647; E.400/5).
Lilburne, John, *Two Letters Writ By Lieut. Col. John Lilburne to Col Henry Martin* (13 and 15 September 1647; E.407/41).
Lilburne, John, *The Juglers Discovered* ([28 September] 1647; E.409/22).
Lilburne, John, *The Grand Plea of Lieut. Col. John Lilburne* ([20 October] 1647; E.411/21).
Lilburne, John, *The Additional Plea of Lieut. Col. John Lilburne* ([20 October] 1647; E.412/11).
Lilburne, John, *A Defiance to Tyrants* ([28 January] 1648; E.520/30).
Lilburne, John, *The Peoples Prerogative* ([17 February] 1648; E.427/4).
Lilburne, John, *The Prisoners Plea for a Habeas Corpus* ([4 April] 1648; E.434/19).
Lilburne, John, *The Lawes Funerall* ([15 May] 1648; E.442/13).
Lilburne, John, *Foundations of Freedom; or an Agreement of the People* ([15 December] 1648; E.476/26).
Lilburne, John et al., *A Plea for Common Right and Freedom* ([28 December] 1648; E.536/22) [signatories led by Lilburne].
Lilburne, John, *Englands New Chains Discovered* (26 February 1649; E.545/27).
Lilburne, John, *The Second Part of Englands New-Chaines Discovered* ([24 March] 1649; E.548/16).
Lilburne, John, *A Discourse betwixt Lieutenant Colonel Iohn Lilburn ... and Mr Hugh Peter* ([29 May] 1649; E.556/26).
Lilburne, John, *The Legall Fundamental Liberties* ([8 June] 1649; E.560/14).
Lilburne, John, *The Legal Fundamental Liberties* (1649, 2nd edn; E.567/1).
Lilburne, John, *An Impeachment of High Treason against Oliver Cromwell and ... Ireton* ([10 August] 1649; E.508/20).
Lilburne, John, *A Preparative to an Hue and Cry after Sir Arthur Haselrig* ([18 August] 1649; E.573/16).

Lilburne, John, *Strength out of Weaknesse* ([19 October] 1649; E.575/18).
Lilburne, John, *The Innocent Man's Second-Proffer* ([22 October] 1649; 669.f.14/85).
Lilburne, John, *The Engagement Vindicated and Explained* ([23 January] 1650; E.590/4).
Lilburne, John, *A Letter ... to Mr John Price* ([31 March] 1651; E.626/19).
Lilburne, John, *L. Col. John Lilburne his Apologeticall Narration* (Amsterdam, [3 April] 1652; E.659/30).
Lilburne, John, *As You Were* (Amsterdam, [May] 1652; Wing L2084).
Lilburne, John, *A Defensive Declaration* (1653: E.702/2).
Lilburne, John, *The Upright Man's Vindication* ([1 August] 1653; E.708/22).
Lilburne, John, *L. Colonel John Lilburne Revived* (1653).
Lilburne, John, Prince, Thomas and Overton, Richard, *The Picture of the Councel of State* (1649; E.550/14).
Livy, *The Romane historie written by T. Livius of Padua*, trans. Philemon Holland (1600).
Locke, John, *Two Treatises of Government*, ed. P. Laslett (Cambridge: Cambridge University Press, 1988).
Machiavelli, Niccolò, *Machiavels Discourses upon the first Decade of T. Livius*, trans. E[dward] D[acres] (1636).
Machiavelli, Niccolò, *Nicholas Machiavel's Prince*, trans. E[dward] D[acres] (1640).
[Marten, Henry], *A Corrector of the Answerer to the Speech out of Doores* (1646) [unsigned].
Marten, Henry, *The Independency of England Endeavoured To Be Maintained* (1648).
Milton, John, *Areopagitica*, in E. Sirluck (ed.) *Complete Prose Works of John Milton*, vol. 2 (New Haven and London: Yale University Press, 1959).
Milton, John, *Tenure of Kings and Magistrates* and *Eikonoklastes*, in M. Hughes (ed.) *Complete Prose Works of John Milton*, vol. 3 (New Haven and London: Yale University Press, 1962).
Milton, John, 'On the New Forcers of Conscience under the Long Parliament', in J. Carey (ed.) *John Milton, Complete Shorter Poems* (London and New York: Longman, 1981).
[Nedham, Marchamont], *The Levellers Levell'd. Or, the Independents Conspiracie to Root Out Monarchie* ([3 December] 1647; E.419/4). [signed 'Mercurius Pragmaticus'].
Nedham, Marchamont, *Case of the Kingdom* (1647).
Nedham, Marchamont, *The Case of the Commonwealth of England, Stated* (1650; ed. P. A. Knachel, Charlottesville: Folger Shakespeare Library, University Press of Virginia, 1969).
Nedham, Marchamont, *A True State of the Case of the Commonwealth* (1654).
Nedham, Marchamont, *Interest Will not Lie. Or, a View of England's True Interest* (1659).
Overton, Richard, *Articles of High Treason Exhibited against Cheap-side Crosse* ([January] 1642; E.134/23).
Overton, Richard, *New Lambeth Fayre* ([March] 1642; E.138/26).
Overton, Richard, *Mans Mortallitie, or a treatise wherein 'tis proved* ([19 January] 1644; E.29/16; unsigned; false Amsterdam imprint).
Overton, Richard, *The Araignement of Mr. Persecution* ([8 April] 1645; E.276/23).

Bibliography

Overton, Richard, *A Sacred Decretall* ([31 May] 1645; E.286/15).
Overton, Richard, *Divine Observations upon the London Ministers Letter against Toleration* ([24 January] 1646; E.317/15).
Overton, Richard, *A Defiance Against All Arbitrary Usurpations* ([9 September] 1646; E.353/17).
Overton, Richard, *An Arrow Against All Tyrants and Tyrany* ([20 October] 1646; E.356/14).
[Overton, Richard], *An Unhappy Game at Scotch and English* ([30 November] 1646; E.364/3).
Overton, Richard, *An Appeale from the Degenerate Representative Body the Commons of England Assembled at Westminster: to the Body Represented, the Free People in General* ([17 July] 1647; E.398/28).
Overton, Richard, *Eighteene Reasons Propounded to the Soldiers of the Body of the Army* ([13 August] 1647; Wing O628A).
Overton, Richard, *Man Wholly Mortal* (1655; Wing O629A; second edition of *Mans Mortallitie*, signed R.O.).
Palmer, Herbert et al., *Scripture and Reason Pleaded for Defensive Armes* (1643).
Parker, Henry, *Observations upon some of his Majesties late Answers and Expresses*, 2nd edn (1642).
Parker, Henry, *Jus Populi* (1644; E.12/25).
Plutarch, *The Lives of the Noble Grecians and Romanes Compared Together by ... Plutarke*, Thomas North (trans.) (1579).
Prince, Thomas, *The Silken Independents Snare Broken* ([20 June] 1649; E.560/24).
Prynne, William, *The Fourth Part of the Soveraigne Power of Parliaments and Kingdomes* (1643).
Prynne, William, *The Lyar Confounded* ([15 October] 1645; E.267/1).
Raleigh, Sir Walter, *History of the World* (1621 edition).
Rastell, John, *Les Termes de la Ley* (1629 edition).
Robinson, Henry, *Liberty of Conscience* (1644; E.39/1).
Rutherford, Samuel, *Lex, Rex* (1644).
Smith, Sir Thomas, *De Republica Anglorum*, ed. Mary Dewar (Cambridge: Cambridge University Press, 1982).
[Streater, John], *A Further Continuance of the Grand Politick Informer* [Thomason: 31 October 1653].
Streater, John, *A Glympse of that Jewel, Judicial, Just, Preserving Libertie* (1653).
[Streater, John], *Observations Historical, Political, and Philosophical* (periodical, 1654).
Streater, John, *Secret Reasons of State* (1659).
Streater, John, *Government Described* (1659) [signed J. S.].
Walwyn, William: works collected in J. R. McMichael and B. Taft (eds) *The Writings of William Walwyn* (Athens, Ga., and London, 1989).
White, Francis, *The Copy of a Letter Sent to his Excellencie Sir Thomas Fairfax* ([11 November] 1647; E.413/17).
White, Francis, *The Copies of Severall Letters Contrary to the Opinion of the Present Powers* ([20 March] 1649; E.548/6).
White, Francis, *A True Relation of the Proceedings in the Businesse of Burford* ([27 September] 1649; E.574/26).

Wildman, John, *A Cal to all the Souldiers* ([29 October] 1647; E.412/10).
Wildman, John, *Putney Projects* ([30 December] 1647; E.421/19).
Wildman, John, *The Lawes Subversion* ([6 March] 1648; E.431/2).
Wildman, John, *London's Liberties* ([14 December] 1650; E.620/70).
Wildman, John, *A Mite to the Treasury* (1653) [signed J. W.].
Wildman, John, *Declaration of the Free and Well-Affected People of England now in Armes against the Tyrant Oliver Cromwell Esq.* (1655) [unsigned; in Wildman's possession on arrest].
Wildman, John, *The Leveller: or, the Principles and Maxims Concerning Government and Religion, which are Asserted by those that are Commonly Called, Levellers* ([16 February] 1659; E.968/3).
Williams, Roger, *The Bloudy Tenent, of Persecution* (1644, E.1/2).
Wither, George, *The Speech without Doore. Delivered July 9. 1644 in the Absence of the Speaker* (1644).
Wither, George, *Letters of Advice: Touching the Choice of Knights and Burgesses*, 2nd edn (1645).
Wither, George, *Vox Pacifica* (1645).
Wither, George, *Opobalsamum Anglicanum* (1646).

Primary sources in modern collected editions

Aylmer, G. E. (ed.) *The Levellers in the English Revolution* (London: Thames & Hudson, 1975).
Calendar of State Papers Domestic.
Firth, C. H. (ed.) *The Clarke Papers*, 2 vols (London: Royal Historical Society, 1992 reprint).
Gardiner, S. R. (ed.) *The Constitutional Documents of the Puritan Revolution, 1625–1660*, 3rd edn (Oxford: Clarendon Press, 1906).
Griffiths, G. (ed.) *Representative Government in Western Europe in the Sixteenth Century* (Oxford: Clarendon Press, 1968).
Haller, W. and G. Davies (eds) *The Leveller Tracts 1647–1653* (Gloucester, Mass.: Peter Smith, 1964).
Haller, W. H. (ed.) *Tracts on Liberty in the Puritan Revolution*, 3 vols (New York: Columbia University Press, 1934).
The Journals of the House of Commons.
The Journals of the House of Lords.
Johnson, R. C. et al. (eds) *Commons Debates 1628*, 6 vols (New Haven: Yale University Press, 1977–83).
McMichael, J. R. and B. Taft (eds) *The Writings of William Walwyn* (Athens, Ga. and London: University of Georgia Press, 1989).
Malcolm, J. L. (ed.) *The Struggle for Sovereignty: Seventeenth-century Political Tracts*, 2 vols (Indianapolis: The Liberty Fund, 1999).
Morton, A. L. (ed.) *Freedom in Arms: A Selection of Leveller Writings* (London: Lawrence & Wishart, 1975).
Roots, I. A. (ed.) *Speeches of Oliver Cromwell* (London: J. M. Dent, 1989).
Sharp, A. (ed.) *The English Levellers* (Cambridge: Cambridge University Press, 1998).

Bibliography

Wolfe, D. M. (ed.) *Leveller Manifestoes of the Puritan Revolution* (New York: Thomas Nelson & Sons, 1944).
Woodhouse, A. S. P. (ed.) *Puritanism and Liberty* (London: J. M. Dent, 1992 edn).
Wootton, D., *Divine Right and Democracy* (London: Penguin Books, 1986).

SECONDARY WORKS

Achinstein, S., *Milton and the Revolutionary Reader* (Princeton: Princeton University Press, 1994).
Adams, D. R., 'Religion and reason in the thought of Richard Overton, the Leveller' (PhD dissertation, University of Cambridge, 2003).
Adams, D. R., 'The secret printing and publishing career of Richard Overton the Leveller, 1644–46', *The Library* 11:1 (2010), 3–88.
Adamson, J., *The Noble Revolt: The Overthrow of Charles I* (London: Weidenfeld & Nicolson, 2007).
Ashcraft, R. *Revolutionary Politics and Locke's Two Treatises of Government* (Princeton: Princeton University Press, 1986).
Ashley, M., *John Wildman, Plotter and Postmaster. A Study of the English Republican Movement in the Seventeenth Century* (London: Jonathan Cape, 1947).
Aylmer, G. E., 'Gentlemen Levellers?', *Past and Present* 49 (1970), 120–5.
Aylmer, G. E., 'Locke no Leveller', in I. Gentles, J. Morrill and B. Worden (eds) *Soldiers, Writers and Statesmen of the English Revolution* (Cambridge: Cambridge University Press, 1998), pp. 304–22.
Baker, P., '"A despicable contemptible generation of men"? Cromwell and the Levellers', in P. Little (ed.) *Oliver Cromwell: New Perspectives* (Basingstoke: Palgrave Macmillan, 2009), 90–115.
Baker, P., 'Rhetoric, reality, and the varieties of civil-war radicalism', in J. S. A. Adamson (ed.) *The English Civil War: Conflict and Contexts, 1640–49* (Basingstoke: Palgrave Macmillan, 2009), 202–24.
Baker, P. and E. Vernon (eds), *The Agreements of the People, the Levellers and the Constitutional Crisis of the English Revolution* (Basingstoke: Palgrave Macmillan, forthcoming 2012).
Barber, S., *Regicide and Republicanism: Politics and Ethics in the English Revolution, 1646–1659* (Edinburgh: Edinburgh University Press, 1998).
Barber, S., *A Revolutionary Rogue: Henry Marten and the English Republic* (Stroud: Sutton, 2000).
Barry, J., 'Literacy and literature in popular culture: reading and writing in historical perspective', in T. Harris (ed.) *Popular Culture in England, c. 1500–1850* (Basingstoke: Macmillan, 1995), 69–94.
Bevir, M., 'Are there perennial problems in political theory?' *Political Studies* 42 (1994), 662–75.
Braddick, M. J., *God's Fury, England's Fire: A New History of the English Civil Wars* (London: Allen Lane, 2008).
Bradstock, A., *Radical Religion in Cromwell's England: A Concise History from the English Civil War to the End of the Commonwealth* (London: I. B. Tauris, 2011).
Brailsford, H. N., *The Levellers and the English Revolution* (London: Cresset Press,

1961).
Brenner, R., *Merchants and Revolution: Commercial Change, Political Conflict, and London's Overseas Traders, 1550–1653* (Cambridge: Cambridge University Press, 1993).
Burgess, G., *The Politics of the Ancient Constitution: An Introduction to English Political Thought, 1603–1642* (Basingstoke: Macmillan, 1992).
Burgess, G., 'The divine right of kings reconsidered', *English Historical Review* 107 (1992), 837–61.
Burgess, G., *Absolute Monarchy and the Stuart Constitution* (New Haven: Yale University Press, 1996).
Burgess, G., 'Protestant polemic: the Leveller pamphlets', *Parergon* n.s. 11 (1993), 45–67.
Burgess, G., 'Radicalism and the English Revolution', in G. Burgess and M. Festenstein (eds) *English Radicalism, 1550–1850* (Cambridge: Cambridge University Press, 2007), 62–86.
Burgess, G., *British Political Thought, 1500–1660: The Politics of the Post-Reformation* (Basingstoke: Palgrave Macmillan, 2009).
Burgess, G. and M. Festenstein, *English Radicalism, 1550–1850* (Cambridge: Cambridge University Press, 2007).
Burns, N. T., *Christian Mortalism from Tyndale to Milton* (Cambridge, Mass.: Harvard University Press, 1972).
Carlin, N., 'Leveller organization in London', *Historical Journal* 27:4 (1984), 955–60.
Carlin, N., 'The Levellers and the conquest of Ireland in 1649', *Historical Journal* 30 (1987), 269–88.
Carlin, N., 'Liberty and fraternities in the English Revolution: the politics of London artisans' protests, 1635–1659', *International Review of Social History* 39 (1994), 223–54.
Christianson, P., *Discourse on History, Law and Governance in the Public Career of John Selden, 1610–1635* (Toronto: University of Toronto Press, 1996).
Churchill, C., *Light Shining in Buckinghamshire* (London: Nick Hern Books, 1996).
Coffey, J., *Politics, Religion and the British Revolutions: The Mind of Samuel Rutherford* (Cambridge: Cambridge University Press, 1997).
Coffey, J., 'Puritanism and liberty revisited: the case for toleration in the English Revolution', *Historical Journal* 41:4 (1998), 961–85.
Collinson, P., 'The Monarchical Republic of Queen Elizabeth I', *Bulletin of the John Rylands University Library of Manchester* 69:2 (1987), 394–424.
Como, D. R., *Blown by the Spirit: Puritanism and the Emergence of an Antinomian Underground in Pre-Civil-War England* (Stanford: Stanford University Press, 2004).
Como, D. R., 'An unattributed pamphlet by William Walwyn: new light on the prehistory of the Leveller movement', *Huntington Library Quarterly* 69:3 (2006), 353–82.
Como, D. R., 'Secret printing, the crisis of 1640, and the origins of civil war radicalism', *Past and Present* 196 (2007), 37–82.
Condren, C., *The Language of Politics in Seventeenth-century England* (Basingstoke

and London: Macmillan, 1994).
Condren, C., 'Liberty of office and its defence in seventeenth-century political argument', *History of Political Thought*, 18 (1997), 460–82.
Condren, C., 'Radicals, conservatives and moderates in early modern political thought: a case of Sandwich Islands syndrome?', *History of Political Thought* 10 (1989), 525–42.
Condren, C., 'Afterword: radicalism revisited', in G. Burgess and M. Festenstein (eds) *English Radicalism, 1550–1850* (Cambridge: Cambridge University Press, (2007), 311–37.
Crawford, P., 'Charles Stuart, that man of blood', *Journal of British Studies* 16 (1977), 41–61.
Crawford, P., '"The poorest she": women and citizenship in early modern England', in M. Mendle (ed.) *The Putney Debates of 1647: The Army, the Levellers and the English State* (Cambridge: Cambridge University Press, 2001), 197–218.
Cressy, D., *England on Edge: Crisis and Revolution 1640–1642* (Oxford: Oxford University Press, 2006).
Cromartie, A., *Sir Matthew Hale, 1609–1676: Law, Religion and Natural Philosophy* (Cambridge: Cambridge University Press, 1995).
Cromartie, A., 'The constitutionalist revolution: the transformation of political culture in early Stuart England', *Past and Present* 163 (1999), 76–120.
Daly, J., 'The idea of absolute monarchy in seventeenth-century England', *Historical Journal* 21:2 (1978), 227–50.
Davies, T. A., *The Quakers in English Society, 1655–1725* (New York: Clarendon Press, 2000).
Davis, J. C., 'The Levellers and democracy', *Past & Present* 40 (1968), 174–80.
Davis, J. C., 'The Levellers and Christianity', in B. Manning (ed.) *Politics, Religion and the English Civil War* (London: Edward Arnold, 1973), 225–50.
Davis, J. C., 'Living with the living God: radical religion and the English Revolution', in C. Durston and J. Maltby (eds) *Religion in Revolutionary England* (Manchester: Manchester University Press, 2006), 19–41.
Davis, J. C., 'Radicalism in a traditional society: the evaluation of radical thought in the English commonwealth 1649–1660', *History of Political Thought* 3 (1982), 193–213.
Davis, J. C., 'Religion and the struggle for freedom in the English revolution', *Historical Journal* 35:3 (1992) 507–30.
Davis, J. C., 'Reassessing radicalism in a traditional society: two questions', in G. Burgess and M. Festenstein (eds) *English Radicalism, 1550–1850* (Cambridge: Cambridge University Press, 2007), 338–72.
Diethe, J., 'The Moderate: politics and allegiances of a revolutionary newspaper', *History of Political Thought* 4 (1983), 247–79.
Donnelly, F. K., 'Levellerism in eighteenth and early nineteenth-century England', *Albion* 22:2 (1988), 261–9.
Durston, C., '"Let Ireland be quiet": opposition in England to the Cromwellian conquest of Ireland', *History Workshop Journal* 21 (1986), 105–12.
Dzelzainis, M., 'History and ideology: Milton, the Levellers, and the Council of State in 1649', *Huntington Library Quarterly* 68 (2005), 269–87.

Firth, C. H. and G. Davies, *The Regimental History of Cromwell's Army*, 2 vols (Oxford: Clarendon Press, 1940).
Fox, A., *Oral and Literate Culture in England, 1500–1700* (Oxford: Clarendon Press, 2001).
Foxley, R., 'John Lilburne and the citizenship of "free-born Englishmen"', *Historical Journal* 47:4 (2004), 849–74.
Foxley, R., '"The wildernesse of tropes and figures": figuring rhetoric in Leveller pamphlets', *The Seventeenth Century* 21:2 (2006), 270–86.
Frank, J., *The Levellers: A History of the Writings of Three Seventeenth-century Social Democrats: John Lilburne, Richard Overton, William Walwyn* (Cambridge, Mass.: Harvard University Press, 1955).
Franklin, J. H., *John Locke and the Theory of Sovereignty: Mixed Monarchy and the Right of Resistance in the Political Thought of the English Revolution* (Cambridge: Cambridge University Press, 1978).
Gentles, I., 'London Levellers in the English Revolution: the Chidleys and their circle', *Journal of Ecclesiastical History*, 29 (1978), 281–309.
Gentles, I., *The New Model Army in England, Ireland and Scotland, 1645–1653* (Oxford: Blackwell, 1992).
Gentles, I., 'The Agreements of the People and their political contexts, 1647–1649', in M. Mendle (ed.) *The Putney Debates of 1647: The Army, the Levellers, and the English State* (Cambridge: Cambridge University Press, 2001), 148–74.
Gibb, M. A., *John Lilburne the Leveller: A Christian Democrat* (London: Lindsay Drummond, 1947).
Gibbons, B. J., 'Richard Overton and the secularism of the interregnum radicals', *The Seventeenth Century* 10:1 (1995), 63–75.
Gimelfarb Brack, M. M., *Liberté, Égalité, Fraternité, Justice! La vie et l'oeuvre de Richard Overton, Niveleur* (Berne: P. Lang 1979).
Gleissner, R., 'The Levellers and natural law: the Putney debates of 1647', *Journal of British Studies* 20 (1980–81), 74–89.
Glover, S. D., 'The classical plebeians: radical republicanism and the origins of Leveller thought' (PhD dissertation, University of Cambridge, 1994).
Glover, S. D., 'The Putney debates: popular versus élitist republicanism', *Past & Present*, 164 (1999), 47–80.
Goldie, M., 'The unacknowledged republic: office-holding in early modern England', in T. Harris (ed.) *The Politics of the Excluded, c. 1500–1800* (Basingstoke: Palgrave, 2001), 153–94.
Gough, J. W., *The Social Contract: A Critical Study of Its Development* (Oxford: Clarendon Press, 1936).
Graves, M. A. R., *The Parliaments of Early Modern Europe* (Harlow: Pearson Education, 2001).
Greaves, R. L. and R. Zaller (eds) *Biographical Dictionary of British Radicals in the Seventeenth Century*, 3 vols (Brighton: Harvester Press, 1982–84).
Greenberg, J., 'The Confessor's laws and the radical face of the ancient constitution', *English Historical Review* 104 (1989), 611–37.
Greenberg, J. R., *The Radical Face of the Ancient Constitution: St Edward's 'Laws' in Early Modern Political Thought* (Cambridge: Cambridge University Press, 2001).

Bibliography

Gregg, P., *Free-born John: A Biography of John Lilburne* (London: Phoenix Press, 2000 reprint).
Gunn, J. A. W., *Politics and the Public Interest in the Seventeenth Century* (London: Routledge & Kegan Paul, 1969).
Gurney, J., 'George Wither and Surrey politics, 1642–1649', *Southern History* 19 (1997), 74–98.
Gurney, J., *Brave Community: The Digger Movement in the English Revolution* (Manchester: Manchester University Press, 2007).
Hampsher-Monk, I., 'The political theory of the Levellers: Putney, property and Professor Macpherson', *Political Studies* 24 (1976), 397–422.
Harris, T., 'Problematising popular culture', in T. Harris (ed.) *Popular Culture in England, c. 1500–1850* (Basingstoke: Macmillan, 1995), 1–27.
Harris, T. 'The Leveller legacy: from the Restoration to the Exclusion Crisis', in M. Mendle (ed.) *The Putney Debates of 1647: The Army, the Levellers and the English State* (Cambridge: Cambridge University Press, 2001), 219–40.
Heinemann, M., 'Popular drama and Leveller style: Richard Overton and John Harris', in Maurice Cornforth (ed.) *Rebels and Their Causes: Essays in Honour of A. L. Morton* (London, 1978), 69–92.
Hessayon, A. and D. Finnegan, *Varieties of Seventeenth- and Early Eighteenth-century English Radicalism in Context* (Farnham: Ashgate, 2011).
Hill, C., 'The Norman Yoke', in *Puritanism and Revolution: Studies in Interpretation of the English Revolution of the 17th Century* (London: Secker & Warburg, 1958), 46–111.
Hill, C., *The World Turned Upside Down: Radical Ideas during the English Revolution* (Harmondsworth: Penguin, 1975; originally published in 1972).
Hill, C., 'From Lollards to Levellers', in M. Cornforth (ed.) *Rebels and Their Causes: Essays in Honour of A. L. Morton* (London: Lawrence and Wishart, 1978), 49–67.
Hill, C., *The Century of Revolution, 1603–1714*, 2nd edn (London: Routledge, 1980).
Hill, C., *Intellectual Origins of the English Revolution Revisited* (Oxford: Clarendon Press, 1997).
Holmes, C., 'The county community in Stuart historiography', *Journal of British Studies* 19:2 (1980), 54–73.
Holstun, J., *Ehud's Dagger: Class Struggle in the English Revolution* (London: Verso, 2000).
Höpfl, H. and M. P. Thompson, 'The history of contract as a motif in political thought', *American Historical Review* 84 (1979), 919–44.
Houston, A. C., 'A way of settlement: the Levellers, monopolies and the public interest', *History of Political Thought* 14 (1993), 381–420.
Howell, R. Jr and D. E. Brewster, 'Reconsidering the Levellers: the evidence of the *Moderate*', *Past and Present*, 46 (1970), 68–86.
Hughes, A., 'Gender and politics in Leveller literature', in S. D. Amussen and M. A. Kishlansky (eds) *Political Culture and Cultural Politics in Early Modern England* (Manchester: Manchester University Press, 1995), 162–88.
Jones, D. M., *Conscience and Allegiance in Seventeenth-century England: The Political Significance of Oaths and Engagements* (Rochester: University of Rochester Press, 1999).

Jones, W., *Thomas Rainborowe (c.1610–1648): Civil War Seaman, Siegemaster and Radical* (Woodbridge: Boydell and Brewer, 2005).
Jordan, W. K., *The Development of Religious Toleration in England*, 4 vols (London: Allen and Unwin, 1932–56).
Judson, M. A., *The Crisis of the Constitution: An Essay in Constitutional and Political Thought in England 1603–1645* (New York: Octagon, 1964).
Kishlansky, M. A., 'The case of the army truly stated: the creation of the New Model Army', *Past & Present*, 81 (1978), 51–74.
Kishlansky, M. A., 'The army and the Levellers: the roads to Putney', *Historical Journal* 22 (1979), 795–824.
Kishlansky, M. A., *The Rise of the New Model Army* (Cambridge: Cambridge University Press, 1979).
Kishlansky, M. A., 'Consensus politics and the structure of debate at Putney', *Journal of British Studies*, 20 (1981), 50–69.
Kishlansky, M. A., 'What happened at Ware?', *Historical Journal*, 25 (1982), 827–39.
Kishlansky, M. A., 'Ideology and politics in the parliamentary armies, 1645–9', in J. Morrill (ed.) *Reactions to the English Civil War* (London: Macmillan, 1982), 163–83.
Knott, J. R., *Discourses of Martyrdom in English Literature, 1563–1694* (Cambridge: Cambridge University Press, 1993).
Koenigsberger, H. G., *Estates and Revolutions: Essays in Early Modern European History* (Ithaca and London: Cornell University Press, 1971).
Kümin, B., 'Gemeinde und Revolution: die kommunale Prägung der englischen Levellers', in H. Blickle (ed.) *Gemeinde und Staat im Alten Europa* (Munich: R. Oldenbourg, 1998), 361–96.
Lake, P. '"The monarchical republic of Queen Elizabeth I" (and the fall of Archbishop Grindal) revisited', in J. F. McDiarmid (ed.) *The Monarchical Republic of Early Modern England: Essays in Response to Patrick Collinson* (Aldershot: Ashgate, 2007), 129–47.
Lamont, W., *Marginal Prynne, 1600–1669* (London: Routledge and Kegan Paul, 1963).
Lamont, W., 'Pamphleteering, the Protestant consensus and the English Revolution', in R. C. Richardson and G. M. Ridden (eds) *Freedom and the English Revolution: Essays in History and Literature* (Manchester: Manchester University Press, 1986), 79–92.
Lamont, W., 'Puritanism, liberty and the Putney debates', in M. Mendle (ed.) *The Putney Debates of 1647: The Army, the Levellers and the English State* (Cambridge: Cambridge University Press, 2001), 241–55.
Levy, M. B., 'Freedom, property and the Levellers: the case of John Lilburne', *Western Political Quarterly* 36 (1983), 116–33.
Lutaud, O., *Cromwell, Les Niveleurs et La République*, 2nd edn (Paris: 1978).
MacCulloch, D., 'Bondmen under the Tudors', in M. C. Cross, D. M. Loades and J. J. Scarisbrick (eds) *Law and Government under the Tudors: Essays Presented to Sir Geoffrey Elton* (Cambridge: Cambridge University Press, 1988), 91–109.
McDiarmid, J. F. (ed.) *The Monarchical Republic of Early Modern England: Essays in Response to Patrick Collinson* (Aldershot: Ashgate, 2007).

Bibliography

McDowell, N., *The English Radical Imagination: Culture, Religion, and Revolution, 1630–1660* (Oxford: Oxford University Press, 2003).

McElligott, J., *Royalism, Print and Censorship in Revolutionary England* (Woodbridge: Boydell Press, 2007).

Macpherson, C. B., *The Political Theory of Possessive Individualism: Hobbes to Locke* (Oxford: Clarendon Press, 1962).

Manning, B., 'The Levellers and religion', in J. F. McGregor and B. Reay (eds) *Radical Religion in the English Revolution* (Oxford: Oxford University Press, 1984), 65–90.

Manning, B., *The English People and the English Revolution, 1640–1649*, 2nd edn (London: Heinemann, 1991).

Marongiu, A., *Medieval Parliaments: A Comparative Study* (London: Eyre and Spottiswood, 1968).

Marshall, J., *John Locke: Resistance, Religion and Responsibility* (Cambridge: Cambridge University Press, 1994).

Mayers, R., *1659: The Crisis of the Commonwealth* (Woodbridge: Royal Historical Society, 2004).

Mendle, M. J., 'Politics and political thought, 1640–1642', in C. Russell (ed.) *The Origins of the English Civil War* (Basingstoke: Macmillan, 1973), 219–45.

Mendle, M. J., *Dangerous Positions: Mixed Government, the Estates of the Realm, and the Making of the Answer to the 19 Propositions* (Alabama: University of Alabama Press, 1985).

Mendle, M. J., *Henry Parker and the English Civil War: The Political Thought of the Public's 'Privado'* (Cambridge: Cambridge University Press, 1995).

Mendle, M. J., 'Putney's pronouns: identity and indemnity in the great debate', in M. Mendle (ed.) *The Putney Debates Revisited* (Cambridge: Cambridge University Press, 2001), 125–47.

Morgan, E. S., *Inventing the People: The Rise of Popular Sovereignty in England and America* (New York and London: Norton, 1988).

Morrill, J. S., 'Mutiny and discontent in English provincial armies, 1645–1647', *Past and Present*, 56 (1972), 49–74.

Morrill, J. S., 'The army revolt of 1647', in A. C. Duke and C. A. Tamse, *Britain and the Netherlands: Vol. VI, Law and Society* (The Hague, 1977), 54–78.

Morrill, J. S., *The Revolt of the Provinces: Conservatives and Radicals in the English Civil War, 1630–1650* (London: Allen & Unwin, 1980).

Morrill, J. S. and P. Baker, 'The case of the armie truly re-stated', in M. Mendle (ed.) *The Putney Debates Revisited* (Cambridge: Cambridge University Press, 2001), 103–24.

Morrill, J. S. and P. Baker, 'Oliver Cromwell, the regicide and the sons of Zeruiah', in J. Peacey (ed.) *The Regicides and the Execution of Charles I* (Basingstoke: Palgrave, 2001), 14–35.

Morton, A. L., 'A still and soft voice', in *The World of the Ranters: Religious Radicalism in the English Revolution* (London: Lawrence & Wishart, 1970), 143–96.

Morton, A. L., 'Leveller democracy – fact or myth?', in *The World of the Ranters: Religious Radicalism in the English Revolution* (London: Lawrence & Wishart, 1970), 197–219.

Mulligan, L., 'The religious roots of William Walwyn's radicalism', *Journal of Religious History*, 12 (1982), 162–79.
Norbrook, D., *Writing the English Republic: Poetry, Rhetoric, and Politics, 1627–1660* (Cambridge: Cambridge University Press, 1999).
Norris, M. A., 'Edward Sexby, John Reynolds and Edmund Chillenden: agitators, "sectarian grandees" and the relations of the New Model Army with London in the spring of 1647', *Historical Research* 76:191 (2003), 30–53.
Peacey, J., 'John Lilburne and the Long Parliament', *Historical Journal* 43:3 (2000), 625–46.
Peacey, J., 'Nibbling at Leviathan: politics and theory in England in the 1650s', *Huntington Library Quarterly* 61 (2000), 241–57.
Peacock, E., 'Notes on the life of Thomas Rainborowe', *Archaeologia*, 46 (1881), 9–64.
Pearl, V., *London and the Outbreak of the Puritan Revolution: City Government and National Politics, 1625–43* (Oxford: Oxford University Press, 1961).
Pease, T. C., *The Leveller Movement* (Gloucester, Mass.: Peter Smith, 1965; originally published in 1916).
Peltonen, M., *Classical Humanism and Republicanism in English Political Thought, 1570–1640* (Cambridge: Cambridge University Press, 1995).
Pocock, J. G. A., *The Ancient Constitution and the Feudal Law: A Study of English Historical Thought in the Seventeenth Century. A Reissue with a Retrospect.* (Cambridge: Cambridge University Press, 1987).
Pocock, J. G. A., *The Machiavellian Moment* (Princeton: Princeton University Press, 1975).
Pocock, J. G. A., 'Languages and their implications: the transformation of the study of political thought', in *Politics, Language and Time: Essays in Political Thought* (London: Methuen, 1972), 3–41.
Polizzotto, C., 'Liberty of conscience and the Whitehall debates of 1648–9', *Journal of Ecclesiastical History* 26 (1975), 69–82.
Raab, F., *The English Face of Machiavelli: A Changing Interpretation 1500–1700* (London: Routledge and Kegan Paul, 1964).
Rahe, P. A., *Against Throne and Altar: Machiavelli and Political Theory under the English Republic* (Cambridge: Cambridge University Press, 2008).
Rappaport, S., *Worlds within Worlds: Structures of Life in Sixteenth-Century London* (Cambridge: Cambridge University Press, 1989).
Raymond, J., *The Invention of the Newspaper: English Newsbooks, 1641–1649* (Oxford: Clarendon Press, 1996).
Raymond, J., 'John Streater and the Grand Politick Informer', *Historical Journal* 41:2 (1998), 567–74.
Roberts, S., 'Local government reform in England and Wales during the Interregnum', in I. Roots (ed.) *Into Another Mould: Aspects of the Interregnum* (Exeter: University of Exeter Press, 1998), 47–69.
Robertson, D. B., *The Religious Foundations of Leveller Democracy* (New York: Columbia University Press, 1951).
Robertson, G. and P. Baker, *The Putney Debates: The Levellers* (London: Verso, 2007).

Russell-Jones, I. 'The relationship between theology and politics in the writings of John Lilburne, Richard Overton and William Walwyn' (DPhil dissertation, University of Oxford, 1987).
Sacks, D., 'Parliament, liberty and the commonweal', in J. H. Hexter (ed.) *Parliament and Liberty* (Stanford: Stanford University Press, 1992), 85–121.
Salmon, J. H. M., *The French Religious Wars in English Political Thought* (London: Clarendon Press, 1959).
Sampson, M., 'A story "too tedious to relate at large"? Response to the Levellers, 1647–1653', *Parergon*, 5 (1987) 135–54.
Sanderson, J., *'But the People's Creatures': The Philosophical Basis of the English Civil War* (Manchester: Manchester University Press, 1989).
Schröder, H.-C., 'Die Levellers und das Problem der Republik in der englischen Revolution', *Geschichte und Gesellschaft* 10:4 (1984), 461–97.
Schwoerer, L. G., *'No Standing Armies!' The Antiarmy Ideology in Seventeenth-Century England* (Baltimore and London: Johns Hopkins University Press, 1974).
Scott, D., *Politics and War in the Three Stuart Kingdoms, 1637–49* (Basingstoke: Palgrave Macmillan, 2004).
Scott, J., 'The rapture of motion: James Harrington's republicanism', in N. Phillipson and Q. Skinner (eds) *Political Discourse in Early Modern Britain* (Cambridge: Cambridge University Press, 1993), 139–63.
Scott, J., *Commonwealth Principles: Republican Writing of the English Revolution* (Cambridge: Cambridge University Press, 2004).
Seaberg, R. B., 'The Norman Conquest and the common law: the Levellers and the argument from continuity', *Historical Journal* 24 (1981), 791–806.
Sharp, A., 'John Lilburne's discourse of law', *Political Science* 40 (1988), 18–33.
Sharp, A., 'John Lilburne and the Long Parliament's Book of Declarations: a radical's exploitation of the words of authorities', *History of Political Thought* 9 (1988), 19–44.
Sharpe, K. M., '"An image doting rabble": the failure of republican culture in seventeenth-century England', in K. M. Sharpe and S. N. Zwicker (eds) *Refiguring Revolutions: Aesthetics and Politics from the English Revolution to the Romantic Revolution* (Berkeley and London: University of California Press, 1998), 25–56.
Shaw, H., *The Levellers* (London: Longman, 1968).
Sirluck, E., 'Introduction', in E. Sirluck (ed.) *The Complete Prose Works of John Milton, Vol. II: 1643–1648* (New Haven: Yale University Press, 1959), 1–216.
Skinner, Q., 'History and ideology in the English Revolution', *Historical Journal* 8 (1965), 151–78.
Skinner, Q., *The Foundations of Modern Political Thought*, 2 vols (Cambridge: Cambridge University Press, 1978).
Skinner, Q., 'Some problems in the analysis of political thought and action', in J. Tully (ed.) *Meaning and Context: Quentin Skinner and His Critics* (Cambridge: Cambridge University Press, 1988), 97–118.
Skinner, Q., *Liberty before Liberalism* (Cambridge: Cambridge University Press, 1998).
Skinner, Q., 'Classical liberty and the coming of the English civil war', in Q. Skinner and M. van Gelderen (eds) *Republicanism: A Shared European Heritage*, 2 vols (Cambridge: Cambridge University Press, 2002), vol. 2, 9–28.

Smart, I. M., 'The political ideas of the Scottish covenanters, 1638–88', *History of Political Thought* 1:2 (1980), 167–93.

Smith, N., *Literature and Revolution in England 1640–1660* (New Haven and London: Yale University Press, 1994).

Smith, N., 'Popular republicanism in the 1650s: John Streater's "heroick mechanicks"', in D. Armitage, A. Himy and Q. Skinner (eds) *Milton and Republicanism* (Cambridge: Cambridge University Press, 1995), 137–55.

Sommerville, J. P., 'History and theory: the Norman conquest in early Stuart political thought', *Political Studies* 34 (1986), 249–61.

Sommerville, J. P., 'Richard Hooker, Hadrian Saravia, and the advent of the divine right of kings', *History of Political Thought* 4 (1983), 229–45.

Sommerville, J. P., *Politics and Ideology in England, 1603–1640* (London: Longman, 1986).

Sommerville, J. P., 'Ideology, property and the constitution', in R. P. Cust and A. Hughes (eds) *Conflict in Early Stuart England: Studies in Religion and Politics, 1603–1642* (Harlow: Longman, 1989), 47–71.

Sommerville, J. P., *Thomas Hobbes: Political Ideas in Historical Context* (Basingstoke: Macmillan, 1992).

Sommerville, J. P., 'English and Roman liberty in the monarchical republic of early Stuart England', in J. F. McDiarmid (ed.) *The Monarchical Republic of Early Modern England: Essays in Response to Patrick Collinson* (Aldershot: Ashgate, 2007), 206–16.

Taft, B., 'Journey to Putney: the quiet Leveller', in G. J. Schochet, P. E. Tatspaugh, and C. Brobeck (eds) *Religion, Resistance, and Civil War* (Washington: Folger Institute Center for the History of British Political Thought, 1990), 63–81.

Thomas, K., 'The Levellers and the franchise', in G. E. Aylmer (ed.) *The Interregnum: The Quest for Settlement 1646–1660* (London, 1972), 57–78.

Thompson, C., 'Maximilian Petty and the Putney debate on the franchise', *Past and Present*, 88 (1980), 63–9.

Tolmie, M., *The Triumph of the Saints: The Separate Churches of London, 1616–1649* (Cambridge: Cambridge University Press, 1977).

Tubbs, J. W., *The Common Law Mind* (Baltimore and London: Johns Hopkins University Press, 2000).

Tuck, R., *Natural Rights Theories: Their Origin and Development* (Cambridge: Cambridge University Press, 1979).

Tuck, R., 'Scepticism and toleration in the seventeenth century', in S. Mendus (ed.) *Justifying Toleration: Conceptual and Historical Perspectives* (Cambridge: Cambridge University Press, 1988), 21–35.

Tuck, R., *Philosophy and Government 1572–1651* (Cambridge: Cambridge University Press, 1993).

Underdown, D., *Royalist Conspiracy in England* (New Haven: Yale University Press, 1960).

Underdown, D., *Pride's Purge: Politics in the Puritan Revolution* (Oxford: Oxford University Press, 1971).

Vallance, E., *Revolutionary England and the National Covenant* (Woodbridge: Boydell and Brewer, 2005).

Bibliography

Vallance, E., *A Radical History of Britain: Visionaries, Rebels and Revolutionaries: The Men and Women Who Fought for Our Freedoms* (London: Little, Brown, 2009).

Venn, J. and J. A. Venn, *Alumni Cantabrigienses: A Biographical List of All Known Students, Graduates, and Holders of Office at the University of Cambridge, from the earliest times to 1900*, 2 parts in 10 vols (Cambridge: Cambridge University Press, 1922–54).

Vernon, E. and P. Baker, 'What was the first Agreement of the People?', *Historical Journal* 53 (2010), 39–60.

Wende, P., '"Liberty" und "property" in der politischen Theorie der Levellers', *Zeitschrift für Historische Forschung*, 1 (1974) 147–73.

Weston, C. C., 'England: ancient constitution and common law', in J. H. Burns and M. Goldie (eds) *The Cambridge History of Political Thought, 1450–1700* (Cambridge, 1991), 374–411.

Weston, C. C. and J. Greenberg, *Subjects and Sovereigns: The Grand Controversy over Legal Sovereignty in Stuart England* (Cambridge: Cambridge University Press, 1981).

White, S., *Sir Edward Coke and the Grievances of the Commonwealth* (Manchester: Manchester University Press, 1979).

Withington, P., *The Politics of Commonwealth: Citizens and Freemen in Early Modern England* (Cambridge: Cambridge University Press, 2005).

Wolfe, D. M., *Milton in the Puritan Revolution* (New York: Thomas Nelson & Sons, 1941).

Woolrych, A., 'Putney revisited: political debate in the New Model Army in 1647', in C. Jones, M. Newitt and S. Roberts (eds) *Politics and People in Revolutionary England: Essays in Honour of Ivan Roots* (Oxford: Blackwell, 1996), 95–116.

Woolrych, A., *Soldiers and Statesmen: the General Council of the Army and its Debates, 1647–1648* (Oxford, 1987).

Woolrych, A., *Britain in Revolution, 1625–1660* (New York: Oxford University Press, 2002).

Wootton, D., 'From rebellion to revolution: the crisis of the winter of 1642/3 and the origins of civil war radicalism', *English Historical Review*, 105 (1990), 654–69.

Wootton, D., 'Leveller democracy and the Puritan revolution', in J. H. Burns and M. Goldie (eds) *The Cambridge History of Political Thought 1450–1700* (Cambridge: Cambridge University Press, 1991), 412–42.

Wootton, D., 'The Levellers', in John Dunn (ed.) *Democracy: The Unfinished Journey 508 BC to AD 1993* (Oxford: Oxford University Press, 1992), 71–89.

Worden, B., *The Rump Parliament* (Cambridge: Cambridge University Press, 1973).

Worden, B., 'Toleration and the Cromwellian Protectorate', in W. J. Sheils (ed.) *Persecution and Toleration* (Oxford: Basil Blackwell, 1984), 199–233.

Worden, B., 'Marchamont Nedham and the beginnings of English republicanism, 1649–1656', in D. Wootton (ed.) *Republicanism, Liberty, and Commercial Society, 1649–1776* (Stanford: Stanford University Press, 1994), 45–81.

Worden, B., '"Wit in a Roundhead": the dilemma of Marchamont Nedham', in S. D. Amussen and M. A. Kishlansky (eds) *Political Culture and Cultural Politics in Early Modern England: Essays Presented to David Underdown* (Manchester: Manchester University Press, 1995), 301–37.

Worden, B., 'The Levellers in history and memory, c.1660–1960', in M. Mendle (ed.) *The Putney Debates of 1647: The Army, the Levellers and the English State* (Cambridge: Cambridge University Press, 2001), 256–82.

Worden, B., *Literature and Politics in Cromwellian England: John Milton, Andrew Marvell, Marchamont Nedham* (Oxford: Oxford University Press, 2007).

Zagorin, P., *A History of Political Thought in the English Revolution* (London: Routledge & Kegan Paul, 1954).

Zagorin, P., 'The authorship of Mans Mortallitie', in *The English Revolution: Politics, Events, Ideas* (Aldershot: Ashgate, 1998), 155–9.

Index

Agreements of the People 5, 12, 20–1, 28, 73–5, 78–82, 121, 134, 136, 139, 157–8, 161–2, 217, 231–2, 234
   First Agreement (1647) 12, 44, 78–80, 130, 136–7, 152–5, 158, 170–1, 175, 178–83, 218
   Jubbes's Agreement (*Several Proposals*, 1648) 130, 187
   'New Engagements' 176
   Officers' Agreement (1649) 12, 75, 136, 159, 162–4, 176, 179
   Second Agreement (*Foundations of Freedom*, 1648) 12, 75, 78–9, 111–12, 132, 136, 142, 159, 162, 176, 179
   Third Agreement (1649) 7, 13, 71–2, 80–1, 110–12, 135, 136, 141, 164, 172, 174, 176, 179, 210–11, 217–18
Allen, William 182, 190
Army 3–6, 11–13, 73, 75, 78–9, 82, 109–10, 132, 136, 141, 150–84, 194, 217, 232–3

Ball, William 65–8, 82
Bastwick, John 9–10, 65, 123
Bodin, Jean 34–5
Bowles, Edward 59–60, 77
Bray, William 156, 186, 222
Buchanan, George 63, 67, 204, 225
Burroughes, Jeremiah 48, 54, 58–9, 77

Case of the Armie 12, 110, 112, 152–3, 156, 169–70, 172, 174–9, 181–3

Catholicism 124, 141–2
Chaloner, Thomas 36–7, 233
Charles I 4, 11–12, 36, 51, 63, 66, 68, 150–1, 156, 158–64, 168–9, 180–3, 232
   see also Monarchy
Chidley, Katherine 139
Chidley, Samuel 144, 191
Cicero 25, 98, 101, 201, 203–4
Cobbett, John 186
Coke, Sir Edward 91, 94–5, 98–104, 106
Council of State 10, 13, 81, 164, 197
Cromwell, Oliver 10, 90, 123, 154–5, 160–1, 170, 181–2, 194–5, 197, 206

Declaration or Representation from his Excellency Sir Thomas Fairfax (June 1647) 152, 167, 172–4
Digges, Dudley 24
Dyve, Sir Lewis 156–7, 181

Edwards, Thomas 5, 9, 134, 142, 209–10

Fairfax, Sir Thomas 157–8, 160, 172, 174, 179, 197
Ferne, Henry 53–5, 58, 63
Foxe, John 9, 123
Franchise 12, 65, 72, 92, 96, 108–12, 135, 158, 175, 177–9, 209
Fry, John 163

Index

Goodwin, John 78, 162
Guicciardini 212

Hall, John 197, 217
Harrington, James 14, 197, 213, 219–20
Harris, John 156, 160, 182, 187, 189
Harrison, Thomas 182, 206
Heads of the Proposals 150, 152, 154, 167–9, 176–8, 180–1
Helwys, Thomas 137
Herle, Charles 34–5, 41, 54–6
Hobbes, Thomas 14, 21–2, 61, 138
Hooker, Richard 25, 28
House of Commons 10–12, 24, 29–32, 35–45, 51–2, 56, 62, 64–70, 76–7, 79–81, 104, 154–5, 163, 171, 173, 177–80, 183, 210
House of Lords 1, 10–11, 31–2, 36–9, 41–3, 62, 64, 68, 73, 80–1, 155, 163–4, 173, 175, 183, 209–10, 219
Huntington, Robert 161
Hunton, Philip 33–4, 60–2

Ireland 142, 145, 151
Ireton, Henry 82, 95, 109–10, 112, 158, 161–2, 170, 178–80, 183

Jubbes, John 130, 187, 189

King *see* Monarchy

Lambe, Thomas 122
Lambert, John 206
Larner, William 5, 144
Liberty of conscience *see* Toleration
Lilburne, John 4–6, 8–13, 31, 37–8, 129, 139–42, 160–61, 169, 180, 195, 230, 232
    and annual parliaments 176
    and appeal to the people 52, 73
    and army 153–8, 171–5
    and classical republicanism 196–207
    and dissolution of government 74–77
    and franchise 108–12, 175, 177–9
    and 'free-born Englishman' 92–7
    Guildhall trial 194
    and law 91, 97–108
    and legacy of levellers 233
    and monarchy 181
    and origins of political power 23–6, 29
    and regicide 161–5
    and religion 119–20, 122–6
    and religious toleration 131–6
    and representation 64–71
Lilly, William 158
Livy 204, 208, 226
Locke, John 64, 148, 233
Lockyer, Robert 157
London 8, 59, 68, 71, 94, 96, 108, 110, 122–3, 140, 150, 156, 168–9, 177, 180, 130
Ludlow, Edmund 160

Mabbott, Gilbert 187, 189
Machiavelli 196, 198–200, 205–8, 213–14
Magna Carta 76, 92–4, 98, 100–1, 103, 105–6, 108, 162, 201, 204
Marten, Henry 6, 10, 29, 36–7, 65–6, 73, 124, 154–5, 160, 196–7, 201, 222, 224, 232
Milton, John 129, 196–7, 212–13
Moderate, The (newsbook) 113, 160–5, 181
Monarchy 1, 10–12, 22–3, 31–43, 51–4, 56, 59, 62–4, 66, 71, 80–2, 155, 162, 168, 175–6, 181–3, 198–9, 202–3, 205–6, 209–10, 213, 216, 219
    see also Charles I
Montaigne, Michel de 26, 130

Nedham, Marchamont 36, 66, 195–9, 201, 204, 207, 210–18, 220, 222, 224–5
New Model Army *see* Army

Out-Cryes of Oppressed Commons 73–4, 76
Overton, Richard 1, 5–6, 8–11, 13, 111, 131, 154–5, 210, 230
    and appeal to people 52, 68–9, 73, 77, 178, 180
    and army 78, 155, 157–8, 170–1, 173–4
    and classical republicanism 198, 200, 202–3

Index

and monarchy 36–7, 175
and origins of government, 23–6, 28–31, 138–9
and Pride's Purge 163
and parliamentary sovereignty 69
and religion 122–7, 131
and representation 38, 43–5, 70–1
and Scots 36–7
and toleration 129, 133, 141–2
in 1650s, 196

Palmer, Herbert 54, 60, 62
Parker, Henry 22–3, 27–9, 34–5, 40–1, 45, 54–8, 63, 107, 136
Peter, Hugh 188
Petitions
  Large Petition 154, 156, 166, 175
  of 11 September (1648) 11, 39, 42, 134, 161–3, 176, 188, 230
Petty, Maximilian 152, 154–6
Pliny the younger 204
Plutarch 226
Putney debates 12, 80, 82, 95, 109–10, 112, 151–3, 155–60, 165, 167–70, 175, 177–8, 182–3
Prideaux, Edmond 198–9
Prince, Thomas 13, 131, 144, 188, 230
Prynne, William 36, 48, 65, 99, 108

Rainborough, Thomas 12, 109, 155–7, 161, 175, 177, 183, 188
Raleigh, Sir Walter 204, 208
Regall Tyrannie Discovered 11, 37–9, 45, 70, 153, 181, 203
Religious toleration *see* Toleration
Remonstrance from His Excellency (November 1647) 158, 160, 179
Remonstrance of His Excellency (November 1648) 161–2, 176, 179, 182
Remonstrance of Many Thousand Citizens 1, 11, 30, 36–9, 45, 49, 103, 130, 137, 154, 177, 202
Remonstrans Redivivus 22–3, 35, 56–7
Representation 10, 40–5, 55–8, 64–72, 82, 173, 177–8, 233
Reynolds, John 157–8, 185
Robinson, Henry 131, 137, 146
Rohan, Henri, duc de 228
Rosier, Edmund 122
Rutherford, Samuel 48, 60, 63–4, 149

Sects 5, 9, 122–3, 141, 232
Sexby, Edward 110, 156–7, 185, 197, 203
Skippon, Philip 66
Solemne Engagement of the Army (June 1647) 152, 167, 173–4
Sovereignty 6, 11, 21–3, 30–1, 33–8, 40–2, 45, 51, 53, 55–6, 58–63, 67–72, 77, 81–3, 138, 183, 204, 207–9, 219–20, 234
Streater, John 195, 197–8, 213, 215–21

Thompson, William 157, 174, 193
Toleration 1, 9, 120–1, 128–34, 140–2
Touching the Fundamentall Lawes 23, 35, 47–8, 56–8
Tulidah, Alexander 156–7

Vane, Sir Henry (the younger) 195, 213
Vox Plebis 86, 201, 204–5, 208, 213, 222, 224

Walwyn, William 1, 5–6, 8–11, 13, 26, 28, 68–9, 92, 166, 172, 175, 200, 230, 234
  after regicide 163, 196–7
  and army 154–5
  and law 102–5
  and religion 122, 124–5, 127–8, 140–2
  and *Remonstrans Redivivus* 35, 56–7
  and toleration 129–31, 134–8
White, Francis 79, 157, 182, 185, 192
Whitehall debates 12, 125, 132, 151, 164
Wildman, John 8, 110, 124, 125, 152, 154–6, 163, 169–70, 172–3, 182–3, 197, 199–200, 220–2, 224
Williams, Roger 137
Wither, George 65–7, 82, 233
Women 111, 139–40

EU authorised representative for GPSR:
Easy Access System Europe, Mustamäe tee 50,
10621 Tallinn, Estonia
gpsr.requests@easproject.com